SCIENCE AND TECHNOLOGY EDUCATION FOR ALL

INTERNATIONAL ENCYCLOPAEDIA OF
SCIENCE AND TECHNOLOGY EDUCATION - 5

SCIENCE AND TECHNOLOGY EDUCATION FOR ALL

By

Dr. Digumarti Bhaskara Rao

M.Sc., M.A., M.A., M.Ed., Ph.D.
Reader & Research Director
R.V.R. College of Education
Srinivasa Nagar Colony
Guntur - 522 006
(India)

DISCOVERY PUBLISHING HOUSE PVT. LTD.
NEW DELHI-110 002

Published by:

DISCOVERY PUBLISHING HOUSE PVT. LTD.
4383/4B, Ansari Road, Darya Ganj
New Delhi-110 002 (India)
Phone : +91-11-23279245; 23253475; 43596065
E-mail : discoverybooksindia@gmail.com
discoverypublishinghouse@gmail.com
namitwasan9@gmail.com
web : www.discoverypublishinggroup.com

First Published: **2001**
Reprinted: **2022**

ISBN: 978-81-7141-548-9 (Set)

ISBN: 978-81-7141-572-4

Science and Technology Education for All

Printed at:
Infinity Imaging **Systems**
Delhi

Preface

Science and Technology have occupied almost all spheres of human life. The wonderful achievements of science and technology have glorified the modern world and transformed the modern civilization into a scientific and technological civilization. Considering the importance of science and technology, they have been incorporated in every stage of education.

This International Encyclopaedia of Science and Technology Education is developed covering a wide range of aspects related to science and technology education for the benefit of all those who are associated with science and technology education. This Encyclopaedia is consisting of eleven volumes, namely:

1. Science and Technology Education,
2. Science Education in Developing Countries,
3. Organizational Structure of Science,
4. Science Education in Asia and the Pacific,
5. Science and Technology Education for All,
6. Values, Ethics, Talent and Girls in Science and Technology Education,
7. Popularization of Science and Technology Education,
8. Science, Power and Society,
9. Information Technology,
10. Teacher Training in Science and Technology Education, and
11. Science, Technology and Society—A Curriculum Framework.

I convey my cordial thanks to UNESCO-PROAP, Bangkok, Thailand; UNESCO-ROSTE, Venice, Italy; UNESCO, Paris, France; IIEP, Paris, France; Commonwealth Secretariat, London, UK; UNCTAD, Geneva, Switzerland, Queen's University, Kingston, Canada; and Alberta Education, Edmonton, Canada for their kind co-operation in preparing this Encyclopaedia.

DR. DIGUMARTI BHASKARA RAO
Secretary
Academy of Communication Culture Education
Science and Service
GUNTUR (A.P.)

Contents

Part II

Science Curriculum for Meeting Real-Life Needs of Young Learners

Part III

Implementing Science and Technology for all: Guide to Better Policy and Practice for Teachers

Part I

SCIENCE FOR ALL AND THE QUALITY OF LIFE

Contents

Introduction

UNESCO PROAP/ACEID, in cooperation with the Ministry of Education and Culture, HM Government of Nepal, the Science Education Development Centre (SEDEC), and the Curriculum, Textbook and Supervision Development Centre, Nepal, convened a Regional Workshop on Science and Technology Education at Lower Secondary Level in Kathmandu, Nepal, from 12-21 March, 1990.

The activity was a component of the 1990 programme of UNESCO/APEID and the UNDP assisted project RAS/86/051—Improvement of Science and Technology Education.

The Workshop supported current deliberations on science and mathematics education of HM Government of Nepal by placing the rich experiences of the region at the disposal of policy planners and curriculum developers of Nepal. It followed a National Seminar on Science and Mathematics Education Policy and Planning held in Nepal between 11-16 February, 1990.

The Workshop focused on:

- Policy and strategy related to science and technology education for all, at lower secondary level;
- Application of learning in science and technology to real life situations in the students' environment, with particular reference to improving the quality of life and productivity;
- Implications for curriculum development and pupil evaluation, including the affective domain;

- Implications for teacher training, and for community/parental involvement; and
- Planning and implementation difficulties.

Deliberations were supported by extensive presentations from countries in the region with several years of experience in reforming science and technology education at lower secondary level. The presentations included examples of curricula, learning sequences, learner evaluation instruments, audio-visual aids, equipment, and teacher training designs, in addition to analyses of new policies.

Participation/Preparations

Eleven countries provided thirteen participants and four observers to the Workshop. Two resource persons assisted in the deliberations.

Mrs. Kristie Regan, Assistant Programme Officer, UNDP, Nepal attended a session of the Workshop, as did experts from Nepal.

Each participant presented and provided an analytical country comment incorporating the following elements, with reference to science and technology education at lower secondary level:

- Recent policies and strategies in science and technology education, with particular reference to Science for All, and implications for curriculum development.
- Planning and implementation difficulties, and actions taken to overcome these.
- Examples drawn from current curricula, of applications of (classroom) science and technology learning in real life situations in the local milieu, with particular reference to improving the quality of life and productivity of the learners and their communities.
- Examples drawn from current curricula, of pupil achievement evaluation instruments, including evaluation of the affective domain.
- Examples drawn from current practice, of designs for teachers education in support of these reforms.

Office Bearers and Resource Persons

The following acted as Office Bearers of the Workshop:

Chairperson : Dr. Thongchai Chewprecha, Thailand
Vice Chairperson : Dr. J.S. Gill, India
Rapporteur : Mrs. Erlinda Y. Basa, Philippines

Ratnaike J., UNESCO PROAP/ACEID, acted as the Secretary to the Wrokshop. The resource persons where Dr. Cliff Malcom, Australia, and Dr. J.S. Rajput, India. Substantive and technical support were provided by Mr. Toran B. Karki, Director, SEDEC and his staff.

Workshop Activities

Deliberations took place in whole group, small groups and individual work sessions. The production of the report was undertaken by two working groups formed by the participants, supported by the resource persons. Presentations, discussions and readings were mixed with writing sessions.

Inaugural Session

The Workshop was opened by the Secretary of Education, Mr. Ramesh Jung Thapa. In his address, he indicated that during Nepal's Seventh Development Plan (1985-1990), HM Government developed a detailed programme aimed to fulfil the basic needs of the nation by the end of the century. In addition to food, clothing, fuel, shelter, drinking water, primary health care and sanitation, transport and security etc., primary education (covering the first five grades) was declared a basic need to be provided to all children of relevant age in the kingdom. Accordingly, primary education has been made free.

Realizing the potential and scope of science and technology in solving such problems and to help achieve the fulfilment of basic needs, policy provisions of HM Government emphasized the development of science and technology through efficient and effective utilization of human and material resources. As a measure of this policy, science has been made an essential component of the school curriculum.

These changes confront HM Government with problems of revision of school science curricula, development of innovative teacher education programmes and preparation of more suitable student evaluation procedures.

Science and technology are recognized as essential factors contributing to progress and peace in the world. The success of a society depends on how effectively and extensively it can absorb and use scientific and technological knowledge and skills in developing its potential. In a modern society, science and technology represent two basic human activities, which relate to asking questions and solving problems. As such, they constitute an intellectual strategy which every learning human being in urban and rural areas alike should adopt for day to day decision-making. Further, they provide powerful tools in finding, knowing, understanding and doing things in better ways. Any education that does not take full cognizance of both science and technology is incomplete, irrelevant, and fails its purpose.

The current cry of "Science for All" reflects the recognition of the capacity of science and technology to improve the quality of life for the individual, community and the nation as a whole. One of the major goals of science education is to generate, develop and transfer such knowledge and skills as are necessary for the promotion of the welfare of the people and socio-economic development of the country. A scientifically informed and technological literate population provides not only the broad base from which qualified manpower can be developed, but also it helps create a climate in which innovative technologies can take root and flourish.

The Secretary of Education wished the Workshop great success in its deliberations and thanked UNESCO for selecting Kathmandu as the venue. He welcomed the participants to Kathmandu and wished them a pleasant and remarkable stay.

Purposes of the Report

The report provided in the first instance a record of the deliberations of the Workshop. It provides also guidance for curriculum and policy development in the member states.

It has been written in the style of a guidebook for reform of science and technology education at the lower secondary level. It discusses the kind of science and technology education required in the next decade. It analyses issues that need to be resolved when reforming science education to achieve current interpretations of Science for All. It offers options, analyses, case studies, and examples rather than prescriptions.

Conclusions

The conclusions and recommendations derived from the deliberations of the Workshop are as follows:

1. The concept of *Science for All* is not to be viewed only in the context of the school curriculum, but as a component of the totality of efforts in universalizing education, including alternative strategies like non-formal education, adult education etc.
2. While the majority of countries in the region have included *Science for All* in their policy formulation and have translated it into school curricula, it is recommended that other countries also do so at the earliest, at least up to lower secondary stage.
3. Each nation may attempt to define and determine the 'learning needs' of the children and also 'quality of life' in the changing context of the growing impact of science and technology. The outcomes, related to 'real life situations' may be utilized in curriculum renewal, which has to be a regular and on-going process.
4. It is to be ensured that a proper mechanism of monitoring and evaluation is established which develops appropriate tools, instruments and mechanisms for the purpose and also trains personnel to perform the tasks objectively.
5. In-service and pre-service teacher education training strategies need to be modified. The programmes should prepare teachers to adopt creative teaching models improvising, experimenting, innovating, and utilizing community resources. Teacher education should encourage teachers to make school teaching more joyful, participatory and related to local needs and aspirations.
6. Apart from teacher training institutions, each country may establish or augment resource centres for

curriculum development and for assisting teachers. These centres would provide regular professional support in solving the problems of teachers which they may experience in the curriculum and in teaching.

7. Policy changes, curriculum renewal and modified strategies for monitoring and evaluation, need to be communicated not only to all education personnel, but also to opinion leaders, and parents with equal emphasis. Acceptance should be ensured as well as modification of curricula.

8. School-community relationships may be strengthened with mutual accountability established. This helps in resource management, better understanding and appreciation of existing community needs, and futures projection. Further, this helps build affective domain components like attitudes, social sensitivity and responsibility, among all concerned, and strengthens the partnership between school and community in the education of children.

9. Teachers' Associations should be established and strengthened. These may function as professional forums and teacher support systems.

10. Whenever feasible, audiovisual aids and electronic technology may be utilized. Teachers may be provided with bulletins, newsletters, new innovation brochures and other print materials as well.

11. Assistance from agencies like UNESCO maybe taken to supplement in-country projects for experience-sharing inputs.

12. Sharing of experiences at different levels amongst countries undergoing similar changes may be encouraged by UNESCO.

1

Emerging Policy and Strategy Aspects for Science and Technology Education at Lower Secondary Level

This chapter proposes a definition of Science For All for curriculum development in the next decade and describes some of the factors which have given rise to that definition. It also examines ramifications of the definition for policies and processes in curriculum development and implementation.

1. Science for All: The New Interpretation

Science and technology are greatly important to human well being and the quality of our environment. Socio-economic progress without science and technology is impossible. Science and technology can help to reduce misery, poverty, hunger, diseases, social injustice, energy crisis, environmental pollution and other global problems.

Universalization of science and technology education is essential. Science and technology education should be available for all human beings without discrimination of race, religion, caste, ideology, socio-economic background, gender, or region.

- All students at the junior secondary levels of schooling should study science and technology.

- All students gain from their studies of science and technology; the objectives, teaching approaches and assessment strategies should be chosen to suit the needs and backgrounds of all students in the group.
- *Science for All* is not only benefiting individuals, but the collective good of the community and humanity as a whole.

1.1 *Features of Science for All*

(i) Schools, teachers, classroom materials, audio-visual aids, workshop facilities and equipment must be accessible to all students.

(ii) The content, language, symbols, designs and purposes of the curriculum should link to the day to day experiences and purposes of the children. This requires some curriculum development at the local level, responsive to the needs and interests of the children in the locality.

(iii) Science and technology education should make a difference to the way students think about their world and the things they do. It should link theory to practice, human purpose and the quality of life; reflection to action; in-school-experience to out-of-school experience.

(iv) Teaching and learning should begin from the beliefs, interests and learning skills that students bring to the classroom, and help each of them to extend and revise their understanding and their ability.

(v) Some learnings have particular value in relation to further learning and employment. Such learnings should be accessible to all students equally.

These features are embraced in an approach which we will refer to as *Science, Technology, Society, Personal Development (STSP).*

Science refers to theoretical knowledge and the processes by which it is generated and tested. This theoretical knowledge is a response to the question "I wonder..."

Technology is the solution of practical problems, and the devices and systems that have been developed as a consequence. It is a response to the question "I want..." Technological development has been greatly enhance by its links to science; science depends strongly on its use of technology.

Society recognizes the social and human context that gives purpose to science and technology, and the impact that science and technology have on our lives. The *society* aspect includes questions "Should we..."

The *Personal Development aspect* recognizes the possibilities within the science curriculum to enhance students' personal skills in logical thinking, expression, personal management, self-directed learning, co-operation, and responsible action. It implies purposes within the science curriculum to assist students to develop and refine their world-view and of take effective and responsible action in their own lives and as part of their community. It recognizes that education needs to address the development of the individual both as an individual person and as a member of society.

The curriculum should give attention to each of science, technology, society and personal development, and they should be integrated in their development.

2. Factors Which Have Led to This Interpretation

2.1 Approaches to social and economic development

The importance of science and technology in science and economic development have been understood for a long time. However, strategies of development have changed over the last three decades.

During the 1960s and 1970s, many countries concentrated on training a work-force who could use technology. The technologies themselves were often imported, and so were the experts who provided the technical knowledge and management. The investment in equipment etc. often came from overseas, and many of the profits went back overseas. Frequently, raw materials were exported for processing and then imported as finished products at high prices.

During the 1980s, the strategy shifted towards creating a work-force which could develop new technologies themselves. By their inventiveness, the work-force produces exportable goods and techniques whose value is much greater than that of the raw materials. This trend continues in the 1990s.

The need in the 1990s is not only for people who can lead technological development and work in science-based industries. The working and living environment is increasingly becoming technological. All people need to be comfortable in that environment and contribute to the use and wise management of technology.

2.2 *Environmental Conservation*

The impact of human activities on the natural environment has become increasingly clear over the last decade. Action at the national, community and individual levels is now imperative for long term survival. We have to use existing technologies more carefully and develop new or alternative technologies which conserve resources and the environment.

2.3 *Basic Needs*

There are some communities and individuals in our countries whose basic needs of hygiene, health, education, nutrition, shelter and clothing are not being met. Their quality of life can be greatly improved if they are educated in simple techniques of, for example, hygiene, use of water, preparation and choice of food, and looking after animals.

2.4 *Educational Purposes*

The achievement of the economic development, environmental management and improved quality of life outlined above, requires education that is aimed not simply at knowledge but at action. This action is required at an individual level, and also at the level of the local community and whole society. Therefore, the curriculum must assist individuals to take action, and to participate in community action.

The curriculum must also address the development of the individual, assisting that person reaches his/her potential as a human being. This requires assisting the student to develop a world view, integrating values and knowledge from different realms of experience and thought, and linking concepts of self to concepts of society and environment, spirituality and justice.

In the 1960s, the orientation of the science curriculum was science is, what scientists do: their methods of developing and testing scientific knowledge, and the concepts and theories that are central to the scientific disciplines. Little attempt was made to link this knowledge to technological applications, social concerns, or the daily experiences of the students.

In the 1970s the orientation shifted to the functionality of science, especially for those who would not enter universities. *Science, Technology, Society* education arose from this trend. It linked science to technology and placed them both in the context of social needs and everyday life. The emphasis shifted from "What do I know", to "What can I do?"

In the 1980s, at least in a few countries, a further change has emerged, with science and technology education becoming a central component of the education of all citizens, so that they can become responsible, productive citizens. The emphasis is shifting towards the social action described above, and the question "Who am I becoming?" This requires more attention to teaching children how to learn, manage their own learning, analyze problems and design and implement solutions. Thus the slogan *Science, Technology, Society* is extended to *Science, Technology, Society, Personal Development* (STSP).

Dimension	Learning for Knowing (1960s)	Learning for Applying (1970s)	Learning for Being/Becoming (1980s)
Philosophy	Positivism	Utilitarianism	Constructivism
Focus	What do I *KNOW?*	What Can I DO?	Who I am BECOMING?
Knowledge produced	Prepositional	Practical	Experiential
Structure	Subject/Discipline	Subject/Discussion Craft/Technology	Issues (micro and macro)/Subject/ Discussion
Teacher Role	Expert/Information Giver	Applier	Facilitator
Teaching/ learning strategy	Didactic	Practical	Real life problem solving

2.5 *Research into Children's Learning*

Recent research provides compelling evidence that:

- Students develop theories and beliefs about the way the world operates, from their experiences with a range of objects and people at home, at play and at school;
- These beliefs are strongly held and little affected by traditional instruction. Traditional instruction often makes little impact on the ways children think about the world or act in it, even when it is coupled with experiments and active learning.

This has led to a view of learning as the construction of new meanings in the light of experience. It is called "constructivist". It contrasts with a view of learning as the reception or acquisition of knowledge.

Students, in the course of growing up, develop their own strategies for learning and constructing meaning. They can be taught to develop effective strategies, and this should be an integral part of the curriculum.

Research has shown also that when students are taught strategies of effective learning in one area (say science), they are able to apply these strategies successfully in other areas.

Constructivist learning requires different approaches to teaching, assessment and classroom management. Teaching needs to start from the beliefs that students already hold and then extend to revise those beliefs.

It is important that students have opportunities to express their current understandings, perhaps through drawing or talking. Similarly, in clarifying their learning strategies, they need opportunities to share with other students, their teachers, and other members of the community.

In expressing their own thoughts and understandings, students take a risk of being seen as foolish by their teachers or fellow students. Hence, it is important that the climate of interaction in the classroom is co-operative.

If student's beliefs and experiences are inputs to the learning situations, then students are effectively involved in developing lessons and planning the curriculum.

Constructivist approaches link to co-operative learning and participative management. The shift towards participative management in classrooms parallels recent developments in agriculture, industry and public administration. In the classroom and in business, an important objective of participative management is to encourage creativity and flexibility.

2.6 *Social Justice*

Over the last two decades, there have been significant shifts in the definition of social justice. In the past "equal opportunity" was presumed to be satisfied if there was freedom for individuals to apply for jobs and promotion, receive health care, enter institutions or obtain services, regardless of their ethnic background, religion, gender, socio-economic background or any disability. However, this apparent access is an illusion if individuals do not have money to pay, if their language is not the language of the institution, if their disability restricts their movement, if prejudice and social structures reduce their prospects of success. Current concepts of social justice recognize these barriers and attempt to overcome them. The shift, in essence, is a shift from "equal treatment" to "equal access" where access is measured not only by availability of a service or opportunity for an individual to use it successfully.

3. Preliminary Considerations: Planning for Science for All

Thorough planning and preparation for educational change and curriculum development are essential for successful implementation. Planning needs to take care of the relationships between educational policies and other policies and programmes; the administrative structures required for formulating, implementing and supporting the changes; and the human and material resources that are necessary. Factors to be considered and issues that arise in planning *Science for All* are discussed below.

3.1 *Dimensions of Policy*

Science education policies are influenced by national policies in areas like agriculture, industry, science, environment, and social welfare. Protection of the environment is now a common component of school science. Policies which shift national priorities from traditional to scientific agriculture, and from *using* to *developing* industrial technology influence the science curriculum. There are also special policies for some categories of people like disabled, women, economically backward, tribal and rural populations.

Policies are developed at different levels, from statements of broad vision and direction to specific arrangements for implementation. The recruitment and preparation of teachers, work conditions, administrative structures at the school and system levels, and provision of buildings, facilities, and instructional materials require policies at the implementation level.

Planning and implementation of curriculum are often worked out in the form of frameworks and guidelines. They spell out curricular content, organization, and the roles of teachers, parents and school administrators. Materials to support curricular implementors and other functionaries are also essential.

Policies in science curriculum for improvement of the quality of life must consider the meaning of "quality of life":

- economic and industrial development
- preservation of national culture and heritage
- spiritual and moral development
- social and economic justice
- equality of opportunity
- respect for individuals, society, constitution and law
- judicious and rational use of the environment and its resources
- maintenance and improvement of the quality of the environment
- understanding the place of science and technology in our society and the role they can have in improving the quality of life

These considerations might lead to objectives of science education like: "The science curriculum will help students to develop progressively to:

- understand some of the methods, concepts and theories that scientists use, and the ways science is applied in our everyday lives
- understanding the role of technology and the world of work
- develop knowledge, skills and attitudes essential for contributing to development and improvement of life
- develop interest, critical thinking and the spirit of enquiry
- develop skills in identifying and solving problems and making decisions and taking action
- develop open mindedness, tolerance and respect
- develop to the full learners' potential for human expression and achievement
- develop habits of team work and co-operation
- expand their vision for global concerns
- respect and use natural resources judiciously and sensibly".

3.2 *Dimensions of the Curriculum*

The curriculum is more than a list of objectives or things to be learned. It includes all the aspects necessary for "good learning" to take place for every student in the class.

Some teaching methods provide better opportunities than others for all students to participate and succeed in the learning. Teaching methods need to be chosen also to suit the different learning styles of individual students and the range of learning objectives of "Science for All".

Assessment strategies are not only methods of measuring educational achievement. They make important statements about the kinds of learning and the kinds of achievement that are valued by the school system, and also influence strongly the learning that occurs. If the curriculum is oriented to problem solving in the context of daily life, students "becoming", and "learning how to learn" as well as "knowing" and "doing", progress in these objectives needs to be part of the assessment. If the only assessment is by national tests at points through the programme, it is unlikely that the curriculum in practice will give serious attention to local concerns and needs.

Facilities, the ways students are grouped, school policies about noise levels and excursions, timetabling, all affect the access that students have to successful learning. Co-operative learning cannot succeed in the general ethos of the school is one where students are ridiculed for wrong answers, or where there is strong emphasis on competition.

If the curriculum is to link to the daily lives of the students there must be mechanisms to strengthen the partnership between parents, students, teachers and the community. Learning is enhanced when there is consonance between school, home and community.

Similarly, learning is enhanced when there is consonance among the curricula in different subject areas. The science curriculum should not be an isolated entity in itself. It should be an integral part of the school curriculum as a whole.

3.3 *Choosing the Content*

In science curriculum which draws its content from science, technology, the cultural and human context of science, and applications of science to improve the quality of life, many topics and approaches are rich with possibilities. No longer is "basic content" defined simply from "the basic structure of the disciplines of science". "Basic" now has to be defined in relation to the needs and aspirations of the students, their communities, and the nation. It follows that the definition of "basic content" must vary somewhat from locality to locality and person to person.

Criteria for selecting content, whether at the central level the local level or both, need to be established as part of science education policy. For example, is the content,

- based on the interests and experiences of the children, founded on action and able to assist students to understand everyday phenomena?
- accessible to pupils through the use of inquiry skills and suited to further development of those skills?
- attainable through materials and equipment that are locally available?
- within the grasp of pupils at their level of cognitive development?
- a basis for further science learning?
- perceived by the students and community as valuable in the world beyond schools?

Decisions need to be made also about the balance that is appropriate between the aspects of science, technology, society and personal development, and about "starting points" in the development of content. For example, development that begins with science and then proceeds to applications and social aspects is likely to emphasize the relationship that the science ideas have to each other, whereas, one which begins with a community issue and looks to science and technology as part of the solution is likely to emphasize the relationship of the science ideas to applications and human purposes. This discussion is taken up in detail in Chapter Four.

3.4 Balancing National, Local and Individual Needs

In the current interpretation of *Science for All,* the curriculum must meet national, local and individual needs. National needs are expressed through national policies and programmes, for example, in agriculture, technological development, conservation and "basic needs". Local needs arise from the community and local environment. Individual needs arise from the purposes, aspirations and daily lives of the students.

It is necessary to specify how the curriculum will provide for common learnings across schools and also for unique learnings in a particular locality.

The options available include the following:

- *A national "core plus options"*. This might be achieved through a given number of units of core and other units to be selected at the local level. An alternative, with less flexibility, is that core units run all year and each unit has an option component to suit different localities. In this model, the options are developed centrally by writing groups who visit different regions of the state, explore the region and consult the local people.
- *A "national core" plus "local options"*. This model is like the one above, but the options are developed at the local level, probably at the level of the individual school. It is possible to build into the model ways of accrediting local units if this is required.
- *"School-based curriculum according to Government Guidelines"*. The responsibility for curriculum development rests with the school. The Government provides guidance on the purposes, approaches to, and general content of the curriculum. The level of detail in the guidelines has to be chosen to provide a balance between Government and school control over the curriculum actually provided. In a decentralized model like this, a large proportion of assessment also is school-based.

A strongly centralized approach to curriculum [often called a "Research, Develop, Disseminate" (RD&D) approach] cannot of itself meet local and individual needs. It can produce highly polished programme materials and equipment and disseminate them to all schools quickly. It has to be coupled with extensive training programmes and support for teachers to achieve effective implementation.

The RD&D model reached the peak of its application in the major programmes in the USA (PSSC, BSCS etc.) in the 1960s. Extensive research has been done since then on their achievements. In spite of the vast resources given to development, training and implementation, the programmes fell far short of national expectations. Even committed teachers often took 5-8 years before they could use the materials expected. By their nature, the materials and teachers' guides could not identify and respond to local needs and resources or individual students.

Many countries have explored variations on the RD&D approach which put the curriculum into closer contact with local needs and allow a component of local curriculum. In Thailand, the Institute for the Promotion of Teaching Science and Technology (IPST) develops complete curricula which schools are encouraged to adapt to meet local needs. Indonesia allows a 20 per cent local/regional component of the curriculum. In India, the National Council of Educational Research and Training prepares 'model curricula' and supporting materials. The curricula are not compulsory. Various state boards of education or certain examining boards modify the materials according to their needs.

"School based curriculum development according to Government guidelines" supports the development of curricula which suit local students and their community. This approach is being carried out in the state of Victoria, Australia. It builds in a partnership between teachers, parents, students, local community and national government. It places responsibility for development and implementation with the school so that, even though the ostensible quality of the materials may be less than in the centralized case, the quality of implementation and the linkage to the lives of the student is much higher. Once again, strong in-service education and systems of support for schools are required, so that teachers and the community understand the guidelines and have the skills to work with them in creative ways. Without this support, some teachers use their "freedom" to teach the same old things in the same old ways.

Lines of accountability and systems of reporting have to be established, to ensure adequate accountability to each of national needs, local and individual needs. This requires clear conception of the balance of central and local responsibility and the mechanisms by which each responsibility is monitored.

The skills required of the teacher are different from those required in curricula designed in detail at the national level. In the latter case, the essential task of the teacher is to implement the curricula as described in the text books and teachers' guides.

If there is a local component, teachers must have also skills in curriculum development including abilities to work co-operatively with other teachers and the community.

3.5 Structures and Processes for Curriculum Management

Successful implementation of educational change requires an efficient mechanism of curriculum management.

It is necessary to establish a communication network, structures and procedures involving governments (national, state/province, and district), schools and communities.

The roles and responsibilities of each government body, administrative unit, schools and the community will vary according to the overall strategy of curriculum development and implementation. In particular, they will depend on the extent to which the management is centralized.

The tasks for which responsibility need to be assigned and administrative structures established include:

- developing curriculum policies and guidelines
- reviewing current curricula and resources in the school and community and gathering information on local needs
- planning for educational change at the school and system levels
- developing syllabi and teaching aids
- preparing guides and support materials for teachers
- preparing textbooks and student materials
- preparing science equipment, kits and audio-visual aids
- training teachers, advisers and inspectors
- developing instruments of educational measurement/assessment
- disseminating and communicating policies and materials to schools, community, commercial publishers, and others
- evaluating the quality of the curriculum and its implementation

- training teachers (in-service and pre-service).

The ways that these tasks are achieved in a decentralized system are very different from a centralized system. For example, if schools have a major responsibility for curriculum development, the responsibilities of district advisers include assisting principals and senior staff with school management, assisting teachers to understand general policies and develop curricula, and assisting the community to be involved in curriculum planning. Alternatively, in a centralized approach, the adviser supports dissemination of the materials and assists teachers to understand and use them effectively. As a second example, policy development is almost entirely a central responsibility in a centralized approach, but schools as well as the central agency must develop curriculum policies in a school-based approach.

The establishment of science and mathematics curriculum development centres such as IPST in Thailand and ISMED (Institute for Science and Mathematics Education Development) in the Philippines, shifted the responsibility of curriculum development from the state to these centres. Teachers and subject specialists can be seconded to these centres to assist the curriculum design team and the editorial committees in all aspects of the work, from curriculum design to the production of teaching materials. The centre's job is not over after developing the curriculum and materials. It also conducts field trails, ascertains research findings and utilizes these for renewal at regular intervals. Mechanisms for passing such findings back to the teacher must be well developed, so that the teacher is constantly updated in all aspects of his/her work. Development of activities and experiments is a major aspect in the universalization of science and technology education. Some of the centres have established instrumentation laboratories/ workshops or are linked to other centres for the development of laboratory equipment. The teams here develop manuals and laboratory guides. They also suggest how modifications and alterations can be effected in local situations.

While the choice of approach will be governed by specific situations and availability of expertise, the point that needs constant emphasis is the involvement of teachers. Their association with the development stage is crucial for success at the implementation stage. It gives them self assurance and a sense of involvement.

3.6 General Strategies of Change

Extensive research has been done over the last two decades on educational change and its management (See for example, Caldwell B., Beare, H. and Millikin, R., *Creating an Excellent School,* Falmer Press, London, 1989; Sergiovanni, T., *The Principalship: A Reflective Practice Perspective,* Allyn and Bacon, Boston 1987; Fullen, M.F., *The Meaning of Educational Change,* New York, Teachers College Press, 1982; Miles, M.B. and Louis, K.S., "Managing large scale change in urban high schools: how to get there", *Knowledge in Society,* 1989).

The success of educational change is greater if we **"Start from where we are, think big, and move forward in small steps".**

If "thinking big" means moving the curriculum towards an Science, Technology, Society, Personal Development (STSP) approach to *Science For All,* strategic options include the following actions:

- Identify content in the present curriculum which could be used to learn science concepts related to technology in the society. Illustrate these processes through adequate examples of application in everyday life.
- Identify situations from the local community which can be applied to various themes in the existing curriculum. Establish training programmes for teachers, and assist them at the local level to understand "Science for All" and make appropriate inclusions in the curriculum.
- Choose topics for the central curriculum such as sanitation, environment, pollution, global warming that relate to local, national and global issues. Design projects for the children through which they develop skills of problem solving, co-operation, applying value judgements in the context of improving the quality of the society they live in.

"Starting from where you are" requires analysis of the current situation. The analysis should consider not only curren structures and current practice, but also resources, trends and emerging needs.

The development of central curriculum guidelines might involve analyses by experts from different backgrounds such as education, agriculture, industry, health and social justice. Alternatively a steering committee might be established with representation from parents, teachers, unions, government, academia and industry. The steering committee might conduct some parts of the review itself and commission other parts.

Research work may need to be carried out. For example, Indonesia conducted a nationwide study of the cognitive development of students in the targeted age range; India gathered data on the needs, motivations, and backgrounds of teachers and students; Philippines completed socio-anthropological research to develop the basis for a needs-based curriculum.

The depth and time required for the preparatory stage depends on the extent of the changes envisaged. For example, major changes to school and curriculum structures, teaching approaches, and assessment at Years 11 and 12 in Victoria, Australia began with the establishment of the Committee of Review in 1984 and led to changes which will operate fully for the first time in 1992. Throughout that period, there has been major discussion of the issues, plans and curriculum designs at all levels to the community, including parliament, educational groups, industry, the public media, schools, parents and students.

Researchers like Matthew Miles consider educational change in stages. The first stage Miles calls *mobilization*, the second *implementation*, and the third *institutionalization*. Institutionalization is the process of embedding the change into life of the school so that it is able to survive changes in leadership or challenges from reactionary groups.

The stages are useful in spite of the facts that they overlap and they seldom occur in simple sequence, because strategies that are especially effective in one stage are not necessarily the ones that are most effective in another stage. For example, mobilization can be led by a small group in a top down way, but implementation cannot occur unless there is wide commitment to the change and wide ownership of the implementation strategy.

Sergiovanni talks about schools being "management loose, culture tight": teachers are loosely bound in the management sense, often making decisions of their own in their classrooms and when planning and conducting their work. On the other hand, they are strongly bound in the cultural sense of having a common view of what "good education" looks like, what "good curriculum" contains and how "good teachers" work. Educational change needs to address the "culture" of education rather than simply work with administrative controls and demands.

Achieving community involvement in the change and community acceptance of the new curriculum needs to be planned. It might involve wide participation in the Review stage, as mentioned earlier. It might involve advertising campaigns and public meetings, videos and explanatory brochoures. Opinion leaders, community leaders and parents must be reached. Government offices, private industry, publishers and voluntary organizations must also be involved so that they can assist in guiding and achieving the changes, and perhaps help in the production of materials and equipment.

Mobilization of the whole of society to support an innovation inevitably results in a feedback from all levels. Provision must be made for this feedback to be received, evaluated and used.

3.7 *Teacher Education and School Support*

The real worth of any curriculum development depends finally on the manner in which it is transacted in the classroom. Quality of learning and social justice depend ultimately on the teacher. Teachers have the moral responsibility of performing the job set for them by the entire cast of policy makers and curriculum designers, head teachers, parents, children, community and colleagues. Everyone expects their own thoughts, expectations, ideas and philosophy to be put into practice.

All teaching staff must understand the changes that are planned and be reasonably committed to them. Teachers who will be directly involved in the implementation must develop the knowledge and skills require—whether in curriculum development (in a school-based strategy) or use of particular materials and equipment (in a centralized approach).

Teacher preparation was often inadequate and underrated in attempts at curriculum change through the 1960s and 1970s. For example, science kits were distributed in several developing countries with little attention to advance preparation of teachers or in-service education. In the majority of classrooms, the kits were not even opened let alone used regularly.

Similarly, attempts to keep teachers informed and supported are often inadequate. A teacher may not receive an educational bulletin or brochure, or its importance and meaning may be lost because no-one is discussing it with the teacher. Solutions include the establishment of "expert groups" to receive teachers' problems and offer solutions, district "schools support centres" and consultancy services, "team approaches" in schools where there are a number of teachers, "networks" of teachers across schools in a district, and professional associations at the state or national level.

Although the head teacher may not be directly involved with the teaching of the new curriculum, he/she must understand it and its relation to the whole curriculum and the operation of the school. Successful implementation requires the support of the school administration and indeed all levels of school support within the Ministry. In-service education programmes are required for teachers and for school administrators. Programmes for school administrators need to address curriculum directions and also processes of management and change.

Training in the use of central policy documents or curriculum materials can be of two kinds. The curriculum developers might train teachers directly in face-to-face encounters. When the teaching force is large and direct training is prohibitive, trainers or consultants have to be recruited and sent out to work with teachers. Distortion of the original idea is likely in the second case, because of the stages in the communication. For this and other reasons, training should not be a "one off" event. The meaning and implications of an innovation become clear to the teacher over time, when he/she is working with it in the classroom. Support should be on-going.

Teacher training must equip the teachers to handle confidently all aspects of the curriculum, including content, teaching methods, development of local curriculum, community involvement, student assessment and programme evaluation.

In-service education for head-teachers, school administrators and members of the local community who work with the school needs to be planned and conducted just as thoroughly as in-service education for classroom teachers. This is so, especially when the school is large and where it has considerable responsibility for curriculum development.

If the school rather than the state has responsibility for designing syllabi and work programmes, coherence and continuity of curriculum must be achieved at school level. Planning and curriculum development need to involve all teachers. If the curriculum is to reflect the needs of the local community and the role of parents in the education of their children, then parents and the community must be involved in the development. If the school is large, formal structures are required for curriculum planning, school management, and professional development.

Colleges of education and teacher education can play a very effective role in assisting with in-service training, curriculum development, and on-going support.

3.8 Evaluation for Quality Improvement

Evaluation should be an integral part of all stages of educational innovation:

- planning (assessing needs, trends, pressures, administrative structures and resources; setting goals and deciding strategies);
- development (designing policies, structures, programmes and/or materials; trialing draft materials);

- implementation (staffing, training, enacting);
- review

Evaluation is an important part of planning and development. It is important also in the accountability of schools, curriculum units and individuals to government and community. It affects decisions about programmes and individuals. Accordingly, it has a political component alongside its objective value in supporting decision-making.

Evaluation needs to be systematic, and it needs to be planned and funded as part of educational change.

At the classroom level, teachers have a central role in evaluation of their teaching programmes and the curriculum materials they use. They need to be trained in advance. Part of their training should be to help them use others—especially students, other teachers, inspectors and consultants, parents, and the community—as part of the evaluation. Assessment of teacher performance must be carried out in a non-threatening manner. It must be seen by the teachers as an aid to improving their professional competence.

The evaluation of published materials during their development should also involve teachers as well as curriculum developers and academics. Many countries, such as Thailand, have carried out small scale trails of books and equipment. Such trails enable the materials to be modified and improved before mass production, but do not preclude other evaluations at a later date.

In addition to the teachers assessing students' and their own performances, education authorities must monitor the implementation and achievements of the curriculum nationwide. The plan should address all aspects of the curriculum, not just teacher performance and student achievement. It should investigate the whole management structure in order to ascertain whether the communication system allows the complete flow of information back and forth between school authorities and classroom teachers, at all levels, and whether the systems of school support, facilities development, teacher education, review and planning etc. are adequate.

The plan is likely to involve various institutions, such as research organizations, and teacher training institutions, and special administrative units within the Ministry, such as an inspectorate or research and evaluation team. It must also involve all units in evaluation of their own functioning and the performance of units around them.

2

Implications for Teacher Training and Orientation of Other Education Personnel, the Community and Parents

The Science-Technology-Society-Personal Development approach (STSP) gives new emphasis to the centrality of the teacher in science education and to co-operation between teachers, parents and the community.

Teachers roles in curriculum design, school management and community interaction are extended in comparison with traditional teaching. Wider subject knowledge and a broader range of teaching skills are also for teachers become critical elements.

The chapter offers guidance under three headings: the professional development of teachers, interactions with parents, other personnel and the local community, and supporting system for teacher improvement.

1. The Professional Development of Teachers

The 1960s approach to curriculum, with its student books, kits, equipments, films, teachers' guides and training programmes was described at the time as the "teacher proof curriculum". The materials kits and guides were seen as the keys to success, as long as the teacher followed the teachers' guide faithfully.

Parents and the local community were peripheral. The curriculum and materials were designed by experts at the national level. The curriculum was intended to be implemented in the same way to all children in all localities.

The strategy was consistent with the learning theories, ideas of social justice, and approaches to management the prevailed at that time.

The Science-Technology-Society-Personal Development approach is very different: constructivist learning theories, participative management, and a view of social justice that has moved away from "equal treatment of all children in all localities" to concern for local and individual variations in purpose and learning style.

The teachers' role becomes pivotal:

- The curriculum has to meet the needs and backgrounds to individual students. The teacher has to be a curriculum designer.
- The student's background and hopes are significant parts of his/her learning and are largely matters of family life. The teacher needs to work with parents to ensure that education at home and school reinforce rather than contradict each other.
- The curriculum should have a local component, linking to the life and problems that belong to the student—the environment, experience, and people of the local community. The partnership between school and community can extend to curriculum implementation as well as design. The teacher needs skills to work effectively with the local community.
- Science knowledge has to be hooked up to applications, problem solving, technological design, social and environmental issues and local questions of quality of life. It has to provide opportunities for students' personal development, assisting them to refine and build their world views, and develop skills in solving real-life problems, expressing themselves, taking effective action, etc. Education has an orientation to

individual development as well as social development. Teachers need broader knowledge and a greater range of classroom skills than in traditional programmes.

The load on the teacher must be shared. Sharing the work and the responsibility supports the teacher. It also ensures that teachers, parents and community have a common view of the goals and methods of the curriculum, and the way that the local and national components fit together. No longer does the teacher work alone in his/her classroom with centrally provided materials, kits and instructions.

If the teacher is working with others in programme development, policy, and implementation, there must be in the school an infrastructure and management expertise to support it. If teachers are to be creative in curriculum design and teaching, the organizational climate in which they work should be both demanding and encouraging. This depends on school management. It also depends on the esteem with which teachers are held by the community generally.

1.1 The Teacher As Learner

Teacher education occurs whenever teachers develop new knowledge and skills, gain new insights into themselves, their work and their students, create meaning from their experience, revise and extend their worldviews. It doesn't happen only in formal settings and course work: it is a part of day to day experience, imagination and reflection.

Teacher education has characteristics similar to education for children, as discussed in Chapter 1. The constructivist learning described there can be rewritten for teacher education:

- Teachers bring to the teacher education situation their own belief about education: what education is, how children learn, what the children should be taught, what a good lesson looks like, how a good teacher behaves. Their beliefs are often strongly held and little affected by simple instruction.
- They have their own views of themselves as learners, their own strategies as learners and problem solvers, their own interests and educational purposes.

Presented with educational theories and curricular approaches contrary to their own beliefs:

- Some become confused, recognizing shortcomings in their own views, but unable to make sense of the contrary views.
- Some ignore the new approaches.
- Some "misinterpret" the new approaches, adapting them or using parts of them to reinforce their own views.
- Some modify their earlier views and explore enthusiastically the ones presented.

Good teacher education, therefore, has the following characteristics:

- It begins from the knowledge, interests and beliefs that the teachers (or student teachers) have. The first step must disclose and clarify these beliefs.
- It challenges teachers to extend and revise their existing beliefs and skills. This development is not a simple yes/no step. It is a progression with different teachers progressing at different rates and with "wrong turns" a natural and essential part of the process.
- It takes time, and opportunities throughout the process for further interaction, challenge, and coaching. It is enhanced by group work and peer support.
- It links theory with practice, and makes clear the purposes and value of the learning.
- It employs a variety of teaching strategies, according to the range of programme objectives and the learning styles of the teachers.

There is a second perspective of "Teacher as Learner": the teacher must have a love of learning as a lifelong activity and must be able to demonstrate good learning strategies to his/her students. These strategies include preparedness to change and explore, open-mindedness, thoroughness, and self-evaluation.

The table in Fig 1 indicates a progression in the roles of teacher and learner that have occurred in the recent past as we have moved towards giving the learner more responsibility for his/her own learning. It applies to a view of the teacher as learner.

(i)	Knowledge based	: I give, you receive, I test
(ii)	Knowledge plus extension	: I give knowledge and suggest extensions; you receive from me, then from other sources; I test.
(iii)	Problem plus resources	: I set the problem and provide the resources to solve it, you do it; I evaluate your ability.
(iv)	Open problem	: I identify the problem; you find the resources and solve it with my help; we evaluate, you evaluate.
(v)	Your problem	: I give experience; you identify the problem; you solve it with my help; we evaluate, you evaluate.
(vi)	Your context	: you choose the issue, you define the problem; you solve it (with help); you evaluate.

Fig 1: Progression in encouraging independent learning. In the table, 'I' am the instructor, 'You' are the learner.

1.2 *Competencies and Roles of Science Teachers*

The basic objective of science teaching is to improve the quality of the life for all students and for society. The workshop listed roles and competencies expected of teachers in the STSP approach:

Competencies

Pedagogical/Classroom Skills: Improvization; teaching processes; meeting specific needs; handling equipment; assessing; relating science technology to real life; classroom management;

managing the learning environment; developing curricula; communicating with students; selecting from and using a wide variety of teaching techniques.

Personal/Professional Skills: Decision making; working with the community to develop curricula and resources; managing the school; communicating within the school system and with the community; questioning; being critical; seeking solutions; evaluating the programme.

Roles

Innovator; developer and implementer of the curriculum; evaluator of learning outcomes; motivator; facilitator of learning; perceiver of children's needs developments; resource manager; communicator of concepts; demonstrator; mediator (for imparting knowledge); interpreter (technological developments); resource of information; community helper/explainer; learner of science and technology developments; theoretician; coach; supervisor; model; designer of activities; coordinator.

These roles can be summarized under headings:

- curriculum developer
- evaluator
- learner
- resource mobilizer
- communicator of change in school and community
- motivator
- innovator
- participant in the total functioning of the school

1.3 Per-service Education

The ideas about education, science, and themselves as teachers that trainees bring to their pre-service course have been acquired mainly from their own experience at school. Their views may be held quite strongly: their propensity will be to teach as they were taught. They come also with a strong sense of purpose, a mission to become good teachers. They have chosen to be teachers.

Consideration of Content

The programme needs to include studies of the science related to the school curriculum. The definition of science needs to include all the aspects that are part of school science: applications, social context, philosophical ideas and social/personal action as well as science knowledge and processes of inquiry.

Trainees need to understand the psychological and philosophical foundations of education, especially the nature of children's learning and the strategies children use to learn.

In addition, teachers have to be aware of educational policies related to the curriculum, socio-economic programmes, technological advances and needs, and have insights into social structures at the state/national level and at the local/village level. These define the context in which education occurs.

Trainees should begin to develop the pedagogical and professional skills listed earlier.

'Value' orientations for developing personal or professional skills have to be addressed. These include 'sensitiveness' to the society for better cooperation through negotiation within the school and communities; achieving personal satisfaction through teaching, observing and enjoying children; and interesting in science and being 'scientific'.

A teacher is a model of scholarship and fairness for children and the local community. The teacher needs to be a professional. The teacher must have leadership skills and personal skills to make learning a lively and enjoyable experience for children. The teacher must love learning and demonstrate good learning strategies to his/her students. The teacher must be prepared to change and explore, be openminded, thorough, and self-critical.

Students Teachers Working with the Community: An Example from India

Working with the community was a required component of the teacher training programme. It was expected to benefit the community as well as the student teachers.

Faculty and trainees discussed possible areas for work. Their list included hospitals, urban slums, rural housing, the School for the Blind, Institutions for the Physically Handicapped, and polluted areas.

The trainees chose a work area and were formed into groups of fifteen or so, according to their choice. It was expected that visits should occur weekly, last about three hours and continue throughout the year. Normally a faculty member accompany the group.

The first visit brought a wide range of reactions from both the trainees and the institutions they visited. Hospital authorities were unwilling to be involved. Organizations working with urban slums and rural housing said no. The School for the Blind and the Institute for Mentally and Physically Handicapped welcomed the involvement. In polluted areas, even where there were voluntary groups already working, more were needed.

Many of the trainees coming from rural areas, although initially hesitant, become excited about the possibilities. In general, trainees from urban areas were less keen.

The different areas held different attractions to the trainees. There was particular enthusiasm for working with the physically and mentally disabled. The experiences of that group are highlighted below.

Working with the Disabled

Education of the disabled is part of the formal lecture programme. The visits were seen by the trainees as complementing the formal programme. The group also received regular informal guidance from faculty members.

In evaluating the visits, the trainees and staff in the programme noted:

- The trainees' social sensitivity in general was enhanced and they felt that the visits would have long term value in their careers.
- The children grew in self confidence. They enjoyed the trainees' visits.

- The interaction helped the trainees to understand the capabilities of disabled persons and the nature of disability. The trainees developed positive attitudes towards the disabled. Misconceptions were removed.
- Only some portions of the formal lecture programme was useful in the practical situation. At the end of the year, the trainees reports of their experiences were passed on to the faculty, as an input to curriculum improvement.
- Techniques for handling disabled children are best learned by actual practice.
- Several members of the group were upset by their first experience working with disabled persons in the institution. They had to be supported, prepared and helped to understand the need before they could proceed effectively.

1.4 In-service Education

Practising teachers come to teacher education programmes with knowledge and experience very different from pre-service teachers. They have direct knowledge of children, schools and teaching, and opportunities to practise new skills and ideas immediately. On the other hand, they may be more set in their ways and sceptical of new ideas. They also face greater difficulties with time constraints and competing responsibilities. The danger with the in-service course becomes "trying to feed too many things in too limited a time".

One of the first steps must be to have the teachers reflect on what happens in their classrooms and evaluate their teaching and the curriculum they offer. They might do this evaluation through reflection and discussion, keeping checklists, talking with students, or having an observer in the school with them. Its purpose is to clarify what already happens in the school, and the teachers' current beliefs about what should happen.

Current practice and the current curriculum need to be challenged, and teachers helped towards "better" solutions. Teachers have to be persuaded that the new approach is better than their current one. Then they must be assisted to understand the new ideas and learn the new skills. This might be achieved in part through argument, but will also need demonstration (whether live or on video), analyses of "good" and "bad" practices, and opportunities to try the new approaches themselves.

In-service courses should address also renewal and extension of knowledge to which the teachers are already committed: new science content, new equipment, management of experiments, assessment, and reporting to parents. This component is oriented not to major change, but helping teachers do better the job they see themselves doing. It is important, even in a programme of "major change ". It recognizes and responds to teachers' knowledge of their work and the interests and in-service purposes they see as important.

A third component of in-service education should be oriented to enhancing the teachers' career prospects: assisting them not only to be "better teachers" but to work as coordinators, department heads, curriculum advisers, head teachers. This career component is more important in the STSP approach than the traditional curriculum because of the greater emphasis in STSP on school based curriculum development and involvement of teachers in school management. It is important also because teachers see that the programme designers are looking at the world from the teachers' perspective, and not simply regarding the teachers as technicians who serve the purposes of the curriculum designers. And it is important for the long term development of schools and the school system because it enhance the quality of school leadership.

The success of a curriculum project and the quality of children's learning depend ultimately on the quality of the teachers. Teachers, much more than curriculum materials and broad educational policies, guide and effect social justice in education, because they guide the progress of each child in their care.

Those who teach the teachers must do their work well. They need sound knowledge of the education in the country and must understand and value the problems of the teachers. The language and images that the trainers use must connect with the experience of the teachers. Teachers are not leaky vessels to be topped up from time to time by an in-service programme, and now and again emptied and filled with a "new oil". In-service education programmes should be models of the good practice that the teachers themselves are expected to use: students centred, experiential, challenging current beliefs and competencies, and extending them.

Professional development does not only occur during in-service education programmes. It occurs whenever teachers seek, try and implement new approaches. The stimulus might come from students, other teachers, reading, or self-analysis. Teachers need to be assisted with the skills of directing their own learning, and they need support structures and opportunities surrounding them which stimulate their own professional growth.

Teacher Networks

Teacher networks are an important part of professional stimulus and growth. For example, consider the introduction of a new curriculum. As more teachers work with it, the opportunities for them to share their problems and successes increase. Also, individuals emerge who very quickly become successful and creative with it. Hence groups of teachers can be formed, with leaders from among them to facilitate further development. In large schools, the teachers within that school are natural groups, and systems of support can even be formalized within the school. For small schools it is necessary that networks form across schools.

However, it is insufficient to leave these groups to themselves. The groups benefit greatly from "external support" from a consultant, academic, or persons involved in the design of the innovation and the conduct of the first phase of training. This involvement also provides opportunities to identify problems the teachers face and give evaluative feedback on the innovation.

Structured Courses, Workshops and Conferences

They can range in duration from half-day programmes to month-long residential courses. They need to be carefully planned, according to the principles described in section 1.1, "The Teacher as Learner".

Preparation needs to be thorough so that leaders know what teachers have been doing in their schools and teachers know the purposes and programme of the workshop. It is helpful if the teachers are consulted during the development of the programme.

Workshops and conferences of this kind need to be part of a longer term strategy. There should be follow-up activities—perhaps further workshops, visits by advisers to the schools, or opportunities for participants in the workshop, to maintain contact with each other and share further progress.

It is preferable to have a number of teachers from a particular school attend the workshop at once, rather than a single representative. This provides an effective means of support for each teacher implementing the ideas at the school.

An alternative to the "one-shot" workshop is to have a number of sessions separated by periods in which the participants work in schools. Teachers come together for a workshop, then try the ideas over a period of days or weeks in their schools, then come together for a further workshop and discussion, and so on. This approach is better able to use the experiences of the teachers and to support implementation of the workshop ideas.

"Action Research" or Project Approaches

By this strategy, teachers are given much greater responsibility to choose the topic or area of their professional development. They choose the area and design a project which will have direct value in their school, and through which they will develop new knowledge and skills. They might choose a process area (such as activity-based learning, co-operative learning, reducing gender bias in the classroom) or a content area (developing units of work, introducing "quality of life" questions in the curriculum, helping students to be effective learners).

To work well, such projects need to have strong support from the school administration, a good group leader, and support from an outside person (perhaps a curriculum adviser, inspector, or lecturer from a teachers' college).

Examples of Workshops Activities

Drafting a Unit

1. Work in groups of four people.
2. Choose a topic area which you want to develop. It should be one rich in possibilities and able to be presented over about three weeks of class time.

Topic: Fuel in the Kitchen

3. Brainstorm possible content for the unit. Do this under headings:

   Science (I wonder....)

   Technology (I want......)

   Society (Should we.....)

   Personal Development

   Special Experiences.

Try to get a similar number of ideas under each heading. Note the rules of brainstorming: Think laterally. Don't evaluate ideas in the list until the list is complete. Encourage all members of the group to contribute, for example:

Science: Different fuels, heat value, where fuels come from, products of burning, combustion, requirements for efficient burning, heat transfer, the effects of cooking on food...

Technology: Types of stoves, designs, choice of materials, efficiency, transport of fuel, cooking vessels, convenience to user...

Society: Environmental considerations: fuel supply, pollution, waste, conservation, economy, safety, health hazards, design, fashion.....

Personal Development: Decision-making, cooperative work, use of time, construction, problem sloving, planning skills, researching, values education.....

Special experiences: Cooking with different systems, exploring foods that are cooked in different ways.

4. Draw concept maps or flow charts which show how ideas/activities might fit together.

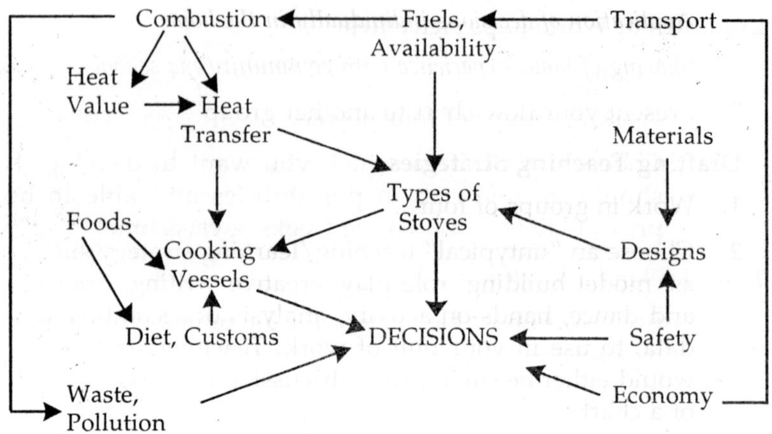

5. Brainstorm a possible "angle" or theme that will give the unit a sense of story, e.g., an environmental theme, a problem to be solved, a story about heroes, a setting. The angle you choose will give the unit character as well as continuity and coherence, as shown in the following example:

   Improving the efficiency of cooking in the students' own homes, looking especially at fuel use, heat loss/saving, and environment aspects.

6. Draw a Flow Chart showing how the unit will develop. Think about:

   (a) what the students will do

   (b) what the students will learn

   (c) how well it relates to the children's interests and experience

This may be shown as follows:

Observation of home situation

Students exchange observations

Study of different designs: disadvantages and advantages

Science of fuels and burning

Decision-making of best cooking methods, and improvements to existing methods

Application of decisions individually in the home

Sharing of home experience with community via school

7. Present your flow chart to another group

Drafting Teaching Strategies

1. Work in groups of four.
2. Choose an "untypical" teaching/learning strategy such as: model building, role play, creative writing, drama and dance, hands-on activity, analysis of second-hand data, to use in your unit of work. Teaching strategies would either be small group discussion or presentation of a chart.
3. Develop an activity to go in your unit (from Part 2) that uses the chosen teaching strategy.

   Example: The group discussion will lead to the preparation and presentation of a chart to the whole class. The chart might be like this:

Type of stove	Number of houses using them	Ease of lighting	Cost	Cooking time	Environ. effects
Wood					
Charcoal					
Kerosene					
LPG					
Biogas					
Electric					
Microwave					

4. Run the activity with the group.

Beyond In-service Programmes

Training programmes are only part of the professional development and support of teachers. Staffing and promotions policies, career opportunities, incentive schemes and professional recognition have important influence on teachers' involvement in professional development and successful implementation. Support through consultancy, resource centres, journals, networks and teacher associations need to be available and well coordinated. Lack of finance, teacher time, and unskilled programme leaders are constraints which can hinder the quality of the in-service courses. These aspects were discussed in Chapter One.

2. Interactions with Parents, Other Personnel and the Local Community

The work of teachers is not simply with the curriculum and children. Teachers work within the organizational structure of the school, and the school in turn is linked to the educational system and the community.

Teachers need to know the formal decision-making structures—the arrangements that exist for leadership, control and support in the school; the requirements of protocol and good manners; the expectations of them in the decision-making processes. They also need skills to analyze the formal and informal structures in the school and community, to work effectively within these structures, and to know where they can get help of different kinds by mobilizing these structures.

Some techniques to develop these skills are offered below:

- *Analyze the organizational structures and power relationships within the school and community.* Teachers can be asked to draw organizational charts that show both formal and informal decision-making structures in the school, and identify "key people" that might assist with particular changes. Similarly, they can identify people in the community relevant to particular ideas and projects.

- *Work effectively as a participant in decision-making and the development of the school.* Teachers can work in "simulation" exercises, acting as group member or in interaction with a superior. Skills in listening, assertiveness, cooperation and conflict resolution need to be addressed.

- *Prepare arguments and information and present their ideas to decision-makers.* Teachers can practise with guidance from an instructor, developing submissions to be put to decision-makers. Both written and spoken submissions need to be considered. Part of the exercise can be the evaluation of other submissions. The preparation and presentation of reports should also be considered, whether they be reports to other staff within the school, or to the community, funding agencies or the Ministry.
- *Negotiate with members of the school and the community.* Teachers need skills to negotiate particular changes, and arrange support and co-operation for particular activities. Through modelling, simulation and coaching these skills can be developed.
- *Examine their own skills, behaviours and career goals and consider how these relate to the life of the school and community.* Teachers can make lists of their strengths and weaknesses as participants in the school and its interaction with the community. They can draw maps which show some of their major achievements and interests, and the way these achievements relate to each other in their career development, they can set goals and plan the next steps in their professional activity.

The details of programme objectives, emphasis and interpretation will vary from one country to another according to the culture of the country, the structure of the society and the expectations and roles to teachers. These interpretations need to be worked through in each country. Variations, even within a country, have to be expected, as the education reforms reach the different ethnic and cultural groups and different physical environments.

Other Personnel, Community and Parents

Other education personnel, parents, and community can have significant roles in the development and implementation of new curricula, a school programme, or a class project. Their contribution comes in several ways—cooperation and assistance, giving direction for further improvement, moral and/or financial support, supervision.

The implications for teacher education come in two ways. First, teachers need to have the skills and strategies for working effectively with the other groups. Second, the other groups need "professional development" that orients them to the work of the schools and assists them to work with schools. There is a sense in which they became "teachers" through their involvement in curriculum design, school operations, and the children's learning.

Parents

Parents should be involved in schools and curriculum planning because of the stake they have in their children's education, the knowledge they have of their children's character, hopes and the activities, their involvement in the local community and their insight into the needs and resources of the community. The achievements of schools are greatest when the values and purposes and approach of the schools are in tune with those the child experiences in family life, peer groups, religious observance, and other community activities.

Arrangements can be made for parent involvement in school activities at different levels:

- *Communication:* Parents need to know what the school is trying to achieve, what the children do at school and how their children are progressing. Teachers need to know about each child from the family's perspective and the family's observation of progress and/or difficulties. Effective communication with parents is not easily achieved. Some parents do not read, or read well in the language used at school. Some find schools and the symbols and language of schools daunting, so that a visit to the school, or discussion with a teacher or head teacher is hard for them. A range of approaches have to be used: meetings of parents of children in a particular grade; one-to-one meetings between a teacher and the parents of a child, perhaps with the child present; social events which enable parents to mix with each other and teachers informally; newsletters, perhaps in a number of different languages.
- *Assistance in the functioning of the school:* Helping with excursions or equipment, working bees to improve

facilities, the organization and conduct of social activities, assistance in communications programmes, collection of data as part of surveys and programme evaluation.

- *Involvement in curriculum planning and school governance:* Informal involvement through participation in programme evaluation and needs assessments; formal involvement through various planning committees, policy committees, or School Council/School Board.

These three levels of involvement imply different levels of input from parents into the purposes and nature of the curriculum in the school. At the "communications" level, the leadership may still be strongly with teachers. At the "school governance" level, the shared responsibility for curriculum planning is formalized through committees and organizational structures, and the balance of responsibility is set in "terms of reference" and membership for each committee.

There is bound to be conflict at times between parents and school, at least for some parents and some teachers or administrators. The conflict can be between educational values and cultures within the school community, between different views of correct processes in communication and decision-making, and between judgements of right and wrong behaviours/actions—whether of a child, at teacher, a parent or an administrator. Conflict is not necessarily negative. It may be simply an expression of different ways of doing things, and as such, a stimulus for better solutions.

For example, a parent may "guide' the child towards a particular field or future in which child is not interested, or the parents may want the child to stay home from school to help the family earn its living. The teacher can play a significant role as a "bridge" between parent and child. But it is not clear where the teachers responsibility or right to be involved starts and stops. The following example may be used:

A Learning Workshop for Parents

1. *Did schooling, does schooling do what it should do?*

   Parents recall the society they lived in as children, and the schooling they had? Did schooling exist for them?

Did it work from them? What are their most vivid memories of their teachers and schools? What were the things learning that have been most useful since? How has the world changed over the last 30 years? How different is their education from what it is now?

2. *Learning is simple, or is it?*

   Parents recall a recent situation where they learned something new: using a total, understanding a situation, etc. They talk to each other about the processes that went through that they thought were important in the success of that learning. Groups attempt to come up with some general statements.

3. *Current approaches to helping children learn*

   A school representative talks to the parents about current approaches to teaching and learning in the school, linking current approaches back to the parents' ideas.

In both pre-service and in-service teacher education, the issues of parent involvement in schooling need to be addressed, and teachers need to be assisted to develop competence in working with parents.

Schools and governments also need to conduct programmes which help parents to understand the roles that they might play in school, and develop the skills they need in order to work effectively in schools. Ultimately, their involvement should make a difference to the learning outcomes of children at the school.

Community

The modern concepts of "community and schools" and their inter-relationships, the study of community groups, identification of resources and their utilization for the well being of the individual and the community, improvement of the environment, population problems, issues related to local and national development, *Education for All* and *Science for All* as we have described them require strong interaction between school and community.

Community involvement can assist and support the school in curriculum development and planning. In this sense it is like parent involvement, improving the school through involvement in the life of the school.

There is a second aspect—the extension of the school into the life of the community. Involvement of the school in the community provides opportunities for the students to link theory to practice, action to reflection; to seek solutions to practical and social problems, to make decision, to work cooperatively.

Community involvement in schooling and involvement in the community both require administrative support and programmes of professional development for teachers and members of the community.

Education Personnel

Educational administrators and support persons, whether at the school level (coordinators and head teachers), the district level (supervisors and consultants), or the regional and state levels have critical roles to play in curriculum planning and implementation.

Workshops for School Administrators and Teachers in their Roles in School Management Focus on Planning

Workshops and discussion sessions can be organized on various themes which need to be supported by programmes for the development of skills and strategies. Questions could be raised like:

- What freedom/responsibilities does/do the school have for planning in curriculum? Resource allocation to the school? Resource allocation within the school?
- What areas of operation within the school can benefit from a co-ordinated approach to school planning? Teaching strategies in different classes? School "climate"? Use of resources? Discipline? Reporting to parents? Curriculum development?
- What are some of the major "problems" that the school is facing? How can they benefit from wide involvement in analysis and planning?

- Do members of the school share a vision of what the school's future development might be?

Existing policies and initiatives in the school can be coordinated so as to reflect that vision? Questions that may be raised are as follows:

- What are the steps in the planning process, and what skills do people have for identifying problems, creating solutions, setting goals, and achieving goals?
- What administrative structures and processes exist for making decisions that have wide effect in the school?
- What is the "work climate" like in the school, for teachers, students and administrators? To what extent is the climate sustained in order to encourage the continuing quest for school improvement?

Curriculum innovation is unlikely to make progress in a school if it is not supported by the head teacher and other school administrators. Educational achievement depends on the administrative climate, and the culture of the school, including a sense of shared vision and common direction among the teachers. School management, and the involvement of school administrators in curriculum leadership has much to do with curriculum innovation.

Similarly, district and regional personnel need to have a good understanding of curriculum changes in progress, and of the processes of leadership and change. Supervisors and consultants need special programmes to acquaint them with new techniques, materials, methods, equipment, concepts, management practices, and structural arrangements. They must understand their role in teacher training, including their responsibilities to support teachers and head teachers in the administrative domain. They must be given programmes which help them develop their skills in consultancy, supervision and school support.

A Summary of Roles: Parents, Community and Education Personnel

The following list provides a summary of the roles of education personnel, community and parents in educational innovation. The lists make clear the importance of including parents and community involvement and educational administrative systems as components of teacher education (both pre-service and in-service) and of providing educational programmes for the community, parents and educational administrators to assist them in their curriculum roles.

Education Personnel

Headmasters/Principals

- provide leadership and effective management in school development and the interaction of the school with parents, community and other agencies;
- administer staff, time allotments, resources, and programmes;
- procure materials, equipment and other facilities;
- assist and supervise teachers in their work;
- encourage teachers and students in curricular and extra curricular activities such as science quizzes, fairs, community intervention.

Supervisors, inspectors, consultants

- assist teachers to understand policy, improve their teaching, develop curriculum, and participate in school planning;
- assist head teachers and coordinators within the school to understand administrative approaches and improve their management skills;
- supervise the activities of teachers and schools;
- work with head teachers in identifying problems in facilities, staffing, curriculum and administrative support, and facilitate the flow of requirements within the system;
- organize training courses/seminars/workshops for teachers, parents, community, and educational administrators.

Directors and Superintendents

- give directions (both up and down the administrative system) about changes needed for the improvement of the system;

- provide educational leadership and effective management of support services, staffing provision, resources and facilities in the region;
- implement curricula and professional development programmes;
- administer examinations and programme evaluations;
- recruit and transfer teaching staff;
- make policies at the district, division, and/or regional level such as those related to the upgrading of teachers, providing incentives for teachers, supervision, tasks of headmasters, and activities for students;
- facilitate the procurement of facilities and equipment.

Community

Community Leaders

- provide an environment (peace and order, structural) and services (transportation etc.) that facilitates effective schooling;
- support the school through provision of resources, access to community resources, and assistance of voluntary organizations, volunteers and donors;
- input to curriculum planning to meet local needs.

Organizations/Associations (including Government Organizations)

- support and assist in extra-curricular activities;
- provide facilities and mobilizing manpower for educational activities;
- promote projects which provide professional development for teachers, head teachers, and other education personnel, and for community leaders, parents, and organizations in their roles in education;
- promote education of disabled and disadvantaged people in terms of moral and/or financial support;
- participate in curriculum planning and implementation;
- improve the coordination of their own programmes with school programmes.

Parents

- motivate and support their children, including expenditures in their children's education;
- guide and assist children in their school work;
- provide moral and financial support for the school;
- attend school functions that promote better relationship between parents, child and the teacher;
- accept the responsibilities that they have to understand what the school is trying to do;
- work with the school to improve the children's educational achievements in terms of their perceptions and values on the education of their children;
- be involved in curriculum planning and evaluation of the quality of implementation in the school.

3. Supporting System for Teacher Improvement

A large number of experiences from different countries are available, which speak of channels and structures available for the improvement of the teacher, and teacher education as a whole.

Inputs through government, voluntary groups and private industry can help science teachers and extend and support the science curriculum. They can provide opportunities for students to see science in the work-place. They can assist students to understand the roles of work in the lives of the individual and society, and develop skills that have value in the workplace.

Examples of support systems are indicated as follow:

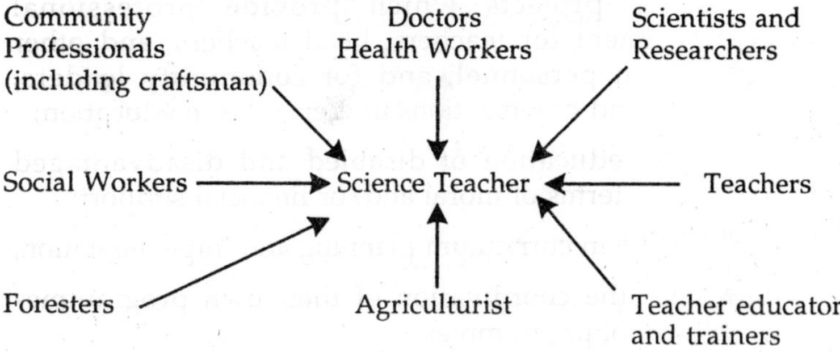

Curriculum developers, teacher educators, consultants, trainers and subject experts may be mobilized though a network of resource centres:

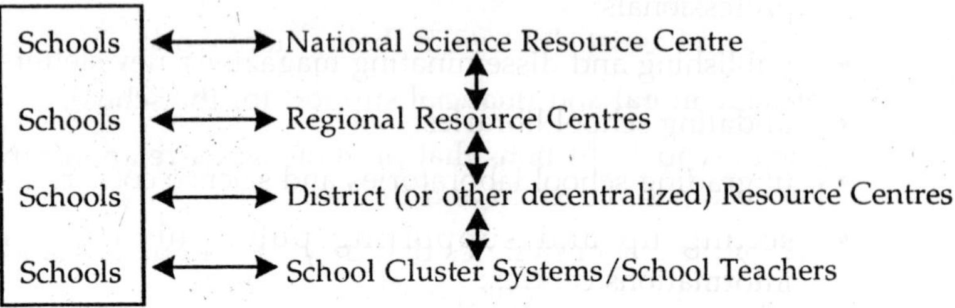

A similar pattern of a network of science clubs help the teacher in carrying out particularly experiments and activities which involve out-of-school situations.

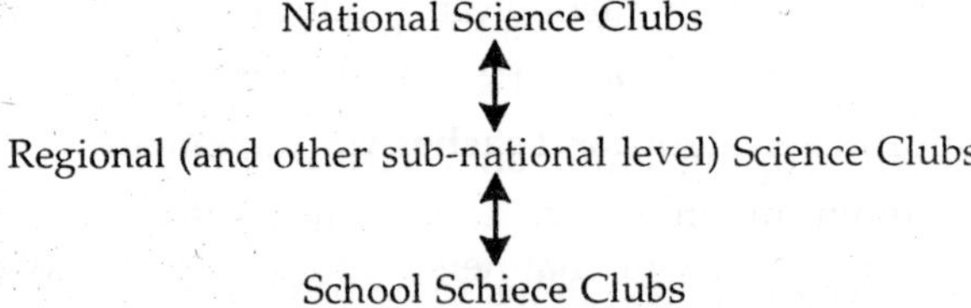

Voluntary groups of science teachers, through their associations, can enrich the teacher for improving the teaching/learning process through mutual interaction and peer learning, by organizing seminars, training programmes and classroom activities.

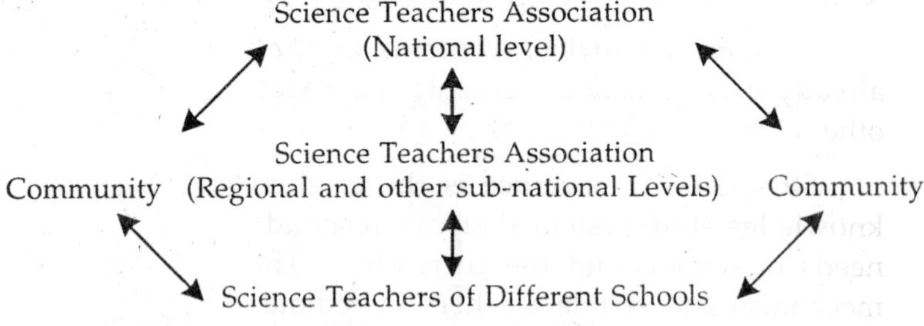

The enrichment of science teachers with science knowledge, skills for interacting with children, community and professionals through the above organizational structures could be possible through activities like:

- organizing seminars and workshops;
- talks from community elders, social workers, professionals;
- publishing and disseminating magazines, newsletters;
- updating school libraries;
- upgrading school laboratories and science corners;
- setting up and supporting public libraries and informations centres;
- organizing science fairs in schools for the community;
- encouraging projects related to science that deal with problems of the community;
- providing incentives through fellowships and leave for self improvement of science teachers;
- developing children's activities based on the local environment;
- developing test items to be used at school level;
- sharing new information among schools;
- discussing problems encountered in the classroom.

Radio and television programmes on science and technology and their usefulness to society, and answering children and teachers querries can be of gainful use to the science teacher.

In many countries, elements of the above mechanisms already exist. Existing elements may need strengthening and other elements may need to be added.

Of special importance is the gradual development of a knowledge flow system that can respond *rapidly* to changing needs of schools and the curriculum. This includes effective mechanisms to enable teachers in remote and disadvantaged areas to indicate their knowledge reference needs and have those needs met. The increasing opportunities for multiple media, including telecommunications and electronics (compact discs, floppy discs, modems) as well as print should be recognized.

Networks, which currently exist independently can be coordinated and linked into a *holistic* national-regional-sub-regional two-way (user—producer) flow structure. Such a network could incorporate all potential resources generators, including those outside the education system (such as agriculture, forestry, fisheries, health, rural development, small industries, information, broadcasting). The development of an integrated national knowledge flow system linked into international networks such as UNISIST and ERIC needs to be considered early, so that the compatibility of systems can be ensured. Plans might include translation of foreign materials into the national language(s).

3

Application in Real Life Situations: Some Examples

A Model for Evaluating Curriculum Units

Progress in science education over the last 30 years can be considered as development in the three dimensions shown in Fig. 2. The three dimensions define a "space" into which curriculum units can be placed according to their treatment of the child as learner, the definition of science, and the extent to which "non-science" is included in the curriculum. Progress has been, in many ways, a move along the diagonal from the "pure science—science as knowledge—child as receiver" corner to the "science/non-science/quality of life—child in community" corner.

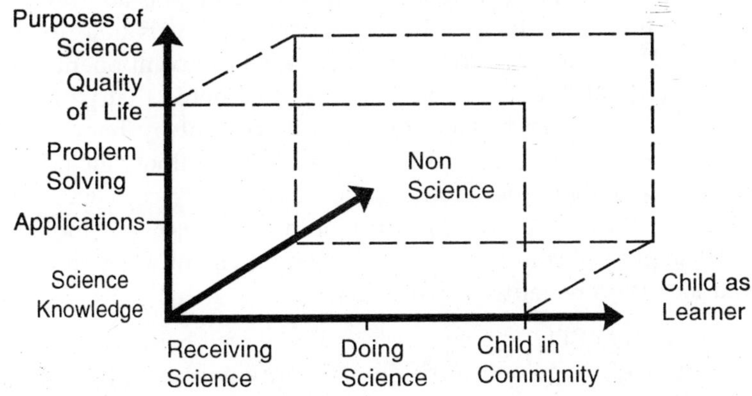

Fig. 2. Model for Evaluating Curriculum Units

The first dimension shows different ways of thinking about the child as learner. It progresses from a subject centred approach (with emphasis on the child receiving knowledge), through a "child and science" approach (with emphasis on learning through doing), to a "child in the community" approach (with emphasis on learning in the context of the child's purposes in the local environment).

The second dimension refers to the definition of "science". It progresses from pure science (theoretical concepts and theories and the processes of generating and testing them), to science and its applications in daily life, to science as a means of solving technical problems, to science as a means of personal and community development. It indicates the extent to which human action, values, personal development and quality of life are admitted as components of the science curriculum.

For example, at the science as knowledge end, a lesson might teach levers and the principle of moments. The children would then be tested on whether they can recite the principle and use it to solve set problems. When the approach is extended to applications, students might examine instances of levers in their community. Extended to solving technical problems, a situation might be presented such as lifting a load, where the lever (or a pulley, ramp, or hydraulic jack) is a possible answer. This is a technical problem only, in so far as it has no values component. There is no concern for whether one solution is "better" than the other, only for a machine that is able to do the job. The next extension introduces a values component and raises issues of "quality of life". It might be noted that workers in the village carry baskets of rocks or cement by hand. The students design and discuss some possible solutions, including the science of their operation. A wheel barrow or a conveyer belt system could be provided, but it would cost the owner money, and it might put some workers out of employment. What should be done? Who benefits? What is lost?

"Quality of life" encompasses material well-being (economic development, hygiene, nutrition, shelter, environment). It also includes personal well-being. Personal well-being is the extent to which individuals realize their humaneness. It has spiritual and moral components. It is a measure of the power that individuals have in their lives, through their abilities to think, respect themselves, communicate, feel, take action, participate fully in the life of the community. It concerns the human being both as an individual persons whose life is unique, and a social person whose life is shared. At the community level, "quality of life" also raises issues of justice in the distribution and accessibility of "goods" in the society.

The third dimension indicates the extent to which the science curriculum extends into "non-science"—especially into economics, social studies, culture, politics, environmental education and moral education. The extension is not into formal instruction in, say, economic theory, but rather to recognize that resolution of "quality of life" problems requires consideration of more than the pure science and technology aspects. Setting science in the context of quality of life places science firmly in the service of the general curriculum and the broad purposes of schooling.

The model in Fig. 2 can be used to evaluate a science unit: the unit can be "placed" in the space according to the way it treats the different dimensions.

It can also be used in curriculum design. The curriculum developers can choose a point in the space which they think is most appropriate in their country or school and design the unit accordingly. It is likely that they will choose different points in the space for different units and so create a range of approaches.

The design of a unit depends on how far the developers choose to move towards the "quality of life" corner of the space. It also depends on the way they choose to start the unit, and the subsequent flow of ideas. Three alternatives are shown in Fig. 3. There are many others.

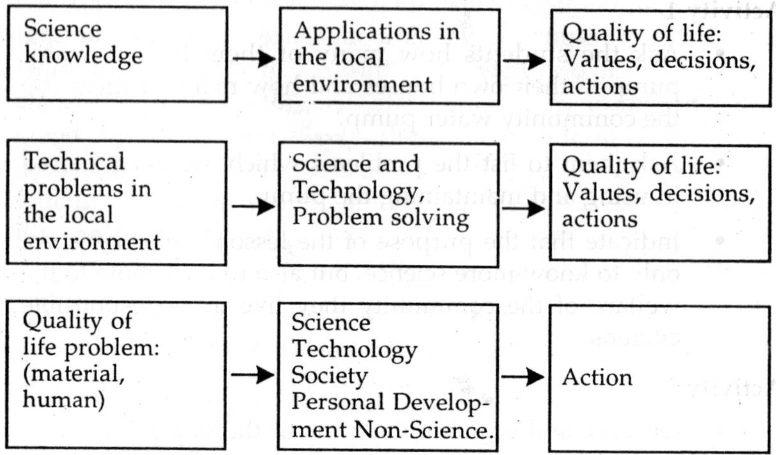

Fig 3: Different approaches to the flow of ideas.
Each approach is concerned with science and the quality of life.

Curriculum Examples

The examples below are from the various participating countries. They illustrate different approaches to science and its application in the local community and to the issues of quality of life. They have been analysed according to the ideas in Fig. 2 and Fig. 3, to provide the commentaries given with the unit outlines.

The first five examples all address question of water supply and water quality. They are included because they demonstrate different teaching approaches and emphasis and the range of approaches that can be used to address particular content and purposes.

Example 1: Hand Water Pump

People in our countries use water pumps abundantly. Often they create problems of malfunction, due to leaking, difficulty of operation, water not lifting up, breaking of nuts, or corrosion. There can also be problems with location of the pump, costs, and whether a new bore is required or the pump placed on an existing well. This sequence addresses the first concern: the functioning of the pump. The other concerns are taking up subsequently.

Activity 1

- Ask the students how many of them have a water pump in their own houses and how many of them use the community water pump.
- Ask them to list the problems which are encountered in using and maintaining the pump.
- Indicate that the purpose of the lesson sequence is not only to know more science, but also to contribute to the welfare of the community they live in as responsible citizens.

Activity 2

- Observe and examine the parts of the pump (on site if possible).
- Discussion and learning/teaching (with relevant student activities) on the mechanism and working principles. Student worksheets related to the lever, water pressure, lift and force pumps, should be used for group work, facilitated by the teacher).

Activity 3

- Divide the students into groups with four or five students in each group. (The criterion for selection is that the students live near each other).
- Assign each group to survey four or five houses which are close to their own homes and do the following (Their own homes may be included in the survey):

  1. Interview the people.
     - List any problems they have with water pumps.
     - List ways they try to solve these problems.
  2. Observe the base and the surroundings of the pump.
     - What materials are used to make the base of the pump?
     - Is there a proper drainage system?

- Is the waste water stagnating near the pump?
- Are the surroundings clean?

Activity 4

- Ask the students to check the problems which they gathered and make one complete list for the class.
- Discuss the problems and classify them under three headings:
  - Problems they can solve themselves.
  - Problems that can be solved with the help of others.
  - Problems that cannot be solved at present.
- Discuss the validity of the criteria used in the classification, in the context of the real situation in the community.

Activity 5

- Give every student the following learning/practice opportunities with real pumps. Support with diagrams. A technician from the community may help. Alternatives to the parts of the pump may be considered (such as for the washer).
  - Changing the washer.
  - Fixing the nut.
  - Oiling the different parts.
- Discuss and plan for the establishment of a student mobile repair team to help the community.

Activity 6

- Discuss the various effects on people of water stagnating near the pump.
- Discuss how the surroundings of the pump may be improved.
- Plan and take action to improve the surroundings of pumps in the village.

  (The local or visiting Health Officer may help with discussion and planning)

Activity 7

Assign to the students the following as homework.

(i) Find out how much water they get in one stroke of the pump. (The students discuss and plan their procedures for this activity.)

(ii) Is the handle of the pump easy or difficult to operate?

(iii) Can a small child (e.g. their younger brother and sister) operate the pump without much efforts or do they need the help of the adults?

(iv) Bring to school some water sample in a clean bottle.

Activity 8

Test a sample of water for turbidity, hardness and softness, colour and smell. If possible, test for the pressure of micro-organisms, by sending the sample to a nearby laboratory. Student worksheets are used for this activity, done as group work.

Activity 9

- For homework, students collect information on local methods for improving hardness/turbidity of water. These are presented in class.
- Do activities for removing the hardness and turbidity of water.
  (Student worksheets are used for this activity, done as group work).
- Discuss the effect on human beings of micro-organisms, if any, found in water.
- Discuss the methods used for the removal of micro-organisms from the water.

  (These could involve expository teaching by the teacher, possibly helped by the local or visiting Health Officers.)

Activity 10

- Ask the students to observe and report the following about the containers which are being used in their own homes for collecting drinking water. Describe the type of container used e.g. plastic, stainless steel, jars made from clay, etc.

- Are the containers washed before each filling? How often? Occasionally, when the look dirty?
- Are the containers covered or kept open?
- What is the condition of the place where the containers are kept, such as dark or lighted, clean or dirty, raised or under the stair case etc.
- Observe and report how water is drawn from the main container into smaller vessels.

Activity 11

Discuss the possible effects or problems that may be created by unclean vessels and containers, uncovered vessels, and the condition of the place where the containers and vessels are kept.

(Assistance may be provided by the local or visiting Health Officer).

Activity 12

- Discuss proper and hygienic ways of cleaning the containers and vessels, and practice using these methods.
- Demonstrate some methods which can be used when drawing the water from the container to the small vessels. Students practice these methods also.
- Discuss and plan how the school can help the community improve the storage of safe drinking water.

Commentary

The lesson sequence addresses the following:

- *Social interaction in relation to a technology:* The lift pump is vital to the quality of life of the communities. The lessons raise the values, benefits, customs and social questions as well as looking at the technology.
- *Science concepts:* These are treated in the context of application in relation to levers and water pressure, learned using pupil worksheets, with group discussion facilitated by the teacher.

- *Personal development:* This includes science process skills such as communicating with people, planning for action (e.g. improving the sanitation near the pump area) observation, data collection inference, etc.
- *Technology:* The repair and maintenance of the water pump; techniques for cleaning vessels to hold water, and for transferring water hygienically.
- *Quality of life:* Contributed to from the above, and collective responsibilities for maintaining the quality of life recognized, including social intervention contributions by the students and the school.

Example 2: Danger In The River

The story was developed by a conference group in Kuala Lumpur in 1989. It shows some of the ways that values and ethics can be integrated into science lessons, and ways students can be involved in lessons planning.

Day 1

Ana walked over to her Grade 8 classroom. During the last week, the class had been working on the topic 'Chemical Pollutants'. Halfway through the lesson, she noticed Lee was scratching all over his body. She went over to him and was surprised to see Lee had rashes all over his body. She asked him what caused the rashes. He said he didn't know. He thought it may be something he had eaten. Some students thought it might be that he had brushed against a particular tree. Others thought it was because he had been swimming the night before in the Sunway River. Ana asked the class for evidences for each of these explanations. Lee had not eaten different foods, or been among bushes or insects recently. He had been in the Sunway River. Another student had also developed rashes after swimming in the river.

Lee was later taken to the hospital for treatment.

Day 2

"Are you okay? What did the doctor say?" Lee replied that he had a reaction to chemicals. "Where do you think Lee got into contact with the chemicals?" "It must be from the river!"

Sarada answered. Ana thought this was a good opportunity to link what has been taught to a real situation. Ana asked her class whether they would like to spend more time investigating this matter and many agreed.

Ana posed the question "How can we find out what pollutants there are in the river that might have caused Lee's rashes". Soon the class had assembled a list of tasks.

Ana wrote them on the board:

1. Collect water sample from the river.
2. Test the water sample.
3. Search any source that is responsible in polluting the river.
4. Interview local residents to see if the water from the river had created problems to them.

She divided the class into four groups. Groups A and B were to look into matters 1 and 2. Ana would take the leaders of these two groups to the river after school so that testing can be done immediately. Sonya, the lab assistant, agreed to help.

Ana assigned tasks 3 and 4 to Groups C and D respectively. Ana requested Abdul, the chemistry teacher, to guide Groups C and D. The visits to the river and the local residents were to be done outside school hours.

Some students volunteered to go to the library to gather information related to the topic, especially for information on chemicals that might be harmful to humans.

Day 3

The water samples from the river were tested using the techniques that had been learned the week before. Ana was pleased at the level of interest that the students had in their work.

Day 4

Testing of water samples was completed. Ana received the results in written reports. For both Groups A and B the results were similar. Sopie the leader of Group A gave a brief account of what they have done and their findings. They found that the percentage of dissolved oxygen was very low. Sopie noted that this explained the fact why there were not many fishes or aquatic animals in the river. Traces of lead and mercury were also found in the water samples.

"Where did these compounds come from?" Sara asked.

Ana explained, "Before we answer that question we should try to make inferences and conclusions about the findings. Should the compounds be in the river in the first place?" "Definitely not", the children answered. Therefore, we can say that the river is polluted.

Day 5

With the help of Abdul the chemistry teacher, Group 3 reported that they had found a paper factory 5 km. North. "This is probably where the pollutants come from". Further investigations needed to be carried out. For example what are the process going on in the factory etc. Lee reported that farmers and villagers along the river also emptied refuse and waste into river. The groups argued that it was unlikely that this waste included mercury and lead. On the other hand, they did not know which chemicals had caused Lee's rashes.

At the same time, Group 4 was having interesting interviews with local residents and employers of the factory. Ana helped them in preparing the interviews and the kind of questions to be asked.

Day 6

From the interviews and investigations, the groups presented some facts and data. It was found that the paper factory was dumping large volumes of chemical waste into the river. Another interesting fact was that almost half of Sunway residents were employers of the factory! Ana posed the question. What action should be taken?

The situation was put on the board:

- River is polluted.
- Factory is polluting the river.
- Factory employs local residents.

The children were eager to give their opinion. To them, the solution was obvious: close down the factory.

Ana pointed out that the problem can be looked at from three different points of view and the implications: the factory owner, factory workers and users of the river. Ana led the class in the discussion and they came up with three options:

1. *Close down the factory.* This implies that the factory owner will lose his business and the workers will lose their jobs.
2. *The owner has to build a proper dumping place or treat the chemical wastes before dumping them into the river.* This will increase the factory's over-head expenses and whether the factory can handle this is yet to be discovered.
3. *Leave it as it is.* Definitely, it affects the users of the river. Lee's rashes was one evidence, lack of fish was another.

Ana was pleased at the end of discussion. Involvement was high and the children had raised good questions. Students were aware of the situation and the difficulties in solving it. They have learnt that they need to be open-minded and willing to accept other people's opinion. She went home thinking about what the next steps for the class might be. She knew that some students wanted to take up the issue with the village factory and with the factory owner.

(From: Values and Ethics in the Science Curriculum, 1989 Workshop Report, UNESCO, in press)

Example 3: Water Pollution and the Growth to Duckweed (an aquatic plant)

Objectives: Upon completion of the unit, students should be able to:

- describe the meaning of water pollution
- describe several causes of water pollution
- identify means to prevent water from being polluted
- take individual responsibility for preventing water pollution

Domestic Wastes:

The teacher leads discussion of waste water from households, to help the students understand the meaning of water pollution, then raises questions about the causes. This provides a lead-in to the activity below:

Activity:

On completion of the activity the students should be able to

- draw conclusions on the effect of concentration of detergent solution on the growth of duckweed;
- describe how domestic wastes can cause water pollution.

Time required: 40 mins

Materials: Duckweeds of equal sizes (50)

Feltpen, syringe (25mL), stirrer, plastic boxes;

Detergent solutions, 0.1%, 0.01%, 0.001%, 0.0001%, tap water. Students will use 20 mL. quantities of the detergent solutions.

Preparations: Preparations should be done five days in advance.

1. Put stalks of duckweed in a plastic bag containing 500 mL of tapwater.
2. Prepare a 0.1% solution by dissolving 1 gram of detergent in 100 mL of water.
3. Prepare a 0.01% solution by taking 50 mL of the 0.1% solution and adding 450 mL of tapwater.
4. Prepare 0.001% and 0.0001% solutions, using the same logic as in (3).

Instructions to students:

1. Set up 5 plastic boxes, each one with a different detergent solution and one with tapwater. Label each box according to the concentration of detergent in it, including the box containing tapwater.

2. Select 50 stalks of duckweed of the same size. Use a stirrer to transfer 10 stalks to each of the labelled boxes. Arrange the plants so the roots are dipping into the solution.
3. Do not let the boxes dry. Add solutions to their respective containers, as frequent as necessary.
4. Place all four containers in a similar environment: similarly exposed to sunlight, wind, humidity, etc.

Discussion of Results:

The detergent solutions of 0.1% caused all the duckweeds to turn yellow and die. The 0.01% solution had no effect on the weeds at the beginning but gradually changed their colour from fresh green to pale yellow. The weeds in the 0.001%, 0.0001% solutions and tapwater grew well. The colour stayed fresh green and some plants grew new leaves. The number of new leaves in the 0.0001% solution was greater than in tapwater. This suggests that large concentrations of detergent are harmful to duckweeds, but very small concentrations may even be helpful.

(The detergent is a phosphate compound. Concentrations of order 15 parts per million help aquatic plants to grow well.)

The effects on other plants can be discussed.

Aquatic plants are useful to the environment. They increase the dissolved oxygen in water through photosynthesis. However, they may cause damage to or impede water flow. In addition, when the plants die, the organic substances which are good nutrients for micro-organisms increase in quantity, and this can pollute the water.

Further Activities:

Similar activities can follow, where students discuss industrial wastes (e.g., high temperature untreated water, toxic substances such as mercury, lead, cadmium, and oil) and then do an experiment where they test the effect of (used) motor oil on Elodea and other aquatic plants. Students can discuss means of removing oil spills, and some of the major accidents that have occurred with oil spills in rivers and at sea.

Commentary

The topic starts from a social problem. The study can lead to an improvement in the quality of life, as students learn some of the effects of water pollution in their community, and ways to reduce them. It also contains the science concepts related to water pollution. Further, the students get opportunity to learn a variety of skills by conducting experiments, discussing and sharing their observations, collecting data and analyzing them.

The topic goes beyond the science concepts. The students are expected to take greater individual responsibility for the prevention of water pollution in their homes and community. This creates a sense of belonging to the community and builds satisfaction and confidence in the students. Such an activity contributes to the personal development of the students and allows them to apply their science knowledge in their real life situation. Science becomes more meaningful for students and gives them opportunity to take part in and make decisions on community development.

Example 4: The Faucet

Water is an important resource which must be conserved. This is the main idea developed in this lesson. The social technological contexts are emphasized. The lessons starts with an activity that presents the social aspects, the community using water, and draws out the attitudes and values of students, raising awareness of the importance of water in their lives. The science aspect of the lesson comes when the water cycle and the sources of water (as ground water and surface water) are discussed. The fact that populations have grown and therefore people have to live further from water sources leads to the problem of obtaining water and distributing it to the users. This is where the technological aspects of the lesson are presented. The water faucet and the water meter are studied to help the students appreciate these technological devices, and develop confidence and a better quality of life through these devices. The necessity for conserving water becomes more evident with the use of the water meter.

Activity 1: The value of water

Ask students to list ways in which the community uses water. Combine the students ideas into a single list the blackboard and ask students to rate their importance. Ask them to defend their positions. Allow time for discussion if students are divided in their ratings.

Conflicts which arose from students' rating on agreement and disagreement is a clarification activity which enables the students to think of the value of water for them.

Activity 2: How different families use water

Let the students estimate the amount of water their family uses for each activity in one day. Call on 5-6 students to fill out a table on the board with estimated averages.

Distribute a worksheet on which they are to record how much water they use in one day, by estimating their water use in different activities. This can be a family activity. Tell them to make a list of the activities that require the use of water, and the amounts used.

If some have difficulty making estimations, give them guidance on the volume of water in a cup, a pail, etc.

Students realize that large amounts of water are consumed in certain activities and the need for water conservation. The data is a basis for discussing issues about lifestyles of people.

Discussion:

Combine the data from different families. Have the students rank the activities from the greatest to the least user of water. Then ask questions like:

- Is the given amount of water used in each activity by each family the same, or is it different? If they differ, what contributed to the difference?
- Could the families use less water for the same purpose? How?
- Would the time of day or month affect the amount of water you used for each activity? Cite examples.

- Ask them to make generalizations from their analysis of the data.

Activity 3: Population and Water Supply

Distribute the UNESCO-UNEP list of 10 worst environmental problems. One of these is the decrease in water supply. These problems arose as a result of increasing demands on infinite resources. These demands came from many sources, but the two significant developments which made this problem critical are:

- the rapid escalation of living standards of most of the industrialized countries since 1950;
- the very significant increase in the population of other countries (which have 75 per cent of world population).

Thus, we have 2 kinds of population:

- One that is static in size with increasing consumption of resources (high consuming population).
- One that is increasing in size with increasing consumption of resources (low consuming population).

On the basis of this information, students have explore ideas about the impact of population growth and people's lifestyle on the water supply. Observations and experiences that will come out will be the basis on which students' decisions will be made.

Activity 4: Sources of water

Ask the students about the sources of their water supply and how do they obtain their water from these sources. Discuss the water cycle to show how surface water, ground water and rain water are formed.

The science part of the lesson is presented—water is a natural resource.

Activity 5: The faucet

Show illustrations of the different types of faucet. Ask them to point out the type of faucet they use at home and the different parts of the faucet. Let them explain how the faucets work in their

The technology aspect of the lesson is developed in this part. Students study the structure of a faucet.

homes. It would be better if you show them actual samples of faucet particularly the screw type. Have at least one working (actual) model.

Find out how often they use their faucets each day and what happens to their faucet if not used properly and with constant use. This will lead them to answer that sometimes their faucets leak. Follow up your questioning as to the causes of a leaking faucet and what is to be done about it.

The idea that technology also fails is presented. Knowing the amount of water wasted from a leaking faucet leads the students do certain actions, in this case preparing a leaking faucet.

Ask how many have leaking faucets at home or once had a leaking faucet. Have them find out how much water is wasted from a leaking faucet. Assign those with leaking faucets at home to make measurements. Tell them to set a container under a leaking faucet for one hour. Measure the amount of water they collected. Then multiply the amount by 24 to obtain the amount of water wasted in one day. Let them estimate how much might be lost in the entire village or city.

Activity 6: Repairing a leaking faucet

Ask them if they know how to repair a leaking faucet. Tell them that they will be doing this in the next activity.

Distribute a worksheet showing the parts of a faucet and the way to change the washer. Have them to do the activity in groups. Have them also inquire about the cost of getting a plumber to come to fix the faucet.

This activity is developed to give students self respect and confidence in themselves with the skills and knowledge they gained in this activity.

Activity 7: Water Meters

Students do a survey to see if water meters in their town are all of the same kind. With the help of worksheets they learn to read a water meter and check a water bill.

Students develop the confidence can understand the bills they have to pay, and no longer see themselves as being governed by the technology.

Example 5: Green Gunge

The unit is for Year 7 students. Its topic is water purity, separation techniques and conservation. It is told as a story to show how students can be a part of lesson planning and managing their own learning.

Maggie introduced the unit to her class:

"There has been an interruption in the normal supply of water because the School Council has not paid its water rates. The only water available for use in the next month is this 'green gunge' from the local creek". She passed a sample around.

"Why wouldn't you use this water for drinking or washing your hands?" Students complained of the colour, the smell, the floating things and the wriggling things. They also suggested that there would be 'germs' in the water, which they could kill by boiling.

"How else do you suggest we can make it suitable for human use?" Maggie asked. Suggestions were written on the chalkboard.

"Which methods do you think are most likely to work?"

The discussion as lively, and a number of the suggested procedures were modified.

Maggie had each student select a method from the list and try it with a sample of the water. Students talked to each other about their successes and failures. Sometimes their failure was due to limitations in their skill, sometimes because of inappropriateness of their method.

Maggie felt that the students were ready for the discussion on how to develop their skills. She used a flow chart of the unit that she and others of the science staff had worked out. She and the students talked about the work plan and worked out the main goals, how the learning would be organized, and the assessment methods to be used.

Maggie explained to the students that, in their groups, they should assess each others' skills in the particular separation techniques. One of the students was worried about this. Maggie suggested that in order to coach and assess each other effectively, all students should select one of the techniques and become an expert in it. This would help them do a useful job of both teaching the technique to other members of their group, and of assessing their performance.

Skill Development

The textbooks used for Year 7 gave details of a number of separation exercises. Maggie had prepared a worksheet detailing additional techniques. The methods considered were:

- sedimentation and decanting;
- filtration (using filter paper, cotton wool, gravel and sand bed);
- flocculation (coagulation of colloid);
- absorption (charcoal filtration); and
- evaporation and distillation.

As the students worked with the skill-development exercises, Maggie led them in developing a list of key words associated with equipment and processes, based on the text and the worksheet. At the end of the section, the students completed a short pen-and-paper test on the basic principles of the different techniques, and their uses.

Purification Projects

Maggie felt that the students were now ready to choose and apply techniques that would succeed in cleaning up the water. She asked them, in their groups, to predict the effects of the different techniques, and to write down their predictions for future reference.

She gave out a worksheet outlining the project, and they went through it together. Each group will be given 100 mL of the "green gunge". Their task is to recover as much clean water as possible. They must decided as a group which technique or combination of techniques they will use. A technique may be used more than once. They must also come to agreement, within their groups, about the ways they will work and the tasks each of them will perform. They should write down their procedure, along with their reasoning. That will help them clarify their plan, and they should inform the teacher of what they are doing. Part of their plan should include record of their work that they will keep: what they have done, what were the effects on the sample, how much water was left, and so on. The teacher will talk to them about their plan when they are ready.

In the earlier exercise on skill development, Maggie had recognized that some groups made quicker progress than others, and these differences had been confirmed in the test. Consequently, she was keen to give the groups considerable freedom to move ahead at their own rates. She invited one group to consider, as well, the viability of their techniques for the large-scale problem: What if the school really did depend on the creek for water?

Maggie monitored the functioning of the groups, encouraging them to involve all members, and to share both the measuring jobs and the recording jobs. She assessed their work from their ability to plan and implement their procedures, and skill with equipment, as well as their observations and results. Students also assessed their own work, writing brief reports of their achievements.

As the groups completed their analysis, their pure samples were displayed and compared. Two other groups was moved on to the "larger-scale" question, while the remaining groups finished their analyses.

Discussion:

Each group presented the result of these work to the class, outlining their procedures and results. Discussion flowed naturally into consideration of which sample was the purest. Maggie suggested that some contaminants could not be detected by direct observation. She demonstrated the measurement of electrical conductivity and compared the different samples. One of the students suggested that dissolved impurities might be found by evaporating the water, and the groups did water evaporation by setting droplets from their samples on glass slides and left them to dry.

Meggie suggested that the idea of "how pure" depended on what the water would be used for. The class briefly discussed the different demands for washing, watering the garden, cooking and drinking. Some of the students who had considered the larger-scale problem led a discussion of the cost of different techniques. Maggie had provided them with some figures on costs. Many students were disappointed at the cost of distillation: they had considered it to be the "best solution". Maggie suggested that, nevertheless, there might be countries in which distillation was carried out perhaps because of lack of alternatives which justified the cost, or perhaps because solar energy was available for the purpose. Four or five students wanted to follow up this idea: which countries, what methods, how would you design a solar still or solar distillation equipment?

One student remarked that he had seen a film on TV involving "moonshiners", and he wondered if water stills and whisky stills worked in the same way. A third group disregarded this change of direction: if distillation was an expensive method of purifying town water, what action was taken by taken the town councils and water boards?

The Rest Laid Plans . . .

Maggie's lesson plan was in disarray, and her unit plan was looking shaky. She called a halt. The class assembled around the chalkboard and listed the questions that had been raised already. Then they added more questions to the list. Based on her original unit plan, Maggie listed the questions in three clusters, relating to: use of water in the home; providing town water; and "individual projects". In the last group came questions from the students and from Maggie's original plan: distillation of sea water and alcohol, solar stills, sewage treatment, provision of clear water in such countries as India and Thailand, finding water in outback Australia, and water diving.

Maggie suggested that the questions which the students had listed under her heading of "individual research" be deferred, and that, in the meantime, half the class might develop a role play on the question of town water, and the other half might investigate water use and water conservation in the home. Both the role play and the water conservation study would complete the "green gunge" story that began the unit; the individual research projects would be extensions of the lessons.

Further Activities

Teacher Maggie offered a scenario for the role play that Con, another teacher, had suggested: "A company wishes to build a factory in our town which will discharge 'green gunge' waste into the river flowing through the town, from which we get our water. The Town Council has to decide whether to issue a building permit. The whole class can play the part of the 'town council', and judge presentations to it by, say, the factory owner, the Chamber of Commerce, the Tourist Association, a local conservation group, and a consulting scientists appointed by the Council. Students can work in three's to develop the presentations to the Council meeting from each of the interest groups. The class will need to talk to some of the people around the town who can help with the arguments. Some contacts have been suggested, perhaps the class can suggest some others ..."

Maggie spent a few minutes explaining what was meant by the Town Council, the Chamber of Commerce, and so on, and discussing with the students the particular interests that the different groups might have.

The water conservation study that Maggie originally had in mind was a speculative problem like: what steps could your family take, if it was obliged to survive on 200 litres of water per day? She needed, now, an exercise equivalent to the role play, and suggested: "The other half of the class can work on a study of water use in the home. It should begin with a survey of the things you use water for and how much is used, say, in one weekend. Students can work in three's to design ways to make the measurements, and to consider their data. The next step will be to suggest ways of reducing water use. Then they can actually put these ideas to their family, try them out for a weekend, and see what reduction that get. The final stage will be to present to the whole class their findings, including the successes and difficulties and their family had in reducing its water use for a weekend".

Maggie asked the students to talk about these ideas with each other and with their families before the next class period, and to think about which project they would prefer to do, or how the projects could be improved.

Maggie was pleased as she packed up at the end of the unit: involvement was high, and the students had raised good questions. She was aware that some of the students remained confused about distillation. She would need to help them in a later unit. She was not clear about when the individual projects would start or how she would organize them, and she needed to give some more thought to the group projects. They had taken on a strong social action orientation. "I should go and talk with the social education teachers," she mused. "I probably should have done that earlier..."

(From Malcolm, C., *The Science Framework*, Ministry of Education, Victoria, Australia, 1987)

Example 6: Malaria As a Human Disease

Activity 1

The teacher explain with the help of charts and/or audio-visual aids the structure of the mosquito and the life cycle of the malarial parasite.

Objectives: The student should be able to acquire knowledge about:

- Mosquito is a carrier of malaria.
- Structure of a mosquito.
- The life cycle of the Anopheles mosquito.
- The life cycle of the malarial parasite.

Teaching Aids:

- Charts showing parts of the mosquito.
- Charts showing the life cycle of the mosquito.
- Films and video illustrating stages of development of the mosquito.

Activity 2

The teacher arranges for a local health inspector to give a talk about malarial disease, its symptoms, precautions and cure against the disease.

Objective: How to take early action to avoid the disease.

Activity 3

The students conduct a study of the locality and identify breeding places of mosquitoes. With the help of the community these places are destroyed and the spread of malaria was controlled.

Objectives:

- How to get rid of mosquito breeding places.
- Awareness of the importance of cleanliness in school, home, community and environment.
- Taking action to remove mosquito breeding places.

Commentary

The unit starts with presentation of the science knowledge relevant to the malarial mosquito. A resource person from the community is invited to discuss the social issues and assist the student to identify problems that they can address. The students work with the teacher and the community to solve the problem through the application of their knowledge. A further step might have been to explore alternative means of solving the malaria problem, and look at side effects of the different solutions.

Example 7: Electric Energy and Power

The unit explores energy and power in the context of electricity in the home, including the costs of using different appliances, and ways in which electricity bills can be minimized.

1. *Knowledge:* The topic is introduced and the concepts of energy and power discussed, through the equation $E = P.t$ (E is energy, P is power, and t is the time for which the power is applied). Units of kilowatt-hour as well as Joule are discussed.

2. *Application, Community:* Students are asked to survey electric energy consumed by home appliances .

Power (P) of appliances in KW	Time (T) consumed in H (hours)	Energy (E) consumed in KWH	Cost in Rs
100 W Bulb .1 KW	1 H 5 H 10 H	.1 KWH .5 KWH 1.0 KWH	
80 W TV .1 KW	1 H 5 H 10 H	.08 KWH .4 KWH .8 KWH	

Table 1

Month	KWH
January	5677
February	6177
March	6680
April	7180
May	
June	
July	
August	
September	
October	
November	
December	

Subscribing-Card

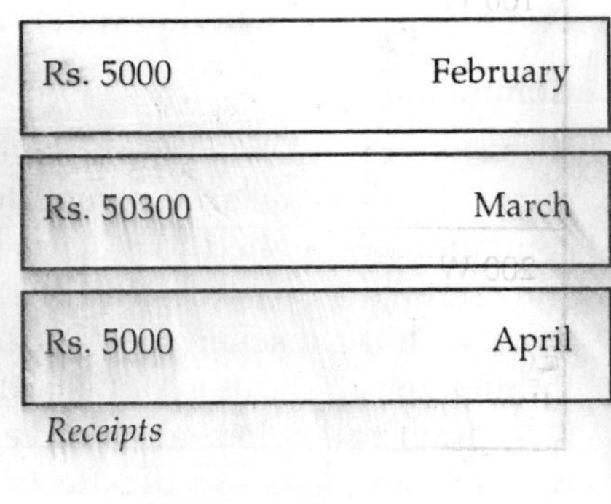

Receipts

Table 2

Months	Energy in KWH	Cost in Rs
Jan-Feb	500	50000
Feb-March	503	50300
March-April	500	50000

Electric Energy Cost Rs.................... per KWH

3. *Non-Science:* Students count the cost of electric energy per KWH, by using data on a Subscribing-Card (see above, Table 2).

They use their conclusions to fill in Table 1.

4. *Improving quality of life, actions:* Students make up Table 3 for distribution to families in their community. The students explain the implications of the calculations for the family budget.

How Much Do You Spend for Your Electric Appliances?

Table 3

Power of the Appliances in W (watts)	Time consumed, in hours	Cost in Rs
100 W	1	10
	6	60
	12	120
	18	180
	24	240
200 W	1	20
	6	120
	12	360
	18	480

Commentary

Concepts: The concepts of energy and power are taught in the ordinary way, through experiment and discussion.

Application, community: Application in a real life situation is explored, using material at the community level and of importance to the community.

Non-science: Activity extends to economics, to count the electric energy cost per KWH.

Improving quality of life, actions: The student is encouraged to share the findings to improve the quality of community life, and use the skills of explaining and persuading. By knowing Table 3 families can be more economical, because they know the amount of money spent everyday for electrical energy consumption.

Example 8: Measurement in Daily Life

Children learn about the importance of measurement and devices used for measuring mass, length, area, volume, time and temperature. They consider accuracy and approximation, and when precision is needed. They handle measuring devices and use their knowledge of measurement in their interaction with their families and others in their life out of school.

Some of the learning situations are:

- Listing instances where measurement of length, area, volume, time, temperature and mass are involved (market, shopkeeper, tailor, milkman etc.);
- Identifying devices used in day-to-day measurements;
- Measurements of mass, length, area, volume, time and temperature;
- Using scales, presenting data in tables and graphs, estimating averages;
- Estimating quantities in everyday situations: the height of a child, tree, building; the mass of a given quality of sugar, potato, books; area of a room, a table top; volume of a tumbler, teaspoon, cup, matchbox, bucket;
- Finding out the probable causes of errors arising from faulty methods of using measuring devices; finding out methods of accurate measurement.

Example 9: Seeds

Children observe seeds and look for similarities and differences, and think about the uses of seeds for food.

Activity 1

We use seeds as tool. The concept that nutritious food is stored within the seed is illustrated through the following questions:

1. How can a seed grow into a tall tree?
2. Which seeds do we eat?
3. Which part of the rice seed can we eat as polished rice? Which part as flour?
4. Which part of the mung seed do we eat mainly?

Activity 2

Compare the seeds of kidney bean and maize. In what ways are they the same? different?

(They are similar in their seed coat and embryo. Among the differences, the kidney bean has no endosperm and 2 cotyledons; the maize seed has an endosperm and one cotyledon).

Activity 3

Plants can be classified as monocotyledons and dicotyledons. List some other plants that you know according to this classification.

Take some other kinds of seeds from home and soak them in water until they are soft. According to the methods you have learned in class, observe their structures and decide whether they are like the kidney bean or the maize seed.

Example 10: Other Examples Linking Science to Everyday Life

10.1 In teaching about the structure of the heart, the class discusses a common heart disease.

10.2 With guidance from teachers, students display at street corners plant specimens they have collected and classified. The students act as little advisers to the public, answering their questions, on uses of the plants.

10.3 Students serve as guides at the National Museum.

10.4 Science Summer Camps provide opportunities for students to learn about the natural environment, cooking, insect and moth control etc., Activities involve learning and app ying through play.

10.5 Students in rural areas learn to prune fruit trees, plant vegetables and breed chickens, using scientific techniques.

The examples presented here produces starting points in presenting lessons in science and technology and their effect in quality of life. More examples can be prepared especially those which relate to the environment of the child.

The exemplar cited offer options for the teachers to use in their particular classroom situations.

4

Country Experiences

1. AUSTRALIA

The Context: Education For All

"Education for All" has to be considered at two levels, which will be called formal access and curriculum access. The first is a precondition for the second; both are necessary.

Formal access is satisfied by the provision of schools, teachers, equipment and programmes to all children regardless of where they live, what they believe, and the financial and social circumstances of their families. In Australia, formal access became policy in the 1870s, promising "free secular and compulsory" education for all students up to a given age. Beyond that age (currently 15), education is not compulsory in Australia but it is available and free to Year 12 level.

Curriculum access requires *Education for All* through a curriculum that connects to the experiences and educational purposes of all students. Such a curriculum is not dominated by the interests, values and learning styles of one or another subgroup in the society. It becomes unacceptable to argue that a science curriculum basic for those who will proceed to further study in science is good for everyone. "Basic", like "relevant", is a word that needs to be qualified: basic for what? relevant to whom? If we allow education to serve truly a variety of needs and a range of groups there can be no longer a single definition of "basic".

In turn, "standards" and a "standard curriculum" become hard to define because there is less standardization: Australians in the desert outback have educational needs different from Australian in flats and factories in industrial Melbourne; Australians recently arrived from Vietnam or Greece bring to the learning situations experiences and expectations different from fifth generation Australians in the same classroom. The curriculum must be able to vary from one school to another and one student to another.

On the other hand, there is more to access than providing opportunities for every student to build on his/her experience and purpose. Individuals and their immediate communities are part of the larger society, with its own needs, rules and traditions. *Education for All* has a responsibility to assist individuals to participate fully in society and work for the good of all people. Accordingly there must be an extent to which schools express a common culture and address a common curriculum.

As well as the common learnings necessary for the function of the society, there are certain learnings that have special currency as "gateways" to higher education, employment and economic or personal power in the society. Subjects like Mathematics and Physics are in this category, and skills like rational analysis, problem solving and facility with computers. *Education for All* must ensure that all students have curriculum access to these learnings.

Participation in Science in Australia

At Junior Secondary level, every student studies science, usually for 2.5-3 hours per week. Classes are typically 25-30 students. Teachers are qualified with degrees in science and education. Equipment and facilities are provided for laboratory work. Excursions are conducted from time to time into the community, industry, the environment, parks, zoos and museums.

Full participation does not apply outside the band of Years 7-9. In many primary schools, there is little science taught. In Year 10 in some schools (a minority) science becomes an elective. Beyond Year 10 science studies are optional in all schools.

In Years 11 and 12 science is offered as Physics, Chemistry, Biology, Geology, Psychology, Environmental Studies and (General) Science. Physics, Chemistry and Biology command the major share of science enrolment. They are differently attractive to boys and girls. The percentage of girls in Biology is approximately 70 per cent, Chemistry 40 per cent and Physics 25 percent.

Beyond Year 10, students can leave school. Retention to Year 12 has increased greatly in all Australian states in the last five years (in Victoria it has doubled) and now stands at about 60 per cent of the age cohort. However this growth has not been reflected in enrolment in Physics and Chemistry.

The low participation of girls in Physics and Chemistry and the failure of senior science subjects to reflect the growth of enrolments of secondary schools generally suggest that girls and "non-traditional students" do not have curriculum access to senior Physics and Chemistry. Their choosing to withdraw from the physical sciences after Year 10 raises issues about the determinants of choice, including their experience in the junior curriculum. Extensive research has been on gender bias in the curriculum. It confirms that access is not the same for girls as for boys. Research for other groups, such as gifted children, disabled, and various ethnic groups, has not been as extensive but confirms that curriculum access in junior science is not the same for all students.

Focus on the Victorian Solution

In Australia, education is a state responsibility. While there is considerable similarity between policies and approach in the various states (achieved through the common culture of teachers, Federal Government programmes, and cooperative projects of the national Curriculum Development Centre) there are important variations.

This paper will focus on the policies and approach in Victoria. One state has been chosen so as to communicate the sense of overall strategy that is clear in a single state, but not across states. Further, Victoria's approach is of spe_ial interest because of the extent and nature of the current reforms: reforms through the 1980s to provide curriculum access for all students compare in importance to the provision of formal access for all students in the 1970s.

The Victorian strategy was published in 1983-4 in a series of *Ministerial Papers*.

Ministerial Paper 6 addressed curriculum development. The strategy is based on two principles:

- access and success for all students; Education for All
- devolution of curriculum planning and management

Devolution

Schools are responsible for curriculum development "according to government guidelines".

The guidelines express the State's responsibility for the curriculum. They set direction by laying out the purposes of education and principles to guide curriculum development. They provide leadership and coordination.

At the school level, school governance (including curriculum planning) is the responsibility of a School Council comprising teachers, parents and students. At the classroom level, students are involved in setting goals and planning programmes.

Devolution is justified on a number of grounds. It supports the development of curricula which suit the local students and their community. It recognizes the partnership in education between teachers, parents, students and State. It places the responsibilities for curriculum development, implementation and evaluation all with the same administrative group (the school). It enables more creative and quicker response to changes in the educational environment.

Access and Success for All Students

All students are to have access to education that has value for them in the settings and roles in which they operate and in which they expect to operate in the future. As well, all students are to have access to particular ways of learning and areas of learning deemed vital for participation in the life of society.

"Access" requires more than a sign on the door saying "welcome". It requires a curriculum which links effectively to the purposes, lives and abilities of the students who enter.

"Success" is based on a definition of education as growth. It recognizes that students start at different points, and focuses "success" on the increments of learning rather than standard end points of learning. Education is successful if the increments are large, unsuccessful if they are small.

"Success" means that learning makes a difference to the ways students think about the world and the ways they act. An effective curriculum links theory to practice and social purpose, in-school experience to out-of-school experience. It promotes problem solving and cooperative action.

Ministerial Paper 6 specifies areas of learning to which all students have access. The areas are specified not as a list of subjects, but as list of 32 goals of education. Goals like:

- listen and talk appropriately in a variety of situations...
- understand and apply the basic concepts of number, quantity and space...
- understand the relationship between physical environment, culture and society...
- participate in democratic processes...
- work with tools and materials on practical tasks...
- develop competence with computers...
- understand natural phenomena and the concepts scientist use...
- be aware of the application of science . . . and the responsibilities...

In schools, science teachers have been asked to choose the ten goals to which they feel Science studies can make particular contributions. The distribution obtained is remarkably flat: science can contribute to all 32. The policy challenges curriculum planners in all subject areas to begin planning not from the traditional bodies of knowledge, but from the broad purposes of schooling.

Questions of Implementation

A central issue in the implementation of the *Access and Success* policy has been the existence of two different definitions of education in the community. The two positions are fundamentally incompatible, but use the same terms. There is endless room for confusion and debate.

One view sees education as transmission of a set body of knowledge and skills or text from teacher to students. The knowledge to be transmitted is that which is considered 'essential' for all educated persons of a given age. Students are assumed to be more or less passive receivers of information, with minds that can be cleared of old ideas and filled with new knowledge by the teachers. Assessment is to identify students for whom the transmission has been successful. The content and its sequence are based on the logical structure of knowledge, and, whether inductive or deductive, have the 'big picture' of the knowledge structure clearly in view. To this extent, teaching is covergent on 'right answers'. The teacher is the authority of knowledge and management. Education is driven by 'the subject' and the (classroom) management system.

In the *Frameworks* approach, teaching starts from the interests, beliefs, and skills that students bring to the learning situation, and individual differences are accepted and accommodated. Learning is seen as an active process for the students, in which they clarify their own views about a particular phenomenon (probably in discussion with each other the teacher), have their views challenged, then seek to reconstruct their views in the light of new information. Education is a continuing development, with good education measured by the size of the increments of growth. Students start at different points, move forward to different points, often in different ways. Assessment is geared to diagnosis and progress. It is used to inform teaching and assist students to manage their owing learning. The teaching sequence is controlled by the usefulness of ideas in solving problems and seeking meaning rather than by the structure of knowledge. Teaching is often divergent.

The two views of education are profoundly different in their definitions of education, their beliefs about justice, about what science is and what science is worth learning, students and learning, the functions of assessment, the teacher's role, and classroom management.

For example, "success for every child" is possible if success is indicated by growth. It is nonsense if every child must successfully receive the same body of knowledge (no more no less). In the transmission model, a child is "successful" if he/she can demonstrate the required knowledge, but there might have been no growth. Alternatively he/she may demonstrate growth, but still not reach the required end point. What one model claims as "good education" the other rejects. The same applies to justice. In the transmission model, justice requires that all students are taught the same things in more or less the same way; all are given the same test under the same conditions. In the growth model, justice requires that different students are taught and assessed differently according to their starting points and learning styles.

At the same time, neither view of education and learning necessarily invalidates solutions developed under the other, just as Einstein's Mechanics do not necessarily invalidate solutions derived using Newton's. One of the challenges facing the teachers currently is to find better ways of incorporating the things the teachers learned, for example, from behaviourist approaches and learning hierarchies.

Neither is it necessary for individual teachers to change their own position before they take action. Indeed changes in behaviour often precede changes in understanding.

Support for the Policy:

The strategy for implementation of the policy has been a careful one, advancing on a many fronts since 1983.

- *Curriculum Framework* were developed in nine subject areas (of which science is one). The *Frameworks* interpret the general policy from the perspective of the subject area, clarify and refine the educational position, and provide illustrations of good practice and advice on implementation. The *Frameworks* were developed simultaneously for all subjects and all grade levels. They reinforce one another, drawing on research and good practice in each subject area from the perspective of "access and success for all". Frameworks in Technology, Mathematics, Social Education and English Language have particular relevance to science.

- Exemplary course outlines and units of work are being published. Many of the units were developed by teachers and teacher-networks in parallel with the development of the *Framework*. A major project is in progress to provide a course outline for Year 7-10, addressing objectives, content, learning experiences and assessment in a fairly detailed way.

- The *School Curriculum and Organization Framework* supports school management and curriculum planning in a decentralized system. It interprets the general policies from a management perspective and provides guidance on administrative structures, management, evaluation and planning. It recognizes the significance of organizational arrangements, facilities, human relationships, school climate, and school-community interaction for the achievement of *Education for All*.

- *Management training programmes are conducted for school principals, curriculum coordinators, and school councillors. There are also regular meetings of school principals with their Regional Managers, to assist in coordination and planning.*

- *Professional development programmes are conducted for teachers. The programmes include teacher networks, conferences, action research in schools, and special courses. As well as after school programmes and special leave arrangements, schools have eight student free days per year. Neighbourhood schools combine for some of these days, to enhance exchange of ideas across schools in a district. Subject Associations, including the Science Teachers Association, and private consultants also conduct workshops and conferences.*

- *Articles were published in teachers journals and Ministry newspapers to explain and promote the policies, and provide case examples and advice on their implementation.*

- *Consultancy services are provided through district School Support Centres.*
- *Schools must document and report their progress, especially through the reports of school councils to their communities and the Ministry.*
- *Curriculum reforms at years 11 and 12 are in progress, consistent with changes at the lower levels.*

All Kind of Science: Science for All

- *All students should study science, and gain value from their studies. The goals, methods and content of science education should provide for the needs and progress of all students.*
- *Science education should be concerned with environmental management, and the survival and quality of life for all.*

Goals: Science, Technology, Society and Personal Development

- *Scientific knowledge, the solution of practical problems, the cultural and human context of science, and opportunities for personal development are four aspects of science. They should be given similar emphasis at all levels of schooling, and should be integrated in their presentation.*

Learning and Teaching: Children's Science Beginning from Children's Perceptions

- *Children (and adults!), by nature, are theorists and problem-solvers, keen to explain and interpret their experiences, to resolve issues they see as important, and to design and build. They bring their perceptions and beliefs to the learning situation.*
- *Children, as experienced problem-solvers, have their own strategies for learning and solving problems.*
- *Science teaching should identify, begin from, and build on the strategies, interests, beliefs and explanations that children bring to the classroom.*

The Role of Teachers: Teacher Development and Curriculum Development

- *The development of both curriculum and teachers' skills in course design and implementation should occur together. Each must be allowed for in planning science education and curriculum revision.*

Curriculum Content: Sampling Scientific Knowledge

- *Any schools can only teach a sample of all the knowledge, skills and experiences related to science. The sample should vary from one school to another, depending in local resources, interests and needs. It should include learnings selected from the board range of scientific disciplines.*
- *Students should truly engage a limited number of ideas rather than seek universal coverage with superficial understanding and application.*
- *Students must have opportunities to feel that they are succeeding, to explore and reflect on their understanding and skills, and use them in a variety of contexts. This takes time, and limits the number of topics that can be covered.*

Fig. 1. The Science Platform

The Science Framework

The Science Framework *is, in the first instance, an educational position. The position is consistent with the policy of Access and Success, but drawn from the language and research base of Science Education:* Science for All, Science, Technology Society, Children's Science. *The position is summarized as a "Platform Statement" (Fig. 1).*

The Learning Theory: Children's Science

The learning theory is "constructivist". Children are seen as serious in their wishes to understand and give meaning to their experience; to refine and extend their world view; to have control over their own lives. They develop theories, beliefs, and learning strategies from their lives in school and out of school, and learning is a matter of reconstructing meaning in the light of new experience. There is extensive research evidence to suggest:

- *the beliefs and understandings that children bring to the learning situation are often strongly held and little affected by simple instruction; they are important inputs to the learning situation;*
- *learning strategies can be taught; being smart can be learned;*
- *the range of learning styles, starting points and interests within a group of children and the range of curriculum objectives require a variety of teaching approaches;*
- *learning is enhanced by consonance between inputs from school, home, community, the environment; education is a partnership.*

Science, Technology, Society, Personal Development

The *Framework* advocates equal emphasis for science, technology, society and personal development. The science is theoretical knowledge and the processes of theory building and testing. It answers the question "I wonder . . ." Technology is the development of artefacts, tools and systems for human purposes. Technology answers the question "I want . . . ." Society is the human context of science; science is a human activity. Personal Development formalizes the opportunities within science classrooms for special experiences (e.g., with nature, machines, animals), and for developing skills in cooperation, personal management, clear thinking, etc.

The *Framework* advocates that science, technology, society and personal development aspects be integrated in their presentation. The entry point is to be sometimes from the Science perspective, sometimes from Technology, sometimes Society and sometimes Personal Development. The choice of entry point is to reflect the "equal emphasis".

Each entry point makes a different statement about what is "worth knowing". For example, starting a topic "conditions for life" from the theoretical perspective, we might seek generalizations about "living" and "non-living", looking to classifications and interactions. Aspects of technology and society would be picked up along the way. Starting from Technology, we might take a farming perspective: what are the conditions required for life, to maximize yield and ensure the long term health of the ecosystem that is the farm. The farm might be cattle, crops, fish or microorganisms. The theoretical and social aspects would be built in, but the selection of ideas and the emphasis would be different from the first case. Starting from a social issue might follow a theme of hygiene, nutrition, or disease, building science and technology in to illuminate the issues and reach for solutions.

This particular strategy overcomes the traditional debate about "process versus product", by shifting attention to the student and recognizing the importance of context. Process has little point if it is not geared to a product; product derives its purpose from context. The context needs to be one which the children relate to—their immediate environment, a fantasy world, a story, a problem, a hero.

Teaching Approach: Examples

The teaching approach should have two features:

- It should employ a range of teaching methods, to suit the different learning styles of students and the different learning objectives (see Fig. 2).
- A complex cognitive skill (designing an experiment, solving a problem, making decisions, judging the likely outcome of events).
- A motor skill (using a microscope, pouring a liquid, using a hammer).
- A social skill (working as a team member, communicating with others).
- A sequence of words to be recalled at will (a definition, a law, order of planets from the sun).
- An image, or sensation (what something looks like, feels like, smells like ...).
- An episode that the student experiences or witnessed (designing and building a parachute, finding a fossil during an excursion).
- A proposition which links ideas, explains a concept or describes a property. A level of understanding beyond simple recall of the words is implied (a seed from a parent plant will produce a similar plant).
- A simple cognitive skill (finding the slope of a graph, balancing a chemical equation, measuring the growth of a plant).

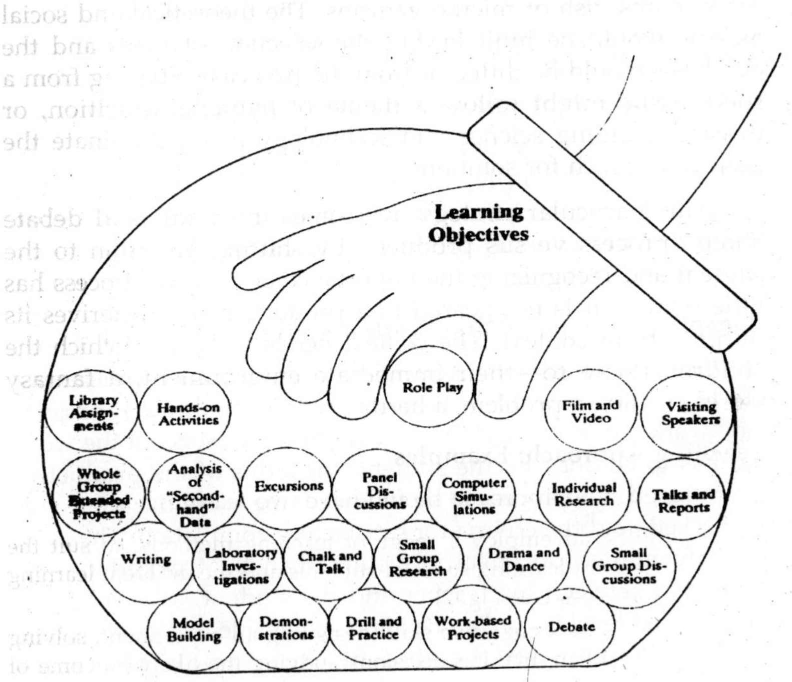

- It should support "constructivist learning" for all students. Accordingly, the first step should give students opportunities to clarify what they already know, set directions, and contribute their own contexts and experiences. The first segment will often be an open exploratory one: brainstorming, concept mapping, drawing, in response to questions like What do we already know about... How many ways can we... What might be the variables that determine.. What would happen if... The second segment is to challenge the students' current knowledge—through an experiment, a demonstration, an argument. The third segment is a teaching sequence which carries forward the students' understanding. The fourth is opportunity to apply and extend the new learning.

Following this broad strategy, topics like cosmetics or machines do not in themselves exclude some groups from the learning and include others. The Cosmetics unit starts with the students doing a survey: What cosmetics are in your home? Used by Mum? Dad? Baby? What is a cosmetic? Collect advertisements on cosmetics. What are the advertising strategies?

An alternative to brainstorming is to start with a story or problem. For example, "Separation of mixtures" can be presented as a technology problem or social issue. The Framework presents this approach in a "case study" called *Green Gunge* (see Chapter 3).

Managing Students' Work: Work Requirements

One way of assisting students to manage their own learning and work cooperatively with other students is through projects and "work requirements". A work requirement sets out the work that has to be done by the students, in terms of the product to be produced, the process to be followed, the ways the work will be checked, and the criteria for satisfactory completion. The level of performance on specific criteria can be worked out in discussion between the teacher and the student, to ensure that the expected level is on the one hand achievable and on the other hand challenging for the student. An example of a work requirements for students in Year 8 are given in Fig. 3.

Unit Plan: Students develop a list of types of accidents requiring first aid. Groups select an accident from the list and develop a presentation to the rest of the class. Groups will: investigate causes of the accident, refer to first aid publications, prepare scripts and rehearse their presentation, develop special effects to simulate the injury or condition, present the information to the class. Each presentation will include a brief description of the body system which is associated with the accident.

All the conclusion of each presentation, each student in the class will construct a concept map that illustrates their understanding of the structure, function and operation of the body system discussed in the presentation.

Work Requirement: The student will present a written report which describes the causes and symptoms of the condition, outline the means of diagnosing the condition, describe past and current methods of treatment and associated technologies, analyze an ethical issue underlying either the diagnosis, selection for treatment, treatment, or rehabilitation of a patient suffering from the condition, and present an argument for the stance that the student would take on the issue.

Fig. 3. Work Requirement Year 8, "First Aid"

Themes

The following themes are to be incorporated throughout the Programme:

- Environmental education and the Australian environment
- Work education
- Science and our way of life
- Australian science

Local science

Topics drawn from current events, weather local area study, national, or international events, as well as student's interests.

- Quarry study
- Investigation of living and non-living things around the local creek
- Butter factory excursion
- Dairying study
- Rubbish investigation
- Supermarket excursion
- The school environment: Keeping the oval green
- The school environment: People paths
- Consumerism and product testing

Experiences

- Using all senses in a wide variety of experiences, with natural phenomena and technologies
- Working together in groups
- Working as individuals
- Finding out in a variety of different ways
- Making things
- Handling animals
- Succeeding
- Enjoying science and science activities

Contexts

Students will use their learning:

- At home: kitchen, garden, workshop

- Farm: machinery, animals, crops, weather
- Current affairs: local, state and national events
- Leisure: sports, entertainments, hobbies
- Work: at home, part-time employment
- At school: further learning

Skills

- Observing: using the senses, measuring, estimating, classifying
- Finding out and experimenting: guessing, creating, making, speculating, using, planning, designing, implementing, interpreting, solving, analysing, evaluating.
- Applying: building, solving, creating, using, making, designing, inventing, planning, organising.
- Communicating: cooperating, examining dilemmas, reporting, recording, explaining, presenting, discussing, writing, reading, listening, debating.

Attitudes and values

- To care for the welfare of people and other living things
- To be open-minded and value objectivity
- To value both natural and manufactured things
- To wish to use science and technology responsibly
- To have a thirst for knowledge and understanding
- To be prepared to work co-operatively

Knowledge

Matter

- Materials around us
- Materials in different forms
- Materials for particular purposes
- Properties, uses and structures
- Manufacture and fabrication
- Planets, stars and galaxies

Energy and Interaction

- Measuring change
- Our energy needs, building and cleaning up, moving and sustaining
- Energy sources and resources
- Energy transfers and transformations
- Change (geological and astronomical)
- Producing new substances

Life

- Growth, and maintenance of individuals and communities
- Ourselves
- Communities and ecosystems and change

- Living and non-living; life and death
- Evolution, life reproduction and death

A Sample Course: (Each unit occupies a quarter of a year)

Year 7	Science Around Me	Caring for Animals	Time and Space	The Environment and me
Year 8	Why Waste?	Electricity for Us	Earthquake in our town	First Aid
Year 9	Have we got the energy	Detection	Everyday Chemistry	Survival
Year 10	Science in the	Moving	The Earth and	Protection

Fig. 4. Science Content

Content

The Science, Technology, Society, Personal Development approach that we are taking was described earlier. The details of content at any particular school are decided at the school level. The *Framework* suggests criteria for selecting content:

- Is it based on the experiences and interests of the students, whether through local or global considerations?
- Does it excite wonder and pleasure in the learning?
- Is it perceived by students and the community as immediately valuable in the world beyond school?
- Does it enable students to develop knowledge and skills relevant to their career and personal aspirations?
- Does it contribute to the programme aims?

The *Framework* suggests content under headings of skills, attitudes and values, concepts, themes, local science, particular experiences, and contexts in which students might be expected to use their learning (see Fig. 4).

Assessment

Assessment serves a number of purposes. One is for credentials or grading. This is "summative assessment". Another is to support and guide learning. The focus of assessment at the years 7 and 8 levels is to guide learning. It follows that assessment is an integral part of classroom activity, and must be a responsibility of students as well as teachers.

Students must be encouraged to ask themselves about their current understanding, to consider how the work they are doing links in to work they have done earlier and experience beyond school.

Teachers must be encouraged to use a variety of assessment methods. These will include direct observation, assessment of the range of products that students produce (written work, talks, drawings, models, constructions), interviews, questionnaires and tests.

Assessment for learning does not occur only at the end of the task: if it is to be a part of the curriculum planning it must occur near the beginning and at appropriate points throughout the task. Concept maps and checklists are two devices that can be used.

Teacher Education

The critical factor in the achievement of access and success for all students is the quality of the teaching.

The quality of the teaching force depends partly on recruitment and pre-service training. It depends also on school factors (management, leadership, organizational support) and the provision of in-service education.

The focus of teacher education, as part of the current changes in Victoria, is in-service education. The number of teachers emerging from college courses each year is only a small fraction of the total workforce, and in any case, new graduates are not in a strong position in the culture and structure of schools to lead school change.

The Victorian reforms require major shifts in educational thought for many teachers. Their beliefs are not changed simply by talking to them about a new policy or handing them a new syllabus and new materials. The required teaching strategy is similar to that listed earlier under the heading Children's Science. Teachers have to be helped to clarify their own educational beliefs and practices, challenged to extend and revise their beliefs, and provided with a teaching programme that supports their learning.

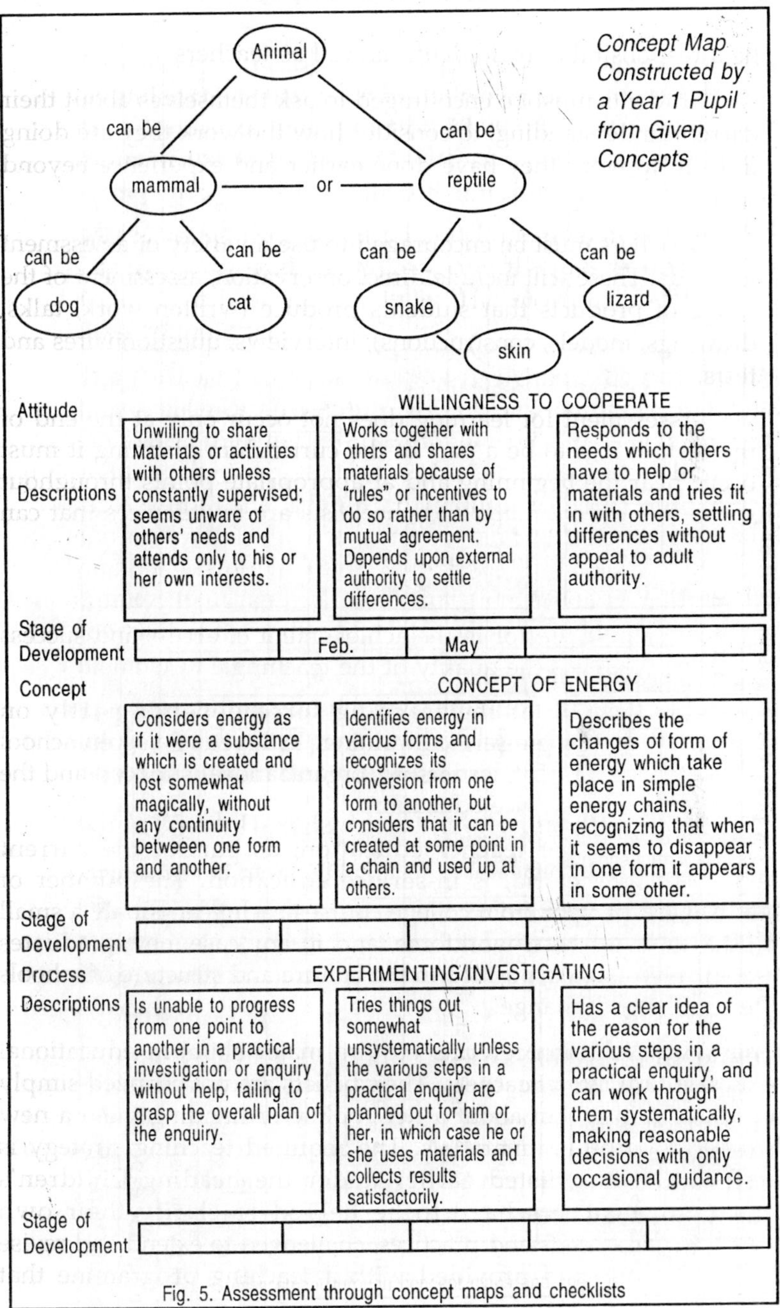

Fig. 5. Assessment through concept maps and checklists

Sample grid for progressive assessment of practical work

	Point scale					
	5	4	3	2	1	
Motor Skills Examples: Organizat ion	Good					Poor
Manipulation	Good					Poor
Follows instructions	Good					Poor
Ability to perform specific task	Good					Poor
Care	Good					Poor
Handling of living material. Sensitive to physiological needs of organisms	Good					Poor
Safety	Good					Poor
Inquiry skills Identify the problem	Identifies problem					No idea
Form hypothesis	Good suggestions					No ideas
Design the experiment	Workable ideas					No ideas
Identify variables	Identifies variables					No idea

	5	4	3	2	1	
Observations	- Accurate - Relevant					Careless Irrelevant
Data collection	Complete					No record
Display data in meaningful way, eg. tabulated, graph, diagrams	Useful					Useless
Interpretation of data	Evidence set out					Statement unsupported
Evaluation of data	Good/critical					None
Predictions based on data	Good suggestions					No ideas
Communication in written report	- Complete - Evidence clearly set out					No report None
Social skills Work with others	Helps others					Unco-operative
Contribution of discussions	Valuable					None
Responsibility	Good					Poor
Persistence	Good					None
Willingness to learn	Good					None

The figure below is from the Framework. It offers self-help for teachers. It says: Consider your current practice. How much do you know about or use the other strategies listed? Reach out and try one, first with a class and in a situation where you are likely to succeed. Talk it over with the Drama teacher or anyone whom you can trust to provide coaching.

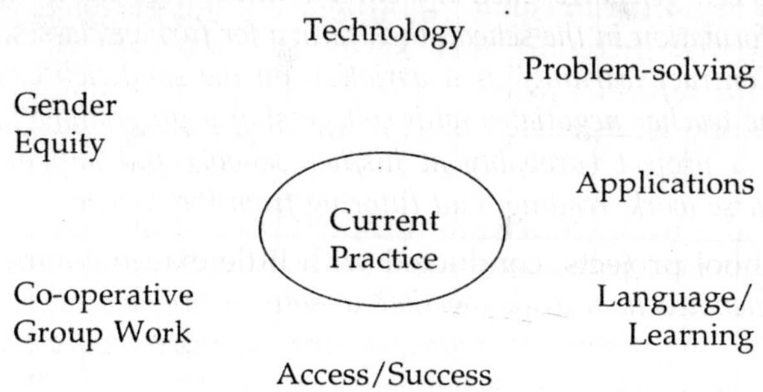

Professional development is being provided by the Ministry on a number of fronts:

- The "one shot": *a motivational speaker, a forum on recent research findings, and explanation of new policies: a speech, a workshop, a one day or two day conference. Such "one shots" need to be part of a larger plan, with lead up and follow on activities. Ministry consultants are available to help schools with this planning.*
- Action Research: *Project teams are formed in schools or teacher networks are formed across schools to address particular problems or develop particular innovations. The teams work systematically through cycles of research and action/development, drawing on their "experiments" in class, reading each other, and outside experts. The Ministry has supported teams working on teaching styles (such as cooperative learning, or students managing their own learning), classroom issues (such as gender bias), course development, and computers in education. The support includes small amounts of money and, more importantly, some release time for teachers and support from outside consultants.*

- Sandwich Courses and Contract Learning: *These are offered by some tertiary colleges and other institutions. The Ministry was conducted for some years a successful sandwich course for Mathematics teachers. It is currently developing others for Junior Secondary Science teachers and Technology teachers. In the sandwich course, teachers attend a class in the college/centre, then try out the ideas or gather relevant information in the school, then return for further classes, etc. "Contract learning" is a variation on the sandwich course. The teacher negotiates with college staff a programme based on a project (probably at his/her school) and supporting course work, reading, and tutoring from the college.*

- School projects, conducted with little external support: *When teachers work together to solve a problem, develop a new programme, introduce a new teaching approach, or define a new assessment policy, professional development occurs. Learning in this way is the same as the learning promoted in frameworks through cooperative approaches, projects and work requirements. This sort of professional development is occurring in all schools in Victoria.*

Government policy makes curriculum development the responsibility of groups of people (the school council, the Science Department of the school) rather than individuals. The policy facilitates coordination of programmes in the school. It also promotes professional development through professional interaction with colleagues.

The challenge to provide curriculum access for all in Victoria has been placed largely with teachers. Teachers are giving their energy and their creativity to it. They are becoming sophisticated in their thinking about educational issues and teaching, and more attuned to their own needs for professional development and planning. The face of education is changing.

2. BHUTAN

The education system is just three decades old. During these 30 years, education has experienced a tremendous number of revolutionary changes. Now there are 152 Primary schools, 21 junior high schools, ten high schools, one degree college, two primary teachers training centres, one secondary teachers training college, two technical institutions and many religious and vocational institutions.

The medium of instruction in all the schools is English, although it is a second language. Dzongkha is the national language and there are several dialects.

The school structure is 7-2-2-3 (seven years primary, two years lower secondary, two years upper secondary and three years at degree levels). Schools throughout the country follow the same curriculum prescribed by the Department of Education. It is imported from other countries. There are no private schools.

The rich and educated people make good use of the available educational facilities. Underprivileged groups do not. They do not understand the value of education. Moreover, the educational services are inaccessible to people in some locations. There are of course some unavoidable factors which contribute to such problems. Until the problems are solved, ideas of equity, "Education for All" and "science for all" are forlorn hopes. The Government of Bhutan is discussing currently a policy of "Universal Primary Education" and its ramifications.

Since the Bhutanese education system is so young and has experienced so many changes, it has not come to a stage of giving special attention to science and technology education, although the importance of it has long been felt.

Bhutan has been importing teachers, curriculum and textbooks, and as a result the children have been learning "Tom Smile lives in London. London is a beautiful city...." instead of learning about their own friends and locality. This is a serious problem. A recent survey reveals that 90 per cent of Bhutanese children knew little about their own country. Consequently, the Government of Bhutan stresses strongly the nationalization of the curriculum to suit their needs and aspirations.

Since 1986, as a result of the 1984 Education Policy, several activities have been initiated: establishment of the Curriculum and Textbook Development Division: introduction of the New Approach to Primary Education for pre-primary to Class III; nationalization of syllabi for Classes IV-VIII; introduction of

Druk Series, Biology, History and Geography for Classes VII and VIII. For the current Five Year Plan, the Government of Bhutan has allocated the maximum budget for the education sector.

Science in Classes I-X is taught as a compulsory subject. Environmental Studies provide the integrating theme for science contents and skills in Classes PP-III. Classes IV-X have separate disciplines. From Classes XI-XV, science studies are optional. The choice normally depends on the marks students obtain in the Class X public examination.

Most of the teachers in lower and higher secondary classes are untrained. Their teaching is usually constrained to the talk and chalk methods of feeding children with ready-made answers for the examination. This includes science teaching.

The whole system is driven by exams and traditional memory tests, in all subjects. There are public examinations for Classes VI, VIII, X, XII and XV. Besides, there are school based examinations conducted by teachers. The examinations hold many pupils back from higher education because they are not able to write the ready-made answers. Examinations are seen more as a means to check the memory power of the children than to find out the achievement problems of the children and try to help them accordingly. Among the subjects offered in the schools, Mathematics and Science are the ones that children are most likely to fail.

Many students complete Class VI, the end of primary education. Only 20 per cent reach Class X level. It is a serious problem. Questions need to be asked, such as: Is there anything wrong with the curriculum? Is the examination system wrong? Is the teacher education system wrong?

Because many teachers lack training in Science, facilities for practical work are often non-existent, schools provide courses for two major groups of students in Classes VII and VIII: those for whom this is their final year at school, and those for whom it is the foundation for further scientific study at higher education levels.

Neither science nor Bhutan will stand still in the next 50 years. All students must be assisted to understand the fundamental and powerful concepts of science and the skills to continue learning throughout their adult and working lives, in order to serve their country to the full. The content needs to be relevant to the needs of Bhutan at present and in the future. It needs to have its roots in sound science. It must enable students to enjoy science, to talk about science, to think scientifically and to start to consider the limitations of science and its interaction with social, economic, technological, ethical and cultural factors.

3. PEOPLE'S REPUBLIC OF CHINA

Recent Guidelines and Policies

1. The Chinese Government issued "the Compulsory Education Law of the People's Republic of China" in 1986 which will further promote scientific and cultural quality of the whole nation. The Law provides that compulsory education should last nine years and that the school system is the Six-Three System (six years in the primary schools and three years in the junior middle school) and the Five-Four System (five years for the primary school and four years for the junior middle school).
2. As most of the graduates of the junior middle schools in the rural areas will go back to work in the countryside, it is therefore quite necessary to have labour technology lessons and professions technology curricula in the junior middle schools, such as planting crops, raising fish and chickens, training to be carpenters and electricians, building houses, etc., which will really meet the needs of Chinese peasants.

Contents of Science and Technology Education in China's Junior Middle Schools

Science and technology education includes physics, chemistry, biology and labour technology. A few junior middle schools in China are still having studies and experiments of comprehensive science lessons. The following are the learning contents and sequences of physics, chemistry, biology and labour technology, with the titles of each chapter and student's experiments only.

Physics (Book 1):

Introduction, simple motion, sound phenomena, heat phenomena, optical refraction, mass and density, force, force and motion, pressure, atmospheric pressure, buoyancy, simple machines, work.

Student's Experiments: Measure length with rulers, measure average speed, measure the temperature of water with a thermometer, study the boiling of water, measure the mass of solids and liquids with a balance, measure the density of solids and liquids with a balance and a measuring tube, study the pressure of liquids, measure the mechanical efficiency of a pulley block.

Physics (Book 2):

Electric current and circuit, voltage, resistance, Ohm's Law, electricity and magnetism, general knowledge of radio communication, mechanical energy, internal energy, heat engines, electric energy, conversion of electric energy and mechanical energy, home circuits, structure of atoms and nuclear energy, development and utilization of energy sources.

Student's Experiments: Connect simple circuit in series and in parallel, measure electric current with ammeters, measure voltage with voltmeters, change electric current with sliding rheostats, measure resistance with voltmeters and ammeters, make electro-magnet and study its effects, measure the electric power of small bulbs, install direct current meters.

Chemistry:

Air and oxygen, molecules and atoms, water and hydrogen, chemical equations, carbon and its compounds, iron, solutions, acids, bases and salts.

Student's Experiments: Appearance of the chemical change, movement of molecules, purification of crude salt, preparation and properties of oxygen, preparation and properties of hydrogen, preparation and properties of carbon dioxide, prepare solution with percentage concentration, properties of acids, properties of bases and salts, experimental exercises, plus 8 selected experiments.

Biology (Book 1):

Unit 1: Plants: Fundamental structures of the flowering plant, germination of the seed, absorption of water and inorganic salts, production of the substance, consumption of the substance and transpiration of water, transportation of the nutrition, blossom, bearing of fruits and nutritional breed, the whole plant: an integration, the main classification of the plants (Algae, Bryophyte, Pteridophyta, seed plants).

Unit 2: Bacteria, Fungus, Virus

Student's Experiments: Observe the plant cell through the microscope, observe the root hairs and the structure of the root tip, observe the structure of the leaf blade, starch produced in a green leaf under the light, observe the structure of the stem, the operation of nutritious plants, collect specimens of plants, observe yeast and mold.

Unit 3: Animals: Main classification of animals, Invertebrates (Protozoa, Coelenterata, Platyhelminthes, Annelida, Arthropoda), vertebrates (Pisces, Amphibia, Reptilia, Birds, Mammalia), behaviour of animals (main types of animal behaviour, physiological basis of animal behaviour).

Student's Experiments: Observe paramecium through the microscope—the form, the main internal structure, motion, the form of the food vacuole, irritability, fill out the sketch of the form and structure of the paramecium. Observe the form, the reaction of stimulus of the hydra, observe the vertical section (or cross section) of the hydra through the microscope, organize the ectoderm, endoderm and digestive cavity, etc., observe the form, motion and reaction for the stimulus of the earthworm, dissect the earthworm and observe its main internal structures, organize the students to collect the specimens of the insects after class and to observe their outside characteristics, methods of mounting insects. Observe the form and structures of the marsh shrimp and others, crustacea animals through the magnifying glass, observe the form of the crustacean and observe the action of each fin and observe the phenomena of how water flow into its oral and out of its gills opening, dissect the crustacean and observe its main internal structures and fill out the sketch with what has been observed, observe the form of the frog, dissect the frog and observe its main internal structures, observe the heart beats of the frog, fill out the sketch with what have been observed, dissect the rabbit or other small-size mammals, observe its main internal structures and fill out the sketch.

Biology (Book 2):

Unit 4: Physiology and hygiene of human body: Brief introduction to the human body, the skin, the skeletal and muscular systems, the circulatory system, the digestive system, the respiration system, the urinary system, the endocrine system, the nervous system, reproduction and development, immunity, infectious diseases.

Student's experiments: Observe the slice of oral epithelial cells of the human body through the microscope, draw a sketch of an oral epithelial cell and indicate the names of each part, observe the slices of four basic tissues through the microscope and contrast the structural characteristics of each one, observe the structures of a long bone, appraise its composition and understand how fragile the calcified bone is, observe blood smear through the microscope and identify the red blood cells and the white blood cells, observe the structures of a mammal's heart, observe the blood flow in the frog's web through the microscope, observe the rhythmic pulsation of the frog's heart, observe the digestion of starch by salivary amalyse, observe the small intestines microvilli of the pig (sheep or chicken) by a magnifying glass, verify that the gas exhaled from the lungs contain more carbon dioxide, test the difference of chest girth between inspiration and expiration, test the lung vital capacity in some schools with better laboratory conditions, do the experiment of knee jerk reflex, do the experiment of frog's scratch reflex, do the experiment of formation of image for understanding the eyeball's function, observe the pathogen through the microscope.

Unit 5: Elementary knowledge about: Heredity, evolution and ecology, heredity and variation, evolution, living things and their environment.

Labour Technology: Woodwork, technology of washing fabrics, cooking technique, knitting and embroidery, how to plant and look after trees, how to plant flowers, how to plant crops, how to breed the cattle and poultry, repairing bicycles, how to sew, photography, hair cutting, typewriting, how to install electric curcuits in the home, how to plant mushrooms, how to cultivate the improved varieties of crops, processing with machines, how to use farm machines, how to process the farm products and by-products.

Characteristics of Science and Technology Education in China's Junior Middle Schools

1. *Fundamental knowledge is paid attention to,* for example: biology as an example, the students may learn the form and structure, physical functions, habits in daily life, classification, inheritance, evolution and ecology of living things, and other systematic and comprehensive knowledge and their application in daily life and production. The students may also learn autopsy and physiology and health, understand the advantages of taking exercise and having good habits of personal hygiene. The contents in every teaching hour are neither too many nor too difficult so that the students will not be burdened.

2. *Experiments are important.* For example: biology observation, illustrations, experiments, visits, practice and experiments after class are carried out during the process of study. While teaching, teachers should raise questions from the above activities and guide the students to think and draw scientific conclusions. By studying biology, the students may develop their observing, experimenting, thinking and self learning abilities.

3. *Science and technology education must take the young age of the lower secondary students into consideration.* It is advisable to use elucidation and interesting methods of teaching. In biology books, there are a large number of pictures, interesting questions, and inspiring outside reading materials.

4. It is appropriate to have some fundamental knowledge of modern science and technology acceptable to students of the lower secondary level. In the biology

class, students are told about tissue culture of plants, behaviour of animals, bionics, immunity, balance of ecology and environment protection, etc.

5. *It is essential to combine theory with practice.* Lessons usually start with practical questions in daily life familiar to students. Then students are guided to the subject and they are allowed to apply science and technology to practical life themselves. The following are real examples illustrating science for all:

   Physics: After studying how to use lenses, the students may known how to protect their eyesight; and after studying an electric lighting circuit, they may understand how to use safely electric devices.

   Chemistry: The students come to know the cause and prevention of air pollution after studying air; and they will be able to determine acidity of soil if they study bases, acid and salts.

   Biology: After lessons on seeds, the students may learn to determine germination percentage; they should be conscious of protecting frogs and birds with the knowledge of higher animals; and they will know more about puberty hygiene if they study the growth and reproduction of human beings.

6. *Organize more and better extra curricular activities of science and technology.* In teaching biology, the teachers should ask the students to collect and make samples, plant trees and work together with them. Such activities beautify the campus, arouse the students' interest and train their abilities, and also improve the teaching conditions.

Some Problems and Their Solutions

1. Only some of the junior middle school students will enter the senior middle schools and universities. The majority of them, especially those from the rural areas, do not possess the knowledge and skills needed to take part in productive labour.

Solutions:

(a) Reform the teaching plan, syllabi and textbooks for the subjects concerned.

(b) Develop secondary vocational and technological education.

2. Lack of teachers and their comparatively low level of education

Solutions:

(a) Increase participation in teacher training colleges and schools.

(b) Offer regular lectures on professional knowledge and teaching theories and sponsor model lessons based on teaching research.

(c) Set up teachers' training colleges at provincial, municipal and country levels and give training courses to teachers who are either released from work or partly released for six months up to three years.

(d) Provide better-quality teaching reference books and teachers' handbooks.

(e) Encourage teachers in the same community to prepare their lessons collectively.

(f) Set up more subject teaching and researching sections and let veteran teachers help inexperienced ones.

(g) China has opened a Television Normal College by using satellite TV channels to train teachers in mountainous and remote regions.

4. INDIA

India is quite diverse both geographically and culturally, with a range of languages, professions and religious. The pattern of education particularly, at the school stage, varies from state to state. The studies and recommendations of Education Commissions set up from time to time gradually brought in changes in policies on school education. At present a national pattern of 12 years schooling has emerged as 10 + 2 with first 10 years as general education. It has Primary (5-10 years), Upper Primary (11-14 years), Secondary (14-16 years) and Senior Secondary (16-18 years). Education is compulsory up to the age of 14. The term lower secondary in the context of this workshop refers to the first ten years, that is up to the age of 16. .

Science has remained one of the essential components of school education from the beginning with slight variations of bifurcation at 8 or 10 years schooling. Science education has come a long way to occupy a central position and has received repeated emphasis from policy consideration as reflected in 1964 Education Commission Report, the 1968 National Policy and successive 5 year plan documents. The implementation phase the (1875-86) of the 1968 policy brought in a shift in science education at the secondary stage towards making it more interesting, meaningful and relevant to the children and their daily life.

The National Policy on Education (NPE 1986) has again stressed the importance of science education. The policy is the culmination of several regional and national seminars and meetings on national goals and curricular concerns. The exercise involved large numbers of educationists, scientists, planners, administrators, teachers and parents. The review of the earlier efforts helped in the identification of weaknesses, strengths, areas of failures and successes (documented as Challenge of Education). The recommendations in the policy document in general and science in particular derived strength from the above document as well as from the study of the Working Group on Science Education set up by NCERT. This group comprised of people from school and higher education, scientists and researchers.

The policy document highlights the need for *expanding* and *extending* the opportunity of science education to larger populations of school childre.ı and through the non-formal system to others of this age group. This strengthens the efforts for providing science to all. Further it emphasized the need for:

- Synthesis of change-oriented technologies and community of the country's cultural traditions;
- Inculcation of scientific temper among the younger populations;
- Incorporating national concerns such as protection of the environment and observation of small family norms as themes in the school curriculum;
- Removal of social barriers and inculcation of world outlook;
- Fostering broad based human values.

The document, while outlining the scope of science education, has made specific recommendations mentioned below, to make science learning more meaningful, interesting and relevant while extending to all.

Science Education

Science education will be strengthened so as to develop in the child well defined abilities and values such as the spirit of inquiry, creativity, objectivity, the courage to question and aesthetic sensibility.

Science education programmes will be designed to enable the learner to acquire problem-solving and decision-making skills and to discover the relationship of science with health, agriculture, industry and other aspects of daily life. Every effort will be made to extend science education to the vast numbers who have remained outside formal education.

Environment and Education

There is a paramount need to create a consciousness of the environment. It must permeate all ages and all sections of society, beginning with the child. Environmental consciousness should inform teaching in schools and colleges. This aspect will be integrated in the entire educational process.

Curriculum Development and Implementation

Curriculum development is an important phase of education and it is an essential component for translating the expectations of the national policy. The Department of Education in Science and Mathematics (DESM) of the National Council of Educational Research and Training (NCERT) is the department entrusted with the development and implementation of the curriculum in science and mathematics. It collaborates with other departments and units of NCERT, SCERTs in states, state departments of education, universities, research institutions and schools. It also works in close liaison with international organizations like UNESCO, UNEP and others.

The present phase of curriculum development in science for different levels of school education is the extension and reinforcement of the earlier curriculum of the 1975 phase along with the incorporation of recent national concerns and recommendations of the National Policy. The steps can be summarized as follows:

1. Review of the earlier policy of 1968 to identify strengths and weaknesses.
2. Reframing of the National Policy (1986) keeping in view the earlier feedback and also the present national goals and concerns including the global concerns and expansion of scientific and technological information (NPE 1986 document).
3. Detailing out the nature of the school curriculum, specially the objectives for each stage, courses to be offered and translation of other expectations of policy (National Curriculum for Elementary and Secondary Education—A Framework).
4. Development of guidelines for curriculum developers and implementors particularly for science education.
5. Development of syllabi in science providing details of course content, activities and expected outcomes.
6. Development of an instructional package comprising of textbooks, teacher resource materials, evaluation materials, laboratory materials and supplementary reading materials.
7. Development of enrichment materials for curricular as well as co-curricular activities such as out-of-school

science activities (science clubs), science exhibitions, science magazines, newsletters and others.

8. Development of guidelines and training of functionaries responsible for curriculum development and implemention at the state level.
9. Training and development of materials for teacher educators/trainers responsible for teacher training.
10. Development of guidelines for strengthening schools specially in science laboratories and libraries.
11. In-depth study of curricular materials implemented to obtain feedback for continual revision, improvement and for the next cycle of curriculum change.

These efforts are expected to help overcome constraints such as lack of detailed guidelines for curriculum development, implementation, strengthening school resources and lack of trained personnel at state level.

Science Curriculum at Secondary Stage

The essential features of the science education curriculum in the light of NPE (1986) are mentioned briefly below:

1. Science teaching continues to be an *essential component* of general education in the first ten years of schooling.
2. Every child has opportunities to learn science during the first ten years of the schooling.
3. Since science would be available to all children irrespective of sect, caste, creed and economic status, attempts have been made to make it more meaningful, and relevant to daily life of children.
4. The science curriculum would provide learning experiences, for developing problem-solving and decision-making abilities, inculcating scientific attitudes.
5. Science up to secondary stage (10 years) has not been presented as disciplines since the child experiences it as a cumulative experience related to life.
6. Efforts in the present science curriculum have been directed to make learning child-centred utilizing daily

life experiences so that the child appreciates the role of science knowledge in the improvement of living and also the quality of the environment.

7. Technology education has been built into science rather than being a separate subject.

The science curriculum developed recently aims at consolidating the abilities, competencies and skills achieved at particular levels, say, after primary, upper primary at the next level. The science curriculum towards the terminal stage of secondary level expects that learners would be able to:

- understand the nature of scientific knowledge;
- apply appropriately the principles, laws and theories of science while interacting with the environment;
- use processes of science in solving problems, making decisions and furthering the understanding of science;
- interact with the environment in a way consistent with science values like keep aside prejudicial, social barriers for environmental protection;
- understand and appreciate the role and relationship of science and technology with society;
- develop interest in science and related issues and enjoy a richer and exciting view of the world around;
- develop manipulative skills associated with science and technology.

Course Content

The science content of the secondary curriculum is based on earlier knowledge at primary level. In addition, the above objectives have been the bases for determining the content (syllabus), which has been framed in detail, listing concepts, sub-concepts, supportive teaching/learning situations/experiences/ activities. The expected outcomes in terms of knowledge, skills, competencies are indicated. The syllabus also provides hints to textbook writers about depth, treatment etc.

The content themes of the syllabus for the age group 11-16 are woven around human beings, their environment, daily life experiences of children and the community. Accordingly the textbook developers have developed instructional packages based on themes such as science in daily life, things and changes around us, important environmental resources like air, water, soil, energy and useful plants and animals. Other basic scientific processes, practices, principles have also been included with examples from and with relevance to daily life.

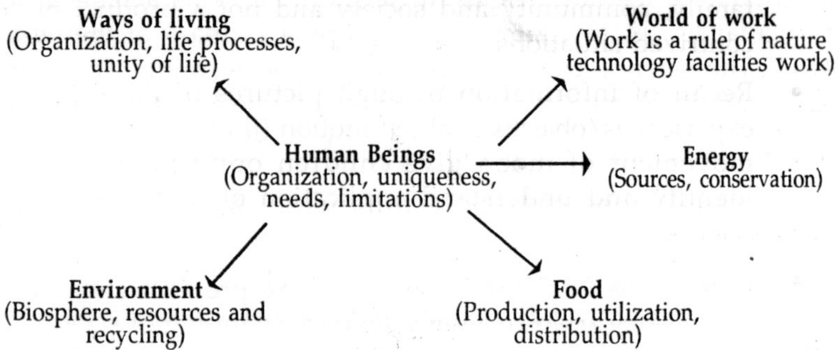

Outline of Basic Themes of the Science Curriculum

Efforts have been made to provide knowledge essential to both rural and urban populations on themes like health, nutrition, diseases, energy, industry, agricultural implements and practices.

The course coverage lays overall emphasis on components of environment, natural resources, relationships between humans and environment, inter-dependence and utilitarian aspects of scientific knowledge and technology, and science applied to understanding the biological unity of the human race, irrespective of caste, colour, creed, religion and language. The terminal part of secondary education (Classes IX-X), covers content from a historical perspective of technology vis-a-vis human needs and gives a feel for the role of science and technology in determining the quality of life and role of the citizens in national development.

Some examples:

- Science in daily life, use of scientific methods such as observation, collection of things around, deal with relevance of scientific knowledge.

- Collection of materials and classification on the basis of solids, liquids and gases. Students also learn to tabulate the information.
- Gathering of information from grocer shops, mechanic shops, framers, fruit and vegetable sellers on diet habits, requirements, sources of pollution make them realise that scientific knowledge is inseparably connected to family, community and society and not a product of contrived situations.
- Recall of information through pictures of daily life experiences/objectives about motion (Jhula), fly player, movement of moon give children opportunities to identify and understand application of principles of science.
- Knowledge on acids and bases is related to acidity in the stomach, acidity of soil, environmental effects.
- Using knowledge of motion, children calculate distance, average speed from their activities like travelling on foot, cycle, bus or train.

Activities based on daily life objects and situations covered in all themes encourage children to question, seek answers, be curious to know, interview elders to gather information on plants, animals, food and fodder production.

The discussion in the course on human beings, their uniqueness and evolution helps children understand more about humans, vis-a-vis other organisms of the environment.

The unit on energy exposes children to sources they use, disadvantages of overuse, hazards of nuclear energy, reducing pollution and need for conservation at individual and group level would help children to apply the basic knowledge on energy gained through this theme.

The examples of food chain giving scientific aspects of vegetarian diet, relate to food chain, biosphere, disturbance to mineral cycles because of the use of fertilizers. The examples encourage children to appreciate the need for harmony between humans and environment.

The examples on soil structure, fertilizer use, and pesticides,. help children to apply the knowledge to growing crops, vegetables and ornamental plants.

Strengthening Teacher Education

Experiences and feedback of curriculum implementation, at the level of teachers, from the beginning and specially during the 1975 phase, helped in strengthening teacher education component. Summer institutes of 2-3 weeks were organized.

It is felt, inspite of all sincere efforts, implementation still was not backed up by intensive training of classroom teachers both in terms of numbers and quality of training.

The curricular reforms after 1986 and review of earlier teacher training efforts necessitated the corresponding strengthening of teacher education both at pre- and in-service levels. The policy document recommended improvement of quality of teacher education and also the working conditions with reinforced school resources in terms of laboratories and school libraries.

Pre-service Teacher Education

As a first step many schemes were launched to deal with teacher training. It was decided to start District Institutes of Educational Training (DIET) at district level. These institutes are responsible for pre-service training of 2 or 3 years for nursery and elementary teachers. They also hold regular training programmes for working teachers on a continual basis.

The National Council for Teacher Education (NCTE) has been framing degree course for Bachelor and Master level as pre-service training in collaboration with university departments of education. Based on present curricular changes in science education curricular contents for a two year programme with details have been worked out and put into practice in some places.

Reinforcing In-service Teacher Training

In order to reinforce the in-service training programmes specially after 1986, many centrally sponsored schemes were started to orient and train the classroom teachers.

1. *A national scheme of in-service training for schools teachers (Programme of Mass Orientation of School Teachers, PMOST)* was planned for training 500,000 teachers each year for the period 1986-90. The short term objective was to create awareness among the teachers about major policy thrusts and curricular changes introduced recently. It was gradually made more of training oriented from awareness, with the strengthening of academic components.

   Ten day Summer Orientation Camps were organized all over the country to initiate, and motivate the teachers so that they appreciate the need for training on a continual basis. The Course Directors/Key Persons were oriented for 3 days in advance to enable them to organize the course successful. They, in turn, organized 5 day orientations of state level rescurce persons. More than 10,000 resource persons have been oriented under this programme.

   Training modules relating to following areas were included:

(a)	Policy issues and thrusts	4 Modules
(b)	Community/School	4 Modules
(c)	Pedagogy orientation	9 Modules
(d)	Attitudes and value development	8 Modules
(e)	Subject oriented material	8 Modules

A telecast in different languages was made during the training camps. Each camp was provided with a TV set.

The programme was monitored through observers and feedback directly obtained from the participants and resource persons. A review for 2-3 days was done with course directors for taking remedial measures for qualitative improvement.

The constraints such as media support, timings and scheduling of camps, board and lodging, were overcome gradually with flexibility at local level.

Constraints include:

- Shortage of suitable speakers;
- Combining of all teachers in one batch overlooking their subject background and level;
- Shortage of relevant media programmes;
- Dilution from key person to teacher through resource team. This was overcome to some extent by introducing more modules.

2. *Scheme for improvement of Science Education in Schools.* For science teachers an additional scheme was launched. Since PMOST was mainly for creating awareness, subject needs of teachers could not be fulfilled. The scheme was started for overall improvement of science laboratories, school libraries and the training of science teachers. The scheme was to help mainly in:

- improving and strengthening science laboratories;
- upgrading library facilities by addition of science books and magazines;
- establishing District Resource Centres in science education for teacher training;
- training science and mathematics teachers;
- seeking assistance and involvement of voluntary organizations.

District Resource Centres are expected to utilize the expertise of DIETs and Colleges of Teacher Education. The resource centres will:

- organize seminars/workshops;
- offer advice on a continual basis;
- help teachers/schools in organizing co-curricular activities for children;
- publish science education newsletters and magazines.

The scheme is sponsored and financed by the Central Government. Initially 500 summer institutes of 3 weeks duration are being organized by NCERT and State Education

Departments. This will be followed by 2 weeks training programmes by the State Governments. The University Departments of Education from the higher education sector are being involved in the training of subject teachers. The teachers for the upper primary or elementary level will be trained by DIETs.

3. *Environmental Orientation to School Curriculum:* Environmental education is a priority. Hence a centrally sponsored scheme was started to strengthen the science curricula with environmental aspects. The scheme is being coordinated by NCERT. Under the scheme, it is planned to set Environmental Education Cells in State Education Departments.

The project areas with specific environmental situations and problems will be identified with the help of voluntary organizations. Short term in-service training courses for science teachers will be organized by voluntary groups working in different areas.

Reinforcing Teaching Resources

The new thrusts in the science curriculum and expectations for developing skills, decision-making abilities and attitudes would require adoption of a variety of teaching resources, educational technologies available and programmes being telecast already on science.

With the introduction of new curricular materials, teachers were invited to sit with pedagogy experts and identify the content areas/topics which needed reinforcement by teaching resource. A set of charts related to biological concepts were developed by the Department of Education in Science and Mathematics (DESM), and the Central Institute of Education Technology (CTET), with the help of University experts and school teachers. These have proved quite useful for clarification of concepts both at the level of the teacher and of the child. They can be used either individually or by groups. Another set is under preparation.

Video Cassettes for teacher training have been prepared on *Science is Part of Life*, depicting the needs and means to link science with daily life situations. A video programme on methods of science has been developed.

Co-curricular Activities to Strengthen Teaching

Other areas which are being fruitfully employed for promoting science education include out-of-school activities, science clubs, science exhibitions and science magazines. They provide opportunities for teachers to involve students in investigatory projects to create interest and develop certain skills like use of tools, kits for carrying out projects and models.

Evaluation of Pupil's Achievement

Evaluation of learning is still continuing through traditional examinations which concentrate on cognitive aspects. The examination system has influenced curricular implementation, and proved to be a severe constraint for curricular reforms. It is conducted for grading the students rather than assessing the learning. The real purpose of pupil evaluation for science learning, to assess the extent of achievement of goals and objective observed as change in behaviours, is largely ignored in the present examination system.

The impact is reflected in:

- reluctance on part of teachers to go for innovations, on alternative teaching strategies.
- children's attitude of casualness towards examinations specially among the brighter ones.
- reluctance on the part of examining bodies, and lack of trained personnel to go for more objective assessment.

Many curriculum developers feel that the present examination system discourages a scientific way of learning, understanding and application of knowledge. The introduction of the present science curricula, with its emphasis on affective objectives, requires drastic reforms in examinations at the secondary level.

Item banks are being developed with the help of teachers and subject experts. Items for different types of objectives are prepared for the whole course. They help the teachers. They can also help pupils train for the examination.

Examination reforms recommended by the 1986 Policy are being gradually introduced. A comprehensive evaluation scheme with evaluation instruments for general topics such as attitudes, interest, have been developed for tryout and introduction in boards of examinations. The number of application type of questions are being used increasingly to assess the ability of the children to apply their knowledge of science concepts. The trend for providing more imaginative and application types of questions have also been introduced in the textbooks.

The possibility of making objective based assessment of achievement even at the school level, where teachers have freedom and evaluate their own pupils, is not being utilized. This probably speaks of lack of the training to assess specially the affective domain and secondly a shortage of appropriate instruments of measurement for the affective domain.

The instruments developed, in a comprehensive scheme of evaluation, such as rating scales and checklists have been prepared for measuring attitudes such as towards studies, teachers, school mates and school programmes. For one activity for observing behaviour, the evaluation tool is given below:

Example: Behaviour Tally Chart

Activity: Field trip to study plants and animals

Name of the learner:

S. No.	*Specific behaviour to be observed*	*Yes*	*No*
1.	Moves in field without anything specific to do		
2.	Break plants without purpose		
3.	Moves from group to group		
4.	Questions other group members		

Likewise behaviour checklists can be framed to observe behaviour with regard to laboratory and project work. Here the pupil can be involved in debates, discussion, individual or group work, to assess the interest, attitude and other objectives of the affective domain. The work in development of evaluation tools and instruments specially for the affective domain has not been undertaken for the science curriculum introduced in 1986. This aspect really calls for intensive inputs both in research and training of teachers.

5. INDONESIA

Development in Indonesia is reaching a critical phase—the last period of the first national development plan. In the past, the country's emphasis was on agriculture. Now, there is a shift in emphasis to agro-industry. According to the current State Guidelines, educational development will focus on the quality of education. The Government intends a basic education of nine years.

The current curriculum is centralized. The system is 6+3+3. Up to year 10 every student has the same programme. At year 11 and 12, there are four optional programmes: physical science, biological science, social studies, and culture and art programmes. Since 1984 process skills have been addressed in all subjects and at all ages. Their purpose is to develop students' creativity, scientific attitude, and self sustaining capacity. However, concept-orientation is still dominant.

The teacher is provided with almost everything he/she needs: background materials, worksheets, equipment, and test items. There is a teacher training system which is believed to be effective. It operates through Teacher Centres:

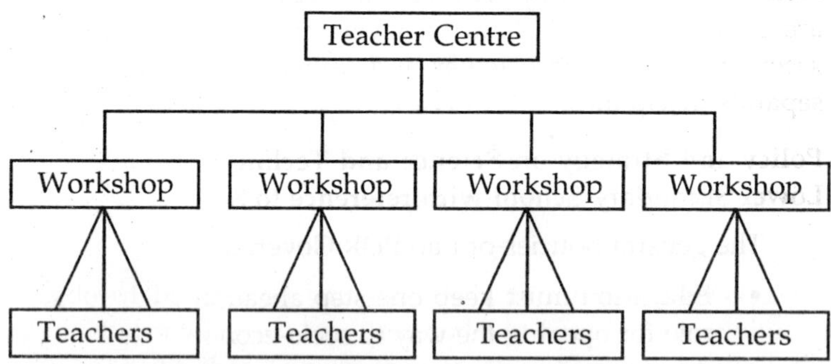

Selected teachers are trained in the Teacher Centre, and then take responsibility to conduct workshops which surrounding teachers attend.

The difficulties that teachers face mostly are lack of resources, too many experiments to be done in class, and an examination system which is concept oriented. Time constraints, consequently, are a major difficulty.

At lower secondary level, even though experiments are carried out and process skills are developed, the teacher is obliged to follow an academic approach. Relating to daily life is difficult. Most experiments are laboratory based, with formal worksheets fixed by central authorities. Creative teachers develop activities which relate science and technology to real life, but mostly as co- and extra-curricular activities.

At the primary level, the situation is better because less concepts are required. The teacher has more time to relate activities to daily life. Concept learning can be linked to improving the quality of life.

The plan to establish nine-year basic education is part of a move towards industrial development. It is an important force in curriculum reform. Efforts are being made at the moment to include the latest issues in education: Science for All; Education for All, and constructivism theory in curriculum planning.

6. LAO PEOPLE'S DEMOCRATIC REPUBLIC

In Lao PDR, education at all levels, and in all grades, is given in Lao (National Language). The school system is 5+3+3 (primary, lower and upper secondary). Science and Technology are compulsory subjects at all levels of general education. At secondary levels (both lower and upper) science is taught as separate disciplines.

Policy and Strategy on Science and Technology Education at Lower Secondary School with reference to Science for All

The general policies of Lao PDR Government are:

- Education must keep one step ahead and play the key role for opening the way to socio-economic and cultural development.
- Education must be closely linked with productive work.
- Social attention should be paid actively to the development of lower secondary school and should consider it as a central task for being able to accept all pupils who graduate from primary school.

Science and technology education at lower secondary school is intended to:

- enable pupils to have a basic and solid knowledge of science, especially in relation to agriculture, forestry, handicrafts;
- encourage them to use the scientific method in resolving real life problems;
- develop scientific attitudes and mind;
- develop scientific and technological thinking.

The existing curricula for lower secondary schools in Lao PDR has been in use since 1976. The time allocated in the teaching is 8 per cent to biology; 8 per cent to physics, 2 per cent to chemistry; 4 per cent to housework and woodwork, 4 per cent to agricultural technology.

Planning and Implementation Difficulties and Actions Taken to Overcome Them

The Educational Science Research Institute is responsible for the research and elaboration of the curriculum, textbooks, and methods of teaching and learning.

The content of curricula and textbooks is well planned and well organized. It reflects the objectives of Science and Technology Education at Lower Secondary School. Science textbooks are in Lao and reflect the scientific nature of education. However the teaching emphasizes recording and memorizing. Demonstrations and pupils' experiments are not common.

The major difficulties are shortages of textbooks, adequate teaching staff, curriculum materials, equipment and laboratories. According to the new education strategy set up in 1986, programmes to revise curricula and textbooks and to train teachers are underway.

Application of Science and Technology Learning in Real-Life Situations

Science and technology education, as taught in Lao PDR classrooms, has had a tangible and positive impact on the learners and society. More and more, now, learners and society are aware of personal and social hygiene, and of the use of scientific techniques in production and improvement of the quality of life. However science and technology education has not yet had profound impact on the ways learners and their communities behave.

Learning and Assessment

In the educational strategy of Lao PDR Government, the assessment strategy is stated: Education Boards must be re-structured at each level—student learning activities should be controlled and assessed through the new examination regulations. Assessment addresses knowledge, skills, attitudes and the intelligence of the pupils. Examinations are set and marked by Boards of Examiners at three levels: district provincial and national. The present system of examining students in Lao schools is not satisfactory and preliminary steps are being taken to change it.

The proposed changes deal with assessment under four headings: open democratic and fair assessment procedures; whole-person assessment; core subject assessment; and assessment of what is actually taught.

Teacher Training

Teacher training aims to develop teachers who possess the following qualities:

- a socialist citizen with qualities of the new working man or woman; correct thinking; and abilities for organizing, administering and teaching.
- ability for developing the role of the school in the context of socio-economic and cultural development of the local community.

To be a teacher in the lower secondary school a candidate must complete the lower secondary school level and then undertake three-years training. It is proposed in the educational strategy to change to completion of upper secondary school plus three years training.

7. MALAYSIA

Current Science Curriculum

At lower secondary level, Malaysia adopted the Scottish Integrated Science Curriculum Grade 7 to Grade 9. At the upper secondary level, the British Nuffield Science Curriculum was adopted, from which two Malaysian programmes were derived: a pure science programme comprising physics, chemistry and biology, and a general science course. The pure science programmes were intended for pupils who are inclined to pursue science. The Malaysian General Science syllabus was meant for those in the non-science stream.

Malaysia has developed an *Integrated Secondary School Curriculum,* locally known as KBSM. It is replacing the above programmes. The KBSM is a curriculum reform aimed to nurture and develop the potential of the individual in the intellectual, spiritual, emotional and physical domains, in a comprehensive and holistic manner. It is based on the National Philosophy of Education:

"Education in Malaysia is an on-going effort dedicated to developing the potential of individuals holistically in an integrated manner so that their development, based on the belief in God, is intellectually, spiritually, emotionally and physically balanced and harmonious. Such an effort is designed to produce Malaysian citizens who are knowledgeable, possessing high moral standards and are responsible and capable of achieving a high level of personal well-being as well as being able to contribute to the harmony and betterment of the society and the nation at large."

The KBSM science curriculum aims to provide learners with opportunities to acquiring scientific knowledge, scientific skills and universal values. The principles which guide the formulation of content in the new science KBSM are:

- Science for understanding of nature
- Science for human well-being
- Science for personal development

The content is organized under four themes:

- Humans and the variety of living things around us.

A variety of living things; the world through our senses; coordination in our bodies; reproduction and growth; variations and heredity; microorganisms and their impact on humanity

- The wealth of the earth and its management.

  A variety of resources on earth; the air around us; water and solutions; Earth and its resources matter and substance; carbon compounds.

- Energy for living.

  Forms and sources of energy; food and the release of energy; nutrition and food production; heat and its transfer; electricity and magnetism; light, colour and vision; energy and chemical changes; force and motion; transportation and communication.

- Humans and balance in nature.

  Interdependence between living things and their environment; balance in nature; Earth and the universe.

In-service Training For Science Teachers

The main purpose of the training programme is to orient teachers to the aims and aspirations of the KBSM and the National Philosophy of Education, and to consider the roles of teachers in the implementation of the KBSM reform.

Centralized teacher training programmes and In-House programmes are conducted. The In-House training package consists of printed documents and video-tapes. The documents and tapes provide the information necessary for those involved with planning and implementing the in-house programme throughout the country.

8. MALDIVES

Since the 1960s, General Science has been taught in the Middle School (ages 12-14 years). Until the National Curriculum was formulated in 1984, schools used science textbooks produced in various neighbouring countries. Teachers usually followed the chapters as presented in the textbook. Frequently, these textbooks were not bought on recommendation but acquired as aid from another country.

The National Curriculum for Grades 1 - 7 includes General Science in Grades 6 and 7 and in the early years incorporates science concepts in the Environmental Studies Programme. A team of two Maldivians drew up the original outline, based on the West Indian Science Curriculum. The syllabuses had to be supplemented with textbooks. However, due to certain constraints, such as limited expertise to prepare textbooks *Integrated Science for Caribbean Schools I and II* has been used to support the General science Course in Grades 6 and 7, since 1985.

In the course of implementing the General Science syllabus, constraints were identified which led to a major review of the programme. A two week workshop was held at the Education Development Centre in 1988. Maximum effort was made to draw to the workshop expertise from within the country and outside.

One of the major recommendations of the workshop was that the aims and objectives of science teaching should be clearly spelt out so that the teachers would be guided by objectives and not merely follow the text books. Accordingly, the participants of the workshop formulated aims and objectives for the middle school. In doing so, the following were kept in view:

- the National Educational Goals:
  - To make education more relevant to the local environment.
  - To train the workforce necessary for national development.
- local needs and environment;
- skills and attitudes required in a rapidly changing world;
- traditional culture and values;
- maturity and age level of the students in Grades 6 and 7;
- the middle school as a terminal stage as well as a preparatory stage for higher education.

Aims of Science Teaching at Middle School Level

1. develop and foster an appreciation of the application of science for human welfare and to instil in them the

importance and need for judicious use of the knowledge of science;

2. promote self-learning of knowledge around them through the processes of science;
3. to foster team spirit and a sense of cooperation in acquiring and sharing the fruits of knowledge;
4. help develop independent and constructive thinking;
5. develop the ability to tackle the problems of daily life situations and to find solutions through the application of scientific knowledge and processes;
6. instil and develop in them a sense of responsibility to apply the scientific knowledge and skills acquired towards improving the quality of life;
7. develop in them scientific attitudes and skills to produce scientific and technological manpower for national development;
8. develop interest and curiosity for knowledge and understanding through scientific processes;
9. develop respect for logic and opinion of others, and concern about consequences;
10. help to acquire practical and work-oriented knowledge and skills through learning science.

Planning and Implementation Difficulties

Among the problems and difficulties faced by the Education Development Centre in its first attempt to implement the Lower Secondary Science Curriculum were the following:

- Shortage of manpower for planning and producing teaching/learning materials. (This problem has been overcome temporarily through involving people from other sectors such as health, fisheries and agriculture.)
- Lack of a science component in the teachers' training programme.
- Science Education is officially to be conducted in the English language. Available untrained teachers are not

able to carry out activity-oriented teaching/learning activities in English. (It has been approved now to conduct Science Education at lower secondary level in Dhivehi, when the English medium is not possible. The new textbooks will be translated.)

- Translating Science textbooks from English into Dhivehi poses a new problem of coining new terms — this in turn leads to shortage of books as the process of forming new words is taking a long time.
- Lack of science teaching aids and supplementary materials. (A basic kit is provided by the Ministry of Education, but it is not adequate.)
- Need for producing improvised aids from local materials.
- Hesitancy of teachers to adopt activity oriented approaches limits students' attainment.

9. NEPAL

Educational Structure

The present educational structure in Nepal is 5-5: five years of primary and five years of secondary. Prior to this, the system consisted of five years of primary, two years of lower secondary and three years of (upper) secondary. A plus 2 stage (higher secondary) will be added gradually to the existing system. His Majesty's Government has already announced that secondary education will be from Grade 6 to 10. Grades 6 and 7 from the previous structure are attached currently either to primary schools or secondary schools.

Changing Face of Science Education

Until 1971, science was taught as an optional subject in high schools (Grade 6-10). At that time there were no standard textbooks. There were no clear objectives for school science.

With the New Education System Plan (NESP) in 1971 there was a dramatic change in science education. One of the significant features of NESP was the establishment of the Curriculum Development Centre, now called the Curriculum

Textbook and Supervision Development Centre (CTSDC). This centre is responsible for developing, implementing and evaluating the science curriculum.

Currently, a centrally—directed model of curriculum development is in operation. National goals were translated into curriculum objectives and programmes. Curriculum guides were prepared in various subjects including science. Activity oriented textbooks were developed. Orientation and on the spot training programmes for teachers were organized. Science equipment were distributed.

The objectives of the new science curriculum are basically the acquisition of knowledge, skills and attitudes of direct use to the students in their daily lives and understanding.

Organization of the Curriculum

The major curricular goals are set at the national level by the Ministry of Education. They are translated into various subject learning objectives by the respective specialists. The current primary science curriculum stresses the teaching of biology and environmental science. At the lower secondary level the emphasis is on physical and biological sciences, while at the secondary level, science is taught as physics, chemistry, biology, geology and astronomy.

The subject specialists in the CTSDC are responsible for developing and evaluating the curricula. The committee system is used to develop curricula. There are three types of committees. The subject committee is composed of members from different educational institutions e.g. the Institute of Education, university campuses, Educational Directorates and School teachers. The chairperson is appointed by the centre. The subject specialist of CTSDC acts as a secretary to this committee.

The subject specialists first prepare a draft curriculum which is discussed in the subject committee. Improvements are made and the revised draft curriculum is forwarded to the next committee known as the Curriculum, Textbook Development and Innovation Committee organized under the chairmanship of the Chief of CTSDC. After approval by this committee, the draft curriculum is sent to a third committee called the Curriculum and Textbooks Coordination Committee headed by the Honourable Minister of Education and Culture. Only after the approval of this committee is the draft curriculum ready for implementation.

Instructional Time

The total instructional time devoted to science education at primary level is 10 per cent and at secondary level is 13 per cent. That means four periods (45 minutes per period) a week in Grade four to five and five periods a week in Grade six to ten.

Evaluation

An examination unit was established with the introduction of NESP. The new scheme is an integral part of the education system. It has produced standardized achievement tests with limited success. There is a lack of suitably trained man power for the purpose. The new scheme for student assessment includes provision for internal assessment. The next step of the new evaluation scheme is to keep records of the *progress* achieved by individual students.

Teacher Training

After the implementation of NESP, the Institute of Education (IOE), now Faculty of Education, organizes different courses at certificate, diploma and degree level, to produce trained teachers. There are pre-service as well as in-service training programmes.

The production of science teachers from the Institute is limited. Lack of qualified and trained science teachers is one of the greatest draw backs, both for schools and for training programmes.

The qualifications required for teaching science at the primary level is the School Leaving Certificate (SLC) and some additional training. At the lower secondary level, one year of science and one year of education with a major in science is required, and in the secondary level, B.Sc. or B.Ed. with a major in science.

The problem with science teachers with M.Sc. or B.Sc. background is that they prefer to take employment outside the teaching profession. They use the teaching job just as a platform for employment elsewhere.

Curriculum Revision

Curriculum development is a continuous process and it has to be adjusted constantly to changing national needs, aspirations and values. In this context, the curriculum has been revised in 1981 and science made optional in grades nine and ten. The main reasons for making science optional are:

- the low achievement of the students
- lack of qualified and trained teachers
- lack of classroom facilities
- high students/teachers ratio
- the teachers are not acquainted with sophisticated equipment.

With the revision of the curriculum, all the textbooks from Grade IV to X are being rewritten so that they suit under-qualified science teachers. Especially in primary and lower secondary grades few experiments were done. So the revised curriculum shifts the emphasis from the student centred textbooks to teachers centred ones.

To overcome the lack of qualified and trained science teachers and to equip the schools with necessary equipment the Ministry of Education and Culture launched a five year programme with the establishment of the Science Education Development Centre (SEDEC) in 1984. This is one of the landmarks in science education in Nepal.

Problems

Most schools, especially primary schools and those in the rural areas, are short of standard classrooms and space. Laboratories, workshops and libraries are almost nonexistent. Nearly, all secondary schools have permanent buildings but the classrooms are crowded. Very few well established secondary school have laboratories for science and collections of books for students and staff.

It is widely felt that the quality of education suffered in the course of the recent significant expansion of schools and enrolments. The deficiency in quality is related to physical facilities, instructional materials, trained teacher supply, and no capacity to translate the national goal and curriculum objectives into textbooks, teacher training and evaluation programmes. Because of these deficiencies teaching-learning and evaluation programmes emphasize objectives in the lower levels of the cognitive domain.

Very little research work has been done in science education in Nepal. In the curriculum development process also there is a great difficulty in developing a balanced curriculum for the whole country because of the great diversity in its people and geographical features. There is also very low participation of teachers from some parts of the country.

Primary education has now been accepted at the national level as one of the basic needs of the people. Recently CTSDC has proposed that science education be made compulsory from Grade one to ten.

The Curriculum, Textbook and Supervision Development Centre has already prepared a proposal to establish an institute to promote school science and mathematics education. It is being on process for approval by His Majesty's Government.

Conclusion

An urgent need to promote science and technology education and relate it to real-life situations in Nepal is strongly felt. The National Science and Technology Policy of Nepal, approved in May 1989, recognizes that the capability of a nation lies largely in its scientific and technological capability. A National seminar on Science and Mathematics Education Policy and Planning held on February 1990 was very timely. So is this Workshop.

10. PAKISTAN

Science and technology have important roles in the current and future well being of humanity. To get rid of misery, poverty, hunger, diseases, illiteracy, social injustice, energy crisis and environmental pollution at national and international levels, introduction of science and technology in the curriculum at lower secondary and higher secondary levels is essential.

The policies of the Government include *Education for All,* and special emphasis has been given to science and technology. Science education is compulsory at lower secondary level (Classes VI to VIII).

Curriculum Development and Implementation

Pakistan has a unique system of curriculum development and implementation. There is a Federal Curriculum Bureau known as the National Bureau of Curriculum and Textbook Development. Under the control of this organization, provincial curriculum development centres develop the initial drafts of the curricula, keeping in view the national and local needs of the students and society. These drafts are submitted to the National Bureau of Curriculum, which finalises and approves them if they are found to be satisfactory. The drafts are then handed over to Textbook Boards situated in each province. Textbooks are developed by the Textbook Boards, and finally approved by the Ministry of Education and the Curriculum Wing. They are printed by the Textbook Boards.

Approach in the New Curriculum

The selection of the subject matter has been made on the basis of:

- the child's intellectual, emotional and physical needs;
- the sciences, especially Biology, Physics, Chemistry and Astronomy;
- the environment, both natural and man made, in which the child lives;
- the objectives we wish to attain; and
- the total school curriculum.

Aims and objectives of science teaching:

- to achieve a broad and genuine appreciation and understanding of different aspects of science and technology;
- to promote scientific literacy and provide scientific and technological manpower for the country's needs;
- to prepare the young generation to solve their own

problems, as well as the problems of humanity, at community and global levels;

- to improve the socio-economic conditions of the country.

Planning and Implementation Difficulties and Actions Taken to Overcome Them

Science and technology education is given a special place in our Seventh Five Year Plan, and foreign aided projects are also functioning to spread science and technology education at lower secondary and higher secondary levels.

The problems faced are shortage of appropriate funds; shortage of highly qualified people to teach at lower secondary level (due to limited financial resources), and population explosion.

Pakistan is assisted financially by organizations like, UNESCO, UNICEF, World Bank, Asian Development Bank and ODA. The problem of getting highly qualified people to teach science at lower secondary level will take time to resolve.

Evaluation of Pupils Achievement

In teacher training programmes, attention is given to evaluation of pupil achievement, including scholastic attainment and attainment in the affective domain. Measurement and Evaluation are taught as subjects in the teacher training colleges.

Examining boards at the provincial and federal levels use written tests for measuring scholastic attainment.

Teacher Education

Elementary teachers complete one year's training after matriculation to obtain the Certificate of Primary Teaching. Teachers for lower secondary classes (VI-VIII) complete one year's training after B.A. or B.Sc., to obtain a Certificate of Teaching.

11. PHILIPPINES

Science education in the Philippines has been revitalized. This was the result of major educational reforms instituted in response to the government's thrust of raising national productivity and economic stability, and the educational thrusts of equity, quality, efficiency and relevance.

Two important developmental programmes for elementary and secondary education were adopted. These were the Programme for Decentralized Educational Development (PRODED) and the Secondary Education Development Programme (SEDP). PRODED was tasked to improve the quality of elementary education while SEDP will upgrade the quality of secondary education. These programmes were designed to:

1. reduce regional disparities in educational resource;
2. improve pupil performance; and
3. improve overall quality and efficiently of elementary and secondary education.

The programmes operated in phases which were in line with the new developmental strategies spelled out in the 1982-89 Medium Term Philippine Development Plan. The implementation of PRODED took precedence since priority was given to the improvement of pupils' performance at the elementary level. Its inputs were a new curriculum emphasizing the 3 R's and Values Education; upgraded instructional materials; retrained teachers, administrators and supervisors; and new and repaired school facilities and equipment.

The implementation of the SEDP coincided with the entry of PRODED educated pupils to the secondary level. SEDP continued the improvement started by PRODED along with the pilot testing of the curriculum and the training of teachers. The expected outcomes of SEDP are:

- increase participation rate (PR) or the number of students per school from 51.5 per cent to 71.5 per cent.
- increase internal efficiently (survival rate) of students entering first year and leaving fourth year by reducing drop-out rate in the public schools from 5.8 per cent to 2 per cent.
- increase achievement scores from 53 per cent to 70 per cent.
- develop a new curriculum and new policies for secondary education.

- build 673 school buildings with equipment packages for science, mathematics and work education.
- improve textbook/students ratio from 1.7 per cent to 1.1 per cent.
- improve teacher/students ratio from 1.53 to 1.40.
- train 140,000 public school teachers, 400,000 private school teachers.
- orient 5,000 school administrators (public and private).

The general plan for revitalizing the secondary education programme involves the implementation of intervening activities on:

- curriculum development;
- staff development;
- provision of instructional materials;
- research and special studies;
- revision of procedures and systems for greater efficiency in the administration and management of the secondary education programme. Preparatory development activities for the implementation of the comprehensive development programme commenced in 1985. In 1989, the new secondary school curriculum was launched and started with the first year curriculum.

Strategies for Implementing the SEDP Goals

To improve the quality of education, SEDP focuses on:

- curriculum reform;
- provision of quality textbooks/teacher's manuals on a 1:1 basis;
- provision of science and work education equipment;
- staff development (short and long term);
- assistance to private secondary education;
- research studies on National College Entrance Examinations (NCEE), Barangay high schools, career guidance, etc.;

To effect efficiency in the system, the SEDP focuses on:

- research studies on school location and distribution, financing schemes, teacher's salaries and benefits, etc.;
- strengthening of sector management and evaluation system.

To expand access to the sector, the SEDP plans to undertake/expand:

- the school building programme;
- the service contracting scheme;
- alternative delivery systems.

To ensure equity in the system, the SEDP plans to undertake/expand:

- the school building programme for local high schools;
- the equipment provision and technical assistance for disadvantage areas.

Policies and Strategies

A. Overall Policies

Major curriculum reforms were carried out in the context of the Medium Term Philippine Development Plan, 1987-92. The policies and strategies to implement these policies are as follows:

Policy: Improvement of the quality and relevance of education and training with respect to Philippine conditions and needs.

Strategies:

1. A general curricular and programme re-orientation which foster knowledge, skills and values.
2. Revision and development of textbooks and learning aids that will reflect Philippine conditions and experiences.
3. In-service training programmes for teachers, administrators and supervisors.
4. Expansion, improvement and maintenance of learning resources, such as libraries, museums and educational media centres.

5. Development of a more efficient system of selection and retention.
6. Increase institutional autonomy to enable schools to strengthen curricular offerings.
7. Create partnership with industry and the rest of society to ensure productivity and enhance relevance of institution.

Policy: Equitable access to education and training opportunities.

Strategies:

1. Development of a socialized tuition fee scheme which is based on the social cost of education and student's ability to pay.
2. Priority in the distribution of teachers' instructional materials, school facilities and equipment to disadvantaged communities and disabled individuals.
3. Provision of alternative training opportunities for the under privileged and disadvantaged sectors of society.
4. Strengthening of the rural based training system.

Policy: Intensification of values education.

Strategies:

1. Identification of traditional desirable Filipino values particularly among workers and potential workers.
2. Integration of values education in the school curriculum using appropriate teaching strategies and character building activities.

Policy: Promotion of entrepreneurial education and training.

Strategies:

1. Emphasis on entrepreneurial training programmes with an agricultural and rural orientation.
2. Installation of vital support systems.
3. Functional linkages with training institutions and industries and non-governmental organizations.

Policy: Increased emphasis on science and technology, indigenous research and experimentation.

Strategies:

1. Institutionalization of the teaching of science and technology in both curricular and co-curricular programmes to promote scientific literacy.

2. Emphasis on pre-service and in-service training of science teachers.

Policy: Full mobilization and utilization of education personnel with an increasingly commensurate system of compensation and incentives.

Strategies:

1. Development of programmes for recruitment, utilization, professional development and welfare of teachers.

2. Provision of appropriate incentives for above average students who have the aptitude for teaching.

3. Creation of a differentiated system of career progression for public and private school teachers and staff.

B. Sectoral Policies

Policies at the sectoral level are concerned with the upgrading of the formal school system, particularly in elementary and secondary education. These policies will continue to emphasize the overall policies of:

- a systematic scheme of student intake retention and progression;
- equity in the allocation of resources based on regional needs;
- a more effective utilization and development of teachers and staff;
- stronger coordination of public and private schools;
- improvement of management capabilities at all levels.

C. *Basic Education*

Policy: Basic science education and science promotion.

Strategies:

1. As foundation for technological advancement, basic education in the sciences will be oriented towards production.
2. Priority in innovations in integrating productive work and in-school science courses.
3. Basic science courses shall serve as an instrument to equip the citizens with skills to develop appropriate technological solutions to specific problems and transform natural resources for productive use endangering the environment.
4. Increase by 30 per cent the number of science and mathematics teachers to be upgraded in teaching competencies.
5. Intensify non-formal education in science through the active promotion and dissemination of science and technology information by the 12 regional science and technology centres.
6. Emphasis on livelihood/employment related technologies.

With these policies a more integrative and in depth evaluation of the formal school system will be done to identify the major problems and issues that affect the sector and to recommend appropriate measures to improve further the delivery system. Public and private schools shall be rationalized to prevent poorly-equipped, understaffed and inadequately financed institutions which turn out poorly-prepared graduates for employment. The revised bilingual education policy will be implemented. The policy states that the medium of instruction shall be in English and Filipino. In addition, the regional language may be used as an auxiliary medium of instruction. Salaries of locally funded high school teachers are nationalized with the implementation of free public secondary education for the school year 1988-89. Moreover, the operating expenses and capital outlays of the schools shall be nationalized. With regards to limited funds, new sources of financing shall be tapped. A nationwide adoption of the educational contracting scheme to make education accessible to all. This scheme allows students not accommodated in public schools to enrol in private schools at government expense.

Upgrading of science education will be done in two aspects:

(a) the updating and the training of teachers in upgraded methods; and

(b) the provision of science apparatus and facilities. The teacher-training component of the new programme will be undertaken by national centres of excellence (CENTREX), selected private institutions of higher learning. Regional Educational Learning Centres (RELCs). Regional Science Teaching Centres (RSTCs) and selected national or accredited high schools. For the equipment component, the Science Equipment Project will oversee the developing, designing and production of instructional science equipment in some selected secondary schools. The project will also conduct a continuous evaluation of science equipment and training for the repair, maintenance and operation of equipment.

Science Education Development Plan (SEDP)

Before the implementation of SEDP in 1989, preparatory activities for a new Development Plan were undertaken. One of these activities is the formulation of the Science Education Development Plan (SEDP).

SEDP is a joint project of the Ministry of Education, Culture and Sports and the Department of Science and Technology (DOST). It was a research-based study and was conceived on the basis of the growing importance of science and technology within the Philippine Development Plan and was designed to upgrade science education systematically at all levels by providing guidelines and priorities for policies, programmes and projects relative to science education. It took two years and hundreds of people from various sectors and parts of the country through a series of sectoral consultative conferences, survey studies, documentary analysis of pertinent documents, analysis of the related literature in science and mathematics education and commissioned studies and paper. The wide participatory mechanism stimulated active deliberation on the directions that science education should take for US Filipinos. By its publication (in 2 volumes), SEDP became a documented basis for describing science and mathematics education in the country.

The policies set down by SEDP were closely linked with the country's development thrust of self-reliance and accelerated productivity. These policies were listed in eight categories in the SEDP's plan of action. These are:

- Organization
- Finance
- Curriculum
- Staff Development
- Textbooks and Instructional Materials
- Equipment and Facilities
- Research
- Linkages.

Science and Technology Plan (STP)

Efforts to build a strong science and mathematics education was accelerated by the creation of the Presidential Task Force on Science and Technology (PTFST). It is a multi-sectoral task force composed of representatives from the government, industry and academic. Its mission is to formulate a Science and Technology Plan that will spur the Philippines to become a newly industrialized country by the year 2000. The Science and Technology Plan is a comprehensive sectoral action plan for manpower development in science and mathematics. It hopes to attract the youth towards careers in science. PTFST, in turn recommended the formation of the Science and Technology Coordinating Council (STCC) to assist PTFST and coordinate in the implementation of S&T Plan. STCC is assisted by two panels, namely, the panel for Higher Level Manpower Development and for Science and Mathematics Education. The sectoral plan on Science and Mathematics Education is now working on the details of setting up a network of high schools. The strategy it hopes to follow in order to achieve its objective is to:

- identify the lead implementation agencies; and
- study teaching-training institution's programmes like the Institute for Science and Mathematics Education Development (ISMED) and Philippine Normal College (PNC) from which future teachers will come by minimizing education course requirements, which would make a teaching career attractive to science majors. Secondary schools which play a key role in developing scientists will also be studied. Activities which identify science talents, such as science quizzes, fairs, etc. will be studied. From the results of the assessment, these institutions will be linked into a strong network, its manpower, science materials and laboratories and other resources will be developed.

Selection of schools which will form the network was done on the basis of their needs, such as teacher training, science equipment, and stronger science environment for students and teacher. Moreover, these schools are mainly located around a tertiary institution which will serve as a node of the network. Some lead persons and institutions were identified and they will assist STCC in the implementation of the Science and Technology Plan.

The process of implementation for school year 1987-88 reported major policy and sectoral developments supportive of the policies and thrusts in education and training. Certain key indicators were identified. The overall enrolment performance at 97.16 per cent fell short of the Plan target. This shortfall maybe attributed by peace and order and poverty-related problems, particularly in the rural areas. Achievement in elementary and secondary levels was higher than the Plan targets. Literacy rates had increased. However, Senator Edgardo Angara, Chairman of the Senate Committee on Education, expressed in an interview that the scientific literacy of a seventeen year old Filipino is only equivalent to the scientific literacy of a 10 year old Singaporean boy. Teacher-pupil ratio of 1.33 in 1987 exceeded the 1.32 ratio of 1986. Textbook-pupil ratio of 1.2 was maintained.

Major reforms were instituted to achieve quantitative expansion and qualitative improvement in the educational system. Salaries of teachers of locally funded high schools were nationalized. This is in preparation for the implementation of the no tuition policy in public secondary schools starting in School Year 1988-89 which had been signed into law (Free Secondary Education Act). Scholarships and loan grants to 16,061 qualified students were increased. The Science Scholarship Fund which provides additional scholarship assistance to poor but deserving students who have the aptitude for science was being discussed. Science and Mathematics teachers were trained by the Regional Science Teaching Centres (RSTCs) which provided in-service and diploma programmes to these teachers.

DECS, on its part, issued an order for a moratorium on the establishment of barangay high schools, to arrest the proliferation of substandard barangay high schools. About 30,285 out-of-school youths went back into the school system through the Philippine Equivalency Placement Test (PEPT). Educational opportunities were extended to cultural minorities by accrediting 15 Muslim Madrasah schools in Region I, employing para-teachers in Colabato, and setting up of tent schools and walking blackboards in the remote areas of Regions I, IX and XII. Mixed classes were set up in areas where the schools' student population did not meet the grade-to-grade class size requirement. The educational service contracting scheme was adopted in Regions VIII and XII. This scheme is an alternative delivery system which is innovative and cost-effective. It allows private schools to take in students who cannot be accommodated in the public schools. The construction of additional classrooms was minimized and maintained the financial viability of private schools. A wider access to education increased enrolment to 14.4 million.

Training programmes were geared in developing the expertise of qualified teachers and enhance the use of technology for countryside development. These covered secondary science equipment improvization, refresher courses in secondary Physics and Chemistry, intensive courses in Mathematics, Chemistry,

Biology and a technician course for science equipment. Eight satellite schools were added to the 13 RSTCs to widen the coverage of the teacher training programmes in the sciences, particularly in the depressed and far flung areas.

Implications for Curriculum Development

"Education is a public function, it is a need as well as a right." This was the strong view articulated by the Fund for Assistance in Private Education (FAPE) President Abraham Felipe during a round table discussion of the Asian Pacific Educational Programme for All. This programme seeks to bring education to all by the year 2000. Yet, Felipe noted that the traditional system is bent in developing people for the labour market which encourages emigration at the expense of the students' rural communities. In this aspect, schools must produce citizens equipped for effective participatory citizenship and committed to the needs, of the country. Thus reforms in the secondary school curriculum is needed. In 1989 the Secondary Education Curriculum was developed through multi-sectoral consultations and conferences. The objectives of the new curriculum are to:

- develop an enlightened commitment to the national ideals by cherishing, preserving and developing moral, spiritual, and socio-cultural values as well as other desirable aspects of the Filipino heritage;
- obtain knowledge and form desirable attitudes for understanding the nature and purpose of man, and therefore, of oneself, one's own people, and other races, places and times, thereby, promoting a keen sense of self, of family and of national and international communities;
- develop skills in higher intellectual operations and more complex comprehension and expression activities, and in thinking intelligently, critically and creatively in life situations;
- acquire work skills, knowledge and information and a work ethic essential for making an intelligent choice of an occupation and for specialized training in specific occupations; and

- broaden and heighten one's abilities in and appreciation for the arts, the science, and technology as a means for maximizing one's potentials for self-fulfilment and for promoting the welfare of others.

The new curriculum is student-centred and community-oriented. Values are being integrated and designated learning competencies are identified. It is cognitive, affective, and manipulative based. Technology is emphasized in Science and Technology. There is emphasis on critical thinking to promote creativity and productivity. Science and technology subjects emphasize the practical application of scientific facts and concepts. The teaching strategies suggested for the teaching of Science and Technology are the discovery and investigative approaches and the Science Technology Society approach. Innovative/creative activities to encourage imaginative and scientific experimentation and discoveries are suggested. Scientific surveys of the immediate environment and related scientific concepts are encouraged.

To ensure the effectiveness of the new curriculum the materials were developed through a review of the 1973 textbooks and other instructional materials. Competencies for each year level were also validated. These were done with the involvement of:

- curriculum writers from the university,
- supervisors, teachers and practitioners,
- curriculum writers of the Bureau of Secondary Education,
- consultants from teacher training institutions, and
- parents and non-government groups.

The curriculum materials were tried out in 80 schools representing 6 types of secondary schools, namely barangay, municipal, provincial, city, vocational, private sectarian and private non-sectarian.

The evaluation of tryout classes showed that the new curriculum was more effective than the 1973 Revised Secondary Education Programme. Pilot classes' scores from pre-test to post test increased. Pilot teachers obtained higher mean scores in competency tests than non-pilot teachers.

First year and second year textbooks and teacher's manuals have been printed in time for School Year 1989-90.

Self Development

The different features of the new curriculum required the training of teachers. These features are the increased emphasis on technology, the new organization of subject, and the setting of desired competencies which must be mastered by teachers and students. Moreover, new strategies have to be learned to teach values education and to promote critical, creative, and analytical thinking.

Training of teachers for the new curriculum followed the scheme used by PRODED which was done by grade level (in SEDP it will be by year level). The training of regional trainers was followed by the mass training of teachers in all regions of the country. In preparation for the mass training of first year teachers, Centres of Excellence (CENTREXES) had been identified to train trainers. One of the CENTREXES is UP-ISMED which handled the training of science and mathematics trainers at all levels. In addition, Regional Leader Schools (RLS) had been identified as centres for the mass training of teachers. Teacher Training Institutions (TTI) were also identified to compliment the RLS. The training design for the mass training were prepared by Regional officers, trainers, RLS and TTI's.

Private schools were involved in the training programmes. FAPE handled the training for the private high school administrators, regional trainers and teachers. The mass training of the private high school teachers would be held simultaneously with the public school teachers. ISMED too was commissioned to train the science and mathematics private school trainers. Private school principals together with public schools principals/supervisors would be oriented on the new curriculum which is being held now at ISMED. However, the intended clientele did not come but instead send their teachers for this orientation.

Staff development for the first year level was completed in 1989 which was the start of the implementation of the first year curriculum. Training of trainers and teachers for the second year level is almost completed which prepared the second year teachers for the implementation of the second year curriculum in School Year 1990-91. The training of third year trainers will be held this May 1990.

The training of trainers and teachers in all year levels and for both public and private school teachers follow the same programme.

Special Features of the Training Programme

Training of Regional Trainers

- One week orientation to values development focusing on personal qualities and using the experiential approach.
- One week for communication skills in English and Filipino.
- Four weeks for content orientation to include an update on content area, strategies and evaluation.

Private Schools

- one month
- Activities cover values development (5 days), technical training (21 days), and action planning (I day)

Mass Training of First Year Teachers

- Public: 3 days for values development, 3 days for communication skills, and 4 weeks for subject area content to cover subject matter, strategies and evaluation instruments.
- Private: 1 day for values orientation and 10 days for subject content, strategies and evaluation.

A complimentary staff development programme was formulated to ensure the effective implementation of the new curriculum. This programme includes the training by selected centres of public and private school Regional Trainers and the mass training of teachers for both public and private high schools. In addition leadership training for secondary school principals/administrators for both public and private schools and fellowship grants on short or long term basis were conducted.

Physical Facilities Development

Research findings of the country's physical facilities and equipment in secondary schools indicated inadequate physical facilities such as classrooms, laboratories, equipment, etc. which contributed to unsatisfactory student performance. There is also inequity and inadequacy in the allocation of resources especially at the local level. Thus, there is a need to provide equipment and technical assistance especially for disadvantaged areas.

Provisions for improved physical facilities and equipment for SEDP included the SEDP Building Package. A package consists of a two-storey building including a workshop and a library. The workshop comes equipped with science and work tools. Other expected grants are the 50 typhoon-proof buildings costing $10 M from the Japanese International Cooperation Agency (JICA) and 186 buildings from an United States Agency for International Development (USAID) allotment, and the setting up of the National Fabrication Centre and the distribution centres by the German Government.

Issues in Planning and Implementation

A number of issues will continue to confront the educational system in the remaining years of the 1988-92 Plan. These are as follows:

Resource generation

This issue is considered to be the biggest challenge to the education sector because of the competing claims of various subsectors on the meagre resources. Additional budgetary support is needed for various activities i.e. full implementation of free secondary education and the financing of the SEDP.

One area where resources for basic education may be tapped is higher education. Expenditures in state colleges and universities (SCU), must be rationalized. The rationale for the proposed solution is that SCUs account for only 23 per cent of the total higher education enrolment and the unit cost per student per year is high. Moreover, SCUs rely on secondary education enrolment for their existence. Other alternatives to make better use of SCUs resources are to allocate SCUs resources to programmes and services which are not provided by the private sectors such as graduate programmes, basic research, etc. and to work out a mechanism for prioritizing SCUs. Savings generated can be channelled to basic education.

The policy of the integration of private education which makes private education a partner of the government may be implemented. The private sector may serve as a resource which can be used to meet the demands of development.

Necessary adjustments have to be made in education manpower and labour with the limited resource availability. In the light of these limitations, a temporary moratorium in the conversion of barangay high schools into national high schools and of public secondary schools into colleges and universities was proposed. The financial plan for the educational system was drawn by the restructuring of the Special Education Fund, a larger share of the Salary Adjustment Fund, and the education lottery scheme.

Education personnel were encouraged to participate in the national productivity programme such as textbook writing, production of desks, equipment, and items needed by schools. Teachers were given flexible schedules so that all teachers can be engaged in income-generating activities. However, sufficient guidelines will be provided so that the quality of teaching will not be affected.

Increasing Mismatch of Supply and Demand

This issue was brought about by the shift in the skills demands of new industries and technology. Plans, policies and programmes should consistently respond to this issue and influence the country's population characteristics and movements to check the uneven distribution and access to employment opportunities. Linkages between industrial plants and educational institutions must be established. Courses should be made relevant to the needs of industry and improve the employment prospect of graduates.

Difficulties encountered during the implementation were gathered from personal interview with certain trainers and administrators involved in the mass training programmes for the lower secondary level. These were:

- Late arrival of textbooks and teacher's manuals for the training period.
- Lack of projection in the distribution of textbooks and teacher's manuals to region/schools. Not all areas received the books, or if ever they received the books, these were in limited amounts.
- Lack of trained personnel to observe and gather feedback for the mass training programme. In some regions nobody observed in the succeeding (first and second) training periods.
- None or very little background in the Earth Sciences was incorporated in the first year curriculum.
- Lack of equipment in most barangay schools.
- The free secondary education programme created large class sizes, averaging 60-70 students in a class. Cost cutting measures such as the limited hiring of additional teachers had aggravated the problem since teachers were handling 7 to 11 classes. As a result teachers were tired, overloaded and underpaid.
- On the administrator's side, difficulties in scheduling of classes and loading of teachers were encountered. This was brought about by curricular changes like the time allotment given to subject areas. Science is now taught 60 minutes/day while the non-science subjects except Technology and Home Economics are taught 40 minutes per day. This results in the overloading of science teachers compared with the non-science teachers. To solve this problem, the time allotment for non-science subjects was raised to 60 minutes a day.

Science I Curriculum at Secondary Level

The Science I curriculum is exploratory and multi-disciplinary in nature. It is developed around basic principles and concepts of chemistry, physics, biology and the earth sciences. It is intended first to serve as a link from the elementary to secondary science courses and second as an introductory course for the biology, chemistry and physics subjects. Its major objective is to develop technological consciousness and scientific literacy among the students who could assist in nation building. Activities are made more meaningful when scientific concepts and principles are made to connect with student's daily living experiences. The relevance of technology and its products are emphasized. Specific examples of scientific studies mostly about the Philippines in focus are incorporated. For example, a scientific study on tilapia is discussed in detail to illustrate all steps in the scientific method. Following are excerpts from Science and Technology I textbook:

"When is a study called scientific?A study of tilapia will clarify the meaning of the term scientific. Tilapia, a food fish commonly seen in local markets, has been subject of scientific and technological studies to improve its size, increase its meat content, and speed up its growth to full size. Dr Deogracias Villadolid, a Filipino ichthyologist (a scientist who specializes in the study of fishes), brought the tilapia to the Philippines sometime after World War II.

"Recently a team of ichthyologists in Hadera, Israel, discovered a technique of changing the sex of a population of young tilapia in a container tank to almost all male.... Male tilapia is desired because they grow faster and develop more meat than the females, The process of changing the female to male, known as sex inversion, consists of feeding them on an androgen diet....

"The sex inversion process is expensive. It requires the use of concrete tanks, large amounts of water, and a supply of food and androgen for the fast-growing tilapia....

One ichthyologist made the hypothesis that sex inversion could be done with much less expense by placing them in a natural body of water such as a river, pond, or lake...

"To try out his hypothesis, he planned an experiment using three cages sunk in a natural pond and one concrete tank filled with water......

(From Cortes, etal, *Integrated Science and Technology for a Better Life I*, Basic Media Systems, Manilla, 1989)

The Science I curriculum is technology and environmentally oriented. Desired learning competencies are prescribed for First Year Science. The competencies expected of students at the end of the first year science and technology programme are:

I. Introduction to Science and Technology

- Appreciate the contributions to science and technology of outstanding Filipino scientists.
- Demonstrate knowledge of the processes of science in solving simple problems in daily life.
- Appreciate the scientific values of open-mindedness, orderliness, patience and sharing ideas with others.
- Appreciate knowledge of how science and technology affect human beliefs, practices and ways of thinking.

II. Some Forces Around Us

- Demonstrate understanding of force and work.
- Develop skill in measuring forces.
- Appreciate the importance of using standard measuring instruments and units of measure.
- Demonstrate intellectual honesty and accuracy.

III. Investigating Matter

- Demonstrate understanding of the properties, identification and classification of matter.
- Appreciate the use of models to explain the behaviour of matter.
- Demonstrate skills in measuring properties of matter.

IV. Forms and Transformation of Energy

- Demonstrate understanding of energy, its forms and transformation.
- Appreciate the importance of using energy wisely.
- Demonstrate understanding of the energy sources in the Philippines and their uses.

- Demonstrate awareness and understanding of natural events and phenomena made possible by energy transformations and biogeochemical cycles of matter in the environment, and concern for their disruption through human intervention.

V. Changes Occur Naturally

- Demonstrate understanding of physical and chemical changes.
- Demonstrate understanding of the changes occurring in the lithosphere, hydrosphere and atmosphere.
- Understand the implications of physical and chemical changes for the environment and for man.

VI. Living Things and Their Environment

- Understand the interactions of living things with their environment.
- Appreciate how nature maintains balance at the individual, population, community and ecosystem levels or organization.
- Gain understanding of the scientific principals and methodology in preventing environmental degradation.
- Manifest appreciation of man's role in improving, conserving and protecting the environment.

VII. Earth's Place in the Universe

- Demonstrate understanding of the solar system.
- Understand the effects of earth's motion, shape and inclination on time and seasonal changes.
- Appreciate the influence of science and technology on space exploration.

Evaluation of Student Achievement

Quizzes, periodic tests and departmental examinations are mostly cognitive evaluation of student's achievement. These are teacher-made tests which are usually of the objective type. Quizzes may be given daily or weekly. Periodic tests and departmental examinations are given at every grading period (usually every 3 months).

There are no public examinations at the end of the elementary level. A public examination, National College Entrance Examination (NCEE) is given to all students who finish the secondary level of education. This examination is conducted by the National Educational Testing Centre of the Department of Education, Culture and Sports. Students who pass the NCEE can qualify for admission in the institutions of higher learning.

Evaluation of the students behaviour and attitudes are included in the student's report card. These behaviours are punctuality, personal cleanliness and grooming, sociability, cooperation, industry and courtesy are examples which the students may be rated. The ratings are in the form of qualitative descriptions such as poor, good and outstanding.

Practical work are seldom evaluated or not at all. Some teachers may evaluate practical work through the use of pencil and paper test or in the form of laboratory reports submitted to every activity/experiment performed by students. Some teachers are reluctant to accept the different ways of evaluating practical work because of the difficulty of the evaluation instruments and much time consumed because students have to be tested individually.

Teacher Education

In the light of major reforms in the educational system, the Sectoral Action Plan for Manpower Development outlined the main strategy for science and mathematics development at the secondary level. Included in this strategy are the teacher-training programmes.

Two kinds of teacher training on programmes were identified. These were the certificate programmes and the diploma programmes. The certificate programmes are geared for teachers with little or no preparation in the science field they are teaching. This will be offered for two summers or part-time studies over three semesters. The diploma programmes are for teachers who need strengthening or upgrading since they have some preparation in their science fields. These will be offered in all fields and it is hoped that teachers move on from the certificate to diploma programmes. Very few slots are allotted for the master's programme. Major effort of the Plan will be in the certificate and diploma programmes than in the master programme since it has been the experience that teachers who finished the master's programme go into college teaching.

Allotment for the two programmes showed that the certificate programmes are for teachers in physics and chemistry. For the 2 summers about 140 teachers (60 per year in physics and 80 per year in chemistry) will be trained for the first year and 200 teachers for the second year. For the part-time three semester programme, again 140 teachers (60 physics teachers/year and 80 chemistry year) will be trained for the first year. Then for the second year, 200 teachers for the first semester and 140 teachers for the second semester.

For the diploma programmes, a total of 360 teachers will be trained for a year. This is a rough estimate based on the teacher-training institutions capabilities, availability of teachers who can be freed from their schools for one year, and availability of funds. Breakdown of these teachers to be trained are:

Mathematics	=	100 a year
Biology	=	80 a year
Chemistry	=	60 a year
Physics	=	60 a year
Integrated Science	=	60 a year

12. THAILAND

The Educational System

The Thai educational system is 6-4-4 (six years at the primary level, three years at the lower secondary level, and three years at the upper secondary level). Educational administration is centralized. All schools throughout the country use the same curriculum authorized by the Ministry of Education.

Compulsory education is six years. At present, about 95 per cent of the children in the 6-11 year age group are enrolled in primary schools.

However, secondary education in Thailand is not compulsory. In 1989, about 47 per cent of the children in 12-14 year age group were enrolled in the lower secondary level (grades 7-10) and about 38 per cent of the 15-17 year age group were enrolled in the upper secondary level. Study at the secondary level depends on the parents' attitude, finance and the student's ability.

Education after the secondary level leads to two types of programmes; the four-year bachelor degree programme, and the one to three year diploma programme. There are about 79 institutions which now offer the bachelor's degree. These include 36 teacher colleges, 27 private colleges, 14 public universities and 2 open universities.

Entrance to any public university is very competitive since only about 20-30 per cent of the applicants can be accepted. For example, in 1989 the institutions of higher learning accepted only 22,282 out of 93,341 applicants. An entrance examination is the main criteria used to select applicants.

The one to three year programmes are offered in more than 100 institutions. These programmes are aimed at training technicians and skilled workers.

Graduate programmes are offered at most universities. Enrolments in graduate programmes are increasing rapidly.

Science Teaching in the Secondary Schools

There are three levels in the lower secondary education programme M1, M2 and M3 (equivalent to Grades 7, 8 and 9). At present, science is a required subject for all students in all grades and is studied four periods a week. The science course offered is an integrated science rather than separate disciplines such as chemistry, biology or physics.

In 1991, science will be required for only three periods a week for all lower secondary students in all grades. Schools are encouraged to offer more science elective courses. Students may be allowed to select to study science up to 10 periods a week. The elective science courses are more locally oriented. Each school can develop its own science course or can select any other science course for their students. It is expected that the study of science, by this approach, will be more locally oriented, and will be more relevant and suitable for the students' interests, needs and abilities.

At upper secondary education (Grade 10-12) students who plan to further their education in science or science related fields would be guided to take discipline science courses such as chemistry, biology and physics up to 10 periods a week for the whole three years.

Students who plan to terminate their studies upon graduation or further their education in fields not related to science are required to take science three periods a week for two years. Physical and Biological Science (PBS) is specially designed for these non-science students. The PBS curriculum is a modular approach and emphasizes more on social issues, the environment, and consumer science. There are 14 independent modules. Students are required to study eight modules in any sequence of four semesters in three years. The fourteen modules are: Solar Energy, Light, Colouring Matter, Electrical Appliances, Invisible Rays, The Earth and Stars, Synthetic Materials, Sound in Everyday Living, Natural Resources and Industry, Good Living, Medicine and Life, Our Body, Evolution, Heredity and Environment.

The Lower Secondary School Science Curriculum Development

One of the most important movements on school science education in the history of Thailand was the establishment of the Institute for the Promotion of Teaching Science and Technology (IPST) in 1972. Many new science curricula have been developed and implemented. The first IPST lower secondary school science curriculum was implemented in 1977 and revised in 1988. The revised curriculum is more technologically oriented. Activities on practical problem solving concerning student's own communities were added. For example problems of hygiene and drinking water for a particular community are posed to a group of students to solve them mentally and practically. Other examples of community problems which are recommended for students to solve are: Soil Quality, Water Quality, Surplus of Agricultural Production in a Particular season, Food Habits Problems of some Minorities, Misuse of Particular Woodland Areas, and problems of Making Fish Sauce in some areas etc.

The Lower secondary school science curriculum is developed by The General Science Design Team which is a division of IPST. The team is made up of classroom teachers, supervisors, teacher college instructors and university lecturers who were recruited as a seconded staff to work part-time with the IPST permanent staff.

The initial decisions concerning the overall organization and philosophies of the new curriculum were made after conducting seminars and after the team completed intensive studies of materials which have already been produced in other countries. The curriculum however, does not follow any particular curriculum from another country. Writers have attempted to develop a Thai-oriented modern science programme for Thai students. The conceptual scheme of science at the lower secondary school level is shown in Fig. 1.

The lower secondary school science courses are interest motivated and involve students in doing science, identifying problems and looking for methods of solving them. All curriculum materials and activities are designed to enable students to observe their environment, enrich their experiences, and develop skills such as observing, communicating, measuring, hypothesizing and experimenting. Through doing science students gain knowledge of scientific facts and principles and have a better understanding of nature and their environment. The practical experience of doing science also develops students' scientific attitudes in hopes of attaining a rational outlook, open mindedness, persistence, co-operativeness, critical and tolerance of opinions, honesty in presenting observations, etc.

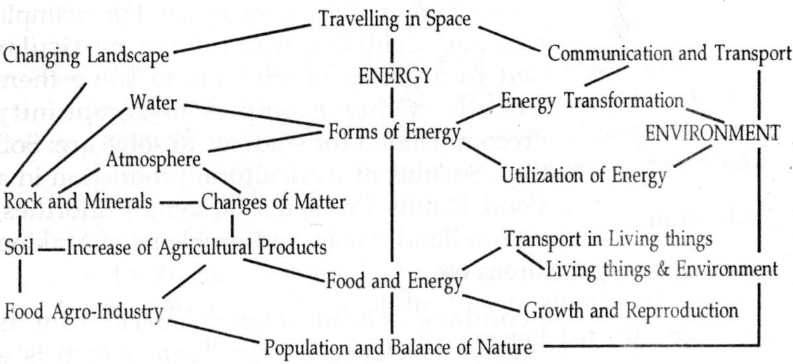

Fig. 1. Conceptual Scheme of Science at Lower Secondary Schools in Thailand (Science Education in Secondary School in Thailand, Dr Nida Sapianchai, former Director of IPST)

Curriculum Materials

In curriculum development at IPST, four areas are developed concurrently: the students' books and teachers' guides, the evaluation, the teacher training and the development of equipment. The IPST approach is shown in Fig. 2.

Students Books and Teachers' Guides

The former Director of IPST Dr. Nida Sapianchai described the specific characteristics of IPST students' books and teachers' guides as follows:

"The students' books contain many activities and experiments around which questions are asked and the students find the answers from observation and from analysis of experimental results. The questions were constructed following analysis of the mental and manual operations required to develop scientific and mathematical concepts. The questions guide the student's learning and place him in the role of the discoverer. The teacher directs the operations, controls the pace and provides assistance when the student or group gets stuck. The teacher also consolidates areas of the subject in more formal presentations. The students' book is not intended to provide the complete story. It is not a text in the traditional sense but a guide to learning."

"The teachers' guides compliment the students' book by providing most of the answers to the questions and by highlighting the important aspects of each section. It gives the teacher additional background material and information on pacing the programme, and on the advance preparation necessary for each experiment. The guides suggest outlines for pre- and post-lab discussions and illustrate how the major concepts in the course might he linked together."

Evaluation

The teachers' guides contain many test items that have been tried in trial schools. It sets out the method of writing items and encourages the teacher to write his/her own items. Teachers are encouraged to assess students' achievements in all three domains namely cognitive, affective, and psychomotor domains.

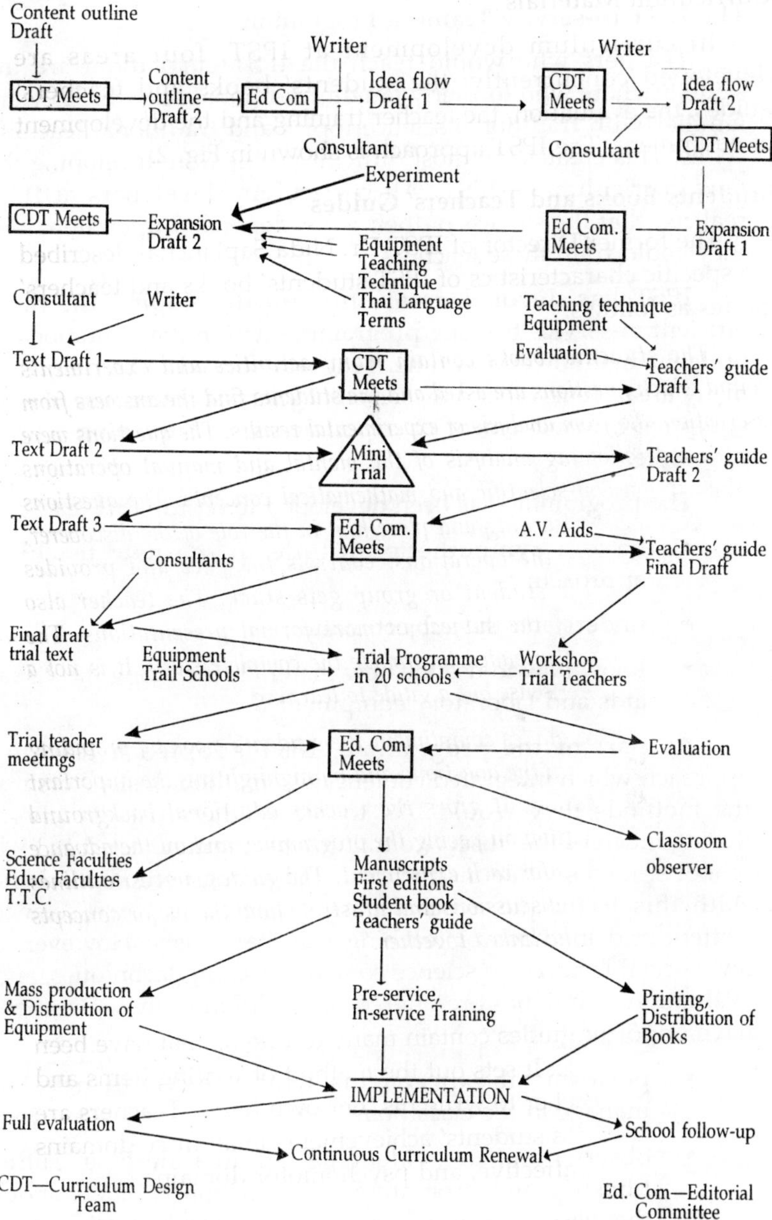

Fig. 2. Development of IPST science curriculum materials

The IPST In-service Training Programme

Teachers who would teach the IPST curriculum are the same teachers who formerly taught traditional science. They are familiar with traditional science topics and traditional teaching styles. This creates the most difficult problem in developing the new curriculum at IPST. All curriculum developers at IPST realized that the success of their work depended upon how well they could train these teachers.

IPST has devoted great effort in developing the most efficient in-service training programme within the limitations of budgets, manpower and time. Teachers needed to be trained in many areas: renewal and extension of science content, use of new equipment, management of experiments, and teaching with a new style.

The programme has been developed to ensure that teachers:

- have a sympathetic attitude to the new teaching approach;
- understand the subject matter;
- know how to use the new materials including the visual aids and laboratory equipment.

As part of the programme, IPST adopted a teaching approach which integrated content with method. Instructors use the methods they would like to see teachers use. Teachers, during much of the in-service training programme acted as high school students while instructors acted as high school teachers. With this technique, teachers are expected to learn science content and methods of teaching simultaneously. However, a few special lectures on science content, teaching techniques, and evaluation techniques are offered. In addition to these, teachers have opportunities to:

- perform all experiments which they will have to manage in the classroom;
- observe and use videotape, audio slide-tape, audio filmstrip and programmed instruction booklets about the classroom management of experiments, laboratory safety, etc. and

- discuss the IPST philosophy and objectives of science teaching, together with its evaluation.

It could be claimed that the development of this lower secondary school science curriculum was among the most important curriculum developments in Thai educational history. All science content have been carefully selected. It is up-to-date and designed specifically for the Thai society.

The inquiry teaching approach was introduced and teachers were strongly encouraged to use it. Teachers attended 3-6 weeks of the IPST in-service teacher training programme at IPST or at the local centres before teaching any IPST courses. The emphasis on the laboratory led the IPST general science design team to search for experiments and to invent new, inexpensive school science equipment which required the use of local materials.

However, 3-6 weeks of in-service training did not necessarily mean that all teachers could teach the IPST courses satisfactorily. This was only the beginning. Many teachers still needed help on a more continuous basis.

IPST Science Equipment

Before the establishment of IPST most of the science equipment used in schools were imported. Now 90 per cent are made in Thailand. IPST has its own Equipment Design and Production Team (EDPT) to develop equipment prototypes. In developing science equipment prototypes, the EDPT works in close co-operation with the Curriculum Design Team (CDT). The CDT provides necessary information about the functions of each piece of equipment to be used. EDPT designs and makes equipment prototypes according to the requests using some criteria that each equipment prototype should:

- give results in accordance with the objectives;
- be used easily and safely, and without any complications, and it should provide apparent results;
- be able to be manufactured inside the country using local materials and in country technology;
- be used in more than one experiment, the accessories of one set of equipment can be used with another;

- be kept in the form of a kit, equipment frequently used in the unit should be in the same kit;
- be inexpensive and durable.

The working process of designing and developing science equipment is shown in the following diagram (Fig. 3):

CDT provides details about equipment requirements

↓

EDPT makes rough drawings of the equipment and specifies materials used

↓

Together CDT and EDPT discuss the drawing

↓

EDPT produces 2-3 equipment prototypes

↓

CDT and EDPT tries out the equipment prototypes

↓

EDPT produces equipment prototypes to test in schools

↓

CDT and EDPT do the follow up of equipment prototypes used in school

↓

EDPT makes detail drawings of the equipment and sends them to Ongkanka* for mass production

↓

CDT and EDPT follow up the use of the equipment in schools throughout the country

Fig 3. The IPST Equipment Design and Production Process.

CDT = Curriculum Design Team

EDPT = Equipment Design and Production Team

* Ongkanka is the business section of the Teachers Association of Thailand.

According to the working process, the EDPT does only research and development of science equipment prototypes. The mass production is under the charge of the Ongkanka, a business section of the Teachers Association of Thailand. However the EDPT and Ongkanka work in close co-operation, by having a Co-ordination Committee which meets frequently.

Generally, Ongkanka produces equipment following the design of IPST. However if Ongkanka wants to change the design to be more suitable for mass production, the design can be negotiated with IPST for consideration and permission. EDPT provides academic assistance to Ongkanka especially on quality control.

The EDPT has already designed more than 300 equipment prototypes both for school science and mathematics teaching.

The design of the inexpensive and locally manufactured science equipment not only makes the equipment affordable, but also creates the industry of science equipment production inside the country, using local materials.

Having EDPT working in close co-operation with the Curriculum Design Team provides more flexibility in curriculum development. The Curriculum Design Team can design activities freely since the equipment needed can be developed as desired.

Implementation

The IPST lower secondary school science curriculum was first implemented in 1977 with an intensive follow up programme. The first revision of this curriculum was done in 1988. It was expected before implementation that teaching techniques and budgets for equipment and consumable materials would be two main problems that would face the implementation. The first problem has been solved through the IPST organized in-service training. In addition, elaborate teachers' guides have been produced by IPST to assist the teachers in their teaching. It is also learned from the follow-ups, that these teachers' manuals have been of tremendous help to the teachers.

School budgets for equipment and consumable materials pose a serious problem. To help the schools, the IPST has designed low cost experiments using inexpensive equipment.

Students use alcohol burners instead of gas burners, measuring spoons as balances, syringes as measuring cylinders. Every group of three students is provided a student kit which contains basic equipment. The IPST has every reason to be proud of its designing of prototype equipment to lower the production cost and render possible the local production.

The implementation of curriculum in such developing countries as Thailand tells us that teachers are the most important mechanism. The training programmes conducted to help them acquire the necessary skills and confidence, are of utmost importance. In this connection, equipment and teaching materials must be readily available so that the schools can purchase them at reasonable prices. The teaching/learning will never achieve its goal if the whole process relies solely on the teachers introducing the equipment and materials needed.

Part II

SCIENCE CURRICULUM FOR MEETING REAL-LIFE NEEDS OF YOUNG LEARNERS

Contents

Preface

Science Curriculum for Meeting Real-Life Needs of Young Learners is derived from reports of two Regional Workshops, one entitled "Meeting Real-Life Needs of Young Children: Science Curriculum Materials", held in Sri Lanka, 22 February to 4 March 1988, and the other, entitled "Science Curriculum Specifications Derived from Real-Life Experiences of Learners", held in Pakistan, 19-28 November 1990.

The objectives of the Workshop held in Sri Lanka were: (1) to create an awareness of the state of the art in the region, regarding the development of new science curriculum and learning/teaching materials, addressing the issues of relevance, real-life needs, scientific competencies, and creativity of the primary school-aged children; (2) to identify and analyse common problems and concerns in relation to the development and implementation of the new materials; (3) to suggest methods and strategies for making science learning increasingly relevant to the children, and of improving teacher competencies in this direction; and (4) to develop exempler curriculum materials, illustrative of the suggested strategies/methods.

The Pakistan Workshop had the following objectives: (1) to observe interactions children have with natural phenomena in their daily life rhythms; (2) to identify natural and scientific phenomena expressed by children off their work situations, and analyse their content and their implications for future new strategies in curriculum development in science and technology education that emphasize learner relevance and the mobilizing of previously under-utilized resources in the learning situation; (3) to identify guidelines for curriculum development in science and technology utilizing real-life situations; and (4) to develop exemplar teaching learning materials derived from real-life situations.

Since the objectives of the two Workshops were somewhat interrelated and directed towards young learners, it was decided that ideas be integrated to form one publication. Both Workshops were convened at the invitation of the UNESCO Principal Regional Office for Asia and the Pacific (PROAP)/Asian Centre of Educational Innovation for Development (ACEID).

The Regional Training Workshop in Sri Lanka was organized by the National Institute of Education, Maharagama; while the Regional Operation Workshop in Pakistan was organized by the Curriculum Wing, Ministry of Education, Islamabad.

The Sri Lanka Workshop was participated in by science educators from Bangladesh, India, Indonesia, Malaysia, Nepal, New Zealand, Pakistan, Philippines, Republic of Korea, Samoa, Sri Lanka, Thailand and UNESCO/PROAP. The officers were: Chairperson: Mr. M.A. de Silva (Sri Lanka); Vice-Chairperson: Mr. Ibrahim (Malaysia); Rapporteur: Ms. Lourdes Carale (Philippines). The resource persons were Mrs. Shukla Bhattacharya (India); Mr. Ross Tasker (New Zealand); Mr. B. J. P. Alles (Sri Lanka); Mr. W. S. Perera (Sri Lanka and Mr. N. A. C. Gunatilaka (Sri Lanka).

The Pakistan Workshop was participated in by science educators from Bangladesh, Bhutan, People's Republic of China, India, Indonesia, Iran, Lao PDR, Malaysia, Philippines, Sri Lanka, Thailand, Socialist Republic of Vietnam and UNESCO/PROAP. The Officers were: Chairperson: Mr. Farid Akhtar Khwaja (Pakistan); Vice-Chairpersons: Mr. K. M. Pant (India) and Mr. Gooi Kee Mein (Malaysia); and Rapporteur: Ms. Lilia Vergara (Philippines). The resource persons were Ms. Lilia Rabago (Philippines) and Mr. Ijaz A. Chaudhry (Pakistan).

Introduction

This publication aims to contribute, through innovations, to the strengthening of national capacities of the Member States to achieve relevant science and technology education for all. There are four chapters.

Chapter 1 presents the country experiences in science and technology of participating Member States, and discusses the current trends and issues in primary and lower secondary science learning in the region.

Chapter 2 provides a framework of real-life needs, scientific competencies, creativity and relevance.

Chapter 3 discusses the guidelines for developing science curricula derived from real life experiences of the learners. Some basic assumptions on developing exemplars are also put forward.

Chapter 4 are the exemplars which are intended to provide models to help teachers bring about effective changes in their teaching.

The ideas presented in this publication proves very valuable if the curriculum truly aims to meet young learners real-life needs, foster desired competencies and encourage their creativity. Implementing at the classroom level will prove to be an enormous task as this will involve a massive change in the primary science curriculum, and the scale and vital nature of the task places a heavy demand on resources. For some countries this is not difficult, but for many developing countries the demand for resources would be the biggest constraint.

The Workshops have made some recommendations in order to achieve real progress in the shortest possible time and in the most economical way, that is, through communication exchanges among primary science curriculum experts from the Member States. The exchange of information would include policy changes, research findings and implementation strategies. Most valuable would be the information on the low cost development of primary science education, and this is by teaching science derived from real-life experiences of the learners.

1

Country Experiences, Trends and Issues in Science Learning

Introduction

Realizing the need to cope with the rapid advances in science and technology and with knowledge explosion, the education policies of the countries in Asia and the Pacific give emphasis to science and technology education as an integral part of primary and secondary education.

For many children of the region, primary and secondary schooling as part of basic education, remains a precious and often the only formal educational experience. Basic schooling must help them meet their needs in terms of their personal requirements, and in terms of the contribution they are able to make towards the well-being of their families, communities and societies. There is a growing awareness among the countries of the region of the need for changes in science learning, in response to the concern for increased relevance of the subject. Some countries have already started to implement new projects, while others are in the process of planning innovations in the science curricula.

Even as these reforms are happening, the science curriculum has not fully responded to the issue of linking science to real life needs and to fostering creativity in children.

The science curricula and teacher education programmes remain frequently discipline-based. Though development of science process skills are mentioned, these are used in most cases, only to develop academic science concepts. To provide relevance from real-life situations are incorporated in the learning activities, but with secondary focus.

Science learning based on real life experiences of young learners has great potential in making contribution to acquiring basic competencies to cope with demands of daily life, as well as to encourage creative abilities which can make better use of existing resources and thus raise the quality of life.

The above discourse is reinforced in the following country experiences presented by the participants to the workshops:

BHUTAN

The Royal Government of Bhutan is determined to make the country scientifically and technologically advanced, especially in telecommunications (including satellite links); jet aircraft, computers, and hydropower to name four. In order to attain this, the country hopes to produce highly skilled scientists and technicians from its population. It is also envisaged that "high- tech" innovations such as solar power installations will become far more widespread. This will also depend on having adequate people with knowledge of the basic scientific principles and the activity to apply them inventively.

The national policies and strategies in science and technology education are set within the other important aims and objectives directed towards the growth and development of Bhutanese children. Science education is regarded as important and an essential part of the country's development plans.

The national education policy puts much emphasis on science education at the class VII and VIII levels. The policy states that "children with more gifts in studies, especially in science, will enter the second level of the school system." The science course will establish "the beginnings of a systematic knowledge of modern science" and that formal subjects should include "a systematic course in education", which emphasizes practical work.

The schools have an important role to play in helping children to understand the world they live in, particularly the sort of environment they are exposed to. This exposure prepares them for life and work. The aims of science education are as follows:

(1) understanding scientific ideas,

(2) developing scientific methods of investigation,

(3) relating science to other areas of knowledge,

(4) understanding the contribution science makes to society,

(5) recognizing the contribution science education makes to personal development, and

(6) appreciating the nature of scientific knowledge.

Bhutan provides free education to children ages 6-14. There are a few who dropout along the way. These dropouts are then absorbed in some form of government employment while a few remain at home to help in household activities.

One of the aims of the primary science programme, is to lay the essential foundation for secondary science. The curriculum in science incorporates substantial learnings about health and hygiene, and the basic agricultural farming practices which are expected to help students when they return to their villages, or those who drop out from schools. Health and agriculture are taught in schools through practical demonstrations, children are also taught the consequences and implications of poor health practices, as well as traditional farming methods. This approach is believed to improve life and develop the individual.

Vocational training centres are being established for the out-of-school youths, such as the Royal Technical Trade Institute where the dropouts undergo a two-year training on carpentry, electricity, plumbing, etc. Upon finishing the training, the students join the private enterprise or government sectors.

The need for an improved school curriculum is very much felt as many developmental activities are launched in the country, especially in science and communication. There are constraints which must be faced through, especially on the need for human and financial resources.

BANGLADESH

The Government of Bangladesh has formulated and launched a number of national science and technology policies. The policies aim to improve the standard of scientific knowledge at all levels, from the school to the university. The science education policy is stated as follows:

> "Adequate emphasis should be given on simple concepts of science and mathematics from the primary stage. The school curriculum should be oriented in such a way that problem solving skills of the pupils are enhanced and the interdisciplinary character of science is reflected."

In curriculum development, efforts have been made to integrate science and technology education with the learner's environment, in order to make it a tool for solving their real-life problems, and at the same time to avoid undue stress to the learners especially on the learning of scientific facts.

At the primary school level for example, science is treated as a part of environmental studies rather than as a separate subject. It is interdisciplinary and it includes information, concepts and principles of natural sciences. Science phenomena is taught in grades I and II in an integrated manner, having the concepts from social and natural sciences. Environmental studies is emphasized in Grades III to V. The science contents are chosen traditionally and emphasizes facts rather than process, science teaching is allocated three hours out of fifteen classes hours per week.

At the lower secondary, science is taught as general science, containing the elements of the natural sciences, i.e. physics, chemistry, biology, geography and their applied aspects in hygiene, health and population education. The content are mostly on facts and theories rather than problem solving and development of inquiry skills. Four, out of 24 hours are earmarked for science teaching.

The teaching strategies at the elementary level is expository and lecture type. At the secondary level, students are allowed to perform experiments (esho prize Kori).

Science teaching faces many problems. At the elementary level some of the problems are as follows:

(1) teachers have not taken any science subject in their secondary school education;

(2) the science courses offered in teacher training institutes emphasize rote-learning; and

(3) common teaching aids needed in science teaching are not available.

At the lower secondary level, some of the problems are:

(1) teachers have no proper training and lack motivation to do their jobs well;

(2) the daily work schedule in schools is rigid and does not normally allow opportunity for outdoor activities, which allow development of process skills;

(3) heavy work load for science teachers;

(4) big classes therefore, hindering demonstration lessons; and

(5) inadequate equipment and laboratory facilities.

CHINA

The National Science and Technology policies of the People's Republic of China, relevant to primary and secondary education, are as follows:

(1) to create an optimum environment for the enhancement of science education;

(2) to include a more advanced, and more practical activities in the curriculum of the schools.

In China, science is taught starting at Grade IV in the elementary level, and is included as a subject up to higher levels of school education. The subject is given an allocation of 3-4 hours per week.

The general nature of science content at the elementary level includes biology, chemistry, physics, astronomy, geology and meteorology while at the lower secondary level, physics, chemistry, biology and geology are included. The natural science subjects provide the pupils with the preliminary knowledge about nature as well as the exploration, exploitation and unification of it by human beings.

Some of the problems faced in science teaching are as follows:

(1) teachers do not have adequate training;

(2) science and technology is not widely accepted in the countryside.

INDIA

The National Council of Educational Research and Training (NCERT), in 1975, published "The Curriculum for the Ten Year School: A Framework". It was an outcome of the discussion of the National Curriculum Committee set up in 1973. The Committee comprised teachers, educational administrators, and educationists.

The framework, among other things, prescribe that the school curriculum should be related to national integration, social justice, productivity, modernization of the society and cultivation of moral and spiritual values. It also states that it should include science and mathematics as an integral part of school education up to class X. Furthermore, the teaching of science and mathematics will have to be upgraded to keep the children in the mainstream.

In 1986, a new policy was enunciated. Science in general education was given an important part, giving emphasis on child-centred curriculum which stressed the need for an activity-based learning of science especially in the primary stage. The new policy also stressed the need for adequate school facilities for the implementation of the school curriculum.

The teaching of science by exploring the environment begins at grade 3. Prior to that, some experiences are provided to the children as specified in the Teachers Guides for Grades 1 and 2. At the lower secondary and secondary levels, an attempt has been made to teach science in an integrated manner. The time devoted to teach science is three hours per week. The science content covered in the elementary and secondary levels are on universal topics but adapted to local context.

The method of teaching used in many primary and lower secondary schools is the lecture method. The teacher depends largely on the information found in textbooks. There are schools however, where teachers are trained and highly motivated. Their teaching involves the experiences of children derived from their environment. Alternatively, for schools where physical facilities are found, activity-based lessons take place. There are also out-of-school science activities as part of non-formal education.

Science teaching in India faces tremendous problems. These are:

(1) physical facilities are inadequate, i.e. small classrooms, lack of equipment, lack of library resources.

(2) teachers are untrained and lack of motivation, especially for single teacher schools in rural areas;

(3) curriculum materials are unattractive, and the books are loaded with facts;

(4) attitude of parents toward school is negative, i.e. reluctance to send their children, especially girls to school.

INDONESIA

The national curriculum which emanates from the Ministry of Educational and Culture gives emphasis on science education. The aims of learning science are:

(1) to help students to understand the environment, and

(2) to understand the ways in which science will affect the quality of life and the future.

Effective education in science at both the primary and secondary levels is a necessary goal of education of Indonesia.

The framework, as stated in the national curriculum is the basis of the uniform and centralized standard of education for the whole population. These are reflected in the curriculum guides, course outlines, and textbooks adopted by the school system.

Science is taught from Grades 1 to 6 as general science. The basic ideas about people is included as part of the social and natural environment, as well as on the development of problem-solving skills of children. This is through actual experience with natural things and phenomena. At the secondary level, grades

7-9 on the other hand, science is taught as combined science. Content is selected from natural things and phenomena, and the growth of human body relating to science in daily life are included in terms of the applications by spontaneous problem-solving.

Considering the advances in science and technology, the learning of science is geared towards familiarization with nature, by observation and experimentation. This strategy is adopted in order to develop skills in problem-solving, scientific view and thinking, interest and attitude towards nature, developing creativity, developing clear thinking and developing the power of expression.

Some of the problems in science teaching are as follows:

(1) Lack of motivation in some teachers;

(2) Lack of adequately trained teachers;

(3) Difficulty in acquiring and maintaining equipment as well as in purchasing materials for use in the conduct of laboratory activities;

(4) Ineffective curriculum development efforts, i.e. books not adequately prepared and designed.

IRAN

The country is currently undergoing a review of its education policies. The present set-up is, the education system is centrally controlled and consists of 3 levels of education:

The primary school level (children ages 7-11)

The guidance school level (children ages 12-14)

The high school level (children ages 15-18)

At the primary school level, science teaching uses the integrated approach; while at the guidance school level, the combined science approach is adopted. High school science is taught by discipline: biology, chemistry, earth science and physics.

The time allocation for the 2 levels of education is shown on the next page. There are 32 study weeks in one year.

<table>
<tr><th>Age</th><th>Grade</th><th>Legal</th><th>Hours/Week</th></tr>
<tr><td>7</td><td>1</td><td rowspan="5">PRIMARY</td><td>2</td></tr>
<tr><td>8</td><td>2</td><td>2</td></tr>
<tr><td>9</td><td>3</td><td>3</td></tr>
<tr><td>10</td><td>4</td><td>3</td></tr>
<tr><td>11</td><td>5</td><td>3</td></tr>
<tr><td>12</td><td>1</td><td rowspan="3">GUIDANCE</td><td>4</td></tr>
<tr><td>13</td><td>2</td><td>4</td></tr>
<tr><td>14</td><td>3</td><td>4</td></tr>
</table>

The entry qualification for primary and guidance school teachers is Grade 12. Teacher trainers at this level follow a 2-year programme in the teacher's college. Further in-service teacher training programmes are provided. These are aimed at:

(a) expanding scientific and technological knowledge; and

(b) developing teaching methods and implementation skills.

There are many difficulties encountered in implementing the teaching-learning of science. Most of the primary and guidance schools do not have sufficient laboratory and library facilities. Furthermore, teachers at these school levels are not adequately trained and are not highly motivated to teach.

LAO PDR

The purpose of the reform strategies on education set up recently at Lao PDR stipulated that the curriculum should be appropriate for all students and for both sexes, in order to develop the following qualities:

- have a scientific outlook,
- be equipped with general knowledge, general technology and vocational training,
- be able to understand basic economics and technology.

Science is taught from grade 1 in an integrated manner under the topic, "The World Around Us". For the upper primary school, science is taught as biology, agriculture and forestry. Biology is taught from grades 6 to 8; agriculture from grades 4 to 7, and forestry from grade 7. The time allocation for the science subject per week are as follows:

The World Around Us:	1 hour/week (for grades 1 to 3) 2 hours/week (for grades 4 and 5)
Agriculture:	1 hour/week (for grades 4 and 5) 22 hours/33 weeks for grade 6 21 hours/33 weeks for grade 7 16 hours/33 weeks for grade 8
Biology:	2 hours/week for grades 6, 7 and 8
Froestry:	12 hours/33 weeks for grade 7

The science content mainly emphasizes agricultural work, as Lao PDR will remain an agricultural country for a long time.

The teaching of science is done by teachers who have low qualifications and inadequate training. What they usually do is read and write on the blackboard, while the pupils listen and copy without understanding the lesson. The priority task of the government therefore, is to improve the qualification of teachers.

MALAYSIA

Primary school education in Malaysia is a 6-year programme. In 1983 the new primary school curriculum "Kurikulum Baru Sekolah Rendah" (KBSR) was implemented nationwide, beginning with all pupils in Grade 1. This new curriculum was formulated based mainly on the Cabinet Committee Report released in 1979. The report stated, among other things, "the present curriculum has been formulated separately according to subjects and there is little integration between subjects". Taking this statement into account, science which was previously taught as a separate subject is now integrated through a new subject "Man and His Environment".

The subject comprises elements of geography, science history, civics, hygiene and other areas of knowledge pertaining to man and his environment. The content is organized along five themes namely: Man and living things experience life processes; Man and living things adapt to the environment; Man manages the environment with responsibility to fulfil his needs; Man interests with fellow human beings as well as with his environment, bringing about various phenomena; and the community and the environment maintain their stability and equilibrium through various processes.

"Man and his Environment" is taught only in Grades IV to VI, but elements of it are integrated into the language programme from Grades I to III. Time allocated for the subject is 16.6 per cent of the total study time per week. The enquiry-discovery approach is used by some teachers in teaching the subject. It involves active participation of the pupils. However, due to big classes (40-50 pupils per class), time constraint and inadequate teacher preparation in using the strategy, many teachers still use the chalk and talk.

The first cycle of the KBSR was completed in 1988, thus the students trained in the new elementary school programme entered the secondary school under the KBSM (Kurikulum Baru Sekolah Menengah) which started to be implemented in 1989.

Secondary school education in Malaysia comprise of 3 years lower secondary education and 2 years upper secondary education. Science is taught through 1 core subject and 4 elective subjects. The core subjects was planned to be taught for 5 years. All the subjects cover knowledge and basic skills in science together with the inculcation of good moral values.

The formulation of the content of the core subject was based on 3 considerations, namely:

Science for understanding of nature,

Science for the well-being of man, and

Science for personal development.

These are organized along 4 themes:

Man and the variety of living things around him;

The wealth of the earth's resources and their management;

Energy for life; and

Man and the balance of nature.

The emphasis along the above themes is placed on teaching and learning strategies that involve active students participation. Four elective subjects (Biology, Chemistry, Physics and Additional Science) however, are taught only in the upper secondary school level and these subjects are provided to cater to the individual interests and talents of the students. The time allocation for any of these science subjects is about 10 per cent of the total time allocation per week. The core science subject is now in its second year of implementation whereas the electives are yet to be introduced in 1991. Due to this early stage of implementation, the problems faced in the teaching for the core subject are yet to be identified in detail.

PAKISTAN

Pakistan is an Islamic country and is a nation committed to the teaching and values of Islam. It is against this background that the Pakistan Education System and policy is being viewed.

The education policy in Pakistan has remained under review ever since its independence. It realizes the need of popularizing science and technology, thus a number of national commissions on education were constituted to suggest reforms in this direction.

The present education system consist of 4 tiers, namely:

Primary:	Grades I to V
Secondary:	Grades VI to X
Higher Secondary:	Grades XI to XII
Tertiary:	Grades XIII to XVI

The National Education Policy of 1972 has made science a compulsory subject at the primary, and the secondary school levels. It is taught as an integrated subject covering basic information on physical and biological sciences. The integrated science programme aims at the "total development of the personality of the learners through the involvement of the senses in observation, exploration and understanding of the natural, as well as man-made environment by means of open inquiry combined with experimentation."

Three underlying themes run in the curriculum development programmes. These are:

(1) the foundation of all learning in Science is the first-hand experience with real things;

(2) science experiences need not involve unusual elaborate or expensive apparatus and materials;

(3) investigating one's environment is an interesting and integral part of an education.

The "Student-centred" model has been suggested as a teaching-learning strategy. The teacher acts as a manager or a guide or a facilitator of learning process, one who should organize the activity so that the child spends more time in observing, investigating, analysing and measuring things in the environment.

Problems and issues related to science teaching were identified during the needs assessment study in 1984, on the status of science education in the country. These are:

(1) science is still taught in school as a dogma;

(2) initiative, scientific inquiry and curiosity is never allowed to grow;

(3) student involvement in understanding scientific concepts is never emphasized;

(4) teachers lack the desired knowledge, skills and scientific attitudes for teaching science;

(5) the traditional 'chalk and talk' monologue rather than dialogue is still in vogue;

(6) investigating, inquiring and problem-solving are virtually missing from science experiments. This has caused absence of learning scientific concept formation, process, methods and principles;

(7) experiments do not develop creative thinking, observation, drawing of inference, and interpretation of results and formulation of conclusions based on evidences obtained in the experiments;

(8) objectives of science teaching at various levels of education have not been clearly stated in activity-oriented terms;

(9) appropriate planning and management of science reforms to achieve the objectives to teaching science, have never been done;

(10) development of curriculum was never based on research. It lacked pre-testing and evaluation; and

(11) progress on science education have been hampered by organizational and institutional deficiencies.

PHILIPPINES

The education system embraces both formal and non-formal education. Within the formal structure are 3 levels of education, namely: elementary (ages 7-12), secondary (13-16) and tertiary or higher education (19-21).

Science is taught from Grade III, and is taught with Health. The minimum learning competencies for science and health from Grades III to VI is built within the conceptual theme of "Man and His Environment". As a science programme, the Bureau of Elementary Education described it as follows:

> "Science and health aims to develop an understanding of how science is related to everyday life and at the acquisition of scientific skills, attitudes and values necessary is solving everyday problems. On the other hand, its goal as a health programme is the development and promotion of knowledge, attitudes, values and behaviour essential to individual, family and community health."

Furthermore, the curriculum in Science and Health spirals from the more basic ones from Grade III to the more detailed and complex in the succeeding grades. Science concepts and skills and health concepts are infused where the 2 disciplines blend naturally and are taken as separate units in other areas. The subjects are taken as one learning area where science compliments Health, and Health reinforces science. Science process skill is being emphasized, in order that the learner would be able to cope with problems related to his expanding school experiences even as he faces problems in daily life.

The secondary school science curriculum is outlined as follows:

Course	*Description*	*Period one week* (1 hour per period)
Science 1 (First Year)	Science and Technology 1 (Integrated Science)	5
Science 2 (Second Year)	Science and Technology 2 (Biology)	5
Science 3 (Third Year)	Science and Technology 3 (Chemistry)	5
Science 4 (Fourth Year)	Science and Technology 4 (Physics)	5

The objectives of the new Secondary Education Curriculum of the DECS are:

(1) to develop an enlightened commitment to the national ideals by cherishing, preserving and developing moral, spiritual and socio-cultural values as well as other desirable aspects of the Filipino heritage;

(2) to obtain knowledge, and form desirable attitudes for understanding the nature and purpose of man, and therefore, of oneself, one's own people, and other races, places and times, thereby promoting a keen sense of self, of family and of national and international communities;

(3) to develop skills in higher intellectual operations and more complex comprehension and expression activities, and in thinking intelligently, critically and creatively in life situations;

(4) to acquire work skills, knowledge and information and a work ethic essential for making an intelligent choice of an occupation or a career and for specialized training is specific occupations; and

(5) to broaden and heighten one's abilities in and appreciation for the arts, and science and technology as a means for maximizing one's potential for self-fulfilment and for promoting the welfare of others.

The features of the new curriculum are self-centred and community-oriented; cognitive-affective and manipulative-based, value education offered as a separate subject aside from being integrated in the teaching of the other subject areas; and desired learning competencies identified in each subject area. Each subject has a 40-minute time frame, except for technology and home economics and science and technology which have 60-minutes daily periods. The work experience concepts are integrated with values education and technology and home economics. Technology is emphasized is science and technology, and in technology and home economics subjects. The emphasis is on critical thinking to promote creativity and productivity at all levels.

The Philippines has a defined programme for Scientific Education Manpower Development. This is to provide a critical mass of literate students who would pursue careers in science and technology. A network of tertiary, secondary and elementary school is being established, managed jointly by both the Department of Education, Culture and Sports and the Department of Science and Technology.

The country has a nationally-funded science high school known as the Philippine Science High School (PSHS), which offers scholarships for secondary school students who are talented in science and mathematics. The school follows a special curriculum in science/mathematics education shown as follows:

Year	*Subject*	*Period/week 1 hour/period*
1	Integrated & Earth Science	4
2	Biology 1	4
	Chemistry 1	4
	Physics 1	4
3	Biology 2	4
	Chemistry 2	4
	Physics 2	4
4	Biology 3	4
	Chemistry 3	4
	Physics 3	4

Elective Courses

Electronics
Geology
Astronomy
Field Biology

There are other science high schools in big cities of the country, which are supervised by the Department of Education, Culture and Sports. The PSHS is under the Department of Science and Technology and its main objective is for science and technology development.

SRI LANKA

In Sri Lanka, science is compulsory in schools from Years 4 to 11, for the age group 8 to 14 years old. The elementary science subjects in the primary schools are so designed in order to facilitate experimental thinking. Every child is taught in his mother tongue.

Teachers of primary science are not specialized. The science topics mostly deal with nature study. A minimum science equipment is provided by the Government for Grades 6, 7 and 8, and the teachers are expected to improvise science apparatus to supplement what is available in schools.

The science curriculum in years 6 to 8 is environment-centred. Science is taught by teachers who have studied the subject. The junior secondary science curriculum is combined-science. The major emphasis of this programme is to impart to the students the methods used by the scientists.

The time allocation for science is as follows:

Years 4 and 5:	2 periods per week at 40 minutes/ period
Years 6, 7 and 8:	6 periods per week at 40 minutes/ period
Years 9, 10 and 11:	7 periods per week at 40 minutes/ period

Textbooks for science are not available for years 4 and 5, but are provided for students from years 6 to 11. However, teachers' guides are provided for teachers of Grades 4 and 5. Every effort is made to incorporate in the teachers' guides simple experimental investigations suitable for the level of the child. Most of the experiments are based on the child's immediate environment.

The emphasis in science teaching are: manipulative skills, making observations and recording, designing simple activities, designing simple equipment, using the environment in learning science, and making investigations about the environment.

VIET NAM

The national science and technology education policies of Vietnam is linked to the socio-economic conditions of the country.

For Grades 1 to 4, the science curriculum is based on "Comprehension of Nature and Society". Grades 1 to 3 takes science for 33 weeks, with one science period per week. Grade 4 takes science for 33 weeks, with two science periods per week. There are two parts to the curriculum, one is "Comprehension on Nature", and the other is "Comprehension on Society".

The contents of "Comprehension on Nature" covers the following areas: biology, geography, chemistry and physics; while "comprehension on Society" has the following areas: the family, the school and the native land, the history and geography of the country.

Science for Grade 5 is called "Popular Science". It comprises of 26 lessons, and one lesson is taught per week. The content areas included are: sanitation, soil, water, air, mineral materials and electricity.

To provide pupils with common, necessary and initial knowledge on nature and society, the topics are arranged according to the scientific logic of the discipline.

The proposed system of science and technology education in Vietnam has been identified to be implemented at different levels. These are:

Level I	-	Ministry of Education and Training.
Level II	-	Programme staff of science and technology education at the Hanoi National Pedagogic University No.1.
Level III	-	Laboratories at the Local Education Services, and the Local Teachers' Training Colleges, Local Pedagogic Universities and Local Higher Schools.
Level IV	-	Teams at Local Vocational Centres and General Schools.
Level V	-	Resource Trainers at Resource Centres.
Level VI	-	Community Members (including families, parents and children) involvement in the popularization of science and technology activities.

There are problems encountered in the teaching of science. The curriculum "Comprehension on Nature and Society" is still on trial at the primary schools. The results show that the materials presented are higher than the cognitive levels of the learners. Popular science has been taught for the last 22 years and has not undergone any reform or innovation. For the out-of-classroom activities, nothing much has been done in this area.

THAILAND

Thailand has a well-defined national science and technology education policy. In primary schools, science education is to provide group experiences for students to learn necessary skills and to utilize scientific procedures in those area of life and society where it is applicable. In lower secondary level, the aim of science education is to pass on skills needed for research in science and technology, and use scientific methods in approaching and solving problems. In addition, the relationship between science and technology and of humanity and environment is stressed.

For the curriculum development efforts, the Institute for the Promotion of Teaching Science and Technology (IPST) is given the sole responsibility for the promotion and development of science, mathematics and technology curricula at all school levels.

The teaching of science stars from Grade 1 up to higher levels of schooling. At the primary level (Grades 1 to 6) science is taught for four periods per week, while at the secondary level, science is taught for five periods per week.

At the elementary (primary) level, science as a subject comes largely from student experiences. The primary science curriculum covers the following areas:

Living Things (Plants, animals, man)

Things Around Us (soil, rocks, water, air)

Energy and Chemical Substances (sound, matter and heat, chemical substance)

Universe and Space

The science subjects in the secondary level is of 2 types: 6 compulsory subjects and elective subjects.

In line with the science and technology development plans, as emphasized by the Department of General Education, Ministry of Education, Thailand, school should provide science and technology activities to encourage students to see the significance of science and technology in their daily lives.

The activities suggested are the following:

- Yearly Science Exhibition
- Contests in the form of Pictures and Projects, Verbal and Written Presentation
- Interschool Science Competitions

- Visual Education and Scientific Exhibitions
- Science Camps
- Science Club Projects
- Mini company Programmes
- Computer Club Activities, e.g. Camps
- Others

Some of the problems encountered in science teaching are as follows:

- Many schools have few teachers who are adequately trained to teach science,
- Classes are too big,
- Resources are few, and
- Equipment for science activities are not sufficient.

A review/revision/updating of the science curriculum is being done in other countries. Samoa, in the Pacific, undertook a revision of the entire primary science programme to make its content suitable to each grade level. In New Zealand, a bottom-top approach to curriculum development is being adopted. In this approach, small groups of 10 teachers discuss among themselves what science to teach, and how they are going to teach it. A separate group within the Curriculum Review Project focuses on identifying strategies and materials which will produce a positive view of science among girls and in the cultural communities. Korea's new curriculum emphasizes problem-solving and inquiry process, as well as the development of practical skills, scientific reasoning, and understanding of the interrelationship between science, technology and society. The learning packages used in schools include optional activities which pupils can choose, depending on their interests.

To prepare the teachers for the curriculum changes, in-service teacher training programmes are available in all the countries. The training, focuses on content, methodology of teaching as well as improvization of equipment.

2

Framework of Real-Life Needs, Scientific Competencies, Creativity and Relevance

Real-life needs, scientific competencies, creativity and relevance are aspects related to science learning. These could be reflected in the science education programme through:

1. describing the social and cultural context;
2. considering a view of science as 'making sense of the world';
3. relating to recent understanding about the ways young children learn;
4. incorporating current initiatives in approaches to teaching science, training teachers and developing a curriculum.

A Social and Cultural Context for Science Teaching

Today's world is full of complexities. The physical-biological systems are under threat; the delicate social fabric is under severe tension; and the survival of humankind itself is in question. There are consequently difficulties involved in helping the young grow up with appropriate competencies for life and work. These require a broad perspective to be adopted by science curriculum developers. It is obvious that real-life performance is much more demanding than simple examination achievement. The educational response must deal with competencies that truly meet functional demands.

There is a further dimension. It must also be recognized that the young pupils in schools are also the same young children in homes and communities. Thus, it follows that real life needs can no long be self-centred. Neither can science remain an exploitation of nature but rather it must be a means to harmonious living with nature.

Viewed in this social/cultural light, "science' competence contributes to (among other things) a nation's political flavour, the standard of community health, and the nature of support for activities, such as those concerning the preservation of the environment.

Against this kind of yardstick, most existing science curricula descriptions and practices in the Asia and the Pacific region fail to measure well. Many pupils judge their learning experiences in Science as of little relevance to the world they know and have understanding about. For these children 'science' has become a discipline belonging to a remote, elite group of clever men who use a special language to describe a world that they cannot relate to, at all, sensibly.

Science As Making Sense of the World

Throughout the Asia and Pacific region there has been a trend towards establishing a science curriculum which emphasizes scientific processes. Teachers are being encouraged to provide activities for children which (they are told) will make basic ideas of science available to the learner and that can promote mental skills and attitudinal development. Unfortunately, recent research has revealed that although these curricula can produce active science classes, there is frequently significant mismatches between the actual ideas, actions and impact on thinking of children and those expected. Furthermore, primary teachers (who typically have a very limited formal science education, relative to the 'experts' who developed the science curriculum they must cover and the textbook they are expected to use) have typically not been provided with a sufficient programme of pre- and/or in-service training to de-emphasize content objectives. Despite an awareness of their own uncertain knowledge of the ideas and explanations of the consensus scientific community, these teachers have clung to what they see as their required role when teaching science, i.e. the provider of 'right' answers. Not surprisingly, most science lessons remain at this level of learning/teaching. Therefore 'what science is' needs to be developed in teachers before science lessons can become relevant to the real-life needs of children and before appropriate scientific competencies can be fostered.

A recent curriculum innovation in the region stresses 'science' as 'making sense of the world'. This definition is not only consistent with what scientists see themselves as actually doing, it also (by virtue of the basic needs for survival) identifies children (even very young ones) and primary school teachers as 'scientists'. This view of science frees teachers and pupils from the 'right answer' syndrome and brings science into the real-world of the learner. It also humanizes 'science' and the scientific competencies that all curricula strive to develop in pupils. The process skills of existing curricula, for example, observation, become the competency to 'look for things, rather than at things'. Provided teachers and parents can be convinced of the validity of science as making sense of the world, there seems much to be gained.

Recent Understandings About the Way Young Children Learn Science

Recent science education research has established much about the way children learn science, which is of significance to science curriculum developers. A summary of some to these understandings (in the context of formal learning) which are beginning to influence curriculum innovations are as follows:

(i) from a young age, children try to make sense of their world, and not infrequently already hold ideas about a topic which a teacher intends to introduce;

(ii) the ideas which children do hold about a topic are not necessarily those held by experts, but to the children they can be sensible and useful. When they are trying to understand a topic, children will draw on their ideas about the topic, or on other ideas which they think might help them, and such ideas can influence their learning in significant ways;

(iii) scientific knowledge based on histories and cultures is something which is neither simply transmitted from teacher to pupil, nor naturally developed from experience alone. Pupils and teachers must interact and discuss ideas derived from common experiences, investigations, reading books and asking experts. It is in these ways that children construct more complete, effective and useful ideas than the ones they currently hold;

(iv) various skills (intellectual processes), particularly those relating to questioning and investigating, are important means by which children can make better sense of their world. But children usually need help to develop such skills. Help will be most effective if given at the time when children see the need for specific skills;

(v) children can begin to take responsibility for their own learning, but this requires an atmosphere where both the teacher and the pupil genuinely care about and respect each other's ideas, an atmosphere which encourages the children to freely and responsibly express their personal views. It also requires that the teacher help the children separate their ideas from themselves so that questioning of ideas is no longer felt by the children to be a threat to self-worth.

Current Initiatives: Approaches to Science Teaching, Training Teachers, and Curriculum Development

An innovative approach to teaching science is being promoted which gives heavy emphasis to the nature of interactions which occur between the natural and technological worlds and the learner, between the learner and his/her fellow learner, and between the learner and his/her teacher.

This interactive approach is an attempt to build on the positive aspects of three major existing approaches to the teaching of science. These approaches are respectively based on the transmission of knowledge, on the discovery of science ideas, and on the development of process skills. In the context of this report, an attraction of an interactive approach to science learning is the acceptance of the learner as the dominant influence in classroom learning. The ideas that pupils relate to the topic under study, and the questions they ask about the topic, are at the very centre of classroom activity. Since learners are young children, their ideas and questions will tend to be intuitive construction and initial descriptions of real-life experiences and needs. Furthermore, since the approach also actively encourages learners to clarify their own ideas and to generate questions based on their own thinking there is a demand on the learners to be creative.

There are further important aspects to be accounted for. One such aspect is associated with the transfer of competencies developed in the classroom to real-life situations. It must be recognized that specially-contrived situations, used to exemplify scientific methods, are usually unproductive in the context of application to real-life situations. Children frequently view school science as belonging only to the classroom. Hence, any teaching strategy should take into account the need for real-life content. When it is emphasized that for many children primary schooling is not only the beginning but also the end of formal education, the critical significance of the need for appropriate content is underlined. Science content at the primary level must have both personal and social relevance, and the science competencies fostered in classrooms must be complemented with the social competencies needed to take action in family and community contexts.

The above views and beliefs about primary school science are not yet those of many teachers. It is, therefore, essential for curriculum developers and teacher educators to begin the task of reorientating the outlook of the teaching force towards its role in science learning. This is a formidable task in every sense and one which is complicated by a growing awareness of the failure of many current practices to impact, as intended, on teacher behaviour. Much research on this problem needs to be initiated. However, it does appear that effective change mechanisms will be characterized by teachers themselves, being given a much more central role in directing change than is currently the case.

Network for Producing Exemplar Materials

To guide the production of exemplar materials, a framework of ideas came about in answer to three questions. These are:

Question 1: What 3 scientific competencies do you consider most important to help young children develop, to meet their real-life needs?

Question 2: What are 3 clear directions that you consider curriculum developers should give teacher so that creativity is fostered in young pupils?

Question 3: What are 3 things that you consider curriculum developers could do to ensure that young pupils and their parents see school science lessons at the primary level as relevant?

Purpose of Science Learning

In order to answer the above questions, the purpose of primary science learning were first identified, as follows:

(1) Should involve children in making sense of their real-life world; and

(2) Should result in the acquisition of competencies that have practical importance, in terms of their daily and longer-term needs, as well as the equivalent needs of their family, community and society.

In the context of learning, the science lessons should be centred on things, events and experiences that children and their parents have in their everyday life. The science activities should use as resources, things, places and people that are part of the children's own environment. The science activities should extend into the home and community and involve the family and society. It has to have application to daily life, e.g. by solving simple problems and creating new ways of doing things.

The Competencies to be Fostered

After varying periods of time in science lessons, children should have improved competency to:

- observe accurately;
- relate what they observe to related existing personal understandings;
- ask questions about things that don't make sense to them;

- identify problems in his/her own real world;
- collect useful data and use it to clarify ideas and explanations;
- use a range of criteria to sort out collections of things;
- find solutions to everyday problems;
- carry out small scale investigations;
- utilize knowledge gained in everyday situations appropriately and use simple tools;
- communicate effectively in a range of ways (orally especially);
- share ideas and be interested in the ideas of others.

The Nature of the Learning Experience

- science activities should match children's perceived needs and interests;
- involve concrete experiences with familiar materials and objects where children are doing things themselves;
- encourage children to come up with their own ideas and share these with others;
- stimulate children to ask questions and provide opportunities for these questions to direct class involvement;
- create challenging situations for the children to cope with, using themselves as the major resource.

The Role of the Teacher

Teachers should not see themselves as a source of all knowledge nor a transmitter of 'right ideas'. Rather, the teacher should:

- act as a manager of resources (including the children themselves) and a faciliator of learning;
- be ready to accept children's own ideas and value all genuine questions they ask;

- accept the limitations of their own ideas and experiences and be willing to adopt the role of fellow investigator;
- be enthusiastic about all topics and activities.

The Classroom Climate

The classroom should:

- be set in a way which allows children to arrange themselves into groups to work on activities;
- have a positive, relaxed atmosphere, where children feel free to express their own ideas without fear of ridicule or disinterest.

The framework discussed can be used as basis for the development of science curriculum materials from real life situation of the child, the community, the society.

3

Guidelines For Developing Science Curricula

Introduction

Even with educational innovations, the teaching of science, especially at the lower level, is still generally confined to the memorization of certain facts and maintaining them for vertical mobility. The major emphasis is on the conceptual and theoretical knowledge which, for many students, are seen as having little or no relevance in their everyday life.

The acquisition of basic scientific attitudes and values and promotion of scientific literacy can best be achieved, if the pupils are allowed to find for themselves, the answers to "what" "how" and "why" certain changes/phenomena occur. This requires a massive re-organization of the curricular contents, because for all practical purposes the curriculum is generally taken as a combination of:

(a) What is to be learned (identified goals).

(b) How it is to be learned (planned experiences).

The planned experiences also include the methods of evaluation of learning outcomes which on their own may also give rise to revision of the planned experiences.

The following is a simplified version of the learner's interaction with the planned experiences.

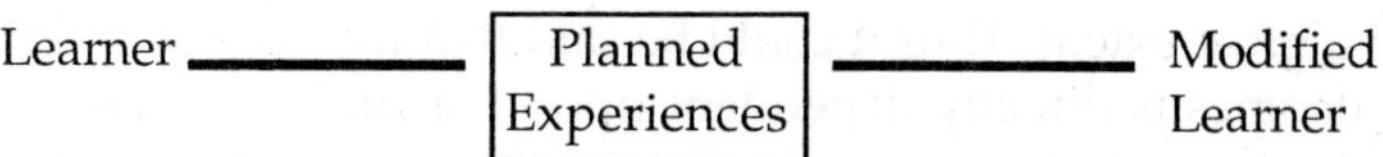

In a formal education system, the level of the learner's achievement depends upon a number of factors. Some of the important ones are:

(a)	Learner factors	(his interest, motivation level, comprehension, desire, etc.)
(b)	Teacher competence	(content knowledge, methodology of teaching, commitment to work, etc.)
(c)	Textbooks	(language, presentation, sequencing the contents, quality of printing, attractive, etc.)
(d)	Teaching aids	(appropriate, interesting, easy to handle, low cost, availability of replacements, etc.)
(e)	Learning episodes	(whether real life situations or experimental investigations of contrived situations, etc.)
(f)	Subject contents (Curriculum)	(appropriate to and consistent with the comprehension level of the learner, grading, application in life, etc.)
(g)	Evaluation	(importance, method, frequency, etc.)

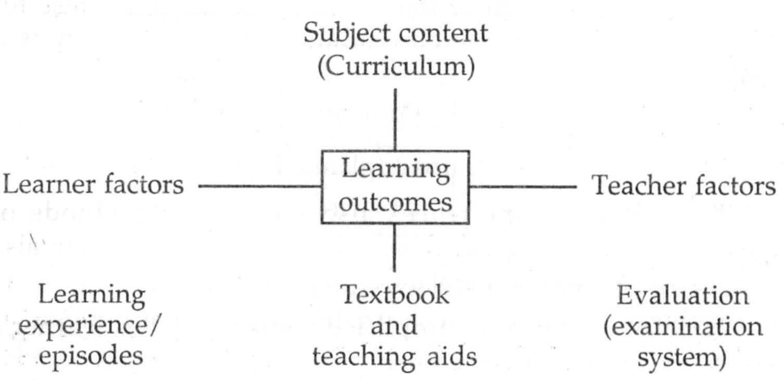

The factors listed above are all influenced by the curriculum to a great extent. Thus it could be said that the quality of learning outcomes is directly dependent upon the curriculum, especially the administration strategy. Experience shows that knowledge imparted by linking the learning experiences with real-life situations is more durable, interesting and useful.

An example of an innovative approach in the teaching of science, wherein the child makes sense of the world, is to let the pupils take part or participate in a livelihood activity (e.g. vegetable growing, fishing, salt-making, etc.) and teach them processes of science and the concepts and principles of different science disciplines (e.g. biology, chemistry, physics, environmental education) involved in said activity. In this approach, real life situations are used as core of the science class, instead of simply integrating them into the course outline of the science subject, usually by citing them as examples or by making the pupils perform activities involving those life situations.

This chapter deals with an innovative approach in science curriculum development and teaching which makes use of the pupils' experiences for classroom instruction. It describes strategies that can guide curriculum developers to choose real life situations and identify science concepts and skills from those life situations. Furthermore, it describes teaching-learning strategies that can help teachers make use of those science curriculum specifications based on the life situations, for the benefit of the learners. The scheme may be visualized as follows:

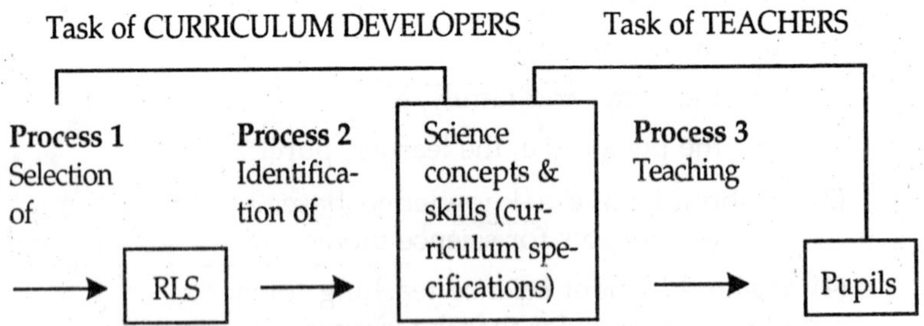

The chapter is organized according to the conceptual scheme shown above. This figure illustrates the order in which different processes for curriculum development and teaching-learning strategies should follow. In the succeeding sections these processes are explained with a view to come up with models for curriculum development and training of teachers based on Real Life Situation (RLS).

Selection of RLS

Real life situations (RLS) refer to: (a) *materials or objects*; (b) *activities or actions*; and (c) *phenomena or events* which are within the learner's realm of experience, or which can be brought to the learner's realm of experience, and which may be utilized for science teaching. Examples of these are:

Objects	bicycle, artesian well (how they work)
Actions	vegetable growing, fishing, farming
Phenomena	flood, erosion, drought

While the countries of the region have many common real life situations, they also have life situations which are unique to them. Thus it is necessary for curriculum developers of each country to choose life situations which are relevant to the various types of communities in their country. To guide them in the selection of those real life situations, the following criteria are recommended:

(1) A life situation should be taken from within the immediate environment of the learners.

(2) It should be relevant to the learners' needs i.e. it should be important to:

  (a) the community;

  (b) the home and family; and

  (c) the person (i.e. the learner/pupil).

(3) It should have a knowledge base, i.e. the necessary science concepts for science literacy.

(4) It should orient science teaching toward the processes of science in order that the learner will attain the higher cognitive skills.

(5) It should provide opportunities for the development of desirable habits, attitudes and values.

Derivation of Science Concepts From RLS

1. *Learning Episodes*

In preparation for the derivation of science concepts from a real life situation, learning episodes are first identified. Some examples are shown below:

Example 1: *Vegetable Growing*	The learning episodes may be as follows:
Objects:	farmer, child, soil, buffalo, hoe, seeds, etc.
Actions:	ploughing, hoeing, seeding, watering the planted seeds, etc.
Events/ Phenomena:	sunlight, shadow, movement of leaves, wind, etc.

2. *Science Concepts*

Having identified the learning episodes, the next step is to list down the science concepts involved in them. Examples of science concepts which may be derived from *vegetable growing* are as follows:

- Proper preparation of the ground will ensure high yield.
- Vegetables do not grow well amidst weeds.
- Tools (machines) are used to do work such as ploughing, hoeing and weeding.
- Muscular force is used to swing the hoe up and down. Some objects are easy to move and some difficult.
- Animals are living things.
- Animals differ in shape and size.
- Plants vary in physical appearance.
- Plants have roots of different sizes.
- Plants have seeds of different kinds.
- Seeds are dispersed in many ways.
- When the hoe comes in contact with the ground, the ideas of friction, collision, momentum and others are involved.

- The sun is a source of light.
- Light enables us to see things.
- Sunlight is necessary for food making in plants.
- Light causes shadows of objects.
- Shadows are produced when the light is screened or blocked by opaque objects.
- Shadows resemble the size and shape of the objects.
- White light is made up of seven colours.
- Images are formed when light is scattered.
- The force of friction makes work difficult.
- The force of an engine can be used to move things easier and faster.

Example 2: *Fertility of Soil* Learning episodes:

Objects:	soil, crops
Actions:	crop rotation, applying fertilizer
Events/ phenomena:	erosion, floods

Science Concepts:

- Soil comes from rocks and decaying plant and animal remains.
- Essential minerals are required for plant growth.
- Soil fertility is lost by flooding, over-cultivation, erosion and leaching.
- Soil fertility is restored by rotation of crops, manuring, use of fertilizers, etc.

Many other examples can be cited from different real life situations.

Organization of the Science Concepts Identified

The science concepts derived from RLS may be organized in a number of ways, three of which are cited below:

(1) By General Topics

Example 1: Vegetable Growing: *Plants, Animals, Matter, Energy, Machines, etc.*

Example 2: Rice Growing: *Nutrients and Vitamins in Food, Diversity, Variation, Complimentary of Organism and Environment, Ecological Relationship, Pests and Diseases, etc.*

(2) By Science Discipline

Those science concepts may also be organized into the headings Biology, Chemistry, Physics etc.

Example 1: Vegetable Growing: *Biology:* Complimentarity of organism and environment; Diversity and variations; Ecological relationships; Pests and diseases. *Chemistry*: pH; Fertilizers, Pesticides. *Physics*: Force; Machines; Pressure.

Example 2: Rice Growing: *Biology*: Nutrients and vitamins in food; Diversity, variation; Complimentarity of organism and environment; Genetics. *Chemistry*: Fertilizers; Pesticides. *Physics*: Machines; Force; Pressure.

(3) By Man's Basic Needs

Those science concepts may also be organized into the headings: Food, Water, Clothing, Shelter, Health, Education, Livelihood, Energy, Transportation and Communication, Sports and Recreation, etc.

Grading the Sc'ence Concepts

In the task of assigning the concepts to the different grade levels, the following should be considered:

(1) The sequencing of the concepts must proceed gradually from simple skills and ideas in the lower grades to the more complex ones in the higher grades. For instance, the concepts for class I should be directly observable to the child.

(2) The content to be assigned to the grade levels must be suited to the mental maturity of the learner and should not be cluttered with materials which are too difficult for them.

(3) The content must include a good balance of materials drawn from the physical biological and earth sciences, with no major gaps and pointless repetitions.

(4) The content must be coordinated with the entire educational programme at each grade level so that science is not isolated from other subjects, thereby giving the child a holistic view of his world.

A learner's knowledge and understanding of science will develop progressively over the years a number of ways. It is necessary and important to find out initial ideas of children in order to identify strategies, to ensure further changes or development of these ideas.

Teaching Strategy

The intended beneficiary of an educational innovation is always the child. Any attempt to improve instruction has for its primary objective to help the child learn more effectively. The science concepts derived from RLS must reach the learners with the help of the teacher; the teacher therefore is the key to a successful implementation of an educational innovation.

To facilitate the utilization of RLS in science teaching the following questions should be answered:

(1) What are the general ways by which RLS can be used?

(2) How would a teacher use RLS in teaching?

(3) How would the teacher organize a RLS-based lesson?

(4) What instructional materials can the teacher adopt?

(5) How can RLS help integrate or unify fragmented concepts within and outside the science subject?

(6) How should a RLS-based lesson be evaluated?

Teachers may utilize real life situations to: (a) *derive, illustrate and apply* science concepts and principles; (b) make the learner perform the processes of science in order to develop those process skills; and (c) give the learner opportunities to develop desirable habits and values.

The use of RLS for science education works on the assumption that the *background experiences of the child* (i.e. the objects, activities and events at home and in his community which he observes or performs) can be used to teach science concepts, principles and processes. The question is, how can the teacher actually take advantage of this background experience of his pupils in the context of the classroom? How would he: (1) select the relevant RLS; (2) focus the pupils' attention on the RLS; and (3) help them learn from it? He may do this with the use of the following strategies:

- field trips/field work
- showing films, video tapes, photographs
- bringing part of the RLS into the classroom such as showing objects from the RLS (e.g. tools, products, etc.), inviting a resource person (e.g. a farmer, community leader, etc.)
- science camps

The teacher's role includes:

(a) finding out what the children's ideas are;

(b) determining where the children are in the progression of concepts and guiding them towards developing more scientific ideas;

(c) providing opportunities to try out the ideas or to have further experiences which challenge them, leading to possible change in ideas; and

(d) assessing or evaluating the change in concepts and skills which have been developed or acquired.

To guide the teacher in organizing a RLS-based lesson and answer the rest of the questions raised, the flow chart in the next page is proposed and subsequently discussed.

Flow Chart for Organizing a RLS-based Lesson

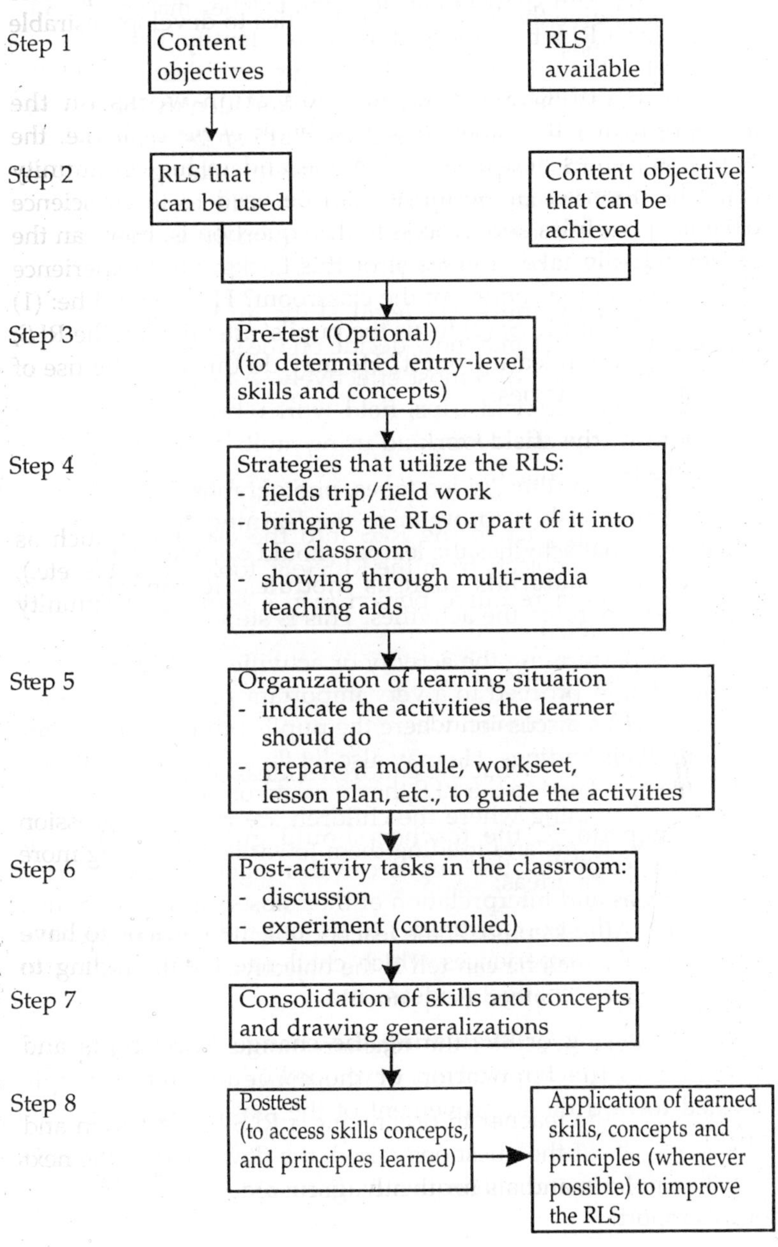

The diagram shows nine steps the teacher may go through to organize a RLS-based lesson. He may identify, first of all, the content objectives (i.e. skills and concepts) and then the RLS that can be used. On the other hand, he may first identify the available RLS and then the content objectives that can be achieved with it. In other words, steps no. 1 and 2 are interchangeable. Either way, the teacher may administer a pretest in order to find out what skills and concepts related to the lesson the learners already know; this is step no. 3 in the flow chart.

Considering the entry-level skills and concepts of the learners, the teacher may now decide on the strategy or strategies that will utilize the RLS most effectively. As mentioned earlier, these may include field trips, field works, bringing the RLS or part of it into the classroom, and using multi-media instructional aids. This is step no. 4.

The next task is to organize the learning situation by: (a) specifying what activities the learner should do; and (b) preparing instructional materials such as modules, lesson plans and worksheets to guide the activities. This is step no. 5

After performing the activity or activities utilizing RLS, the teacher should proceed to a very important part of the learning process, a class discussion where the pupils present, analyze and interpret their findings. He may also let them perform controlled experiments related to the RLS they worked on. This is step no. 6.

In step no. 7, the teacher should guide the classroom discussion such that the pupils can draw generalizations from their analysis and interpretation of their observations or findings in the RLS. After step no. 7, the teacher may administer a posttest by means of which he can tell if the objectives of the RLS-based lesson has been attained (step no. 8).

Whenever possible, the teacher should bring the pupils' attention to the application of the concepts and principles learned toward the improvement of the real life situation (step no. 9).

Exemplar materials for this diagram are found in Chapter 4 of this report.

Preparation of Instructional Materials

1. General guidelines for developing curriculum and curriculum materials derived from RLS

The following steps are suggested to be followed by the developers of curriculum and curriculum materials:

(a) Identify the needs of the community as perceived by its members and leaders, teachers and pupils.

(b) Identify the science knowledge and skills (appropriate to the particular grade levels in the school system) that are necessary to satisfy those needs and which may be taught using the available community resources.

(c) (i) Study the curriculum guide or scope-and-sequence chart of the science course and find out at what points the knowledge and skills identified in (b) can be entered.

(ii) Or, if certain knowledge and skills in (b) have no entry point in the chart in *c*(i), revise the chart and provide entry points for those additional knowledge and skills.

(d) Use various techniques and instructional tools to operationalize the integration of the knowledge and skills in *(b)*. Examples are: field trips, lectures or demonstrations by resource persons from the community, use of modules and other instructional materials on specific topics.

(e) In connection with, *(d)* above, conduct workshops for science teachers and supervisors with these objectives: (i) to map out the programme of community-oriented class activities for the year; and (ii) to construct lesson plans and modules on specific topics and other instructional materials.

(f) Regularly monitor and evaluate the strategy being implemented.

The teaching of science and technology, utilizing real life situations, is of course not limited to only the needs of the community in general. As mentioned earlier, its target groups also include the family and the individual pupil.

2. *Module Making*

Modules differ structurally in the length and writing style; the main parts, however, are generally the same (see list below).

Main Parts of a Module:

(1) Cover page

(2) Title page

(3) Table of contents

(4) Body of module

(5) References and suggested readings

For purposes of utilizing real-life situations for instruction, modules may be knowledge oriented or skills-oriented. Examples of these are shown in the titles of modules as follows:

Knowledge-oriented	1. "The Truth About Drugs" 2. "Your Family's Electricity Consumption" 3. "Harmful Effects of Dynamite Fishing"
Skills-oriented	1. "Vinegar Making" 2. "Preparation and Use of Organic Fertilizers" 3. "Constructing a Fuel-Saving Cooking Device"

Because of this difference in orientation, the body of the model (*d* in the list of parts) varies markedly in structure. For knowledge-oriented modules, the one presented below has gained wide acceptance among teachers and students alike.

Parts of Module Proper:

(1) Purpose (general objective or goal)

(2) Instructional Objectives..................based on no. 1 (specific, behavioural objectives)

(3) Prerequisite Concepts and Skills

(4) Pretest.................based on no. 3 and partly on nos. 2 and 5

(5) Lesson proper ....based on no. 2 (discussion of content; activities)

(6) Post-test..................based on no. 5.

(7) Keys to Correction; Interpretation of Scores.

For modules intended for primary and secondary school pupils, the writers may find the following writing tips and reminders useful:

(1) Make the style conversational but *not* informal. Address the reader. Imagine that you are teaching in a class but you are writing down what you are supposed to be saying. Avoid abbreviations and contractions of words. Avoid dangling sentences.

(2) Observe proper use of punctuation marks, paragraphing, indention and other mechanics of writing.

(3) Beware of plagiarism. Always document and acknowledge your outside sources of information and ideas.

(4) Sample interpretation of scores.

(a) Pre-test (10 items)

"If you get five points or better, you may proceed to the lesson proper. If you get lower than 5, review the prerequisite concepts and skills and see your teacher for a second pretest."

(b) Post-test (10 items)

"If you get 5 points or better, see your teacher for the summative test. If you get lower than 5, go over the module again and see your teacher for a second post-test."

For skills-oriented modules, the parts of the module proper are reduced to five:

(1) Purpose

(2) Instructional Objectives

(3) Introduction

(4) Activity (Procedure)

(5) Evaluation

3. *Evaluation of the Module*

Evaluation of the effectiveness of any educational programme, teaching method or instructional material (such as books, modules, etc.) is based on the educational goals or objectives, which include *knowledge, skills* and *attitudes*.

To evaluate the modules to be prepared specifically for science education utilizing real-life situations, the following guidelines are recommended:

(1) Have the module evaluated by both teachers and pupils;

(2) Adapt the evaluation instrument to the pupils, i.e., use simple language and simple instructions;

(3) Pay attention to both the content and the mechanics of the module;

(4) Have two separate instruments for evaluating knowledge-oriented and skills-oriented modules (see Instrument 1 and 2). If a skills-oriented module requires an output (e.g. a fuel-saving cooking device, a product such as a new fertilizer or chicken feed, etc.), evaluate the output also; and

(5) Aside from the cognitive/psychomotor objectives of the module, evaluate also the affective objectives, such as *attitude towards work*. This entails preparation of a third instrument such as an attitude scale (see Instrument 3).

Instrument 1 (for knowledge-oriented module)

Evaluation of Module

Module No.:..................................

Title:..

To the Pupil:

This is NOT a test. We only want to know what you think of this module to help us improve it.

I. Below are eight sentences about the module. Opposite each sentence are three numbers; their meanings are as follows:

1. I agree.
2. I am not sure.
3. I disagree.

Tell us what you think about each sentence by encircling the number of your choice.

1.	The objectives of the module are clear.	1	2	3
2.	The discussions are easy to understand.	1	2	3
3.	The things discussed in the module are useful to pupils of my age.	1	2	3
4.	The size of the letters (in which the module is written) is just right.	1	2	3
5.	The pictures are clear (i.e., not blurred).	1	2	3
6.	The number of pictures is just right (i.e., neither too few nor too many).	1	2	3
7.	The length of the module is just right.	1	2	3
8.	The cover page of the module is attractive to pupils of my age.	1	2	3

II. For no. 9 and 10 complete the sentences:

9. This is what I like about this module:

____

____

10. This is what I do NOT like about this module:

____

____

Instrument 2 (for skills-oriented module)

Evaluation of Module

Module No.: --------------------------

Title:------------------------------------

To the Pupil:

This is NOT a test. We only want to know what you think of this module to help us improve it.

I. Below are eight sentences about the module. Opposite each sentence are three numbers; their meanings are as follows:

1. I agree.
2. I am not sure.
3. I disagree.

Tell us what you think about each sentence by encircling the number of your choice.

1.	The objectives of the module are clear	1	2	3
2.	The steps of the procedure (or the instructions) are clear and easy to follow.	1	2	3
3.	The activity or project is useful to pupils of my age.	1	2	3
4.	The output of the activity works (i.e., the project is successful).	1	2	3
5.	The size of the letters (in which the module is written) is just right.	1	2	3
6.	The diagrams are easy to understand.	1	2	3
7.	The length of the module is just right.	1	2	3
8.	The cover page of the module is attractive to pupils of my age.	1	2	3

II. For nos. 9 and 10, complete the sentences:

9. This is what I like about this module:

____

____

____

10. This is what I do NOT like about this module:

____

____

____

Instrument 3 (with skills oriented module)

Attitude Scale

After using Module No.:------------------------

Title:---

To the Pupil:

This in NOT a test. We only want to know how you feel about WORK after going through the module.

Below are fifteen sentences. Opposite each sentence are three numbers; their meanings are as follows:

1. It is true of me.
2. I am not sure.
3. It is not true of me

Tell us how you feel about each sentence by encircling the number of your choice.

1.	I enjoyed doing the activity (or project) in the module.	1	2	3
2.	I helped my team do the activity in the module.	1	2	3
3.	I did my best in working on the activity.	1	2	3
4.	I did not care whether or not I finished doing the activity in the module.	1	2	3
5.	I admire people who are hardworking.	1	2	3
6.	Working no the project gives me self-confidence.	1	2	3
7.	I felt self-pity while working on the project.	1	2	3
8.	I respect people who work hard.	1	2	3
9.	I would rather work alone than work with others.	1	2	3
10.	I am ashame to be seen by my friends while working.	1	2	3

11. I like to teach my friends what I learned from the activity.	1	2	3
12. It is all right to work like this on a project but not often.	1	2	3
13. I look forward to working on another activity in the next module.	1	2	3
14. As soon as I reached home, I told my parents about the activity I did in the module.	1	2	3
15. I will do the project again at home.	1	2	3

4. *Lesson Planning*

The tool which will directly enable the teacher to effectively utilize real life situations for instruction is the lesson plan. The format of a lesson plan varies widely among teachers, among schools, among disciplines. But the main parts are more or less the same.

Parts of a Lesson Plan

1. General Description

   Title

   Grade/Year Level

   Time Allotment (number of minutes or class meetings)

   Materials (books, modules, references)

2. Objectives

3. Contents	4. Strategies
(a) Topical outline	Motivation
	Guide questions
	Activities
(b) Summary	

4. Evaluation
5. Enrichment/Remedial Exercises (optional)

6. Assignment

   Application of the concepts learned in the lesson.

   Preparation for the next lesson.

The flow chart for organizing a RLS-based lesson (page 223) suggests the following modifications of the list above:

1. General Description

   Title

   Grade/Year Level

   Time Allotment

   Materials

2. Concepts (which may be taught using the RLS)

   Skills

   Attitudes

3. Objectives

4. Pre-test (about the RLS, optional)

5. Introduction (optional)

   This may include: (a) a general introduction of the main subject of the lesson; (b) activities which the teacher may do in preparation of the lesson; (c) possible modifications of the lesson plan; (d) reminders or cautions; etc.

6. Teaching Hits (Strategies)

7. Evaluation (Post-test)

8. Enrichment/Remedial Exercises (Optional)

9. Assignment

Another format for lesson-planning, would include the following:

1. Topic/Theme: Real-life needs, relevancy, scientific competencies and creativity.

2. Background: A rationale that supports the topic/theme.

3. Objectives: Need to be clearly stated, emphasize involvement and provide for open-ended outcomes.
4. Activities: Should provide direction, but not be in detailed lesson-plan form. Some justification for each focus suggested should be given, while all activities should be described so that pupils' active involvement is emphasized.
5. Follow-up Activities: Some comment should be provided which indicates the further potential of the topic/theme.
6. Evaluation Strategies: Suggestions which broaden the base that teachers tend to use to assess involvement and achievement, should be included.

While the mechanics of lesson planning is very easy to follow, the greater consideration is what should go into the plan.

The use of materials and situations within the pupils' realm of experience is one of the universally accepted principles of teaching and learning. Educators agree that the practice facilitates learning because the pupils learn faster and more effectively when the learning materials and situations are familiar and meaningful to them, especially if the pupils see the importance of the subject matter to them and if the learning experience is pleasant and enjoyable to them. In addition to this pedagogic advantage, utilizing appropriate home and community resources and tackling real life issues and problems in teaching may actually help solve environmental problems and improve the people's quality of life as well as contribute towards the fulfilment of certain national development goals of the country.

4

Exemplar Instructional Materials

Teachers play a key role in determining the quality of learning in the classroom. They are the makers of the curriculum in action. If their attention is to be focused on issues of relevance, real-life needs, scientific competencies and creativity, they must be able to recognize the shift in emphasis from the traditional content/concept-based teaching of science, to a mere practical approach. A practical view is seeing science as making a better sense of the world, coming to terms with real-life situations.

The exemplar materials shown in this chapter are intended to provide models to help teachers bring about effective changes in their role. This change is directed towards making them *agents of change*, held them view afresh that science teaching is not the mere dispensing of facts and information.

Underlying these exemplar are the following basic assumptions:

1. Teaching by telling is not effective. It typically lacks relevance to the child, who cannot relate it to daily life, and hence learning is NOT PERMANENT.

2. To become consistent with the view that science as making better sense of the world and to be relevant to the real-life needs of the learners, classroom practice has to be shifted closer to the world of the children. It has to be CHILD-CENTRED rather than SUBJECT-CENTRED.

3. Classroom/laboratory practice have to be based on collective investigations involving teachers and pupils, where the teacher's role is as a fellow investigator who has the advantage of wider experience, and is perhaps better equipped with more mature common sense. The science classroom should be characterized by open dialogue between pupils, and between pupils and teachers.
4. It is necessary to give due cognizance to the intuitive ideas or real-life experiences that children bring to topics and activities. Often those ideas/experiences appear very sensible to children and have a critical influence in their learning. They need to be encouraged to express freely their ideas or share their life experiences, and teachers should use these to develop the specific topic/ activity.
5. Teachers need to create an atmosphere in the classroom which encourage pupils to take responsibility for their own learning.
6. Activities will promote the development of mental processes and other competencies and be open enough to allow pupils to use their own ideas/experiences to enhance creativity. Some competencies to be emphasized are the following:
   - looking for real-life needs or things and happenings in the environment, and exploring ideas/ experiences that are attempts to make sense to the learners;
   - asking useful questions which lead to further investigations;
   - identifying real-life needs/problems and finding ways to meet these needs or solve these problems;
   - seeking explanations for things that are not well understood, but are encountered in daily life activities.
7. Activities will use resources which are locally available, e.g. human material, and equipment. (Note: the

equipment should be those basic equipment available in the locality and not those found in science laboratories).

8. Strategies for developing the topic should be anchored in local resource and the learning must have an effect which is relevant and useful to the child, ultimately resulting in better quality of life.
9. It should be noted that while the practical real-life experiences/activities are discussed, planned for, and implemented, the corresponding science facts/ information, generalization and principles/ concepts should be incorporated/ integrated into the learning/ teaching situation.

The exemplars shown in this chapter are for teaching science and technology for pupils; and for teacher training.

Exemplar for Pupils

There are 2 exemplars for pupils. Exemplar 1: A Farm is for Class 1, includes a worksheet and a pre-test and Exemplar 2: Agriculture is for Class 5 includes 2 lesson: Sowing Seeds and Preparing the Soil.

1. A Farm (for Grade 1)

STEP 1

RLS: Visit to a farm.

STEP 2

Learning episode: Animals

Concepts:

- Animals differ in shapes and sizes.
- Animals move. They differ widely in the way they move.
- Animals need food. They eat. They differ in the food they eat and how they eat.
- Animals differ in the place where they live.
- Animals need water.
- Animals are useful to man in many ways.

Skills:

- Observing, meaning, comparing, communicating, predicting

STEP 3

(See the sample pre-test on page 250).

STEP 4

Strategies:

The teacher may bring his class to a farm where they can observe animals. He may also use photographs or pictures of animals.

STEP 5

Instructional Materials:

The teacher may prepare worksheets that will show the pupils what they will do in the farm.

STEPS 6 and 7

The teacher must conduct a post-activity discussion for: (a) analysis; (b) interpretation of the pupils' observations and findings; and then (c) synthesis of concepts and principles.

STEP 8

The teacher may administer a post-test similar to the sample pre-test and covering the concepts identified in step 2.

STEP 9

Going back to the list of concepts (step 2) related to animals, the teacher may choose "animals need food". The class may discuss the following:

(a) What do you think will happen if chickens are given plenty of food (e.g. rice, corn, etc.) and water instead of just letting them look for their own food in the yard?

(b) What do you think will happen if chickens are in a coop for many days without food and water?

Sample Pre-Test

(Shown in pictures, instructions to pupils given orally by the teacher.)

1. Which of the following objects are animals? Encircle your answers.
   - plow
   - dog
   - seeds
   - horse
   - tree
2. How many legs do these animals have?

Animal	*Number of legs*
Buffalo	________
Donkey	________
Chicken	________

3. Which of these are covered with hair (fur)? Encircle your answers.
   - sheep
   - mountain goat
   - chicken
4. Which is bigger? Encircle your answer.
   - horse
   - duck
5. How do the following move (meaning, do they walk, fly or crawl)?
   - horse
   - snake
   - butterfly
6. Where do these animals live?

Animal	*Where it lives*
Goat	____________

Eagle ________________

Fish ________________

7. Which of the following, help us in the field? Encircle your answer.
   - Cow
   - Crow
   - Locust

8. How do these animals eat?

Animal	*Its food*
Buffalo	________________
Chicken	________________
Grasshopper	________________

9. Which of those help us carry heavy load? Encircle your answer.
   - Donkey
   - Goat
   - Chicken

10. What sort of food do we get from animals?

Animal	*Food we get from it*
Buffalo	______________
Goat	______________
Chicken	______________

Sample Worksheet

(Shown in pictures, instructions given orally by teacher)

Directions:

Look at some animals. Then answer the following questions for *each* animal.

1. What is its name?
2. Describe its appearance by answering these:

2.1 Does it have legs? If yes, how many?

2.2 Does it have a long, slender tail?

2.3 Is it bigger than you or smaller than you?

3. How does it move? Does it walk, fly or crawl?
4. Where does it live?
5. What food does it eat?
6. Is it useful to people? If yes, how?

Draw your answer to these questions in the chart below:

Question	Animals		
No.1			
No. 2.1			
No. 2.2			
No. 2.3			
No. 3			
No. 4			
No. 5			
No.6			

One of the important features of the use of RLS in science teaching is emphasis on the science process skills. The teacher should always bear in mind that his lesson *objectives, activities* and *assessment* of learning performance should all reflect the importance that the proponents of this innovation have assigned to science process skills. This can be seen, for instance, in the sample worksheet for class I. The questions call for the simplest levels of *observing, measuring* (to indicate both number and size), *comparing* and *evaluating* (particularly No. 6, where the pupils judge whether animal is useful to people or not). The instruction to record (or draw) the observations in tabular form promotes the skill of *communicating* and facilitates *comparing* the animals based on the information called for in this particular set of questions.

2. Agriculture (Grade 5)

Concepts from Real-life Situation:

1. There are various ways of sowing seeds.
2. Tools/machines may be used for sowing seeds.
3. Seeds should be sown in proper depth and at proper distances from one another.
4. Proper environmental conditions are required for the seed to grow.
5. There is a proper time for sowing different kinds of seeds.

Process skills: Observing, comparing, analyzing, planning an experiment, communicating.

Manipulative skills: Preparing seeds for sowing; sowing seeds.

Attitudes: Love of work, patience.

Teaching hints:

1. Take the class to a farm. Request a farmer to demonstrate and explain the following tasks: selecting good seeds, preparing them for sowing, and sowing them in different ways.
2. Prepare an interview guide or worksheet which the pupils can refer to during the farmer's lecture and which, at the same time, calls the pupils' attention to the main points of the lesson.
3. Back to the classroom, conduct a class discussion where the pupils can: (a) report; (b) analyze; and (c) interpret their observations and findings, and then (d) synthesize concepts and principles.
4. Let the pupils read a *Farmer's Handbook* to get an idea of the planting schedule for common agricultural crops (i.e., proper time to plant them) as well as the conditions of the soil, climate, etc. best for them.
5. Let the pupils perform a laboratory activity similar to the RLS. (See the sample activity next page).

Activity: Sowing seeds

Objectives

In this activity, the pupils will be able to:

(a) Separate good seeds from seeds of poor quality.

(b) Treat the seeds with a chemical (fungicide) to protect them from diseases.

(c) Sow the seeds.

Materials

Kidney bean seeds, 50

Beakers or wide-mouthed bottles, 2

Clean cloth or paper towel

Fungicide

Water

Tray with soil

Procedure

1. To separate the good seeds from those of poor quality, put all the seeds in a beaker or jar of water. The good seeds will sink while the defective ones will float. Remove the floating seeds, and pour off the water. Keep the good seeds in the same beaker. Examine the good seeds and the defective seeds; compare them.

2. Your teacher has prepared for you a certain amount of fungicide solution. Pour it into the beaker containing the good seeds. Set the beaker aside for about 10 minutes. Then wash the seeds with plenty of clean water, and dry them.

3. Place the seed on the tray of soil; count them.

4. Observe the seeds daily at a specific time. Count how many seeds germinate every day; record your observations in the form of a chart.

Discussion

1. Describe the good seeds and the defective seeds. Why do the defective seeds float?

2. Why is it advisable to treat the seeds with fungicide?
3. How many seeds germinated at the end of the activity? Compare it with the total number of good seeds that you placed in the tray (this will give you the percentage of germination).
4. Seeds of some plants are first allowed to germinate in a seed plot before planting, while others are sown directly either by scattering or by sowing in holes or grooves made during soil preparation. Give one or more examples of these kinds of seeds.
5. Some seeds are soaked in water before planting, while others are not. Give one or more examples of these two kinds of seeds.
6. Suppose we want to find out why seeds are sometimes soaked. What should we do? In other words, plan an activity to find out the purpose of soaking seeds. Use white kidney bean seeds for the activity.

Teaching hints:

Conduct a final discussion where the class will answer the following questions:

(a) What ideas about sowing seeds did you learn from this lesson?

(b) What crops does your family grow in your farm? List them down. Describe the ways their seeds are sown.

(c) Indicate the month when those seeds are sown, the climate during which they grow best, the type of soil where they grow best, etc. Then refer to a *Farmer's Handbook* (if one is available); are your answers the same as the information in the handbook? If no, try the suggestions in the handbook.

Lesson: Preparing the Field

Concepts from Real-life Situation:

1. Soils are of various types. They may either be clay, sand or loam.

2. Simple tools or machines can be used to till the soil.
3. Soil must be free of weeds before planting vegetables or other crops.

Process skills: Observing, comparing, analyzing, planning an activity.

Manipulative skills: Ploughing, hoeing, tilling the soil, crushing lumps of soil, removing weeds, using a yoke.

Attitudes: Love of work, patience.

Objective of the lesson:

Students should be able to:

1. Identify the types of soil.
2. Describe the various steps needed or taken in preparing a field.
3. Select the tool suitable for preparing a particular type of soil.
4. Describe how a hoe or plough is used.
5. Use the hoe or plough to remove the weeds as well as to loosen the soil.

Teaching hints:

1. Take the class to the field to inspect the whole area.
2. Invite a farmer from the community to explain how a field is prepared for planting. Instruct each student to note the step-by-step process involved in field preparation. Each one should have a notebook and pencil with him.
3. Alternatively, an agricultural extension worker can be invited to explain how a particular type of soil prepared for a certain type of crop.
4. If the farmer in the community is explaining the procedure while someone is actually preparing a specific field, let the students observe and take down notes, specifying the type of soil, tools used, etc.

Activity: Preparing the Soil

Time to complete: 3 hours

Materials

Plough	Crusher for breaking clods
Yoke	Power tiller
Hoe	Tractor
Spade	Leveller
Harrow	

Objectives

The students should be able to:

1. Use a hoe or a native plough and bullock.
2. Level the field by using a leveller.
3. Remove the weeds by using a hoe.

Pre-activity instruction

1. Before going out to the field, find out whether you have the needed tools or material with you. Brings also your notebook and pencil.
2. Then go to the field and inspect the whole area to know the following:
   (a) the type of soil in the area: clay, sand or loam or a combination of these;
   (b) the tool or machine needed to clear the area or to loosen the soil (hoe, spade, plough, harrow, etc.);
   (c) the terrain (rugged, needs levelling, evenly flat, etc.); and
   (d) the weeds abundantly growing in the area.
3. Start preparing the soil or observe how the soil is prepared; note each step taken and the tool used in the process.
4. Once the field had been cleared, determine what plant would grow best in the area.

Post-activity discussion:

1. Does the field cover a wide area?
2. What kind of soil is found in the field? Describe what you have observed.
3. Describe the tool(s) or the machine you used in clearing the field.
4. Was the soil easy to loosen? Why or why not?
5. If the particular soil in the field was difficult to loosen, would the use of another tool make the process easier?
6. What weeds did you find in the area? Describe them.
7. Name and describe the steps involved in preparing the field.
8. What crops do you think would grow best in the area?
9. Sketch the following tools used in soil preparation:
   (a) plough
   (b) spade
   (c) yoke
   (d) hoe
   (e) harrow

Exemplar for Teachers

Exemplar 1—Lesson: Water in the Home and Water in the School

(For Grade 4)

The following exemplar shows one of the many ways teachers could adopt in the effort of making their lessons (teaching and learning experiences) more relevant, meeting children's real-life needs, and need to achieve meaningful and useful scientific competencies.

Background:

Water:

- is a material that is closely linked to the child's life/ activities;

- is used in many aspects of life-drinking, bathing, irrigation;
- is enjoyable to play with (e.g. when bathing);
- lends itself to many other activities that a child can do, without using any complicated or sophisticated equipment.

The ideas that could be brought into focus are that:

- water is freely available around us. But it could get limited. Therefore, storage of water and preservation of water is important;
- water used for drinking is usually clean. It can get spoilt in many ways: in storage, in actual use, in transport etc. It is important to safeguard water from getting spoilt;
- if clean water is used for drinking, one remains free of many diseases.

Objectives:

1. To think about and share experiences regarding the different ways is which the water supply is obtained.
2. To share the experiences among learners about the different uses of water.
3. To recognize that water used for different purposes must meet different requirements.
4. To compare the different samples of water on the basis of its colour, smell and appearance. (Often the differences are not at all that sharp.)
5. To share experiences of ways is which water gets spoilt at its source, between the source and the user, on standing, and in use.
6. To develop simple skills in keeping well water from getting polluted, and to apply simple precautions when drawing water from a well. (Similar comment for storage vessels, and taps.)
7. To develop simple skills of making water safe for drinking.

8. To develop simple skills in safe handling of drinking water at home and in the school.
9. To recognize or identify the ways in which water is wasted, and ways of preventing wastage of water.
10. To develop positive attitudes on the effect of preventing wastage of water at home and in school.

Some Possible Activities

The activities for this topic may weave around certain key questions the would arouse pupils' interests and put them in a "problem-considering (solving) situations."

Stimulating Questions and Motivating Issues:

1. Where do you get your water supply at home?

   As an entry point, teachers could open a discussion in order to get pupils' ideas/experiences by posing above question. Response may be varied e.g. Water from an open well, stream, tap, tube-well, rain water etc.

2. How do you make use of water in your daily life, at home and in school?

   While posing a set of structured questions, pupils should be allowed to discuss among themselves in small groups about the different uses of water in their daily lives, and identify water that could be used for different purposes. The idea would be to draw pupils' attention to the fact that we may use different types of water (condition of water) for different purposes (work).

3. What are these different types of water?
   Are they all safe for drinking?

Activity: Pupils fetch 'clean' and 'unclean' water.

Put them in clean containers.

Compare the colour/odour/physical appearance.

Look for sentiment/stains on standing.

Observation:

Observation	Sample 1	Sample 2	Sample 3 etc.
Colour			
Odour			
Sediment			

Activity: Consultation with a resource person/public health personnel.

The imparting of simple skills and the awareness of the importance of safe-handling of drinking water at home and in the school could be done by posing the questions such as the following:

Stimulating Questions and Motivating Issues:

4. How do you usually store your water so that spoiling is minimized?

The first question may elicit answers such as a clay pot, aluminium vessels, plastic or metal containers etc. A discussion on the advantages and disadvantages of the different types of containers would be useful.

The answers to the second question may lead to ideas of purifying water, followed by an activity to discuss how to develop their own storage systems (container) whereby it can reduce the possibility of getting the water spoilt when drawing it from the container. This can be done by allowing them to develop to build their own storage containers in the forms of 2 or 3 dimensional drawings, or building a prototype from easily available raw material.

Discussion:

If the pupils notice that certain types of water are not 'clean', lead the discussion to give reasons.

Stimulating Questions and Motivating Issues:

5. If water is 'cloudy'.
   - What makes it cloudy?
   - Can we make it clean? How? (Suggest methods).

Pupils may suggest methods such as the following:

- Let water stand for a time until sediment collects at the bottom.
- Add 'Alum' and let it stand.
- Add some chlorine compound (Bleaching Powder).
- Construction of a simple filler containing layers of sand, gravel and pebbles.

At this stage, students could be stimulated to plan out a simple types of filter using the above materials.

Samples given below:

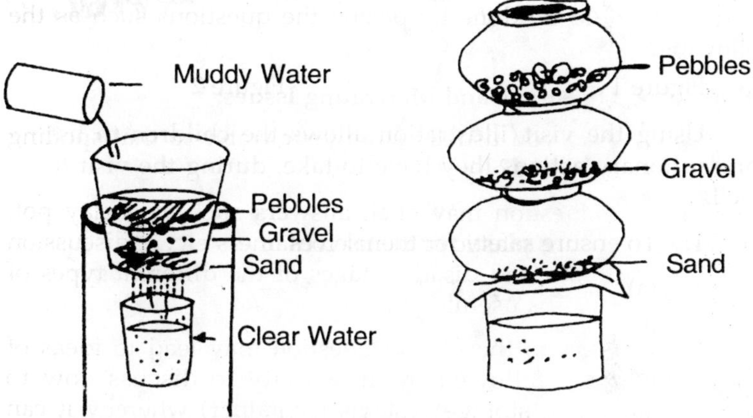

Following the above activity a question may be posed, such as:

- Is this water safe for drinking?
- Can you suggest another way to prepare drinking water?

Lead the discussion to highlight the following issues:

- Why water needs to be boiled before drinking.

Stimulating Questions and Motivating Issues:

6. How does water become unsuitable for drinking?

Activity: A visit to the community/school well (studying an illustration of a wall as shown below if more is available at the vicinity of the school).

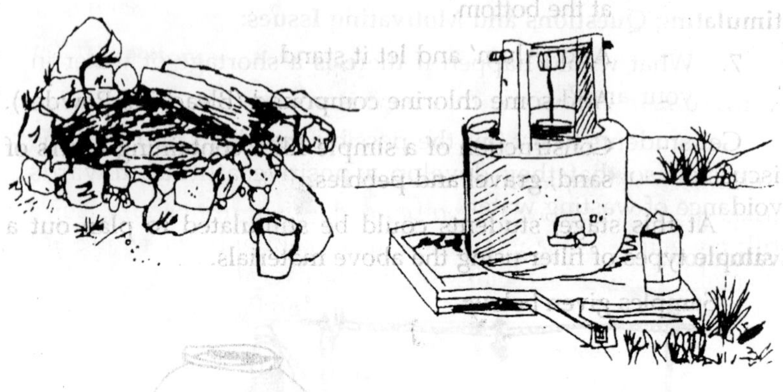

Figure 1 Figure 2

Using the visit/illustration allows the children to list the precautionary actions they have to take, during the visit to the well:

1. To ensure safety for themselves.

   (a)

   (b)

   (c)

2. To ensure that the well does not get spoiled/polluted.

   (a)

   (b)

   (c)

Through this exercise, try to highlight the safety measures that should be taken, e.g. not to peep in too far, etc. and measures to prevent polluting well, e.g. not allowing waste water to run back into the well, keeping the bucket up side down when not in use.

Extend this activity to the situation where tap water is available. In all of these activities try to get suggestions from children about the uses for which waste water could be put—

e.g. direct the waste water to a vegetable plot in order to make use of it for another purpose.

Stimulating Questions and Motivating Issues:

7. What would happen if there is a shortage of water in your area?

Get students to list out the possible problems and lead the discussion so that they develop a positive attitude towards avoidance of wasting water.

Evaluation:

Refer to the picture above and answer the following questions :

1. How could the water in the well get spoiled?
2. If it gets spoilt, describe the steps you would take in order to make it safe for drinking.

As a follow up of the above activity, the teacher may like to bring to the children the real-life situations and problem in their neighbourhood. One such activity has been suggested as example.

Activity:

Possible extension for the topic.

Focus: Real-life Problem

Problem:

Our water sources often get polluted due to human activities.

Key Question:

How do human activities/actions make water dirty/spoiled? Can we take some steps to prevent it?

The purpose of this activity is to focus pupils' attention to a real problem in their surroundings. It would also help clarify the pupils' existing ideas as to how water sources may get dirty and extended their ideas about how they view this problem and what they can do about it.

Competency:

- Share experiences with others
- Ask the right kinds of questions
- Make meaningful observations
- Collect information from others

Suggested Steps

This activity may be done in groups. Each groups may be asked to study one aspect of the problem. A class report can be prepared on the basis of the group report.

Each group may visit the water source. They may make a selection of more than one source, if available. Prior to the visit, the teacher may ask pupils, their own ideas about the topic. (Remind the class about safety.) The teacher may ask the pupils to focus their observations and collect information on reaching the site. Some of these could be:

- Observe the different activities going on in and around the water source.
- How do these activities generate waste water?
- What happens to the used or waste water: Does it flow back to the well?
- Is there a way by which the water may be carried away from the water source?

- Do you think these activities pollute the water source?
- Is there a way to prevent the pollution?

In case the source of water is an open well, pupils may also find out:

- If the source is a well and has a platform around it, how is the platform constructed.
- Whether there is an outlet for used water, away from the platform.

In regions where wells are not available as a water source, the rivers/stream etc. could be visited. Observe where the water waste is directed.

Each group presents a report of their visit to the class followed up by a class discussion.

Let children suggest some ways in which they can help in reducing this pollution, and in taking the message home and influencing their parents to take better care of the water source. Allow the children to think of the follow up action.

Exemplar 2—Lesson: Shelter: A Roof Over My Head

Background:

All living beings need shelter in one form or another. It is a basic need for all. The type of shelter required by people differs from the type needed by other animals. Existing human shelter reflect social and cultural values, as well as the wealth of its people and the condition in which they live. Obtaining a shelter that meets reasonable basic needs, remains a major difficulty for the poor.

The following aspects are considered worthy of discussion within this lesson.

1. Human beings use houses for their shelter.
2. A house is a place where people live with other members of the family.
3. Shelter protects humans from heat and cold, rain and storms and dangerous animals.

4. Shelters are necessary for rest and comfort, and for storing and preserving possessions.

5. Houses differ from place to place in their form and structure. There are,

   (a) thatched houses

   (b) wood houses

   (c) tin sheds

   (d) houses made of clay/mud

   (e) houses made of bricks and stones

   (f) houses made of concrete and cement.

6. Different kinds of materials are needed to make different houses, such as straw, leaves, bamboo, tin, bricks, stones, sand, clay, iron, glass, cement, wood etc., depending upon the types of houses.

7. In building houses, services of people like, masons, carpenters etc., are used.

8. The beauty of a house, and the comfort for living it provides, depends on its design and cost.

9. Proper use and maintenance of the house depends upon the people living in it.

10. Like people, other living beings also need shelter, e.g.

    (a) wild animals live in caves, holes, nests, trees etc.

    (b) domestic and pet animals live in specially made places for them, such as cowsheds, cages, stables etc.

With all these possible aspects to consider, there are many opportunities for pupils to explore ideas and interests as these relate to their environment and daily experiences.

To raise children's awareness of practical ways their houses can be made to be better places to live in.

This could be achieved by:

1. sharing ideas about shelters;

2. extending ideas about the usefulness of adequate shelters;

3. broadening understandings of the role of shelters in daily life;
4. enhancing understandings of materials used in building and maintaining a house;
5. introducing children to the skills involved in building and maintaining a house.

A Way of Developing the Lesson

Initial activities should provide a chance for pupils to clarify their own concept of a shelter and the usefulness of a shelter, by sharing ideas with their peers. Follow-up activities should be build upon the ideas and questions pupils show most interest in, following these initial activities.

Possible Activities Include the following:

1. Where do you go after school:

The purpose of this question is to eventually focus pupil thinking and discussion on 'house' and 'home'. Once this focus has been achieved, other questions like,

- why do we have a home?
- what do we use our houses for?
- what things do we do in our homes?

can focus on the requirements of an adequate shelter.

Teachers will be well aware that some pupils may live in very humble circumstances. Where this is the case, they will need to be very cautious about the questions they ask, and the activities they involve their class in. Strategies which enable the children to present honestly their ideas and experiences, without being identified with a particular idea will be very powerful. One such strategy is described in the 'Food for me and my family' exemplar.

Following the activities centred in the above questions, further activities leading to a wider exposure of the environment of the pupils can be carried out. Examples of such activities are as follows:

Activity 1: What are houses built of?

This focus involves pupils in activities that explore:

- the different kinds of materials houses are built of;
- the different ways the materials are used to build houses;
- the range of skills and craftsman involved in building a house.

Activity 2: How do you use and maintain your house?

This offers the opportunity for activities that explore:

- the internal arrangements of houses
- the sizes, shapes and features of houses.

The intention is that children will think more deeply about the purposes for which a house, and its rooms or different portions are used. Hopefully, some children will discover practical ways of making their home more comfortable. By including activities related to maintaining a home, children will be encouraged to accept more responsibility in looking after the physical conditions of the home, including how clean it is.

For all these activities the teacher should act as a manger of resources (including the children's own ideas), and facilitate group work and interaction. They will be able to enhance all activities by anticipating resources which can stimulate thinking and extend ideas. For example, building up a collection of photographs/drawings of different houses, cutting out article from newspapers about houses and housing, locating building projects in the local community which could be visited by the class and negotiating with local experts to demonstrate their skills and talk about their craft. Obviously the ability to do this will depend upon what is reasonably available in the community of the school.

Possible follow-up activities

The initial focus on homes can be extended in many ways. Two possibilities are as follows:

- buildings in our community other than homes, e.g. shops, the schools, a factory, the temple or church.

Whatever buildings are considered, the relationship between its physical characteristics and its use, and the skills associated with its construction and maintenance, will be worth exploring;

- shelter for domesticated/per animals, e.g. cowsheds, cages, stables.

The main emphasis here will be on providing activities which explore the best possible physical conditions provided for domesticated animals to live in.

Evaluation:

Approaches to determine the impact on the pupils, of the activities undertaken in this lesson, could vary from simple routine formative test developed by teachers, to group reports (including use of visual materials, e.g. charts and/or displays as well as written statements) developed by the pupils. The emphasis being placed on group and individual reporting is recommended strongly.

Exemplar 3—Lesson-Making Sense of Distance, Direction, Time and Space

Background:

Young children's perception of distance, direction, time and space keeps on changing, as their experiences are extended and as these experiences are slowly assimilated. In our daily life, we often use these ideas with different and varying degrees of precision. These changing perception, are seen in words and phrases such as those often used by children:

- How far?
- How near?
- How long?
- How short?
- How fast?
- How slow?
- How vast?

Many of their experiences are intimately linked with their feelings:

- How soon the holidays have ended?
- How long it takes for my birthday to come again?

These qualitative notions linked to their feelings are "changeable". These need many concrete experiences for further consolidation and continued development, to form a usable conceptual framework.

To begin with, it is necessary to give the children simple activities of ordering, rearranging and comparing, 'inventing' their own "tools" of measurement of time and distance. These activities would help develop some important aspects of creativity. This exemplar is focused on children's perception of distance, direction, time and space. The activities suggested are based on these perceptions. It is hoped that through these, their ideas could be strengthened so that they see those relationships that help to make sense of the 'little world' around them.

The activities suggested here are initial concrete experiences for children, which would help enhance the simple patterns they are continuously evolving.

Objectives:

1. Make rough estimates of direction of movement relative to different objects.
2. Measure distance using simple units like number of hand spans, foot lengths etc.
3. Make rough estimates of time taken for moving from one place to another (counting hand claps, tapping a drum, etc.).
4. Recognize the relationship between time taken and distance covered, e.g. walking, running, etc.
5. Make simple sketches maps of the classroom, the school compound and their own home environment.
6. Plan a small trip to a nearby place keeping account of the distance, direction and time involved.

An approach to the lesson:

A set of questions can be posed to the pupils for which they find their answers through the activities suggested below. Through these activities, they would get the feel of time, distance and directions, and also be made to feel the necessity of developing standard units of measurement.

Motivating questions:

- How far is your school from your home?
- Does your friend (X) stay 'near to' or 'farther away' from your school?
- Is your friend's house on the same route as yours?

The responses received for the above questions could lead to an activity as mentioned below, confining it to the school compound.

Activity 1: Making Sense of Distance

Divide students into groups and get different groups to walk from their classroom to

- the front gate
- Headmaster's office
- the perimeter of the fence/wall etc.

(Each group can select a different route)

While doing this the pupils should note down the distance covered by counting the number of steps taken or by using a stick as a unit of measurement, as shown below:

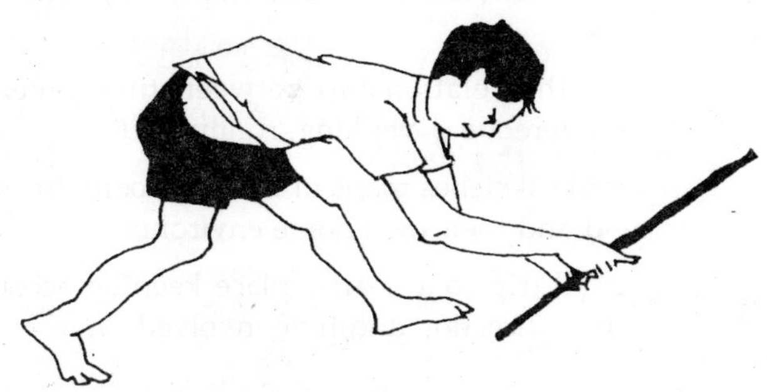

When the children are back to the classroom, the teacher should collect the information of the different groups and put them up on the blackboard as shown below:

Gr. No.	*Place*	*Distance* *Steps*	*Stick length*
No. 1	Gate	20	15
No. 2	Gate	-	-

Discuss the result with the pupils. From this discussion, the teacher may draw their attention to the idea of 'farther' and 'nearer'. It may be possible and useful to let them feel the necessity of having a common unit for measurement.

Activity 2: Making Sense of Direction

Pupils are made to go out into the school garden. Encourage them to note the answers to the following questions in their notebooks.

(a) From which direction does the sun rise?

It is likely that varied response will be received, such as "In front of the school gate?" "Behind the tree." etc. The teacher discusses their response to introduce the ideas of East and West.

(b) Looking at the rising sun can you determine the direction of North and South?

A possible way to find this out is to ask one pupil to stretch both arms, with the right hand pointing to the rising sun. In this position the pupil would be facing the North. Pupils may be asked to find out South direction.

(Introduce the words North and South)

With this activity, pupils may note the direction in their notebook as shown below:

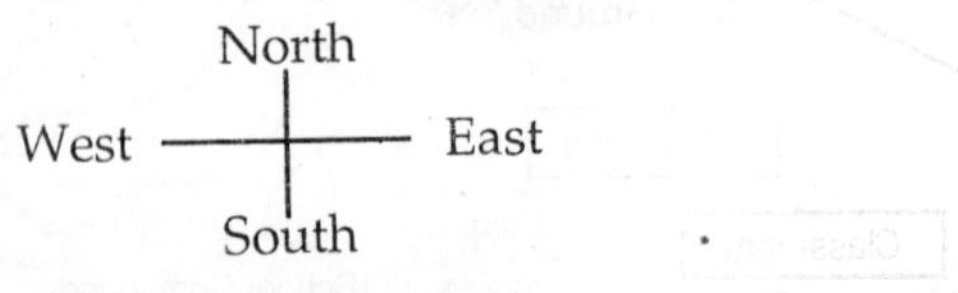

Using the above diagram, the following questions may be posted:

(c) From where you are, in which direction is the classroom? (Indicate in their drawing)

(d) From where you are, in which direction is the Principal/ Headmaster's office/school gate/school well?

In this manner, pupils may be encouraged to complete a simple sketch map of the school compound.

Activity 3: Making Sense of Time

Get pupils to do the following activities and note the results in their notebooks:

(a) How long does it take for you to - walk to the gate?
- run to the gate?
- hop to the gate?

The timing would be done by counting the number of steps or by beating on a drum, or clapping hands.

Result could be tabulated as follows:

Activity	*No. of steps taken*	*No. of drum beatings taken*
Walking		
Running		
Hopping		

Through this activity, lead the discussion to highlight, that when the pupils use the methods listed above, they get different results. This could be a starting point to introduce the need for a standard unit to measure time.

Additional Activity: Making a rough map of the school compound as a follow-up, e.g.

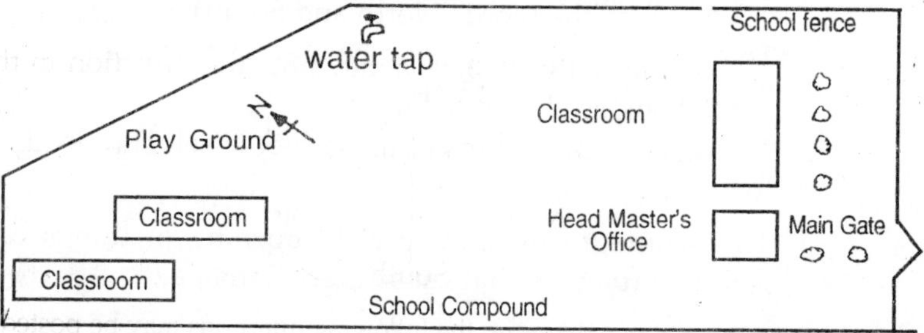

This acvitiy could be extended to make simple sketches of their home environment.

Evaluation:

1. *Treasure hunt (game)*

   Pupils are invited to find a treasure that is hidden some where in the school compound. The whereabouts of the treasure are given by the teacher, indicating the distance (steps) and direction (N/W/E/W). The time taken to set to the treasure could be considered.

2. Plan a trip to a nearby market/store, discussing aspects of the distance, direction and the time that would be involved.

Exemplar 4—Lesson: Things that burn

Background:

Burning, to children, is a very familiar experience. They have seen firewood burning in the kitchen, oil lamps and candles burning at home and in place of worship, garbage, burning in the garden, etc. Burning usually gives hear and light. Careless burning of things can cause great damage by causing house fires and accidents.

Objectives:

1. To identify burning as an important process in everyday life.
2. To identify, from the many things that are found in the environment, those that burn.
3. To become aware that during burning, heat and light are given out.
4. To identify things that could be used as fuel from among the many things that burn.
5. To create an awareness of using fuel wisely, not leading to wastage.
6. To become aware that careless burning of things can lead to situations that cause great damage.

7. To develop basic skills to prevent fires from spreading and causing damage.

Focusing questions	Possible activities
• Have you seen things burn?	Discussion among pupils of instance where they seen things burning, in their own experiences.
• What things generally burn and what things do not burn?	Collecting things from the environment and observing what happens when they are held in oil lamps or candle flames. Pupils may present their observations in tabular form. A possible presentation is:

Things that burn	Things that do not burn
1.	
2.	
3.	
…	
…	

Focusing questions	Possible activities
• What changes do you observe when things burn?	Possible resources: • Burning things give of—smoke —smell. • The size of the thing being burnt becomes smaller. • Ash is formed. • Black soot is produced. • The hand feels warm when brought near the burning object. • When burning takes place in a dark place, the darkness is removed (light is removed (light is given off). • Burning produces sound.
• What fuel do you use to cook food at home?	Possible answers: … firewood … wood charcoal … kerosene … liquefied petroleum gas (LPG)

- Why do you not use other forms of fuel to cook food?

Possible answers:

... not available in quantity
... expensive
... produce bad semll
... produce lots of soot

- What do you use to light your home?

Possible answers:

... kerosene
... candles
... coconut oil/plant oil
... electricity

- Why do you not use other sources of light?

Possible answers:

... does not burn well
... is expensive
... does not give enough light
... not available in the community

- What do you to put out a fire?

Possible answers:

... Pour water
... Cover with cloth
... does not give enough light
... not available in the community

- What would you do if you see your friend's shirt burning?

Possible answers:

... Pour water
... Shout for help
... Ask the friend to roll on the floor
... Cover him with a wet cloth
... Remove the shirt

Read the picture story and answer the questions given below.

Evaluation 1

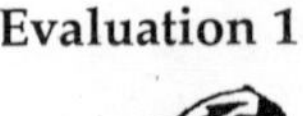

Padma: Shall we burn this garbage?

Raja: I know a way to burn it. We will put pieces of paper and set fire to it.

Raja: I don't think it will burn. It is wet.

Padma: Look! It is burning now and ants are leaving it. When we burn things the animals living in the soil die. It is not a good thing.

Raja: It is not burning well. Shall I see what is wrong?

Padma: No, don't use your hand, you will burn yourself. Use a stick and rake it.

Raja: There, it is burning better now.

Padma: Get away now! Look how beautiful is the flame.

Raja: Look at these leaves. They have changed.

Padma: Not only the leaves, the soil too has changed.

Padma: Raja look, that tree too has caught fire. It might spread. The wind too is blowing. What can we do?

Raja: We will put some water on it.

Raja: There the fire is gone.

Padma: But don't step on it. You will burn yourself.

Raja: Now let me see what happened to the piece of glass I put there.

Padma: After that, let us go home. But let us make sure that the fire is completely out before we leave.

1. In (2) suggest any other things that can be used instead of paper.
2. Suggest a way of using paper to burn for a longer time.
3. Why do you think that ants started leaving the place?
4. Quote two good things that Padma has uttered in this picture story.
5. Write three precautions that you should take in handling fire.
6. What do you think raking did to make it burn better in (4)?
7. Why did Padma say that the flame is beautiful. Do you think a flame is beautiful? Can you write some statement about a flame?
8. What changes would there be in leaves and soil in (5)?
9. In (6) why was Padma worried that the wind was blowing?
10. What else could they have used to put the fire out instead of water?

11. Why did Padma asked Raja not to step on it in (7)?
12. What changes do you think Raja saw in the piece of glass in (8)?
13. How can they make sure that the fire was completely out in (8)?

Evaluation 2

From the items mentioned, choose which one fits the description given below:

Sand, wax, wood, wet, cloth, dry leaves, crackers, kerosene, green grass, cotton, glass, iron nails, polyethylene, piece of rubber, polystyrene, sugar, salt, etc.

1. Easy to burn..
2. Does not burn...
3. Is burnt for fuel...
4. Is difficult to control burning...................................
5. Gives out a smell when burning..............................
6. Leaves a lot of ash when burning.........................
7. Gives a bright flame when burning......................
8. Does not give a flame while burning....................
9. Burns for a long time..
10. Produces a sound when burning..........................

Exemplar 5—Lesson: Food for Me and My Family

Background:

Food is a basic need of living organisms, including our own. Its efficient production, distribution and use is of critical importance to all societies, communities, families, and individuals. Even young children have extensive experiences with food, and can bring many ideas on this topic for class discussion. Their ideas and experiences are a rich resource in which the teacher can base her class activities.

Objectives:

To enhance pupils' understanding relating to the part played by food in their own lives, in their family life, and in the community they live in. In particular, to extend understandings about production, selection and use of food:

1. by clarifying pupils' ideas about 'What is food';
2. by helping pupils appreciate, that sufficient food for a day will include a range of different food in appropriate quantities;
3. by broadening pupils awareness of where their food comes from;
4. by enabling pupils' to select and use good quality food (in both economic and nutritious terms);
5. by developing pupils' abilities to help produce healthy and cheap food; and
6. by encouraging pupils to use food wisely without waste.

A Way of Developing the Topic

Initial activities should provide ways for pupils to define the topic. By 'define' it is meant that each pupil will be given the opportunity to:

(i) clarify his/her own existing ideas relating to food; and

(ii) describe the particular aspects of 'food' he/she has questions about, and is interested in findings out more.

Follow-on activities should be influenced by the pupils' response to (ii).

A possible development could be:

A. Initiating/Focusing Activities (which can help define the topic)

Focus: What do I (each pupil in a class) think of 'food'?

The purpose of this focus is to clarify pupils' existing ideas 'What is food', and to extend the views of any child who holds a limited view. For example, some pupils do not include 'drinks' in their meaning of 'food'. For such children, it will be useful to have their meaning challenged by being made aware of a broader way of thinking about 'What is food'.

Activity: What did your family take yesterday?

Every pupil in a class is required to keep a diary of the food his/her family takes on a day, or (more simply) each pupil is asked to recall yesterday's meals to make up a list during the lesson itself.

Teachers should recognize that "food we take" can be a sensitive request for some pupils (e.g. those who have had little to eat). It may be necessary to devise a way that makes public this information, without identifying exactly which pupil has listed what food. One way of achieving this is set out as follows:

> Each pupil's list (without his/her name on it) can be placed in a container, the lists can be mixed up and randomly redistributed. Then working in groups, the pupils can use the lists they now have (and their own ideas), to make up a more extensive list of food. These group-lists can then be displayed, compared and contrasted. In this sharing time, the pupils' ideas and questions should form substance of the discussion. Finally, a class definition of 'What is food' could be drawn up and displayed. Teachers need to recognize that their role in a lesson of this kind is not of a provider of information, but of a manager of pupil-pupil interaction.

Once a class has a sensible working definition (in terms of the teacher's adult common sense), further focusing activities which expose pupils' ideas, interests and questions (needs) can be introduced.

Focus 2: What food does your family take in a day's meals?

This focus can lead to activities that relate to what nutritionists call a 'balanced diet', but what common people think of as 'a day with a mixture of sufficient food'.

Focus 3: Where does food come from?

Such a focus can be successfully sharpened in a way which enhances relevancy and fosters creativity, if each pupil is able to contribute to the thinking of the class, and be involved in the planning as well as the action that forms at least part of the class activities. For example, Focus 3 'Where does food come from? could be initiated with the following activity.

Activity: From where does your family get its food?

The pupil-generated list of ideas can again be a useful starting point, with the teacher's main role being that of a manager of pupil-pupil interaction. The ideas that gain wide support can then, themselves, become foci for further activities, Possible foci could include:

(i) How do you select the best vegetables at the market?

(ii) How does your family help your home garden grow well?

(iii) How does your family help your animals grow well?

Each of these focusing questions are capable of initiating much useful pupil-led work. To show this more clearly, a possible development of (iii) above is now given. The development described is based in a country setting where almost all rural families raise chickens for eggs, meat, money and manure.

Sub-focus 1: What things do chickens need to live well?

This sub-focus would offer opportunities to involve children in activities to do with.

(i) What foods do chickens need?

Possible pactivities include:

- preparing a list of items of chicken food;
- feeding chickens at home or at school;
- bringing samples of chicken food from home or the market;
- rearing chickens at school.

(ii) What is a good chicken house like?

Possible activities include:

- pupils' own drawing of their chicken house;
- visits to homes and farms to identify different kinds of chicken house;
- constructing models of chicken houses with clay, wood and paper;

- looking for features of chickens and chicken behaviour that indicate their physical well-being (e.g. conditions of plumage, number of eggs being laid).

(iii) How can we tell if our chickens are well cared for?

Possible activities include:

- looking for signs of disease;
- measuring the rate of weight-gain in young chickens;
- making charts of different kinds of chicken diseases and matching these with preventions and cures;
- discussion with animal husbandry officers/workers and parents who are 'local experts' in chicken diseases.

Sub-focus 2: How productive are my chickens?

This sub-focus would offer opportunities to involve pupils in activities to do with the following:

(i) How many eggs are my chickens laying each day?

Possible activities include:

- Keeping a daily record of eggs laid and relating these to the number of chickens you have;
- how many eggs are big, how many eggs are small.

(ii) How can we get the best price for our chicken eggs at the market?

Possible activities include:

- examining eggs for size and freshness including testing eggs in water and light,
- visiting shops/stalls and relating condition of eggs to price;
- finding ways of keeping the eggs fresh.

(iii) How fast are my young chicks growing?

Possible activities include:

- weighing chicks over a period of time and comparing weight gains (including the weight gains of different kinds of chicks).

Sub-focus 3: How do we keep the right number of chickens?

This sub-topic would offer opportunities to involved pupils in activities to do with the following:

(i) How can we get the most eggs to hatch?

Possible activities include:

- visits to homes and farms to observe different methods of hatching eggs.

(ii) How can we make sure most chicks grow up well?

Possible activities include:

- observation of rearing chickens at home and on farms;
- observing photographs of rearing chickens on farms;
- investigating what the needs are of young chickens, e.g. food, water, shelter etc.

The above range of foci and activities is quite extensive, but by no means includes all possibilities. Pupils and teachers will be able to think of many more interesting and worthwhile things to do. Whatever activity is included; the key to success (in terms of meeting pupils' real needs, making science relevant and encouraging creativity) lies with the ability of the teacher to provide a supportive classroom climate in which pupils can offer and share ideas, ask questions and suggest investigations. The teacher who inhibits these behaviours and who is unable to resist teaching by telling will not only prevent his/her programme from achieving the goals of this approach to science, but will also reduce the pupils' level of enjoyment, involvement and sense of success.

Evaluation:

Approaches to determine the impact on pupils of the activities undertaken in this topic, could vary from simple routine formative tests developed by teachers, to group reports (including visual materials e.g. charts and/or display as well as written statements) developed by the pupils themselves. The emphasis being placed on group and individual reporting is supported strongly.

Exemplar 6—Lesson: Preparing Food for the Family

Background:

Food is a basic life requirement. All children have their own ideas about food and its importance, based on their own experience. These ideas can be used as significant entry points to create a meaningful learning situation.

The following points are considered worthy of concentration under this topic:

1. Food is a precious commodity and it is everybody's concern not to waste food.
2. We use various methods of preparing food. Some of these methods,
   (a) improve the test of food;
   (b) make it safe to eat;
   (c) make it keep longer.
3. When we select food for preparation, it is good to consider the needs of the body to grow, to work, and to have protection from diseases.
4. In preparing food, care should be taken to retain as much nutrients as possible in the food.

Objectives:

1. To clarify pupils' ideas about food by,
   (a) identifying sources of food in the community;
   (b) sorting out different kinds of food using different criteria, e.g. food they like to eat, food they do not like to eat, food eaten raw, food cooked before eating, etc.

2. To describe various ways of preparing food to
   (a) make it tasty, look good, and have a good smell;
   (b) make it safe;
   (c) keep it for a long time.
3. To find out the traditional ways (practiced in the locality) of preparing food in the community to make it stay long.
4. To appreciate the importance of:
   (a) avoiding wastage of food;
   (b) cleanliness in preparing food.
5. To select and prepare food considering,
   (a) the nutrients that the body gets from food;
   (b) ways of avoiding loss of nutrients from the food.

Activity Cluster 1: Clarifying One's ideas on food

Focusing Question	**Possible Activities**
• What food do you find in the community?	1. A visit to the school garden, a nearby farm, or the market, from where pupils can make a list of foods that are available.
• What foods would you like to have?	2. Making a list of foods they would like to have for a meal on ordinary days, and a meal on a special day.
• Why do you like them? What foods do you think you should have? Why?	3. Making is list of foods they think are important for their health. Do they eat these foods often? If not, why not?
	4. Sorting out food samples (or pictures; or names of food written on cardboard), using their own criteria. Possible basis of classification are: what I like to eat; and what I do not like to eat; food eaten raw and food cooked before eating; food taken from plants and food taken from animals, and so on.

These activities will indicate the pupils' ideas about food.

(Detailed description of activities are given as Sample Activity 1 and Sample Activity 2.)

Activity Cluster 2: Describing Various ways of preparing food

Focusing Question	Possible Activities
• Can you thing of 2 or 3 dishes that you enjoy having? • How do you cook rice? (or meat vegetable) • Why do you cook rice? (or vegetable	1. Sharing of experiences on the dishes they particular enjoy and why. Discussion may lead into the preference of many people, including themselves, or perhaps their parents, for sample inexpensive meals, not only for economic reasons, but also for the sheer enjoyment of it. Discussion may also lead into the aesthetic values of food, such as the colour, smell and of course, the taste, or a combination of these properties. 2. Observing ways of preparing food at home or in the school cafeteria, that may bring out various methods such as boiling, frying, roasting and baking. In the class discussion, children may suggest that some foods are eaten. Children may want to give examples of foods prepared in a particular manner. 3. A project in which some children may write on a topic like My favourite Food' which

includes a description of the food or picture, why the pupils like the food, how it is prepared, etc. Pupils' work could be up on the wall of the classroom which the class can observe and discuss.

4. Comparing the taste of food before and after it is cooked, which may initiate a discussion on why food is cooked. In addition to reasons like, to make it better, to make it easy to digest, to make it soft enough a chew, pupils may even say to make it safe to eat. This last idea could include the killing of "germs" and also the removal of toxic substances. For example, in the Philippines and in Sri Lanka, a particular root crop (tapioca) is boiled in an uncovered pot, to allow a poisonous substance to escape. (The poison is really cyanide which escape as hydrocyanic acid but this need not be discussed with pupils).

(A detailed description of an activity for this cluster is given as Sample Activity 3.)

Activity Cluster 3: Finding out how food is prevented from spoiling in our community

Focusing Question	Possible Activities
• What are some properties of spoiled food?	1. Sharing experiences on properties of spoiled food (how spoiled food tastes, smell, looks like, etc.). Giving possible causes of spoilage,

- What happens to you when you eat spoiled food?
- Why do you think spoiled food make you ill?
- What are the preserved food that you know?
- How does a preserved food sample compare with the fresh sample?
- Can you describe how to preserve some foods?

based on their own experiences, like flies feeding on the food, worms found on the food (which come from eggs laid by flies), dirty of the food and leaving the food in a warm place (encouraging bacterial spoilage).

2. Narrating occasions when they themselves or other people got sick diarrhea and other such problems) form eating spoiled food; why they think spoiled food makes people sick (spoiled food has germs, spoiled food contains poisons)
3. Asking parents and other people about the different ways certain kinks of food are preserved. Sharing gathered information with the class.
4. Sampling certain kinds of preserved food at home and in the classroom, and comparing them with the fresh samples. In addition to making the food keep longer, some effects of preservation can be brought out by pupils from this experiences, such as better taste, more pleasing colour, softer texture, different smell, and other observations.
5. Linking up with the home economics class where ways of preserving foods using traditional methods are being taken up.

(For a more detailed description of an activity for this cluster refer to Sample Activity 4.)

Activity Cluster 4: (a) Observing cleanliness
(b) Avoiding food wastage

Focusing Question	Possible Activities
• What do you think we should to have enough to eat?	1. Start with a sharing of actual stories related to effects of unhygienic handling and preparation of food, for example a case of food poisoning during a festival. Use this as the basic for a discussion on what to do and what not to do. Stress the importance of cleanliness in handling and preparing food.
• There is much food wasted (or allowed to spoil) in our community. Do you think this should happen? Why do you think so?	
• There was food poisoning in a particular village during a festival. What could have lead to this situation? What can be done to prevent this form happening again?	2. Start with a description of how some of the most delicious recipes in the community have been developed, to make full use of the food instead of throwing away some parts. Some Chinese dishes, enjoyed by people worldwide, were originally thought of, for this purpose.
	A dramatic, though negative, way is to focus on food shortage in other parts of the country, and its effects on children. This will pupils rethink some of their wasteful habits relating to food.
	If the problem of food shortage is already in the community, the discussion can channelled to constructive measures like raising their own food, or making full use of all edible portions of a plant or animal.

3. Make a list of what to do and what not to do, in relation to the problem of food wastage.

4. Link up with practical arts and the home science subjects regarding these issues. Maximum utilization of food by recycling materials otherwise thrown away such as producing vinegar from coconut water; making attractive food preparations from parts of vegetables, can be cited as examples.

5. In some communities fruits and vegetables, when plentiful, go to waste. They are too common and there is no "prestige" attached to them. If this happens in your locality, you may ask a prominent figure's help in promoting these "lowly" foods. You can also help your pupils think of attractive and varied ways of preparing these foods.

Activity Cluster 5: Groups of food

Focusing Question	Possible Activities
• What foods do you like to have? What do you think these foods do for the body?	1. A discussion of the kinds of food enjoyed and not enjoyed by children and the reasons for their answers.
• What foods do you *not* enjoy? Do you think these foods are also important to your body?	2. Sharing possible experiences on how some pupils started to eat from they did not previously enjoy and eventually learned to like them.
• Can you think of ways to getting the necessary materials that the body needs, from your food.	3. Relating interesting stories to pupils that bring out the importance of a meal, with a variety of foods that are not necessarily expensive.

4. The teachers may then introduce the idea of the important food groups and the food samples under each.

GO foods	(make the children GO, walk, jump, play)	root crops, rice, enlarged stems, peanuts
GROW foods	(makes the body grow)	beans, eggs, milk, fish, meat, sea food
Glow foods	(makes your face glow, makes the body healthy)	fruits and vegetables

In introducing this concept, the teacher was to be conscious of selecting proper examples that will not offend the pupils, e.g. food chosen should be affordable and within their reach; it should be acceptable within the cultural/religious context.

By having pupils examine their food choices for their snacks and their meals, they may realize the need to try changing some unsound practice, e.g. buying 'junk food' for snacks.

Promote discussion to lead them to buy inexpensive food like bananas or papaya, eating mostly GO foods for their meals, etc.

5. Choosing from a selection of meals, which ones are better because they contain foods coming from the GO, GROW and GLOW food groups. Honestly assessing, if they can try having more to these meals.

   If possible, pupils may try planning their own meals and try preparing such meals for the family.

6. Discussing proper ways of handling and preparing food to keep the nutrient value, e.g. washing vegetables before cutting or peeling; cooking vegetable within the proper time duration. (Overcooked vegetables are not tasty and overcooking destroys nutrients).

Sample Activity 1: Sorting foods into groups

You may start with a discussion with pupils, using some entry questions such as:

1. What foods do you find in your community?
2. What foods do you like to eat?
3. Can you bring some samples or pictures of food?

Some pupils may want to bring some samples of food to the class. Others may choose to bring pictures. It will be desirable if foodstuffs like milk, coconut, drinks and fruits are represented.

Pupils will sort out the food, using any criterion.

Pupils will discuss their basis for grouping.

The discussion may be expanded along the criteria brought out by the pupils, such as food eaten raw, and food cooked before eating.

Possible discussion questions are:

"What properties do you like about foods eaten raw?

(Perhaps the discussion of these properties will invariably lead to the idea of freshness as a desired quality).

"Why do you think you have to cook some food?"

(This may provide a good spring board for another activity on cooking food).

Sample Activity 2: Where do you get your food from?

1. Ask a few questions to stimulate the pupils' interest in the activity (Note: You may want to rephrase the questions if you feel they would embarrass some pupils in your class).

   What kind of food do you normally eat?

   What kind of food do the village eat?

   What are the sources of food in the community?

2. Make a list of food available in the village.
3. Where do the food items in the list come from?

   Some pupils may sort them out in this ways.

Food	Source				
	Market	Store	Sea/River	Backyard	Farm
Crab					

Others may think of sorting them out as to whether they come from plants or from animals.

4. Encourage pupils to discuss their findings and solve any problems arising from "contradictory" ideas on certain food sources. For example, fish can either be obtained from a store, market, sea, river or lake.
5. Display some of the pupils' work on the wall. These can be viewed and discussed.
6. As a written activity, pupils could make a short narrative on what they have done.
7. For informal evaluation, ask simple questions orally to summarize what they have learned in their activity.

Sample Activity 3: Why do we cook our food?

A. Groups of pupils may be given about 1/3 cup of grain (or corn or peanuts). The pupils may be asked to cook the food samples in several ways and to observe the food after cooking. What changes have happened to the food? Take the necessary safety precautions in this activity so that pupils will not be harmed. The pupils can put their obsevations in tabulated form. Pupils will share their work with the class.

   Some methods of preparing food in their homes may be discussed.

B. If fish or a fruit can be made available in the classroom, you may present a problem to the pupils through a series of questions like:
   What can you do so that it does not spoil in a short period?
   (Possible answers are:
   Cook it. Put salt on it. Dry it in the sun and so on).

   Are you sure the fish will keep longer, if you do as you suggested?
   Would you like to find out?

You may want to discuss pupils' own plans for a simple activity to answer the problem. What will they do? What will they look for? How often will they make their observations? How can they tell, following their method that the fish/fruit really stays unspoiled for a longer time? (This could lead to a need for control).

A similar activity can be done by using other available inexpensive foodstuffs.

Pupils can be encouraged to do other simple investigation like comparing the results when different amounts of salt are used, or different degrees of drying, or using salt versus the same amount of sugar or using combination, and so on.

Sample Activity 4: Would you let food be wasted?

Make a list of fruit (or vegetable) found in the community or seen in the market at different times of the year. Pupils may show the information they gathered in a table. The table may indicate that some fruits (or vegetables) are found throughout the year, while others are plentiful only in certain months.

Name	Jan.	Feb.	Mar.	Apr.	May	Jun.	Jul.	Aug.	Sep.	Oct.	Nov.	Dec.
A												
B												
C												
D												
E												

Pupils may narrate pleasant experiences about fruits. The discussion can later lead to the wastage commonly observed when fruits (or vegetables) are in season. The teacher may raise a few questions, such as:

How much olives/rambutan/passion fruits/mangoes does a tree produce during the season?

(Can you guess? Can you work it out? Can you keep a count?)

How many do you actually eat? What do you do with the others?

Possible answers are: We sell them. We give them to friends.

Are some fruits (or vegetables) wasted?

How can you keep them from getting spoiled?

Can you ask your parents and other older people about ways of preserving food.

Pupils will bring to school a description of what their mother or other people do at home to preserve some kinds of food, e.g. lime pickle. Pupils may even bring samples to class. Some may be able to get the following information on the effects of preservation.

1. Drying or loss of water helps to keep foods for a longer time.
2. Salt and vinegar improve the keeping qualities of some foods and make them taste better.

Evaluation

Get the pupils into groups. Ask them to display the picture cards of foods in front of them. Get groups select pictures that will fit into the groups of food that the teacher reads out. Evaluate on the cards selected. Get groups to display and discuss. Some questions could be:

1. Select foods that can be eaten raw.
2. Select foods that rot easily.
3. Select fruits/vegetables that are preserved in your locality.
4. Select foods that can be eaten boiled, fried or both.
5. Make a group of foods that is taken in a meal.

As mentioned earlier, the exemplars presented can be used as curriculum models by curriculum developers, science educators, science teachers, and adapted according to the situation where they are in.

Part III

IMPLEMENTING SCIENCE AND TECHNOLOGY FOR ALL: GUIDE TO BETTER POLICY AND PRACTICE FOR TEACHERS

Contents

1

Background

> Science Teachers' Associations should enter into partnership with the United Nations, Intergovernmental Organizations; participate in programmes on Science and Technology education for all.
>
> —*Project 2000⁺, International Forum*

The Advisory Committee on the Renewal of Science and Technology Education in Africa (Okebukola, 1993) take *Science and Technology (S&T) education for all* to be the provision of learning experiences in science and technology to the formal school population, the out-of-school population, the work force (including vast number of functional illiterates) the educated adult population, girls and women that are usually marginalized; and people with special needs in the population. These learning experiences in science and technology, according to Okebukola, are in the form of knowledge, attitudes, skills and values and have to be given to all individuals irrespective of state, gender, creed, political affiliation or other peculiarities.

These views are in consonance with those of the participants at the *World Conference on Education for All in Jomtien, Thailand* in 1990. The participants at the conference agreed that basic education was the foundation for lifelong learning and human development. And shortly after the Jemtien Conference, UNESCO in conjunction with the International Council of

Associations for Science Education, in recognition of the growing need for a scientifically and technologically literate society, especially its contribution to the enhancement of lifelong education, initiated *Project 2000*$^+$. The three-phased project, now entering Phase III, among others, encourages the formation of national task forces involving personnel from government, IGOs (inter-Governmental organizations) and especially, NGOs (non-governmental organizations such as Science Teachers' Associations) of initiate local programmes for greater scientific and technological literacy.

Against the backdrop of Project 2000$^+$, it should not be an overstatement to say that there is a compelling need to work towards the attainment of scientific and technological literacy for all. However, while S&T illiteracy may be said to be a global problem, the fact remains that there is a great disparity in the current level of S&T literacy in the various regions with the balance tilting lopsidedly in favour of the developed nations. For example, a survey conducted by UNICEF revealed that in Nigeria (Okebukola, 1993:26):

- 30 per cent of children are unable to attend primary schools for a host of reasons including socio-economic, cultural and difficulty of access of the schools.
- 77 per cent of the pupils lack textbooks including primary science books
- 47 per cent of the school furniture are inadequate for the use of the pupils.
- 38 per cent of the classrooms have no ceiling.
- 36 per cent of the pupils have no writing materials.
- 3 per cent of the schools have no chalkboard.
- 12 per cent of the pupils sit on the floor for lessons.
- 31 per cent of the teachers observed used no teaching aids.
- 80 per cent of the schools have no equipment and materials for teaching primary science.

But if in their present state, the developed nations are conscientiously pursuing programmes that will lead to further increase in the level of S&T literacy, this should be a 'food for thought' for the developing nations, particularly those in Africa. This concern has been expressed in a number of quarters. For example, while delivering a public lecture at the 33rd Annual conference of the Science Teachers Association of Nigeria, Bajah (1992:17) lamented:

> My burning concern, now, is what will be facing humanity at the turn of the century, and how well we in Nigeria will prepare the young ones to face a world in which human beings will be competing with robots. Trips to outer space will be common place in some parts of the developed world. The computer will organise our work as well as our play ... This is the time to begin to plan ahead so that we can avoid our age-old 'Fire Brigade Approach'.

Prof. Sam Bajah was not alone with this view at the said conference. In fact, delegates to the ICASE/UNESCO/STAN seminar held as a feeder meeting to phase 1 of *Project 2000⁺* as part of the 33rd Annual Conference of STAN were not enthused over the existing level of S&T literacy in Nigeria in particular and Africa in general. Expectedly, STAN proposed a target date of 2057 for the attainment of the goals of project 2000^+ in Nigeria (the date coincides with the centenary celebration of the founding of STAN). Similarly, African delegates to the International Forum of Project 2000^+ in Paris France, July 5-10, 1993, agreed to form *national task forces* for the prosecution of the ideals of the project. In Nigeria, the proposal for the formation of the task force anchored by the STAN President Prof. Uduogie Ivowi, is currently receiving the attention of government.

Of particular significance is the *Declaration* by the participants in the international forum of Project 2000^+ *urging* non-governmental organizations such as *Science Teachers' Associations to:*

- enter into partnership with, and make their knowledge and experience available to, United Nations and other inter-governmental bodies as well as establish innovative programmes in a common effort to achieve the goal of scientific literacy and technological literacy for all; and

- participate in national, regional and international programmes for the enhancement of scientific and technological literacy for the improvement of the quality of life in all societies and for the achievement of sustainable development.

It is this aspect of the *Declaration* (Appendix A), that forms the pivot of this study. Thus, while there is a general consideration of the tenets of scientific and technological literacy, particular cognisance has been taken of the role which Science Teachers' Associations (STAS) could play. Similarly, and udnerstandably, much of the focus is on Africa.

2

National Policies on Science and Technology

Disparities are discernible in national S&T policies. Even so, in Africa, the *African Primary Science Programme* set the pace, leading to integrated approach to S&T teaching in many countries.

Science and Technology (S&T) have consistently been given prominence in the educational policies of most countries. A survey conducted by the United Nations Educational, Scientific and Culture Organization (UNESCO, 1986) has shown that science, technology and mathematics are taught in the schools by several nations though to varying degrees.

Table 1 provides an overview of the percentage of time allotted for science and mathematics in school curricula. Some disparities are discernible. For example, Sierra Leone allocates a dismal 11.3 per cent for Grades 1-2 compared to the averages of 27.4 and 29.2 for Africa and the world respectively.

Table 1: Percentage of time allocated to Science and Mathematics in school curricular

	Grades 1-2	Grades 3-6	Grades 7-9
Botswana	23.5	23.4	27.1
Ethiopia	26.5	26.5	26.0
Ghana	25.4	25.4	23.7
Kenya	17.1	24.8	29.6
Lesotho	19.0	23.4	44.6
Mauritius	20.5	19.0	39.7
Nigeria	39.1	36.3	22.8
Seychelles	26.2	25.5	37.2
Sierra Leone	11.3	18.8	25.9
Tanzania	30.0	25.4	33.3
Zambia	25.7	26.9	26.9
Africa	27.4	30.8	37.0
Arab States	23.8	24.7	26.8
Asia and the Pacific	31.4	27.4	35.9
Europe	30.8	30.9	37.1
Latin America and the Carribbean	30.0	32.7	39.3
World	29.2	29.9	36.3

Source: Adapted from UNESCO (1986).

In Africa, a lot of input was created by the African Primary Science Programme (APSP) and the African Mathematics Programme (AMP). Both Projects were initiated by the Educational Services Incorporated (ESP which later became known as the Education Development Centre, EDC) based in Newton, Massachusetts, U.S.A. Urevbu (1990) reports that the two projects were offshoots of the famous summer study in African Education at the Massachusetts Institute of Technology in 1961.

The African Mathematics Programme, funded by USAID and Ford Foundation, aimed at improving the quality of mathematics teaching and to develop in each participating country a nucleus of people knowledgeable in mathematics and capable of undertaking improvement of mathematics curriculum. By 1969, the AMP had produced a complete textbook series from Primary one to Primary seven (Pupils books and accompanying teachers' guides); a manual for teacher training, basic concepts in mathematics and two alternative series for secondary schools—67 volumes of prototype materials. The series have been criticized for heavy reliance on language (particularly descriptive terminology), a constant pre-occupation with classroom and textbook centred examples at the expense of using the rich mathematical resources in the immediate environment, as well as the rigid, class by class progression of texts. The series were used in several English speaking countries including Nigeria.

The African Primary Science Programme (APSP) on the other hand was initiated in February 1965 at Kano, Nigeria. Like the AMP, the APSP was founded by the USAID and the Ford Foundation. It aimed to enable the African child to:

- be familiar with a variety of biological, physical and man-made phenomena in the world around him;
- show interest in further exploration of the world around him on his own initiative;
- acquire ability to find out for himself—to see problems and to be able to set about resolving it for himself;
- demonstrate confidence in his own ability to find out for himself and do things for himself;
- acquire ability to share in a common development of knowledge (SEPA, 1975 in Urevbu, 1990).

By 1970, the APSA was able to produce fifty units, six films and some apparatus. Appendix B lists some of the titles produced by APSP.

However, the management of the APSP was in 1970 taken over by eleven participating governments under the auspices of the Science Education Programme for Africa (SEPA) with headquarters in Accra, Ghana (Yoloye, 1978). Participating countries in SEPA included Botswana, The Gambia, Ghana, Ethiopia, Kenya, Lesotho, Liberia, Malawi, Nigeria, Sierra Leone,

Tanzania, Swaziland, Uganda and Zambia. SEPA was founded by African Governments, USAID, UNESCO and Carnegie Corporation of New York. The objectives of SEPA included:

- facilitation of excellence and relevance in the learning of science at all educational levels in Africa;
- development of manpower resources in science curriculum development;
- development of instructional material for teacher training institutions and for schools;
- development of instructional material for teacher training institutions and for schools;
- promotion of information exchange.

SEPA's approach to science education took the view that science is a medium through which a child might develop his natural curiosity, his powers of observation and enquiry, and constructive attitudes to problem-solving and decision. In its handbook for teachers of science (Appendix C), SEPA (1978) places a high premium on integration.

It is, therefore, not unexpected that even though SEPA is virtually moribund, the current approach to primary science in most African countries as Chisman (1988) reports, is, invariably an integrated one—a reflection of the philosophy and practice of the Science Education Programme for Africa (SEPA). In fact, Chisman contends that some of the original units and teaching materials are still in use as part of the primary school courses in some countries. This has necessitated an overview of current science education policies in a few countries in Africa, namely, Ghana, Nigeria and Zambia.

Ghana

The current Education system for Ghana which came into effect in 1986, provides for in nine-year basic First Cycle education made up of six years primary plus three-years Junior Secondary, compulsory for all children of school-going age. The second cycle appears only in one phase, the three year senior secondary school, while the third cycle includes the universities, polytechnics and diploma colleges (see Appendix D).

A spiral primary science curriculum has been designed with the aim, among others, of providing an atmosphere in which pupils are sufficiently stimulated and encouraged to become well informed, capable of using their hands and of doing clear logical thinking. According to Ajeyalemi (1990), the Junior Secondary School Science syllabus, developed in 1987, provides a system of science course such that all pupils, whatever their academic abilities and career intentions, receive an appropriate science education.

In Ghanaian Secondary Schools (Second Cycle) General Integrated Science is a compulsory subject. Other subjects include Biology, Chemistry, Physics, General Science, Additional General Science, Agricultural Science, Home Science (Home Economics) and Health Science, out of which a student can select two in the last three years of secondary education. Ajeyalemi (1990) has reported that the course contents for these subjects are defined by syllabuses issued by the West African Examinations Council (WAEC) which has imposed conditions to ensure practical orientation of the science courses.

Tertiary (Third Cycle) institutions prepare science teachers, engineers, agriculturists, medical officers and scientists with most programmes modelled after those in British universities, for obvious reasons.

Junior Secondary Schools teach technology in order to promote skills that will familiarize the students with technology, science and various vocations (Ministry of Education, and Culture, Ghana, 1987). At the secondary level, objective of technology education include the production of skilled, middle-level manpower for industry and commerce. Technical education at the tertiary level is carried out in the University of Science and Technology, Kumasi and the polytechnics.

Nigeria

Nigeria runs a 6-3-3-4 system of education (Appendix E) anchored on the need to integrate the individual into a sound and effective citizen and the provision of equal educational opportunities for all citizens at the primary, secondary and tertiary levels, both inside and outside the formal school system (Federal Republic of Nigeria, 1981). Some of the general objectives of primary education are:

- the inculcation of permanent literacy and numeracy, and the ability to communication effectively;
- the laying of a sound basis for scientific and reflective thinking;
- developing in the child the ability to adapt to his changing environment;
- giving the child opportunities for developing manipulative skills that will enable him to function effectively in the society within the limits of his capacity.

A core curriculum for primary science (see Appendix F) has been developed with the objectives of enabling the Nigerian child to:

- observe and explore the environment;
- develop basic science process skills, including observing, collecting, manipulating, classifying, communicating, inferring, hypothesizing, interpreting data and formulating models;
- develop functional knowledge of science concepts and principles;
- explain simple natural phenomena;
- develop a scientific attitude, including critical reflection and objectivity;
- apply the skills and knowledge gained through science to solving everyday problems in his environment;
- develop self confidence and self-reliance through problem solving activities in science;
- develop a functional awareness of and sensitivity to the orderliness and beauty in nature (Federal Ministry of Education, 1981 (a):8).

At the Junior Secondary level, Integrated Science is a compulsory subject. The core curriculum for integrated science (Federal Ministry of Education, 1981 (b):3) adopts a *thematic* approach and is aimed at enabling the pupils to acquire the following skills:

(i) Observing carefully and thoroughly.

(ii) Reporting completely and accurately what is observed.

(iii) Organizing information acquired.

(iv) Generalizing on the basis of acquired information.

(v) Predicting as a result of the generalizations.

(vi) Designing experiments (including control where necessary) to check predictions.

(vii) Using models to explain phenomena where appropriate.

(viii) Continuing the process of inquiry when new data do not conform to predictions.

Introductory technology is also taught in the Junior Secondary.

At the Senior Secondary level, science is taught as separate subjects of Agricultural Science, Biology, Chemistry and Physics. Mathematics and technical subjects are also taught. The Physics curriculum for Senior Secondary Schools, for instance aims, among others, at providing the student with basic literacy in physics for functional living in society.

A national Agency that co-ordinates all curriculum development efforts, *The Nigerian Educational Research and Development Council (NERDC)* was established in 1988 through a merger of four bodies—the Nigerian Educational Research Council (NERC), the Comparative Education study and Adaptation Centre (CESAC); the Nigerian Book Development Council (NBDC) and the Nigerian Language Centre (NLC).

In addition to the curriculum documents, Nigeria has two other important documents on S&T. These are the *National Policy on Science and Technology* as well as the *National Policy on Science and Engineering Infrastructure.* The objectives of the Nigerian Science and Technology Policy (Federal Republic Nigeria, 1986:10) are to:

- increase public awareness in S&T and their vital role in national development and well-being;
- direct S&T efforts along identified national goals;

- promote the translation of S&T results into actual goods and services;
- create increasing and maintain an indigenous S&T base through research development;
- motivate creative output in S&T;
- increase and strengthen theoretical and practical scientific base in the society; and
- increase and strengthen the technological base of the nation.

On the other hand, the National Policy on Science and Engineering Infrastructure (Federal Republic of Nigeria, 1992) provides for the prosecution of a Science and Engineering Infrastructure Development Programme (S-EIDP) aimed at catalysing the emergence of endogenous capacity able to supply a progressively increasing percentage of delivery/production systems needed to support the efficient production of goods and services locally. Consequently, a National Agency for Science and Engineering Infrastructure (NASENI) has been established. In the implementation by NASENI of its science and engineering infrastructure development mandate, four subjects have continuously attracted attention, namely:

- manpower development;
- science, engineering, and technology information services;
- science and engineering infrastructure development complexes; and
- independent infrastructural industries.

Zambia

In Zambia, the aim of education is to develop the potential of each citizen to the full for his own well being as well as that of society and for selfless service to his fellow men. Consequently, the nation's Educational Reform Document (Ministry of Education, Youth and Sports, Zambia, 1977) provides for a three-stage structure of education, namely:

- Basic education in grades 1-9.
- Second stage education—secondary school (vocational training) 3 years;
- Third stage education.

The Reform Document also provides for a basic science education that will enable the pupil to master useful practical skills which they would apply in life in various ways, adopt a scientific approach and attitude, observe, collect information, draw conclusions and apply what they know. A new environmental Science syllabus which forms an integrated course of science for grades 1-9 has replaced the old syllabuses of primary science and junior secondary science. Science courses are also taught in the secondary schools while technology education takes place mainly in institutions of higher learning. A British Council project—the Zambia Mathematics and Science Teacher Education Project (ZAMSTEP)—has helped in no small measure in science teacher training. ZAMSTEP provides, among others, a secondary science and mathematics upgrading programme, open to teachers with college Diplomas plus at least five years teaching experience.

Of special significance is the role of the Junior Engineers. Technicians and Scientists (JETS) of Zambia. Established in 1966, the main objectives of JETS include the popularization of science and technology among secondary school pupils. In pursuance of this, JETS clubs here been established in secondary and primary schools. A 'JETS and, of, ZAMBIA' magazine has also been published.

3

Science Teachers' Associations (STAS)

The NSTA, ASE are the leading STAS in the world. However, in Africa, STAN is the most virile STA, being the only STA in the region to have a permanent Secretariat.

Worldwide, Science Teachers' Associations (STAS) have played significant roles in STME. However, before a more detailed consideration of the role of STAS (especially in Africa) can be made, it would be necessary to provide brief profiles of some STAS. A comprehensive list of STAS is given in Appendix G.

National Science Teachers Association, U.S.A.

The National Science Teachers Association (NSTA) is the largest non-profit educational organization in the world dedicated to improving science education at all levels—pre-school through college. Founded in 1944, NSTA has a membership of abcut 50,000 which includes science teachers, science supervisors, administrators, scientists, business and industry representatives, and others involved in science education. NSTA offers the following services: four journals *(Science and Children, Science Scope, The Science Teacher and The Journal of College Science Teaching)*, a newspaper *(NSTA Reports!)*, regional and national conventions, awards programmes, teacher training workshops, educational tours, an employment registry, professional certification, and position statements on a variety of science education issues. The Association has, for instance, published a *Lead paper on Science and Technology Education for the 21st century.* The Association believes that (a) scientific literacy must be a major goal of science education worldwide and for all children and (b) national and international professional organizations and agencies and institutions must work together to ensure effective science teaching around the world (NSTA, 1990).

To exchange ideas with international colleagues, NSTA held its first international conference in Moscow in 1991 and the second international conference near Mexico city in 1993. NSTA and its British counterpart, the Association for Science Education, conduct a lecture exchange each year. In addition, NSTA has special representatives serving on the Executive Committee of ICASE. NSTA staff and members attend conferences and meetings of science and/or education organizations, institutions, and agencies around the world. It welcomes international members and invites international colleagues to attend its conventions. The NSTA has set up task forces on:

- Articulation with school Administrators.
- Child Advocacy.
- Developing a Research Agenda.
- Developing a Science Education Research Database for teachers.
- Developing standards for identification of courses for science credit.
- Elementary Scope, Sequence and Co-ordination Project Development.
- An Expanded view of Assessment.
- NSTA/NCTM Areas of Co-ordination.
- NSTA Sponsored sessions at Non-NSTA Conventions/ Meetings.
- NSTA visions for the 1990's and beyond.
- Past Presidents.
- Science Teacher Professionalization.

According to NSTA (1993b) of the Association was expected to have purchased a new headquarters building in Arlington, Virginia, a suburb of Washington D.C., by June 1993. The four storey red brick office building, located at 1840 Wilson Boulevard costs US $5.45 million. The building offers a three-level underground parking garage for 138 vehicles and outside parking for 16 vehicles. At present, NSTA plans to occupy all of the third floor and parts of the first and second floors. The remaining space will be rented to tenants. NSTA is purchasing the building to consolidate all of its operations—once scattered in three locations and later at two facilities in Washington, D.C., and Arlington, Virginia—into one building.

The NSTA headquarters is headed by an Executive Director. The Association has a Board of Directors with the President serving for one year—two other years as elect- and retiring-. There are Directors for the following Divisions: Preschool and Elementary School, Middle level, High School, College, Research, Supervision, Teachers Education, and Multicultural Education.

Association for Science Education, United Kingdom

The Association for Science Education (ASE) located at College Lane, Halfield, Herts, U.K., was constituted under a Trust Deed dated 5 January, 1963. The objects of the Association are to promote education by:

- improving the teaching of science;
- providing an authoritative medium through which opinions of teachers of science may be expressed on educational matters;
- affording means of communication among all persons and bodies of persons concerned what the teaching of science in particular and with education in general.

The ASE is governed by a council comprising: Association chair, Regional representatives, Immediate Past chair, Chair-elect, Active Trustee, Treasure, 4 co-opted members and the General Secretary (in attendance). The General Secretary, a full time employee, represents the Association nationally and liaises with a wide range of similar professional Associations and industrial and commercial organizations. He is responsible to Council for the day-to-day running of the Association.

The Association has three groups—interest, service and tasks groups—working independently to advance the aims of the Association. Interest groups (e.g. Science Advisory Teachers Group) support the interest of sub-sets of members with a self-defined brief, but to the mutual advantages of the Group and the Association. Service groups (e.g. The Primary Science Committee), are established by the Association to provide a continuing contribution towards its (ASE'S) work and effectiveness. Task Groups (e.g. Post-16 Working Party) are established by the ASE to tackle a clearly defined task.

The ASE has a number of periodicals. These include the *School Science Review, Primary Science* and *Education In Science*. In also has an insurance scheme which protects individual members in the U.K. against any civil action taken against them in the courts for the death of, or injury to, any person and loss of, or damage to, property either happening, or caused, during the performance of members' professional duties. In terms of scope of activities, the ASE is indeed, a model in Europe and second only to the Washington, D.C.-based NSTA in the world.

Science Teachers Association of Nigeria (STAN)

Established on 21 June 1957, STAN has the following aims:

- To promote co-operation among science teachers in Nigeria with a view to raising the standard of science education in the country.
- To provide a forum for discussion by science teachers on matters of common interest.
- To help science teachers keep in touch with developments in science and its applications to industry and commerce.
- To popularize science.
- To co-operate with and affiliate to other societies and bodies with related interest.

The functions of the Association which was about 1000 members include the following:

- Encouragement of the interchange of ideas among science teachers through meetings, conferences, workshops (see Appendix H for schedule of workshops for 1994), exhibition of science materials, books and periodicals.

- The publication of the Journal of STAN, position papers, STAN bulletin and conference proceedings.
- Interaction with all bodies concerned with science and science education.

STAN is administered by three separate but mutually supportive organs: the Annual General Meeting, The Governing Council and the National Executive Committee (STAN, 1991). It has ten subject panels: Agricultural Science, Biology, Chemistry, Integrated Science, Mathematics, Physics, Primary Science, Science, Technology & Society, Teacher Education and Technology Education. There is a branch in each of the nation's 30 States as well as a Federal Capital territory branch. The Association maintains a Secretariat at the premises of Government College, Ibadan, Oyo State headed by a full-time Administrative Secretary whose functions include, among others, the effective day-to-day running of the Secretariat and keeping the Association's books and records. Though its Secretariat is yet to be fully equipped, STAN is the only STA in Africa "with a permanent Secretariat and vehicles, and it's been a leading light in the various attempts to develop an African super-association, its publications, courses and conferences being highly regarded" (Deeson, 1993:1). The African Forum for children's Literacy in Science and Technology, in the May 1992 edition of its newsletter also describes STAN as a 'successful model'.

Ghana Association of Science Teachers (GAST)

GAST was formed in 1956 to promote science teaching in Ghana. The Association has a number of subject Panels (Biology, Chemistry, Elementary Science, Junior Secondary School, Laboratory Technicians, Physics, and Teacher Training). It also has regional groupings: Brong-Ahafo, Central, Greater Accra/ Eastern, Northern, Upper East, Upper West, Volta and Western Region. Each region has its offices but overall co-ordination is the responsibility of a national executive comprising President, Secretary, Assistant Secretary (2), Treasurer, Public Relations Officer, Science Fair Organiser, Immediate Past President,

Curriculum Review and Development Chairman, Chairman, Publication Committee and Chairman, Instructional Materials and Equipment Committee. There are no full-time staff and no permanent Secretariat.

Zambia Association for Science Education (ZASE)

ZASE was inaugurated in 1966 with the task of improving the teaching of science in schools. It has published teaching notes for teachers and has compiled a large stock of examination papers. It organizes conferences where exhibition of laboratory equipment and books is carried out. However, its bid to buy a group insurance for members failed due to non-payment of dues by members. Still, ZASE has made immense input through its involvement in the activities of the JETS of Zambia and in some international activities such as the 1st African Sub-Regional Science Olympiad held in Lusaka, Zambia in 1990. Its inability to establish a permanent secretariat has meant that much of its activities revolve around personalities. The ICASE Secretariat for instance, has lost contact (temporarily?) with ZASE following the death of the Secretary General of ZASE Mr. T. Varghese.

New Zealand Science Teachers Association (NZSTA)

NZSTA is a national organization made up of 15 regional Science Teachers' Associations under the leadership of a national executive elected for a period of two years. It is committed to:

- providing information and advise to teachers of science on resources, teaching methods and curriculum;
- promoting the development of effective links between teachers of science in primary, intermediate, and secondary schools, to enhance the quality of learning in science at all levels.

The NZSTA has a Working Party developing guidelines for Professional Standards and negotiating a contract with the Ministry of Education to set up Professional Standards for Science Teachers. It is also developing teaching resources to complement the new science curriculum. According to Anne Hume, the President of NZSTA, this is their first commercial activity. He is hopeful of expanding the area in future. At the 1993 AGM, the NZSTA voted to form a National Executive with a permanent paid Secretariat. It has the support of the Royal Society of New Zealand in this regard. The NZSTA is a member of the Society. It publishes a journal *NZ Science Teacher* three times a year and a newsletter about five times a year. Biennial conferences are also organized. The membership of the NZSTA is about 500.

Science Teachers Association of Singapore

The Association was formed in 1965. It is an Association for science and mathematics teachers and has seven subject committees—biology, chemistry, physics, general science, maths (primary), maths (secondary) and science (primary). Recent publications include a handbook of practical activities in the Biology (plus slides); Chemistry board games; a booklet on process skills test items for primary schools. The Association produces yearly three issues of its bulletin and its journal *SCIENATAS*. Activities include involvement in the Singapore science fortnight with Science Centres and especially the science camp and science fair, Primary Science Club activities (young scientist badge award scheme) and Questa (for secondary school students). It is involved with subject curriculum committees and contributes to the primary and lower secondary subject groups. It is involved in vetting science materials for schools. The Association raised the idea of making senior teachers hold positions of Head of Department which was implemented in 1985. It assists in courses for teachers.

Sri Lankan Association of Science and Mathematics Educators (SLASME)

SLASME was formed in 1984 to develop and improve the quality of science education in Sri Lanka, to share knowledge and trends in science and science education, provide a forum for people of similar interests to meet and have fellowship. The Association is not currently involved in curriculum development, but is able to put suggestions to the Ministry of Education e.g. introduction of continuous assessment in Sri Lanka. Activities include a regular newsletter 4 times a year, meetings 3 times per year (in a rural area) and committee meetings very month (in Kandy or Colombo). There is emphasis on increasing membership by getting media to help publicise the annual meeting. SLASME is also involved in supplying materials for a weekly commercial science newspaper.

Hong Kong Association of Science and Mathematics Educators (HKASME)

HKASME was founded in 1964 to promote science and mathematics education in Hong Kong. Its membership is about 1000 and is affiliated to the Association for Science Education in the United Kingdom. Its aims are to improve the quality of science and mathematics education, to provide a means of communication for science and mathematics teachers, provide a medium for teacher to express opinions and extend the professionalization of teachers. Activities include lectures, seminars, workshops and field trips. It also sells low cost equipment, publishes a newsletter monthly and a journal twice per year. It is heavily involved with the work of the curriculum development committee (CDC) and the Hong Kong Examinations Authority (HKEA). Special functions include an annual conference each June.

Nepal Science Education Society (NESES)

The NESES was established in 1991 as a non-profit organization of science teacher educators, science teachers and those interested in the dissemination, promotion and innovation of science education in Nepal. NESES aims to promote and propagate the teaching and learning of Science from primary to higher education, to disseminate the importance of science education, to promote the exchange of innovative ideas among members institutions, to develop co-operation among those involved in science education, and to contribute to science education policies, planning, implementation and evaluation.

Brunei Association of Science Educators (BASE)

BASE was formed in 1977 and its activities can be divided into 2 parts; those for teachers and those for students. For teachers, BASE organizes seminars, work-shops, talks, courses (e.g. on computers). The main target has been secondary school teachers, but more emphasis is now being placed in helping primary teachers. For students, a number of activities are organised e.g. the science project competition, the science quiz and a 3D art photo competition. BASE publishes a journal once per year (if possible) and a newsletter 3 times per year.

Korean Science Education Association (KSEA)

KSEA was formed in 1970. It holds national conventions twice each year, one in the summer vacation and the other in the winter vacation. Science educators are sometimes invited from foreign countries. In the summer, a science camp is also organized for teachers to exchange ideas on science teaching. Students also attend the science camps.

Umbrella Organizations

Apart from the Science Teachers' Association listed above, there are a number of regional and international organizations which have contributed immensely to STM education. These include the:

West African Association of Science Educators (WAAST)

WAAST was established in 1977 to, among others, establish an all-embracing Union of the STAS in West Africa with a view to promoting interchange of information and ideas about professional matters. The Association became inactive after a few years due to lack of funds.

Forum of African Science Educators (FASE)

FASE was inaugurated in Lagos, Nigeria in 1980 under the auspices of the Science Teachers Association of Nigeria. It sought to:

- promote co-operation among STAS in Africa.
- encourage the formation of STAS in Africa.
- promote good science teaching in schools in Africa.
- co-operate and/or affiliate with any organization whose aims and objectives are in accord with the above objectives.

Now becoming virtually moribund, FASE drew its membership from STAS in Botswana Ethiopia, Gambia, Ghana, Kenya, Lesotho, Malawi, Nigeria, Sierra Leone, Swaziland, Tanzania, Uganda, Zambia and Zimbabwe. Its President is still Prof. O.C. Nwana, a consultant with the Nigerian Educational

Research and Development Council, Abuja. However, there is yet no replacement for its late Secretary General/Treasurer Mr. Thomas Varghese of Kitwe, Zambia.

The experience of FASE (and to some extent WAAST) is a sad one. Its activities are virtually paralysed due to financial constraints.

African Network for Research and Development in Science and Technology Education (ANERSTE)

ANERSTE was formed in January 1993 by African delegates who attended an international conference in Israel. Immediate activities of the Network include publication of the *ARNESTE Newsletter* and *Who's Who in Science and Technology Education in Africa*. The group met again in Paris, France, in July 1993 during the International Forum of Project 2000^{+} and informed delegates about its progress so far.

African Forum For Children's Literacy in Science and Technology

This *Forum* is an informal association of African educators, scientists, technologists, media specialists and international resource people. It is financed and supported by the *Rockefeller Foundation*. The Forum has an Advisory Board that overseas policy, and a Grants Committee which recommends proposals to the Rockefeller Foundation. Its Secretariat is housed in the Regional Rockefeller Foundation office in Nairobi, Kenya.

The Secretariat solicits proposals and recommends them for peer review before presentation to the Grants Committee. A *resource bank* is being established at the Secretariat for use by science educators throughout the continent. The Forum has for example, given a grant to the *Lesotho Science and Mathematics Teachers Association* to publish its journal for a year.

Commonwealth Association of Science, Technology and Mathematics Educators (CASTME)

Inaugurated in 1974, CASTME is supported and funded by the Commonwealth Foundation, Commonwealth Secretariat, Marlborough House, Pall Mall, London. It has a Council headed by a Chairman with the Chief Programme Officer (STME) at the

Commonwealth Secretariat as the Honorary Secretary. *CASTME* has an *awards scheme* which is intended to encourage teaching of the social aspects of STM with particular reference to third world countries in the Commonwealth. The scope of the awards is interpreted broadly and the phrase 'social aspects' includes the relevance of the STM curricula to local needs and conditions and also to the impact of technology, industry and agriculture on the local community. According to CASTME (1992), its strength lies in its ability to attract the commitment of specialists from all parts of the world.

International Council of Associations for Science Education (ICASE)

ICASE was established in 1993 to extend and improve education in S&T for all children and youth throughout the world by assisting STAS that are members. It is particularly concerned in providing a means of communication among individual STAS and to foster co-operative efforts to improve S&T education. Activities of ICASE include:

- publishing a journal *Science Education International;*
- issuing a *Directory* of STAS worldwide;
- publishing the *Who's Who in STM Education around the world;*
- disseminating information about activities of national and regional groups;
- arranging regional activities in association with other organizations such as UNESCO;
- promoting exchanges of science personnel;
- using its endeavours to promote research in science education.

The Governing Body of ICASE is the General Assembly consisting of one delegate from each member Association together with any members of the Executive Committee who are not delegates. The Executive Committee comprises President, Past-President, President-elect, and up to eight members elected on a geographical basis. The Executive Secretary, Treasurer and Editor are appointed by the Executive Committee. ICASE is financed, in part, by annual fees from member associations, institutions, foundations, and companies. But because it is *not a Foundation* (and is *not* funded directly by any Foundation), *it has no means of assisting member associations financially*. ICASE has no permanent Secretariat. The full list of member association as of August 1993 is as shown in Appendix G.

4

Role of Science Teachers' Associations

> A powerful kind of organization that stimulated development in science education in practically all the countries was the association of science teachers. Everyone of the countries studied had such an association in one form or another. There were variations in the magnitude of contributions made by these organizations from country to country.
>
> —*Bajah and Yoloye (1981)*

As earlier stated, Science Teachers' Associations (STAS) have been known to play significant roles in STME. Silber (in King 1991:47) sees STAS as performing the following functions:

- Communications—Journals, conferences, publications.
- Representation—To teachers and government, liaison with other groups and participations in international activities.
- Services—continuing education, employment, low cost equipment and out-of-school activities.
- Leadership—Curriculum development, teacher benefit, guidance on new developments in science education.

In fact, STAS such as NSTA and ASE have had tremendous influence on STM education not only in their countries but also in foreign nations. For instance, Holbrook and Chisman (1988) report that in the U.K. the ASE was responsible for producing *Science in Society* and *Science in a Social Context* courses.

In *Africa*, Bajah & Yoloye (1981:27) while evaluating *Science Education Programme for Africa* had this to say:

> A powerful kind of organization that stimulated development in science education in practically all the countries was the association of science teachers. Everyone of the countries studied had such an association in one form or another. There were variations in the magnitude of contributions made by these organizations from country to country. Gambia, Liberia and Lesotho report negligible contribution. At the other end the Ghanaian and Nigerian associations have exerted tremendous influence on the training of science teachers, the curriculum, and educational policies. STAN in Nigeria, produced its own books in integrated science for the first two years of secondary schools.

Others (Sharma, 1974; Bajah, 1983, Dienye and Gbamanja, 1990; King, 1991) are in general agreement with the above assertion. According to King, the achievement of STAN in the pursuit of quality education in science in Nigeria is a record of which it should be justly proud. This is because, STAN has produced curriculum materials and support textbooks which have gone a long way towards the establishment and maintenance of STM.

In general, the STAS in Africa have made contributions in STEME in the following areas:

(a) Curriculum Development

STAN is probably the leader in this respect. In 1968, a request was made to STAN by the West African Examinations Council (WAEC) to make recommendations on the review and improvement of the then GCE 'O' level science syllabuses. A revision was thought necessary due to developments in science education all over the world. Consequently, STAN set up four curriculum development committees, one each in Biology, Chemistry, Physics and Mathematics. The project was funded by the *Ford Fundation* (through the Comparative Education study and

Adaptation Centre CESAC), *Curriculum Renewal and Educational Development Overseas* (CREDO) through the British Council. Support in the form of curriculum materials was received from UNESCO and from Longman (Nigeria) publishing company.

Later on, additional Committee was set up to take care of integrated science. The publication of Curriculum Development Newsletter No.1 (STAN, 1970a) meant that things could not be the same again in Nigeria with respect to science teaching. In a *Foreword* to the newsletter, the then General secretary of STAN Rev. P.S. Samuel (STAN 1970a:3) said, *inter alia*:

> The need for curriculum Reform in Science Education in Nigeria has been felt by the members of the Association for some time and especially since the great Curriculum Reform movements, such as B.S.C.S., P.S.S.C., Chemstudy and C.B.A. in the United States, the Nuffield Teaching Project in the United Kingdom and the work of the Scottish Education Department, began to influence the general educational atmosphere everywhere. However, professional associations are seldom strong enough financially or sufficiently strong enough to carry out such important task alone. The Science Teachers Association of Nigeria nevertheless felt that it was time to do something about the development of a new science teaching curriculum for our schools ... We hope that this is the beginning of a long and important process and we invite comments, criticisms and suggestions on the contents of our work so that we may improve upon it in future. With this hope and prayer, we present the first *fruits* of our Curriculum Development work to teachers and other science educators.

The document proposed that the integrated science course should enable the Nigerian child to:

- be *actively involved* in the learning process;
- develop the motivation and ability to work and think in an *independent fashion;*
- *recall* information and experiences;
- *devise* schemes for solving problems;
- *use* and classify given information;
- *apply* previous knowledge to new situation;
- *interpret* information showing evidence of *judgement* and *assessment;*

- *communicate* selectively and effectively;
- *relate* his experiences in each subject area to other areas and to live in his society.

Accordingly, the course envisaged that the following skills would be acquired by the child:

- *Observing* carefully and thoroughly.
- *Reporting* completely and accurately what is observed.
- *Organising* information acquired by the above process.
- *Generalising* on the basis of acquired information.
- *Predicting* as a result of these generalizations.
- *Designing* experiments (including controls were necessary) to *check* these predictions.
- *Using models* to explain phenomena where appropriate.
- *Continuing the process* of inquiry when new data do not conform to predictions.

The course, initially planned for two years (Fig. 1), is now a three-year course following the introduction of the 6-3-3-4 system of education in Nigeria. The present course has the following themes:

- You as a living thing.
- You and your home.
- Living components of the environment.
- Saving your energy.
- Controlling the environment.

A spiral arrangement is adopted for each theme.

Following the publication of the Curriculum Development Newsletter No. 1, three others were subsequently published:

- Curriculum Development Newsletter No. 2: Chemistry Syllabus (STAN, 1970b).
- Curriculum Development Newsletter No. 3: Biology Syllabus (STAN, 1971a).

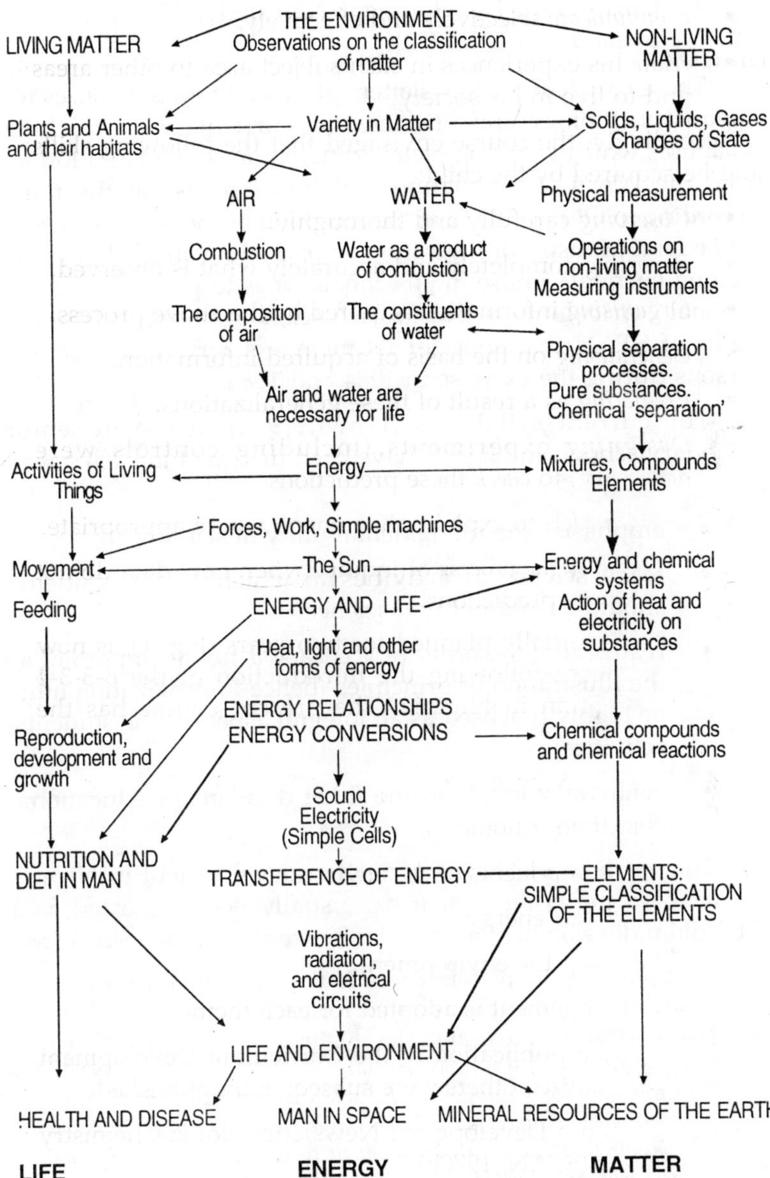

Figure 1. Integrated Science: A course for the first two years of Nigerian Secondary Schools A Flow Chart of the Outline Content

- Curriculum Development Newsletter No. 4: Physics Syllabus (STAN, 1972).

These Curriculum Newsletters produced new syllabuses for Chemistry, Biology and Physics. The curricula were teaching syllabuses which were completely different in content and format from the WAEC Examination Syllabuses in use at the time. According to Otuka (1993), at the inception of the 6-3-3-4 system, the Federal Ministry of Education embarked on streamlining the existing curricula in use in all schools so as to produce a single national curriculum content in each science subject. It is to the credit of STAN that some of its members served as resource persons during the exercise in 1984 and 1985.

The current syllabuses (Ivowi, 1990) in use in senior secondary schools in Nigeria have been designed in such a way as to:

- emphasize the fundamental unity of science;
- teach science as activities to which extent, students should *do* and not *read* science;
- realize that the order of accuracy is not as important as the illustration of principles (hence improvization must be highly practised as an integral aspect of the students' activities);
- evaluate students in the three domains of educational objectives.

The work of STAN in curriculum development in Nigeria has been so pervasive that it has usually been regarded as a curriculum development agency. In the words of Ivowi (1993:353):

> In appraising the performances of the curriculum development agencies (in Nigeria), five such bodies, namely, the Nigerian Educational Research and Development Council, West African Examinations Council, National Teachers Institute, National Commission for Colleges of Education and the *Science Teachers Association of Nigeria have been singled out. STAN, a professional association that has contributed much to curriculum development in Nigeria is here regarded as a curriculum development agency*. It is a very typical and foremost example of such a professional association in Nigeria.

association in Nigeria.

(b) Production of Textbooks

A number of STAS have been involved in the production of textbooks for use by pupils and teachers. The *Zambia Association for Science Education* (ZASE) has produced a series of *Teaching Notes* for the Junior Secondary School Leaving Examination in General Science. The handouts are published and distributed by the Curriculum Development Centre of the Ministry of Education.

These notes (Nwana, 1980) which have been written by classroom teachers have dealt with such topics as Water, Air, the Sun, the Universe, Life, Force and Energy. They are an invaluable supplement to existing texts in a effort to make science practical and relevant. The notes are moulded out of the Unit Plan idea and each topic or content thereof has the intended teaching outcomes quite clearly spelt out for the guidance of the teacher.

The *Ghana Association of Science Teachers (GAST)* has also created a lot of impact on the production of textual materials GAST has published, Core Science Biology, Chemistry and Physics textbooks for Senior Secondary Schools. The books are produced in collaboration with Macmillan Education Ltd. and Unimax Publishers and are based on the syllabuses drawn up by the Ministry of Education. Each book follows a rational teaching plan covering the syllabus in the approved sequence.

However, by far, the greatest and most remarkable contribution in the area of textbook production by STAS in Africa is from the *Science Teachers Association of Nigeria (STAN).* Following the successful production of an Integrated Science Curriculum by STAN, a panel of authors was constituted to write Integrated Science textbooks for students and teachers. The major writing effort took place at the Conference Centre, University of Ibadan, in September 1970. According to STAN (1971b:iv) *'the seminars which preceded the actual writing should be properly recorded and studied as a successful model for achieving an integration of knowledge and methodology.'* It is worth noting that the STAN Integrated Science writing team combined the basic requirement for expertise, with broad geographical representation. A two-year course comprising Pupils' Textbooks, Pupils' Workbooks (for practical work) and Teachers' Guides was produced. First published in 1971, the books have since been revised and restructured into a three-year course comprising Pupils Textbooks, Pupils' Workbooks and Teachers' Guides. Between 1971 and 1993, several other titles have been published by the Association. Below is a full list of textbooks published by the Association:

Publisher: Heinemann Educational Books (Nig) PLC

Titles: Nigerian Integrated Science Project (New Edition) Pupils' Textbooks 1-3

Nigerian Integrated Science Project (New Edition) Pupils' Workbooks 1-3.

Nigerian Integrated Science Project (New Edition) Teachers' Guides

Chemistry for Senior Secondary Schools

Biology for Senior Secondary Schools

Physics for Senior Secondary Schools

Publishers: University Press PLC

Titles: Primary Science, Pupils' Books 1-6

Primary Science, Teachers' Guides 1-2

Primary Science, Work Book 1

Publishers: Longman Nigeria PLC

Titles: Science Teachers' Handbook

Agricultural Science for Junior Secondary Schools, Books 1-3

By August 1994, other titles are due for publications. These are the *STAN Mathematics for Junior Secondary Schools Book 1-3 with Teachers' Guides* to be published by University Press PLC and the *STAN Agricultural Science Textbook for Senior Secondary Schools* to be published by Logman Nigeria PLC. It is worth nothing that some of the books written by STAN are used by some other countries.

An interesting dimension to textbook writing by STAS in Africa has been that some of the members of these STAS have through their experience in the activities of the Association, acquired competencies in book writing. In Nigeria, Prof. Sam Bajah, a fellow and Past President of STAN has been a renowned author. His book, *Teaching Integrated Science Creatively* (Bajah, 1983), has continued to serve as a useful companion for student teachers, science educators, administrators and researchers. This book is currently undergoing revision. In conjunction with Anthony Youdeowei, Prof. Bajah in 1982 published a series on Primary Science that has helped in no small measure in revolutionising science education in Nigeria.

The course (Bajah and Youdeowei, 1987) is presented in the form of six Pupils' Textbooks, one for each year of primary schooling. There are two accompanying Teachers' Guides. One Teachers' Guide covers Textbooks 1-3 while the other covers Textbooks 4-6. The series is also currently being revised to take care of the current requirement of the Primary Science Syllabus. Prof. Bajah is also currently being engaged in developing a pool of relevant *popular science series for 6-12 year-old in Africa.* The project involves a package of video to accompany the series. Focused on the objectives of Project 2000$^+$, the series should attract the attention of such agencies as UNESCO, the *African Forum for Children's Literacy in Science and Technology* and the *Commonwealth Foundation.* Like Prof. Bajah, many others have used their experience in writing individual texts. The current President of STAN, Prof. Uduogie Ivowi, is one of them. In his newly published book, Ivowi (1993:1) has this to say:

> My involvement with curriculum development in Nigeria started in 1968 when I was elected a member of STAN Curriculum Development Committee that produced the STAN syllabuses in Integrated Science and Physics. I also served on the STAN Committee that produced the Nigerian Integrated Science Project (NISP). Science then, I have played prominent roles in a number of other curriculum projects.

Such has been the impact to book writing by STAS in Africa. The *multiplier effect* has indeed been remarkable.

Elsewhere, Ivowi (1984) has elaborated on the *prospect from writing projects.* According to him, the sale of project materials (textbooks) could be very lucrative as STAN has, for example, been able to raise some revenue through royalties from books to organize conferences, seminars and courses, and sponsor its members to activities of similar professional bodies outside Nigeria. Even so, the Association has often found itself in very difficult financial situations as royalties from its titles are sometimes not sufficient for its pressing needs. This is so because the books are sold at considerably moderate prices to ensure 'grassroots' patronage and to achieve the goals of the Association.

(c) Organization of In-service Training for Teachers

The organisation of in-service training has been one of the major functions of STAS in Africa. This is usually done through conferences, workshops and seminars. These provide avenues for the exchange of information and interaction between designers and implementers of curriculum projects thereby leading to the professional growth of teachers and school administrators (Ivowi 1983). Virtually all STAS in Africa have been involved in teacher training. The Ghana Association of Science Teachers holds conferences each September. It also runs national and regional workshop in the various subject panels.

Similar workshops and conferences have also been conducted by the Zambia Association for Science Eduction (ZASE). In Nigeria, STAN has been holding annual conferences. Apart from the workshops organized by the 31 branches of the Association, 10 national workshops are conducted each year (Appendix H). Bajah (1993) reports that STAN conducts workshops for primary science teachers annually through its Primary Science Panel. According to him, over the period 1982-92, STAN conducted eleven in-service workshops which involved an average of 136 primary science teachers in each workshop. Okebukola (1993) also reports that over 900 teachers benefit from the in service training offered by STAN. According to him, by the year 2000, STAN would have been involved in the retraining of over 40,000 science teachers since it was founded in 1957.

Besides, the Association served as a consultant in the *World Bank-Assisted Primary Education Project* in the training of Master trainers in Primary Science (STAN, 1992a). This, obviously, was in recognition of the capability of STAN to offer high quality training for primary science teacher trainers. According to Otuka annually on in-service teacher training. Similar commitments have been made by other virile STAS. Table 2, for instance, gives the budgetary provisions of a STA. In-service training (workshops, conference, science fairs) gets a substantial provision of twenty per cent.

Even so, STAN'S role has often been misunderstood. Deeson (1993:6), for instance had this to say:

> Despite its name, STAN is not an association for science teachers, but a professional institute. It seems to offer quite a lot to such people as teacher trainers (and even to pure scientists and engineers), but I am concerned that the practical needs of the people in the science classrooms and laboratories are addressed by nobody. School teaching (in all subjects) is extremely theoretical: chalk and talk; most teachers have inadequate knowledge of how to use even the few resources they have, and many, for sure, do not understand many basic science concepts.

Table 2 : Percentages of provision in a national science teachers' association budget

Sub-Head	*Provision*
Transport & Travel	4%
Office & General	5%
Meetings	10%
Staff Emolument	15%
Publications	18%
Workshops, Conferences, Science Fairs	20%
Capital Development	28%
	100%

Nothing can be further than the truth. There are definitely problems yet unsolved, but STAN'S effort so far in STM teacher training and retraining within the limits of its lean resources is enormous, remarkable and worth of emulation by other STAS.

(d) Organization of Science Fairs

Science Fairs provide opportunities for individuals and groups to display the various science projects which they have undertaken. A project may set out to make discovery, develop new ways of demonstrating important principles or attempt to demonstrate practical applications of a known principle.

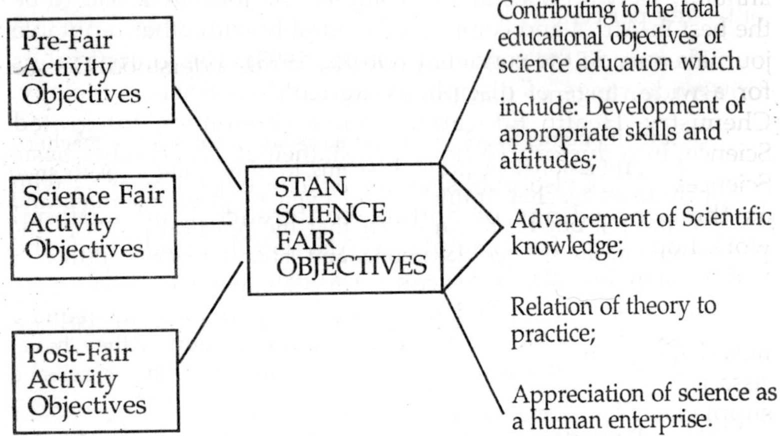

Fig. 2 Objectives of STAN Science Fairs

Source: Obioha (1983:82)

Figure 2 gives a schematic representation of the STAN Science Fairs.

The Science Teachers Association of Nigeria and the Ghana Association of Science Teachers have in addition to organizing Science Fairs in their respective countries (like other STAS in Africa) been engaged on discussions that will lead to joint Science Fairs in the near future. Some modalities have already been worked out and it is hoped that funds (which is the major impediment) will be available for this laudable scheme to take off very soon.

(e) Publication of Periodicals

STAS have also embarked upon the publication of periodicals such as Journals, bulletins (newsletters) and proceedings of conferences and workshops. These publications feature articles, research reports, innovations, science notes, reviews, approaches to science teaching, trends in science teaching worldwide and updates on members.

teaching worldwide and updates on members.

The Journal of the Science Teachers Association of Nigeria originally published twice a year, is now published once annually as two issues in one volume. The Journal is said to be the best in Africa and compares favourably with other reputable journals outside the continent (Otuka, 1993). The Journal caters for a wide range of disciplines; agricultural Science, Biology, Chemistry, Health Education, Home Economics, Integrated Science, Introductory Technology, Mathematics and other basic Sciences. STAN also publishes the *bulletin* twice a year as well as the proceedings of annual conferences and national workshops (see, for example, STAN, 1992). In addition, the various state branches of STAN have their bulletins.

Other STAS in Africa have floated their periodicals. The newsletter of the *Lesotho Science and Mathematics Teachers Association* comes out six times a year. The newsletter has a supplement for students that contains mathematics puzzles and games, a competition and suggestion for science activities. The February 1993 issue had ideas for activities with *water drops, growing spores* and *investigating balloons*. In 1992, the African Forum for Children's Literacy in Science and Technology provided a small grant for the Lesotho Science and Mathematics Teachers Association to publish its journal for a year.

(f) Research Work

STAS have been involved in a number of research projects in STM education. The Science Teachers Association of Nigeria (STAN) for instance has embarked on several research projects. Some of there efforts have led to the publication of the following position papers by the Association:

STAN Position Paper No. 1

What is Science?

STAN Position Paper No. 2: *Women in Science, Technology and Mathematics: The Nigerian Experience*

STAN Position Paper No. 3: *School Industry Link*

STAN Position Paper No. 4: *Raising the Standard of Performance in Public Examinations in Science, Technology and Mathematics.*

5

Problems Encountered by Science Teachers Associations

Financial and Communication problems beset STAS

A number of factors have continued to militate against the performance of STAS. The two outstanding factors are of course, poor finance and lack of communication. In terms of finance, it would be said that, save for the NSTA and the ASE, STAS are virtually having financial difficulties though to varying degrees. Much of the revenue of each STA comes from dues from members. But because of fluctuations in membership strength, some STAS occasionally are unable to raise enough funds from this source to finance their programmes. According to Ikeobi (1993:2), 'nearly every STA in Africa is unable to survive, grow and flourish because the only regular source of fund—members' dues—is subjected to entry and withdrawal of members from the Association.' Similarly, at the inauguration of FASE in Lagos, Nigeria, Nwana (1980: 92) had this to say:

> The future for an association of science teachers and science educators in Africa should certainly be bright especially if one were to judge only by the enthusiasm with which the idea has been received . . . But we must not overlook the fact that problems abound and there are many hurdles to clear . . . We have much more to do in inaugurating this association than passing resolutions ... We need to give serious thought to the financing of the Association.

Those were the prophetic words of Professor O.C. Nrwana, and today, FASE is virtually moribund, due largely to financial difficulties. The story has been the same for several STAS in Africa. Even those STAS that are moderately active, has been unable to set up permanent secretariats with the result that such STAS have been built around personalities, making perpetuity difficult if not impossible. The Zambia Association for Science Education (ZASE) is a good example. With the passing away of its General Secretary Mr. Thomas Varghese, the activities of the Association have been paralysed. ICASE has, in fact, reported a loss of contact with ZASE (see Appendix G). Even ICASE is not left out. Its Secretariat had to move recently from Hong Kong to Cyprus due to the movement of its Executive Secretary, Dr. Jack Holbrook. In Africa, the financial problem is further compounded by the non-sponsorship of the activities of STAS by industries and companies. This is contrary to what obtains in the U.K. and the U.S.A. where industries and companies sponsor several programmes of the ASE and the NSTA respectively.

The other major factor, *lack of communication,* which militates against the proper functioning of the STAS is partly a product of their poor financial position. Both Nwana (1980) and Ikeobi (1993) agree that poor communication has continued to threaten the activities of STAS as letters are often not replied to or received. And in the words of Holbrook (1993):

> The biggest problem that I face as Executive Secretary of ICASE is correspondence and obtaining information on concerns, developments and in general, on ways in which ICASE can play a role as an umbrella organization. Currently I can cite the Singapore science teachers association which has recently closed their P.O. Box. (I know because mail was returned). As yet I have not been able to re-establish contact.

The problem is not only between STAS. It also exists within STAS. The Science Teachers Association of Nigeria, for example, sends out from its Secretariat, a few thousand mails to its members annually but only receives a few hundreds in return. At the other extreme, however, some STAS in Africa do not correspond with members regularly.

6

Relationship of STAS with the Machinery of Government with Respect to S&T Policy Formulation

STAS influence S&T policy through conferences, workshops; collaboration with government agencies, etc.

Science Teachers' Associations have been involved in S&T policy formulation by governments through the following ways:

(a) Floating of a policy document

According to Holbrook (1993), STAS such as the ASE in the U.K. are able to influence policy by creating their own policy statements and floating these so that the membership can interact and even vote. He maintains that among the membership of the ASE are influential governmental policy makers and hence the ASE dissemination process of floating policy statements and encouraging discussion in its publications influences science education thinking as documentation produced by the ASE is easily tabled during governmental policy meeting.

(b) Adoption of STA-initiated project by government

Sometimes a project embarked upon or initiated by a STA

is adopted by government. In Swaziland, Slimming (1976) reports that the impetus for that country's Integrated Science project came when, in 1971, the *Swaziland Science Teachers Association (SSTA)* brought to the attention of the Ministry of Education's Science Teaching Panel their dissatisfaction with the existing Junior certificate syllabuses in Introductory Science and Biology. There was concern that the new course should encourage the study of science with an emphasis on individual experimentation and on understanding and constructive thinking; and it was strongly stressed that full account should be taken of the cultural and physical environment of the country. A set of proposals was put forward and the Ministry of Education invited all science teachers to a meeting to consider these. After a lively debate the proposals were unanimously accepted and the Swaziland Integrated Science Project (SWISP) thus came into being in March 1972. Similarly in Nigeria, the Nigerian Integrated Science Project (NISP) earlier reported on is the brainchild of STAN.

(c) Membership of Decision-Making Bodies

The Science Teachers Association of Nigeria has been able to influence S&T policy partly through its membership of the Joint Consultative Committee on Education (JCCE). The JCCE, inaugurated on 30 September, 1955 is Nigeria's highest advisory body on education to all governments of the Federation. It meets twice yearly and makes recommendations to the National Council on Education (NCE) for consideration and ratification. At each meeting of the JCCE, STAN presents a report on its activities. Occasionally, the Association in addition to the report, presents a memorandum on a particular subject. One of such memoranda in 1989, led to the establishment of special science secondary schools in Nigeria. More recently, on 9 December, 1993, STAN presented a memo to the JCCE plenary session calling on the Nigerian Federal Government to set up a *National task force on Project 2000^{+}*. Membership of the JCCE has, therefore, enabled STAN to be aware of the direction of government policy well in advance and to influence it where possible. It is interesting to note that many members of the JCCE are Co-opted members of the Governing Council of STAN. These include: the Federal Ministry of Education, Nigerian Educational Research and Development Council, West African Examinations Council, National Teachers Institute, Joint Admissions and Matriculation

Board, National Board for Technical Education, National Commission on Colleges of Education, National Board for Educational Measurement, and the National Business and Technical Examinations Board.

(d) Collaboration with Government Agencies

Active collaboration of STAS such as STAN with government agencies has led to new science education policies. The development of the *Nigerian Secondary Schools Science Project (NSSSP)* which produced textual materials in Biology, Chemistry and Physics was due to the collaborative effort of STAN and the then Comparative Education Study and Adaptation Centre of the University of Lagos. In fact, the writers of the series were guided considerably by the syllabus outlines earlier developed by the Science Teachers Association of Nigeria at the instance of the West African Examinations Council (WAEC). Other Nigerian government agencies such as the National Teachers Institute have also been collaborating with STAN either directly or by assigning some work to some of STAN's veteran members.

(e) Membership of Task Forces, Commissions, etc.

STAS do influence government policy on S&T through membership of special tasks forces, commissions, conferences, etc. For Instance, STAN in Nigeria participated actively during the nation's curriculum conference in 1992 in Kaduna. In fact, the STAN President, Professor Uduogie Ivowi served as the Rapporteur General. Similarly, the Association was represented at the workshop that led to the formulation of the Nigerian National Policy on Science and Technology.

(f) Holding Seminars, Workshops and Conferences

Holbrook (1993) has cited the holding of seminars, workshops and conferences as a means of influencing S&T policy. He believes that the involvement of governmental personnel as participants in these workshops can strongly influence policy and gives, as an example, the increase in the level of in-service provision for teachers in Hong Kong following the 4th ICASE-ASIAN symposium held in Hong Kong. Similar activities by GAST in Ghana, STAN in Nigeria and ZASE in Zambia have always received government attention and patronage. The Science Teachers Association of Nigeria usually publishes its conference communique and copies are made available to government. These communiques are highly regarded. Appendix I gives the 1993 conference communique of STAN.

7

How Science and Technology Policies Get to Teachers in the Grassroots Classrooms

STAS play a very important role in the transmission S&T Policy to Teachers.

Figure 3 is a schematic diagram showing how national S&T policies get to teachers in the grassroots classrooms. Once a policy on S&T has been formulated, the relevant (Education) ministry collaborates with specialists—in Universities, other Higher Institutions as well as STAS—in producing the syllabus. In some countries, the syllabus—appropriately called teaching syllabus—provides the performance objectives, teaching content, activities to be performed by the children as well as evaluation procedures. Nigerian syllabuses are typical examples. In others, the syllabuses serve examination purposes mainly. Textbooks are thereafter written by individuals and groups. In some countries (such as Nigeria), STAS produce textual materials for both secondary and primary school teachers who make use of these in their interaction with students. The secondary and primary school science teachers along with lecturers in higher institutions and ministry officials constitute the membership of the Science Teachers' Association (STA). Where the STA is virile, its workshops, conferences and other teacher training programmes serve as veritable avenues for mutual exchange and updating of information on developments in STM education. There is therefore a lot for the system to lose wherever there is no STA or the STA is not active. In all, the scenario shows a lot of interactions with each unit lending support to the other in one form or the other. Even the students who are the last recipients of a S&T policy, must necessarily participate either directly or indirectly at each stage in the scheme since the focus is, without doubt, on them. Students' participation in science fairs in Ghana and Nigeria has for example, helped to improve the standards of fairs organized by STAN (GAST in Ghana and STAN in Nigeria) in these countries.

An aspect which can not be ignored is the central role which Science Teachers' Associations play in the propagation of S&T policy to the grassroots teachers. STAS play active part at all stages as aptly illustrated by the following two Case Studies from Nigeria.

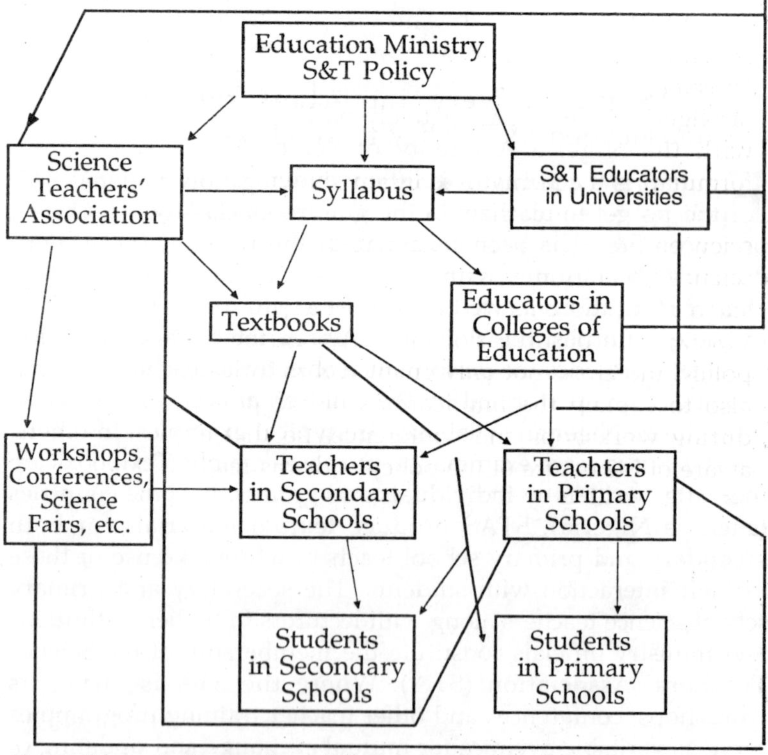

Figure 3. Schematic diagram showing how national S&T policies get to teachers

Case Study 1

An example of the introduction of a new S&T policy in Nigeria was the change from the 6-5-2-3 system of education to the 6-3-3-4. Here the Science Teachers Association of Nigeria participated in conferences leading to the change of policy, was instrumental to the production of syllabuses in science subjects and, in fact, went ahead to produce some textual materials. The Association also organized workshops, conferences and seminars on the new system for its members. Some of those conferences drew membership from Ministry of Education officials, science teacher educators, publishers, and students. *Thus, through the effort of STAN, teachers were aware of the demands and modalities for the implementation of the new system of education well in advance.*

Case Study 2

Another case study showing the role of STAN in the transmission of policy on S&T was the formulation of the *Nigerian National Policy on Science and Technology* (Federal Republic of Nigeria, 1986). STAN actively participated (and collaborated with the Nigeria Academy of Science) in the process of formulating the policy. It is little wonder then that some aspects of the policy emphasize the need for sound basic education in science. The policy, for instance, states that "in the teaching of science, local examples should be used particularly at the early stage of introduction to science" (Federal Republic of Nigeria, 1986:7). The participation of STAN in the formulation of the policy, therefore, not only enabled it to influence the policy but also to explain the implications of the policy to its members during workshops and conferences so that each member was aware of the nature of the policy and was ready to implement it.

8

National Science and Technology Policies and Felt Needs of the African Community

African countries possess laudable S&T policy documents which focus on *relevance*. But implementation problems have occasionally dwarfed these ideals leading to loss of opportunities. Still, the African remains resilient, looking into the future with renewed hope.

Science and Technology (S&T) are crucial factors of economic and social development of any country. The adoption of a sound S&T policy in national life makes the difference between a developed and a developing country. The developed countries such as the U.S.A. and Japan have made tremendous use of S&T. They now dominate the world markets. On the other hand, the developing countries such as Nigeria and virtually all African countries (except, perhaps, South Africa) have been barely managing to survive. African countries lack sound S&T infrastructure with attendant abject poverty, huge debt, low literacy, etc. In consequence, each African country has formulated its own policy on S&T to cater for the *felt needs* of its citizens. There has, therefore been, of recent, a conscious efforts to seek for *relevance* of S&T policies vis-a-vis the contemporary problems in Africa. In Nigeria, the National Policy in Science and Technology (Federal Republic Nigeria, 1986:7) states, inter alia:

> Science must . . . be domesticated for it to be effective and its teaching in the institutions of learning, made purposeful and *relevant* to the country's cultural milieu. Accordingly, in the teaching of science, local examples should be used particularly at the early stage of introduction to science.

In order to ensure that the S&T policy is relevant, the Nigerian government seeks to:

- make it possible for the average child to have early contacts with the concepts of, and materials related to, S&T even before attaining primary school age.
- ensure a sound science foundation during the first six years of the 6-3-3-4 educational structure.
- enforce strictly an absolute minimum of 60:40 ratio of science—based to other disciplines in student yearly enrolment into the nation's universities with the target ratio of 70:30.
- work towards establishing at least on Trade Centre/ Vocational School in each Local Government Area of the country.
- ensure that adult education includes, in addition to learning how to read and write, learning how things around us work.

Similarly, the *Nigerian National Policy of Education* clearly states that secondary education (for instance) should serve as a preparation for *useful living* with in society and for *higher education*. According to lvowi (1990), these two factors are satisfied at the senior secondary school by the provision of *vocational* and *academic education*. He contends that the science and mathematics curriculum contents are comprehensive, relevant and widely appealing in scope, depth and application.

In Botswana, Nganunu (1992:120) reports that in developing the science syllabus, the approach used was:

- to identify the needs of the society through consultation with various departments and organizations; areas of national interests and concern included issues like water conservation, diarrhea and death from dehydration, car accidents, mining and pollution; these areas had to be covered in the syllabus; and

- to identify the needs of the individual by identifying the activities people do in their daily lives (e.g. describing the activities done by a school-boy in town, a woman in the rural areas, a city worker, and a mother); then identify what science is needed to do these activities; from there, syllabus activities were framed and finally the objectives sorted into topical themes such as *Water for Living, House Construction, and Keeping Healthy*.

According to Nganunu, the outcome was a syllabus that contained topics and skills not found in the traditional academic science curriculum such as *building solar devices.* (Botswana has 320 cloudless days per year), *preparing an oral rehydration therapy* (because diarrhea is a major killer of children).

Ghana is another country that is seeking the *relevance* of its S&T policy through the *science in Ghanaian Society Project*. Funded by the British Council and UNESCO, the project has the following objectives (Yakubu, 1992:14):

- To study local industries in order to identify the scientific concepts and processes embedded in them.
- To produce books on local industries and other aspects of Ghanaian culture relevant to science teaching.
- To develop industry-oriented or interdisciplinary methods of science teaching.
- To investigate ways of improving the image of the world of work of Ghanaian youth, especially senior secondary, junior secondary and technical school leavers.

In the same vain, Ajeyalemi (1990) surveyed science and technology offerings in Ghana, Nigeria, Uganda, Zambia, Zimbabwe, Lesotho and Swaziland and noted that all the science curricula recently developed in these countries placed less emphasis on the purely academic curriculum and more on *relevant* and functional education. For example, Zimbabwe has an issues-oriented curriculum dealing with the following themes:

- Science in Agriculture
- Science in Energy use
- Science in Structures and Mechanical systems

- Science in Industry
- Science in Community.

Bajah (1982) has equally advised that a science programme which strives for *relevance* in Africa must take into consideration most of the points relating to *need, usefulness, modernity* and *acceptability*. Elsewhere, Bajah (1988) contends that many African countries have evolved their own educational systems in which education at all levels focuses on *relevance*.

However, it does appear that in spite of the good intentions of the various national S&T policies in Africa, namely, that of seeking relevance, the situation on ground can hardly justify this claim. In the words of Ajeyalemi (1992:117):

> Whether in Zimbabwe or in any of the other countries (eight African countries were studied) . . . the classroom implementation is contrary to expectations of the science curriculum developers. Science instruction is teacher-directed, theoretical and textbook-bound . . . Nor has science education in these African countries succeeded in meeting the needs of the very few college and university bound students with science career aspirations. It has certainly not been appropriate for the larger majority who need science for meeting personal needs, for resolving societal problems, or for developing career awareness . . .

Ajeyalemi lists poor economic conditions of most African countries, centralization of the educational system, limited public awareness of, and possibly support for, science and poor quality of teachers as some of the reasons for the discrepancy. Similarly, Ogunniyi (1984) has stated that science teaching in Africa is being hampered by inadequate teaching facilities, lack of funds to purchase equipment, poor readability of textbooks, large classes, lack of well-trained science teachers, poor motivation of teachers and the negative influence of external examinations. It is with this avalanche of problems that Ogunniyi feels that *education for rural transformation* is not only hypocritical but unattainable in the present circumstances. In his words (Ogunniyi, 1984:23):

> Those advocating for *rural transformation* by means of appropriate science education programmes are neither living in rural areas nor are they contemplating that they themselves nor any member of their family would do so now or in the future .

> . . The lack of virtually all the basic amenities of life . . . the conspicuous absence of youthful energies among the farming communities and so on make education, and science education in particular, orientated towards rural life, to say the least, a hollow and a bogus propaganda.

What all this means is that there is a discrepancy between S&T policy and practice in Africa. If S&T education must be truly *relevant,* governments in the various countries in the continent must as a matter of deliberate policy ensure that relevant education, particularly S&T education, is not only on paper but actually put into practice. It is only in this way that the continent can hope to benefit from the tenets of Project 2000+.

9

Guide Framework for Science and Technology Education for All

- COMSEC, UNESCO, others should support virile STAS and resuscitate ailing ones.
- Governments should give priority attention to adequate funding of S&T education.
- A Foundation should be established for ICASE.
- NSTA, ASE should assist other STAS.
- STAS, schools, parents, industries, others should work in concert.

The discussion so far inevitably leads to recommendations for the implementation of S&T education for all. Of paramount importance is the fact that the provision of *S&T education for all, in all countries* requires concerted efforts of several agencies, governments, the public and individuals. Accordingly, the approach adopted here is to highlight some of the roles in which the following agencies/groups are expected to play in our bid to provide S&T education for all:

- International Agencies—Commonwealth secretariat, UNESCO, etc.
- Governments.
- International Council of Associations for Science Education (ICASE).

- National Governments.
- Science Teachers Associations (STAS).
- Schools.
- Industries.
- Parents.

Role of International Agencies

As earlier highlighted, STAS have a major role to play in the implementation of S&T for all. However, in many African countries, their impact is either very low or non-existent. International agencies such as the *commonwealth secretariat* and *UNESCO* are hereby called upon to assist in resuscitating all ailing STAS and also to further strengthen those that are currently virile before they too become moribund. For a start, the Commonwealth Secretariat is called upon to assist in the following areas in the developing countries of the Commonwealth:

- Where STAS are ailing, support should be provided for their resuscitation.
- STAS should be encouraged to set up permanent paid secretariats to enhance their effectiveness. GAST in Ghana, for example, is long overdue for a permanent secretariat. A delay can only lead to further deterioration in the scope of its activities. The Commonwealth Secretariat should provide technical expertise preferably from within Africa. The STAN Secretariat in Nigeria could be helpful in this direction. Similar efforts should be made in countries like Botswana, Zambia and Zimbabwe.
- Financial support should be provided for projects embarked upon by STAS especially in furtherance of Phase III of Project 2000^{+}.

Role of Governments

Governments are expected to do the following:

- Support for STAS—These are in the areas of funding, representation on governing bodies of STAS, patronage of programmes such as workshops, conferences and seminars. Award of contracts to STAS to strengthen their revenue base—such contacts are usually cheaper for governments and better executed since STAS have the human resources.

- *In-service training for teachers:* This should be done in close association with STAS to avoid duplication of efforts. In addition, Educational Institutes should be encouraged to embark upon distance education.
- *Books and Library Development:* Governments should as a matter of urgency procure S&T books for schools and libraries. Support should also be given to STAS to publish S&T textbooks.
- *Personnel Management:* This involves provision of adequate data and effective (even) distribution of teachers. In Nigeria, for instance, S&T teachers, are in short apply in rural schools.
- *Admission Policy:* Entrants into the S&T teaching profession should be those with reasonably good qualifications. Mediocres should be discouraged.
- *Conditions of Service of Teachers:* S&T teachers like other workers require a high morale to operate effectively. Policies and positive actions in this direction are needed.
- *Public Awareness:* By and large, the public has a role to play in S&T education. Government should help to create this awareness via deliberate campaigns in hand bills, posters, radio/television programmes and newspaper articles.
- *Fund Allocation:* This is where the problem lies. Most governments will give on paper very lofty objectives in S&T. However, the release of budgetary allocations very often proves difficult. On the contrary, African governments easily and willingly sponsor sporting and other activities that tend to boost their political egos. STAN (1992b) feels that this implies paying *'lip-service'* to S&T education.

Role of ICASE

As one of the initiating agencies of project 2000$^+$, the central role of ICASE towards the success of the scheme cannot be underestimated. ICASE is expected to play a co-ordinating and supervising role. But more importantly, *ICASE should support STAS financially*. Unfortunately, ICASE doesn't have funds of its own. This brings to the fore the need to establish a *foundation* to support the activities of ICASE. Until this is done, much of the lofty ideas of that organization will remain unfulfilled and all nations will be worse of for the inaction. It is hoped that this will receive a favourable attention of the governing body of ICASE. This will inevitably lead to the establishment of a permanent secretariat for ICASE which is highly desirable.

Role of Science Teachers' Associations

To enhance the attainments of S&T literacy for all, STAS are expected to:

- strengthen themselves through more membership drive, functional structure, establishments of permanent secretariats and revenue generation. Revenues could be sourced through commercialized book-development efforts and the provision of consultancy services to governments, industries, etc.
- execute S&T programmes such as S&T fairs, camps, workshops, lectures, seminars, symposia, films, conferences, newsletters (bulletins), journals, science prizes, badges and road shows. STAS could also sponsor S&T radio and television programmes as well as the activities of S&T clubs in schools.
- embark upon international co-operation with other STAS. More privileged STAS such as the NSTA and the ASE should consider offering support to the less privileged. Both organizations (NSTA & ASE) have, for instance, been co-operating with STAN in the areas of training, conference participation and exchange of publications. Fortunately, the International committee of the NSTA recently voted to provide more support in this direction to STAS in all countries.

According to NSTA (1993a), the Association is determined to:

- promote formal partnership and exchanges with other science teachers and among science teacher associations worldwide.
- promote international conferences, seminars, and sessions fostering global awareness of issues, ideas and trends in science education.
- promote multicultural science education.
- encourage global transfer of information related to science teaching and learning.

Similarly, the ASE's teacher scholarship scheme is a worthy and commendable effort and there is the desirability that the scheme, which aims to promote the exchange of curriculum development ideas in the teaching of science between the U.K. and Australia, be extended to cover other regions, particularly Africa. The Commonwealth Secretariat should assist in this respect by liaisoning between the ASE and STAS.

Role of Schools

Schools are expected to encourage their teachers to participate in the activities of STAS by authorising their release and sponsorship. Schools should also provide the enabling atmosphere for S&T teaching as well as conduct career counselling service for students.

Role of Industries

Industries are called upon to sponsor S&T programmes. In Nigeria, an education tax has been introduced. The policy aims at compelling industries to pay 2 per cent of their earnings as education tax. This is a commendable effort. What remains is to see how government will channel such income to education, particularly S&T education. By the large, other countries are advised to follow suit.

Parents

Parents are implored to provide S&T toys to their children, embark on home teaching and visit S&T centres. These reinforce the activities that take place at school. Parents should also encourage the children to use S&T badges and join S&T clubs such as the Junior Engineers Technicians and Scientists Clubs in Zambia and Nigeria. Incidentally, the United Nations has declared 1994 as the *International Year of the Family.* It is, therefore, hoped that every family in every nation will work towards the enhancement of S&T education for *all,* in *all* countries in 1994 and beyond.

10

Conclusion

The Experience of Virile STAS are vital for all

This study has revealed the enormous impact which Science Teachers' Associations (STAS) have created on Science and Technology education in countries where they are virile. This has been the case of NSTA in the U.S.A., the ASE in the U.K. and STAN in Nigeria. STAS' influence has been experienced in the area of curriculum development, production of textual materials, organization of training programmes and formulation of S&T policy. STAN, in Nigeria, has expected so much influence in S&T education that it is difficult to imagine what would have happened without it.

Unfortunately in Africa, virile STAS are few. But this should not be the case because as the world awaits the implementation of the Phase III of Project 2000^{+}, it can ill afford to ignore the positive role of STAS. The experience of STAN is a pointer to the enormous gap that must be existing in the African country with an ailing STA. This is why positive action is needed in continuing support for virile STAS and the resuscitation of ailing ones. Both the Commonwealth Secretariat and UNESCO should consider taking urgent and decisive action in this direction.

In the same vein, there is the need to establish a Foundation for ICASE as well as encourage closer patnerships among STAS in the various regions. The NSTA and ASF are implored to collaborate and co-operate more actively with STAS in Africa.

Finally, governments, IGO, NGOs and other agencies of education must work in concert within the framework of Project 2000^+. It is only in this way that we can ensure, as Goldsmith (1991:17) has stated "that the illiterate, numbered in millions, are provided with means of learning to become an unchallengeable and vital nation resource." This is, essentially, the basis of *S&T education for all.*

References

Ajeyalemi, D. ed. (1990). *Science and Technology Education in Africa: Focus on Seven Sub-saharan Countries, Lagos, Nigeria: University of Lagos Press.*

Ajeyalemi, D. (1992). The Status of STS in Africa. In R.E. Yager (ed.), *The Status of Science-Technology-Society Reform Efforts around the world*. ICASE year book, 116-18.

Bajah, S.T. (1982). How Relevant is Science Education to the school leaver in Africa? *Journal of STAN*, 4, 20 (2) 179-92.

Bajah, S.T. (1983). *Teaching Integrated Science Creatively*. Ibadan: Ibadan University Press.

Bajah, S.T. (1988). Recent developments and key issues in Integrated science Teaching in the African Region. In Recent Developments in Integrated Science Teachings. A report of a meeting held in Canberra, Australia, 281-22.

Bajah, S.T. (1992). Public Understanding of Science: seeing with both eyes. Special lecture at the 33rd Annual Conference of STAN, Enugu, 17-22 August.

Bajah, S.T. (1993). *Shortage of Science and Mathematics Teachers: A Nigerian Case Study*. London: Commonwealth Secretariat.

Bajah, S.T. and Yoloye, E.A. (1981). A Report of twenty years of Science Education in Africa. Ibadan, Nigeria: Science Education Programme for Africa.

Bajah, T. and Youdeowei, A. (1987). *Primary Science for Nigerian Schools, Books 4-6, Teachers' Guide*. Ibadan: Heinemann Educational Books (Nig.) Ltd.

CASTME (1992). *Handbook on Commonwealth Association of Science, Technology and Mathematics Education*. London: Commonwealth Secretariat.

Chisman, D. (1988). Review of Developments in Integrated Science Teaching in the African Region. Recent Developments in Integrated Science Teaching: A Reporting of a meeting held in Canberra, Australia, 56-63.

Deeson, Eric (1993). Report on the 34th Annual Conference of STAN.

Dienye, N.E. and Gbamanja, S.P.T. (1990). Science Education: Theory and Practice. Abuja, Nigeria: Totan Publishers Ltd.

Federal Ministry of Education (1981a). *Core Curriculum for Primary Science*. Lagos, Nigeria.

Federal Ministry of Education (1981b). *Core Curriculum for Integrated Science. Lagos, Nigeria.*

Federal Republic of Nigeria (1981). National Policy on Education, Revised. Lagos: Federal Government Press.

Federal Republic of Nigeria (1986). *National Policy on Science and Technology. Abuja Directorate of Social Mobilization, MAMSER.*

Federal Republic of Nigeria (1992). *National Policy on a Science and Engineering Infrastructure.* Lagos: National Agency for Science and Engineering Infrastructure.

Goldsmith, M. (1991). Education for All. Presidential address of the CASTME/COL North American Regional Seminar on Quality in Science, Technology and Mathematics Education, University of British Columbia, Vancouver, Canada, 15-19 April, 16-18.

Holbrook, J.B. (1993). STAS and S&T Policy. Contribution to the study on implementing S&T education for all. Guide to better policy and practice for teachers.

Holbrook. J. and Chisman, D. (1988). Review of Integrated Science Education worldwide. Recent Developments in Integrated Science Teaching. A report of a meeting held in Canberra. Australia, 13-28.

Ivowi, U.M.O. (1984). Curriculum Innovation in Nigeria. *Journal of Curriculum Studies,* Vol. II, No. 2, 1-13.

Ivowi, U.M.O. (1990). The philosophy and objectives of the Science and Mathematics Curriculum at the Senior Secondary School levels in Nigeria. *Journal of STAN,* 26 (2), 3-8.

Ivowi, U.M.O. ed. (1993). *Curriculum Development in Nigeria,* Ibadan: Sam Bookman.

Ikeobi, I.O. (1993). Report on African Region to the ICASE General Assembly held at the UNESCO Headquarters, Paris, France, 11th July.

King, W.R. (1991). Ensuring Quality Science and Technology Education: The role of agencies outside of the school. Proceedings of the CASTME/COL North American Regional Seminar on Quality in Science, Technology and Mathematics Education, University of British Colombia, Vancouver, Canada, 15-19 April, 44-53.

Ministry of Education and Culture, Ghana (1987). *Things you need to know about the Junior Secondary School Programme. Accra-North: Nsamankwaw.*

Ministry of Education, Youth and Sports, Zambia (1977). Education Reform Document. Lusaka.

Nganunu, M. (1992). Inclusion of Indigenous Technology in School Science Curricula—A Solution for Africa. In R.E. Yager (ed.), The Status of Science-Technology-Society Reform Efforts around the world. ICASE Year book, 119-24.

Nwana, O.C. (1980). Co-operation among Science Teachers' Associations in Africa. *Proceedings of the Inaugural Conference of the Forum of African Science Educators. Lagos, Nigeria, 74-95.*

NSTA (1990). Science Teachers Speak out: the NSTA Lead Paper on Science and Technology Education for the 21st century. Adopted by the NSTA Board of Directors, January.

NSTA (1993a). NSTA Position Statement: International Science Education. Adopted by the NSTA Board of Directors, January.

NSTA (1993b). NSTA buys New Headquarters, staff to begin moving this fall. *NSTA Reports*. May/June, p. 1.

Obioha, N.E. (1983). Science Projects and Fairs in Science Education. Journal of STAN, 22 (1), 79-84.

Okebukola, P.A.O. (1993). Perspectives from Nigeria on the implementation of Project 2000+—an International Project on Scientific and Technological Literacy for all. A background paper on Africa's contribution to Project 2000+ forum held in Paris, July 5-10.

Ogunniyi, M.B. (1984). The Rhetorics of Science Education for rural transformation. *Journal of STAN*, 22 (2), 20-25.

Otuka, J.O.E. (1983). Contribution of the Science Teachers Association of Nigeria to Curriculum Development. In U.M.O. Ivowi, (ed.) *Curriculum Development in Nigeria*. Ibadan: Sam Bookman.

SEPA (1978). Handbook for Teachers of Science. Accra, Ghana: SEPA Secretariat.

Sharma, G.N. (1974). The role of the Science Teachers Association in the improvement of Science Education in Nigerian Schools. *Journal of STAN,* 12 (3) 24-25.

Slimming, D. (1976). The Introduction of Integrated Science Teaching in Swaziland 1972-76. *Journal of STAN,* 15 (1), 13-23.

STAN (1970a). *Curriculum Development Newsletter No. 1: Integrated Science,* Ibadan: Yokele-Pekun Press.

STAN (1970b). *Curriculum Development Newsletter No. 2: Chemistry Syllabus.* Ibadan: Yokele-Pekun Press.

STAN (1971a). *Curriculum Development Newsletter No. 3: Biology Syllabus, Ibadan: Yokele-Pekun Press.*

STAN (1971b). *Nigerian Integrated Science Project, Pupils' Textbook one.* Ibadan: Heinemann Educational Books (Nigeria) Ltd.

STAN (1972). *Curriculum Development Newsletter No. 4: Physics Syllabus.* Ibadan: Yokele-Pekun Press.

STAN (1992a). Proceedings of the World Bank-Assisted Primary Education project. Master Trainers workshop in Primary Science. Ibadan: STAN Secretariat.

STAN (1992b). Position Paper No. 4: Raising the standard of Performance in STM in public examinations. Ibadan: STAN Secretariat.

UNESCO (1986). The Place of Science and Technology in School Curricula: A global survey. Paris: Division of Science, Technical and Environmental Education, UNESCO.

Urevbu, A.O. (1990). Curriculum Innovations in Africa: Successes and Failures Benin City, Nigeria: University of Benin Press.

Yakubu, J.M. (1992). Indigenising the Science Curriculum in Ghana through the Science in Ghanaian Society project. *Science Education International,* 3 (3), 14-19.

Yoloye, E.A., ed. (1978). *Evaluation for Innovation: African Primary Science programme Evaluation Report.* Ibadan: Ibadan University Press.

Appendix A

Project 2000+: International Forum on Scientific and Technological Literacy for All

Declaration

At the conclusion of the International Forum on Scientific and Technological Literacy for All Held at UNESCO Headquarters, Paris 5-10 July 1993, about 400 participants from more than 90 countries endorsed the following declaration.

We, participants in the Project 2000+ Forum meeting at UNESCO, Paris, France from 5-10 July 1993:

1. *Recalling* the World Declaration on Education for All, in particular its recognition that sound basic education is fundamental to the strengthening of higher levels of education and of scientific and technological literacy and capacity and thus to self-reliant development and further recalling recent worldwide expression of concern for the environment and for quality of human life especially those contained in Agenda 21, the output of the United Nations Conference on Environment and Development, Rio de Janeiro 3-14 June, 1992.

2. *Believing* that scientific literacy and technological literacy are essential for achieving responsible and sustainable development.

3. *Declare* our full commitment to the promotion of science and technology education for all in keeping with the World

Declaration on Education for All, and our readiness to contribute Project 2000+ to the concerted action set out in the Framework for Action to Meet Basic Learning Needs.

4. *Call* on government, industry, public and private sector interests, and education and other authorities in all countries to:

(a) review critical existing provisions for science and technology education at all levels and in all settings with the aim of giving appropriate attention to development and maintenance of learning programmes responsive to the needs of individuals and communities;

(b) assign such steps as may be necessary to ensure equity of access for everybody to science and technology education, notably for all with the aim of achieving responsible and sustainable development;

(c) take such steps as may be necessary to ensure equity of access for everybody to science and technology education, notably for women and girls, young children and other under-represented groups.

(d) develop appropriate in-school and out-of-school opportunities, programmes, curricular and assessment procedures for science and technology education responding to the human needs of a scientific and technological society;

(e) ensure and support appropriate pre-service and continuing in-service provisions for those responsible for all forms of science and technology education;

(f) encourage and support evaluation, research and development in science and technology education in both formal and non-formal sectors;

and to this end:

(g) establish and support task forces involving partnership with public and private education bodies and councils; these might include universities and other institutions of higher and further education, research institutions, libraries, interactive science centres, environmental areas, nature reserves as well as public and private bodies active in the fields of agriculture, natural resources, environment, health, industry, commerce and the media, and also organizations and individuals specially concerned with science and technology education.

(h) recognize the central role of teachers in achieving scientific literacy and technological literacy for everybody and enhance the status of careers in science and technology education at all levels;

(i) recognize the capital role of institutions of non-formal education, such as museums and scientific centres, of the media (radio, television and the press) and of all other out-of-school channels for communicating knowledge of science and technology, in fostering scientific and technology literacy for all; and develop activities designed to set science and its applications in a wider social and cultural environment;

(j) ensure that adequate resources are available to achieve these aims.

5. *Urge* United Nations Agencies and other inter-governmental organizations to work together to initiate and support programmes which will advance the ability of countries and of populations to shape their own future in a scientific and technological society and which will increase the capacity of countries for designing, planning and implementing scientific literacy and technological literacy programmes.

6. *Urge* non-government organizations active in fields of science and technology education, as well as the social science, and professional associations of teachers and educators and educational organizations at all levels to:

enter into partnership with, and make their knowledge and experience available to, United Nations and other inter-governmental bodies as well as establish innovative programmes in a common effort to achieve the goal of scientific literacy and technological literacy for all; and

participate in national, regional and international

programmes for the enhancement of scientific and technological literacy for the improvement of the quality of life in all societies and for the achievement of sustainable development.

7. *Recommend* that UNESCO make provision, within its Medium Term Plan (1996-2001) in the field of education, and in the context of Project 2000+, for an international programme to develop co-operation among all countries in the field of science and technology education, with particular reference to the promotion of scientific literacy and technological literacy for all.

This programme, conducted in partnership with the relevant and competent government and non-governmental organizations and agencies, should focus on regional and sub-regional co-operation and on strengthening networks for exchange of ideas, information, human and material resources for science and technology education, and actively seek to promote world-wide:

(a) understanding of the nature of and the need for, scientific literacy and technological literacy in relation to local culture and values and to the social and economic needs and aspirations of each country and its peoples, and also in accord both with the general aims of education for the all-round development of human personality and with human rights and basic freedoms;

(b) identification of those issues concerning the applications of science and technology which are of special importance for personal, local and national development and their embodiment in educational programmes;

(c) establishment of teaching and learning environments as well as supporting structures conducive to the achievement of scientific literacy and technological literacy for all;

(d) formulation of guidelines for the preparation and continuous professional development of science and technology educators and leadership coupled with assistance to countries in giving effect to them;

(e) development of effective communication both verbal and

visual, assessment strategies and evaluation programmes designed to enhance general levels of scientific literacy and technological literacy;

(f) support for the non-formal and information sector in its own right and support for development strategies which will help to stimulate and maintain lifelong scientific literacy and technological literacy.

8. *Recommend* that by the year 2001 there be in place appropriate structures and activities to foster scientific literacy and technological literacy for all, in all countries.

Appendix B

African Primary Science Programmes (APSP)

SELECTED TITLES

1. How the sky looks.
2. Stars over Africa.
3. Strangers in the sky.
4. Using the sky.
5. Common substances around the Home (mixing powders and liquids).
6. Measuring Time.

   Part II: Making clocks that measure hours
7. Colours, Water and Paper.
8. Construction with glass.
9. Activities for lower Primary: Water.
10. Chima makes a clock.
11. Activities for lower primary: Cooking.
12. Estimating Numbers.
13. Ourselves: Activities and Experiments.
14. Seeds.
15. Sinking and Floating.
16. Small Animals.

17. Tilapia.
18. Chicks in the classroom.
19. Ask the Ant Lion.
20. Activities for Lower Primary: Dry sand.

Appendix C

Science Education Programme for Africa Handbook for Teachers of Science

CONTENTS

Appendix D

New Structure of Education in Ghana

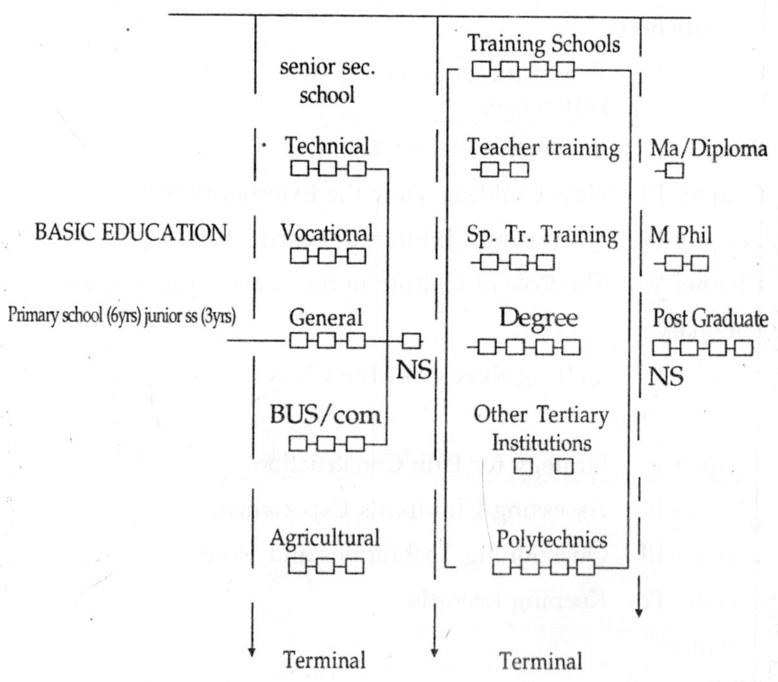

Appendix E

Nigerian Education System (6-3-3-4)

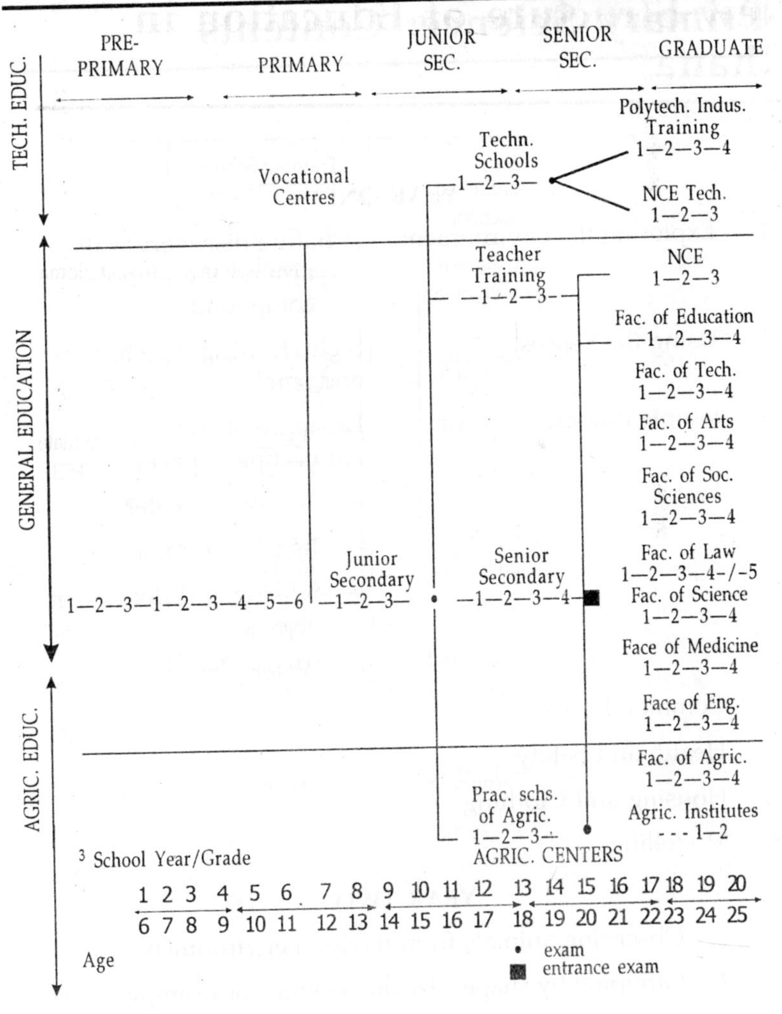

Appendix F

Nigerian Core Curriculum for Primary Science: Contents

YEAR ONE

1. Exploring the environment: A nature discovery walk around the school compound.
2. Using the Senses: Sight, hearing, touch, taste and smell.
3. Simple Properties of Air: Existence of Air
   Air occupies space.
4. Water:
   — Sources of water
   — Its uses at home
   — Sinking and floating of objects
   — Water play.
5. Common Foods
6. Health and Safety
7. Housing and Clothing
8. Modelling

YEAR TWO

1. Observing animals from the local environment.
2. Grouping by shape, size and colour (for example, leaves,

bottoms, etc.) making leaf print.

3. Ordering of objects by comparing volumes, weights and lengths.
4. Growing plants from seeds.
5. Air and Wind: Moving air from one container to another.
6. Further activities with water.
7. Health and Safety: Care of the body.
8. Housing and Clothing.
9. Making figures and models of simple objects using match box and clay and making leaf print.

YEAR THREE

1. Further activities on plants and animals—comparison of major characteristics.
2. Further activities on Air and Water.
3. Force as push and pull.
4. Measurement: Length, Time and Mass: Comparing Volume.
5. Simple activities with mirrors and images.
6. Making sound with different local materials.
7. Colour: Dyes from plants and soil.
8. Technology: Local examples of things and practices we try to do to make work easier or more identification of simple machines and tools.

YEAR FOUR

1. Soil: Types and Constituents.
2. Gardening—Growing better plants, Growth and Food (practical, observation and measurement).
3. Food Types and Uses—Food gives us energy which we need to grow and work.
4. Simple ideas on heat and temperature.

5. Water Cycle—Evaporation and Condensation: Things which dissolve and things which don't. Filtering and Purification.
6. Weather—Regular observation and recording.
7. Further activities on measurement of length in metre, centimetre, and volume in litre.
8. Names of colours, different shades of the same colour, making rainbow, observing natural colour and changes.
9. Exploring the human body—Bones, Joints, Muscles and Movement.
10. Health and Safety: Simple First Aid.
    — How to clean wounds, stop bleeding.
    — Treatment of stings, bite (dog, snake, scorpion, wasp bites).
11. Technology: Identification of materials:
    — Metallic, Wood, Rubber, Plastic, Glass and Ceramic.

YEAR FIVE

1. — Pressure
   — Propulsion, Glider, Flight of Birds and Kites
   — Burning.
2. Domestic Farm Animals: Visit to farms, Raising and Maintenance of Chicken Poultry.
3. Electric Circuit:
   — Ways of Lighting Bulb
   — Conductor and Insulator (non-Conductor)
   — Uses of Electricity in everyday life.
4. Heat, Energy and Temperature.
5. Rocks: Classification: Constituents: Uses of Rocks.
6. Soap and Alkali.
7. My Body at Work:

   Breathing System

Feeding System

Excretory System.

8. How life begins in:

   (a) Plants

   (b) Animals.

9. Health and Safety: Common Diseases.

YEAR SIX

1. Simple machines, types and uses.
2. Improving crop yield (project essential).
3. Simple ideas about magnets.
4. Minerals: Types and Uses.
5. Our Earth and Sky.
6. More about the Environment.

Appendix G

Communique For The 34th Annual Conference of the Science Teachers' Association of Nigeria

1.0 The 34th Annual Conference of the Science Teachers Association of Nigeria (STAN), was held at Government College, Katsina, Katsina State from 16-21 August, 1993. Teachers of Science, Technology and Mathematics from 27 States of the Federation and the Federal Capital Territory, Abuja attended the conference. A delegate from the Association for Science Education (ASE), Mr Eric Deeson and the Director of the British Council Assisted Nigerian Integrated Science Teacher Education Project (NISTEP), Mr. Paul Turton, based in Zaria, Kaduna State, actively participated in the conference.

2.0 The theme of the conference was "Professional Development and Retention of Personnel for Effective Science, Technology and Mathematics Education in Nigeria."

3.0 The conference was declared open by the Executive Governor of Katsina State, His Excellency, Alhaji Saidu Barda. In his speech, he enumerated the efforts of his government in promoting STM, through the provision of science equipment in Secondary Schools and payment of science allowance to teachers in his state. He also reiterated his government's commitment to the provision of STM education in Katsina State. He donated a handsome sum of money on behalf of the government and people of Katsina

State. The address of the STAN President, Prof. U.M.O. Uvowi, FSTAN focused on "Instructional Competencies". In his address, he stressed the competencies required of STM teachers as:

(i) entry behaviour into the teaching profession;

(ii) the training and retention of teachers, and

(iii) a proper match amongst the elements of teachers, non-teaching staff, students and materials.

The Commissioner for Education, Hajia Rakiya Abdullazia Jibia delivered a short welcome address while the Principal of Government College, Katsina, Alhaji Rabe Musa Maiadua also presented a welcome address.

4.0 The Keynote Address was presented by Professor Emeritus E.A. Yoloye, FSTAN. His address, supported with relevant data revealed that professional development was not merely professional training in science, technology and mathematics education leading to professional certificates, but was more of broadening the knowledge base, skills and understanding of science of STM personnel. Retention, he stated, dealt with the motivation of the personnel to continue on the job.

5.0 The following sub-themes were discussed:

(a) Professional Development and Retention of Personnel for Effective STM Education in Nigeria: Socio-cultural factors.

(b) Professional Development and Retention of Personnel for Effective STM Education in Nigeria: Implications for the Learner.

(c) Professional Development and Retention of Personnel for Effective STM Education in Nigeria: Implications for Meaningful National Development.

(d) Professional Development and Retention of Personnel for Effective STM Education in Nigeria: Comparative Analysis.

6.0 Other highlights of the conference.

6.1 *Launching of Books:*

Position Papers 1, 2 and 3, authored and published by STAN were launched during the conference.

6.2 *Conferment of Fellowship of STAN:*

Two distinguished members of STAN namely: Dr. R.L.N. Offurum and Mr. P.P. Udofia were conferred with FSTAN Award for their invaluable contribution to the Association and science education in Nigeria.

6.3 *Special Lectures:*

Dr Kabir Ahmed, Provost, College of Education (Technical), Dutsin-Ma delivered a lecture entitled "Science Education Today". This lecture focused on:

(i) meaning and implications of scientific knowledge,

(i). essence of science education, and

(ii) the interaction of science education and society.

Alhaji Is'haq Nuhu, Chairman, Katsina State Implementation Task Force on the National Policy on Education centred his lecture on "Administrative and Financial Factors Affecting the Development and Retention of Personnel for Effective STM Education."

The lecture focused on:

(i) source and supply of STM teachers;

(ii) administrative factors militating against the development and retention of STM teachers.

6.4 *STAN Symposium*:

The theme of the symposium was "Professional Development and Retention of Personnel for Effective STM Education in Nigeria: Contributions from States." Representatives from the following states participated in the Symposium: Katsina, Kano, Lagos and Ogun.

6.5 *Science Quiz:*

Cross River State represented by Federal Science College, Ogoja won the first prize of the quize competition, Katsina State came second while Bauchi State took the third position.

6.6 *Election:*

Mr John Ogu, MSTAN was elected General Secretary of the Association during the conference.

7.0 *Resolution:*

Having deliberated extensively on the theme: Professional Development and Retention of Personnel for Effective Science, Technology and Mathematics (STM) Education in Nigeria, the conference observed that there was much room for improvement in the professional development and retention of STM teachers and resolved as follows:

7.1 *Commendations:*

STAN commends the Federal Government for:

7.1.1 mounting the Annual Teacher Vacation Course (TVC) for the professional development of STM teachers;

7.1.2 upgrading the Grade II teachers professionally through the NTI Distance Learning System (DLS) to the NCE level, thus encouraging their retention in the teaching profession;

7.1.3 making a deliberate policy for the production of STM teachers;

7.1.4 promulgating an enabling decree for the professionalization of teaching;

7.1.5 establishing more Federal Colleges of Education (Technical) to produce more teachers of technology;

7.1.6 encouraging computer literacy for STM teachers, educators and administrators.

STAN commends that State Government for:

7.1.7 sponsoring the STM teachers to the annual TVC;

7.1.8 paying science inducement allowances to STM teachers;

7.1.9 encouraging computer literacy for STM teachers, educators and administrators;

7.1.10 institutionalizing in-service courses for STM teachers;

7.1.11 providing funds, materials and equipment for STM education.

7.2 Observations:

In spite of the commendations listed above, STAN observes that:

7.2.1 teaching of STM subjects still continues to be devoid of innovative teaching strategies;

7.2.2 a high proportion of equipment in school science laboratories and workshops are in bad condition due to poor maintenance culture;

7.2.3 less than 4 per cent of schools subscribe to any journal and STM journals available to STM teachers have drastically reduced;

7.2.4 some Nigerians that were trained under the Technical Teachers Training Programme (TTTP) in the 80's to teach technology have found their way to commerce and industry due to dissatisfaction and lack of incentives;

7.2.5 Discipline in schools today is at a very low ebb;

7.2.6 STM laboratory personnel are few in the secondary schools and non-existent in the primary schools;

7.2.7 problem of inadequate of funding, poor conditions of service and loss of morale militate against teacher motivation and desire to remain on the job;

7.2.8 an inter-disciplinary approach to the teaching of STM is desirable, and should be extended to include studies in population/family life education, environmental education, citizenship education, drug abuse education and the like.

7.3.0 Recommendations:

STAN therefore recommends that:

7.3.1 Deliberate efforts should be made to train STM teachers in:

(a) group and individual methods of working with students;

(b) greater use of co-curricular activities such as guest lectures, excursions, science fairs and exhibitions;

(c) greater and effective use of home work, assignments and projects.

7.3.2 The provision of laboratories and equipment should be carefully planned and executed so as to effectively support the teaching of science, mathematics and technical subjects.

7.3.3 The curricular of professional training for STM teachers should be broadened to include knowledge of world problems such as population, environment, drugs and peace as well as the wider implication of science such as the philosophies of STM and society.

7.3.4 Proper foundation should be laid for STM education at the primary school level through employing specialist science and mathematics teachers.

7.3.5 The use of non-formal education delivery systems and out-of-school co-curricular activities such as JETS competition should be intensified.

7.3.6 STAN should intensify and formalize its own teacher training efforts and curricula/instructional materials development programme and request government for demonstrable support.

7.3.7 NTI should intensify efforts to operate the section of the decree establishing it which deal with providing teaching with regular in-service training opportunities.

7.3.8 Adequate allocation of funds for Research and Development in Science and Engineering

Infrastructure should constitute a land mark in government's national development plans.

7.3.9 The Federal Ministry of Education and Youth Development should put in place the necessary machinery to establish the National Teachers Registration Council.

7.3.10 States that have not started paying science allowance to their STM teachers should do so in order to encourage them.

7.3.11 Incentives for STM personnel should be made vis-a-vis their participation and effective contribution in workshops, conferences and seminars.

7.3.12 Discipline in schools should be stepped up by involving PTAs.

Professor U.M.O. Iwovi, FSTAN
President
21 August, 1993

Part IV

FUTURE CONTENT IN SCIENCE AND TECHNOLOGY EDUCATION AT SECONDARY LEVEL

Contents

Introduction

The UNESCO PROAP/APEID Regional Workshop for the Development of Science Education at the Secondary Level with Special Reference to Futures Content was held from 29 November to 5 December 1989, in Beijing, People's Republic of China. The Workshop was co-hosted by the National Commission of the People's Republic of China for UNESCO and the Professional Technical Training Centre (PTTC), Beijing. This activity was a component of UNESCO's 1988-89 Programme and the Programme of the UNDP assisted project on the Improvement of Science and Technology Education (RAS/86/051).

Participants/Resource Persons

Fifteen Participants/Observers and resource persons from eight countries attended the Workshop (vide Annex 1—List of Participants).

UNESCO was represented by Dr. F.C. Vohra, CTA, UNDP/UNESCO Science Education Project, Nepal, and Ratanaike, J., Specialist in Science and Technology Education, ACEID, UNESCO/PROAP, Bangkok.

Inauguration

The Workshop was inaugurated by Mr. Jia Xueqian, Deputy Secretary General, Chinese National Commission for UNESCO.

Mr. Lu Yu-Cheng, Deputy Mayor of the Beijing Municipal Government and Mr. Shi Shao-Qi, Chaoyang District Government stressed the importance of the Workshop theme and provided greetings to the participants. A statement about the purposes of and the expectation from the Workshop was made by the UNESCO PROAP/ACEID representative.

Office Bearers

The following were selected unanimously as Office Bearers of the Workshop:

Chairperson	:	Prof. Li Chun (P.R. China)
Vice-Chairperson	:	Dr. Chaleo Manilerd (Thailand)
Rapporteur	:	Dr. T. Freeman (Australia)
Ratnaike, J.	:	UNESCO PROAP/ACEID acted as Secretary to the Wrokshop.

The Agenda

The following Agenda acted as a guiding framework for the deliberations at the Workshop:

1. Opening Ceremony
2. Election of Office Bearers/Discussion of Schedule of Work
3. Exchange of Country Comments
4. Future science content areas at secondary level/ importance/content analysis
5. Recommendations for action in regard to sources, learning/teaching methodologies; learning/teaching experiments/activities, materials
6. Consideration of Draft Final Report
7. Closing Ceremony

Workshop Activities

The Workshop Schedule reflected the following three major components of the Workshop deliberations:

1. country experiences in regard to new trends in science and technology education at secondary level, future content and curricular designs in science and technology education at secondary level, and current status of the development work in this regard;
2. future content, its justification and its analysis;
3. potential sources for reference and consultation, possible learning/teaching activities, investigations and

experiments for the secondary level in regard to this content, and likely implementation difficulties.

The country experiences were presented and discussed in plenary. In particular, country experiences dealt with current work in regard to science and technology education after the Year 2000; and the curriculum models, structures, and strategies envisaged for the purpose.

The other two components were discussed both in plenary and in two groups, the Physical Science Group; and the Biological Science Group. Potential content from different significant issues in science and technology of the future, such as new frontiers of science; global issues related to science and technology; and science issues derived from technological advancement, were taken up for discussion.

The discussions on the identification and analysis of content and its justification were triggered by the following four brief presentations looking into the above issues:

1. The Use of Computers and Calculators in preparing for a Career in Engineering or the Physical Sciences by Dr. T. Freeman (Australia)
2. Laser as High Tech for Development: A Case Study from Thailand by Dr. Chaleo Manilerd (Thailand)
3. Biology-based Technology by Dr. F.C. Vohra, CTA, UNESCO/UNDP Science Education Project, Nepal

Similar brief presentations by:

1. The P.R. China delegation, on New Trends and Implementation Difficulties;
2. Dr. Wongchan Wongkaew (Thailand), on possible experimental work on bio-technology; and
3. Dr. T. Freeman (Australia), on possible experimental activities in computer/physics, stimulated discussion on potential directions for the conversion of future content into learning/teaching episodes.

During Group Work, the participants considered further details of the content analysis, the justifications, the experimental work for learning and teaching, and potential resources for reference and consultation.

Interactions with Secondary Education

The Workshop schedule included visits to secondary schools in Beijing, in particular vocational schools, which were incorporating future requirements for socio-economic development in China in their training programmes for students. Indeed, participants had intimate and practical interactions with these training programmes in that the entire service operation at the Workshop, from hotel and food service to the AV and duplication services, were entirely, and highly competently, provided by upper teenage secondary vocational students. This underlined a very real, highly admirable and deeply appreciated dimension about futures in secondary education.

Closing

Prior to the Closing Session on 5 December, the Workshop considered recommendations for further action at national and regional levels, and at the Closing Session, adopted the Draft Final Report of the Workshop.

The Closing Ceremony was conducted by the Chairman, Dr. Li Chun.

Participants, resource persons and observers, and the UNESCO staff, were unanimous in their deep appreciation of the excellent services, generous hospitality and warm personal care and concern provided to them throughout the Workshop by the Organizers. The rich and varied experiences enjoyed by those who attended the Workshop were both unique and rewarding.

The participants, resource persons and observers expressed appreciation of the opportunities provided by UNESCO to share and investigate together a new area of science and technology education.

1
Country Comments

Each participating country provided a document and presentation on the thinking, priorities, strategies, design and content being considered nationally for the future science and technology education at secondary level. Each presentation was followed by intensive discussions and clarifications on the various issues involved, both substantive and feasibility.

The following represents a brief summary of the country experiences, and of significant trends and issues, in the development of future science and technology education at secondary level.

PEOPLE'S REPUBLIC OF CHINA

Science and technology are developing rapidly at the present time. It is necessary to let middle school students do, as early as possible, new and developing subjects that represent the future of science and technology. China is making great efforts in the reform of the educational system, content and methods so that education serves better the socialist modernization.

There are five strategies being experimented for introducing new science and technology: (1) to open up the content in parts of teaching materials with knowledge of new subjects; (2) to offer optional courses on new subjects; (3) to organize extracurricular groups for educational activities; (4) to carry out the new subject education in senior vocational middle schools according to specialities; (5) to let after-class organizations organize students in study and research. The contents include environmental science, genetics, space science, biological engineering, super conduction technology, electronic technology, remote sensing technology and microcomputers. The teaching methods vary according to the content and educational equipment; knowledge introduction, experiments and observations, and scientific research. The municipal and district (county) educational administrations, schools and after-school organizations are responsible for the organizational and administrative work. Promotion methods are exchanging experience and citing the advanced workers.

With such efforts, the new subject education, in Beijing middle schools, has obtained the following development and achievement in recent years.

Environmental education was started in 1987 in 15 ordinary middle schools. They have given elective courses like Environmental Chemistry and Environmental Physics to the senior middle school pupils and organized some of them to take part in surveying environmental pollution and writing theses. The experts gave great attention to *"Noise Pollution Circumstances of No. 15 Middle School and Propositions for Control"* written by the pupils in the No. 15 Middle School and *"Survey on Pollution of Liangma River"* and *"Survey, Analysis and Design of the Social Environmental System of Bai Yang Dian"* written by the pupils in the No. 80 Secondary School. Some of vocational schools have established the speciality of environmental control.

In recent years, 176 middle schools have opened computer courses for senior middle school students, with successful results. The students majoring in computer in senior vocational middle schools, could master several computer languages, and they all receive training in programming and software making.

A biological research group of the Middle School attached to Qing Hua University, with the help and instruction of the Biology Department of Beijing University, found out a new breed of fruitfly while researching a new mutant breed of Beijing fruitfly. Even schools are equipped with electron microscopes of 200,000 times magnification. Some senior vocational middle schools for horticulture set up special tissue culturing laboratories. Some senior vocational middle schools in the countryside applied knowledge of hereditary breeding to productive practices.

Students from the No. 2 Middle School attached to the Normal University, Ba Yi Middle School and Changxindian Middle School for the children of railway workers and staff, took part in the national youngsters competition in designing the space shuttle load project.

The senior vocational middle school of Haidian district offered the laser photo-composition speciality, and students could operate skillfully the computer for composition, and use the laser printer.

In recent years, the Science and Technology Centre for Youngsters of Chongwen District has been popularizing knowledge of super conduction among middle school students, carrying out low temperature super conduction experiments, and have made a superconductive materials with help of the Physics Research Institute of Academic Sinica. This centre is also spreading laser knowledge among middle school students, doing optical experiments with lasers, and students learn to make microfilms with laser technology. Some senior vocational schools have opened microfilming courses.

The aeroplane model group of the Youngsters Science and Technology Centre of Xuanwu District has recently made a low-altitude micro-aircraft controlled by sensing, in co-operation with the Agriculture University. This micro-aircraft can monitor dynamically crop growing. The electronics group has applied electronics technology to musical instrument making and developed many kinds of new electronic musical instruments.

The radio group of the Children's Palace of Haidian district, has organized 15 middle school students, under the instruction of the engineers from the National Meteorology Satellite Centre and the counselling teachers from the Children's Palace, to develop in two years, a small unit able to receive cloud atlases from the Japanese GMS static satellite and the American NOAA Satellite. This satellite cloud atlas receiver adopted IC phase-lock demodulation technology, and made a breakthrough in smallness and multi-functionality. It's technical specifications, such as receiving sensitivity, has surpassed the present level of domestic products, and some specifications reached the level of international advanced products. The biology group has been carrying out botany tissue breeding experiments under the guidance of the Botany Research Institute of Academia Sinica.

The Municipal Science and Technology Centre for the Young organized 10 middle school students to develop low altitude photographic techniques.

Presently, there are two problems in developing the new subjects in education in Beijing's middle schools: (1) the class hours of present subjects are too many to arrange new subjects; (2) teachers are short of knowledge for new subjects. In order to develop the new subject education, it is necessary to make great adjustments, to subject arrangement and content, and to train teachers. The task is difficult, but these problems can be solved while the education reformation is deepening.

INDONESIA

Various conceptions about the future have been worked out. Some concern the negative side of the future, such as the fear of nuclear disaster, polluted environments, depleted resources and the energy crisis. The world will be full of catastrophe and the ones who survive, will have the enormous task of rebuilding a whole new world almost from the beginning. Some conceptions are concerned with the positive side of the future. In the mental make-up of humans, there are creative faculities such as wisdom and good sense. There will be innovative ideas in developing the new modern world. This conceptions are used to chart out the concept of education, education for awareness and education for mankind. Communications and information systems are developing rapidly and effectively so that if we are not aware we will be left behind by the modern world.

Indonesia and other developing countries have the same problems, that is to breakthrough the low economic growth and to put a foundation for improving the quality of life. This needs a big effort in national development. There are two main problems in the process of development. Firstly, the problem of life environment caused by povert and by the big population.

Secondly, the problem of managing the existing natural resources. The destruction of the life environment is caused by the problems themselves and the science and technology used to overcome the problems. This means that the science and technology know-how and its applications given to students should be selected in accordance with environmental problem.

The 1988 National Workshop and Seminar on Future Science Curriculum in Jakarta agreed to use the following strategy and framework of thought to develop the Future Science and Technology Education Programme.

The Strategy of the Development of Future Science and Technology in Secondary School Curricula.

The Determination of
Science and Technology Education Goals

↓

Institutional Goals of Science and Technology Education

↓

Curricular Objectives of
Science and Technology Education Programme

↓

Instructional Objectives
of Science and Technology Topics and Sub-topics

↓

Science and Technology Curriculum Content

The translation of Science and Technology Education Goals into Institutional Goals should be carried out by representatives from research, development and implementation bodies in the Ministry of Education and Culture, various universities, related ministries, related private and public institutions, and related industries.

The movement of institutional Goals into Instructional Objectives is supposed to be carried out by experts in education and psychology, scientists, science educationists, professional leaders in education, supervisors, headmasters and teachers.

The Development of Future Science and Technology Education in Indonesia (A Framework of Thought)

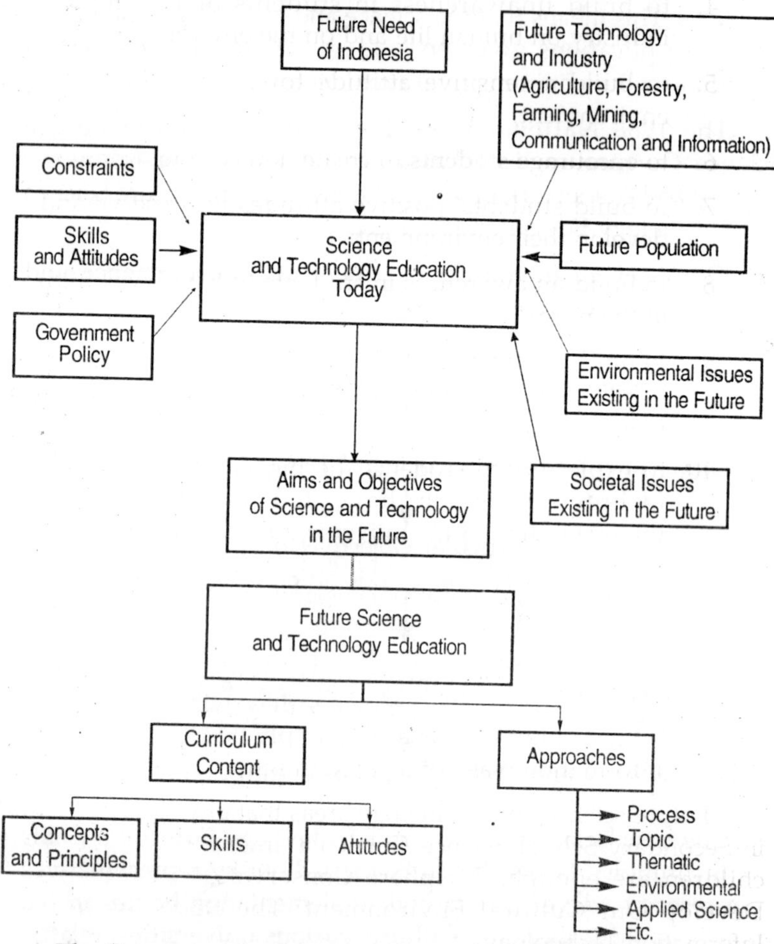

The Science and Technology Education Programme has the following aims:

1. to provide students with concepts and principles relevant to the implementation and problems of science and technology today and tomorrow;
2. to encourage students to think systematically, constantly and accurately;

3. to provide students with basis skills for entering the world of work;
4. to build unawareness in students of the impact of industry on human life and on the environment;
5. to build a sensitive attitude towards changes in the environment;
6. to encourage students to create new technology;
7. to build students' positive attitudes to preserve and to develop their environment;
8. to build an awareness in students to have two children at the most;
9. to build an awareness in students of the important role of scientists in the building of an improved future for mankind;
10. to explore with students the big ideas of science and technology which have led to man's current understanding of the universe, resulting in far-reaching technological achievements, which figured in civilization's major problems and presented some of the most exciting challenges for the future;
11. to ensure that students learn how to learn, so that solutions to future problems they will be confronted with will not be prevented simply because the relevant information was not learned in school.

Future science and technology areas that are likely to appear in Secondary School Science Curricula among others are: Two children are enough; Biosphere Conservation; Preserve and Develop Our Cultural Environment; The Rapid Growth of Information Technology.

List of Contents of Air and Water Conservation

A. We need air

1. What is air?
2. Do we need pure oxygen?
3. The importance of nitrogen.

4. The importance of carbon dioxide.
5. The greenhouse effect.
6. Photosynthesis and respiration.
7. The noble gases.
8. Some experiments on air:
   (a) Some experiments on photosynthesis
   (b) Measure your lung power
   (c) Volume of air that passes through your lungs in 24 hours
   (d) Does the air you breathe out contain more carbon dioxide?
   (e) How do clouds form?

B. *Pollutants*

1. What are pollutants?
2. Smong: the silent killer
3. Photochemical smog
4. Temperature inversion
5. Sulphur dioxide strikes again
6. Acid rain
7. Aerosols and the Ozone layer
8. Lead in petrol: knock anti-knock compound
9. Carbon monoxide: the invisible killer
10. Mercury: the Mad Hatter's complaint
11. Fluorides
12. Cigarette smoke
13. Radioactivity
14. Nuclear power stations
15. Testing of nuclear weapons
16. Storage of radioactive waste

17. Some pollution activities:
    (a) How pure is the air you breathe?
    (b) Collecting dust
    (c) Looking at smoke
    (d) What gases are put into the air when coal burns?
    (e) What gases are put into the air when petroleum products burn?
    (f) Making and testing sulphur dioxide
    (g) Does sulphur dioxide affect plants?
    (h) What do cigarettes deposit in your lungs?

The Boundless Sea

1. Ways of cleaning oil-soaked feathers
2. Pollution and conservation

We Need Water

1. Can you imagine life without running water?
2. Drinking-water from river-water
3. How water is treated in a modern sewage-work
4. The oxygen needs of some animals
5. Study the animal life in a river
6. How much water do you use?
7. Construct a model water-purifier
8. Some chemical experiments on water
9. Questions on water treatment

Water for Agriculture

1. Case history: damming the river
2. Plants and water
3. Some experiments on plants and water
4. Questions on water and agriculture

Water for Washing

1. What is soap? How does it work?
2. Detergents
3. Hard and soft water
4. Soap or detergent: Which is better?
5. Construct a model water-softener
6. Make a bar of soap
7. Experiments on soaps and detergents
   (a) Which disperses dirt better—soap or detergent?
   (b) Which is better at making oil mix with water—soap or detergent?
   (c) Do soap and detergent lather in hard water?
   (d) Which are the most alkaline detergents?
   (e) Which are better—enzyme detergents or non-enzyme detergents?
   (f) Which detergent gives you the most for your money?
   (g) What makes algae grow?

MALAYSIA

There are several reasons as to why the Ministry of Education in Malaysia has to review the present curricula of science education. Society today seems to be experiencing a very serious spiritual and moral crisis. Drug abuse, drug trafficking, corruption, misappropriation of funds, personal aggrandizements and hedonism are some examples of the societal problems that Malaysia faces. The Ministry feels that it is time for the educators to devote more efforts into finding ways to minimize these problems. Educating the youngsters with proper moral values for example, may help solve some of these problems.

The education system today is still geared towards equipping students with certificates and occupational skills only. The education system should be restructured to give due emphasis to the overall development of the individual who will later help contribute to the progress of the religion, race and nation. Neither do we consider a student as a total person if he or she is equipped with occupational skills only. However, Malaysian society continues giving emphasis to academic achievement and excellence, to the exclusion of other factors contributing to the well-being of young people.

Science education has to be closely linked to technology. Much of the advance in scientific researches aimed at the alleviation of human problems has been due to applications of technology. Technology has a close link with personal, social and economic affairs, and has become a part of the culture of this era of modern living. To cope with the knowledge explosion, it is perhaps pertinent to include in the science curriculum the study of new technology. The objectives in exposing study areas in technology should not only provide students with basic technological literacy and skills, but also aim at helping them develop an awareness of the social consequences of technology. This will gear science education towards increasing students' understanding about the interactive role of science and technology in improving society.

An appropriate science education programme has to be designed to produce the most effective form of training that is sensitive to the changing needs of a country gearing towards industrial progress. The science curriculum should not only be designed to provide the foundation for further education in science and technology, but also to give direct support to vocational and technical training to develop technical skills. This will contribute towards the manpower requirements of a nation progressing towards becoming an industrialized nation.

In the search for new content areas in science education at secondary level in Malaysia, it is necessary for every curriculum planner to review the scenario of scientific and technological advancement in the 21st century. One of the major emphases is to develop in students the ability to acquire intellectual skills and positive values that are required to deal with social problems in everyday life. The inquiry skills, through experimentations and other activities taught in schools, are not sufficient to help students understand the resolution of human issues and problems. The intellectual processes should also be emphasized to develop in students the skills required for analyzing, validating, synthesizing information in making responsible decisions.

The following is a listing of futures science content areas that have been drafted by the Curriculum Development Centre in Malaysia.

1. Science for an Understanding of Nature
2. Science for the Well-being of Man
3. Science for Personal Development

The content is organized thematically and integrates scientific knowledge and its application, scientific skills and sound moral values. Such an approach follows for a wider coverage of several inter-related concepts in a particular theme as well as basic knowledge in science. Four themes are identifie for study. These are:

1. Man and the Variety of Living Things around Him
2. The Wealth of the Earth's Resources and their Management
3. Energy for Life
4. Man and the Balance of Nature

For each topic in the syllabus, specifications are provided. These specifications outline the emphases given to each topic and the main content to be covered, including scientific knowledge and applications. Moral values to be inculcated are also defined.

MONGOLIA

The Mongolian People's Revolutionary Party and the Government, having analyzed the present situation and the prospect of developing education, in 1986 worked out the project of *"The Improvement of the School System"* to reflect the scientific and technological achievements of the leading branches of science essential for school education, to develop democracy in schools, to perfect the school network and its development.

The learning of Physics, Chemistry, Biology and Geography has been reformed into a course of natural science having taken the logical connection between these subjects and the rinciple of transferring the curricula from general to special modern scientific and technological progress, development of industrial technology and their prospects. Computers are widely used. So informatics and principles of computing techniques are now taught.

One of the modern key-problems which occurs from scientific and technological progress and human activity, is the question of given children ecological education. While elaborating curricula, the principles of heritage the reform are the main principles in the curricula of these subjects. In elaboration, curricula are enriched, on the one hand with the rich historical tradition of the people, which always treats nature with great care, love and humanism, and on the other hand, with achievements of modern science in this branch and its ideas. At the same time, excursions and practical classes in laboratories are to be organized widely. The people have a historical tradition tradition of developing cattlebreeding on pasture. The development of this will be continued as it is very economical. On the base of social requirements and traditions, the curriculum for teaching cattle breeding, agriculture and industry has been worked out. In the curriculum, not only problems of tradition, but also of modern mechanized agriculture, and industry are included. Besides special classes were opened for the 6-8th Form, in order to prepare young cattle-breeders. Pupils enter this class on their own or at their parents' request. These pupils learn general education like other pupils. But they do practical work on cattle-breeding. The experiment has shown that the lessons, which were taught by the front-rank cattle-breeders and specialists, were useful. After the 8th Form, pupils may continue their study or became cattle-breeders and may choose one of the following schools: technical-vocational school, or specialized agricultural secondary school. This form of teaching corresponds to the specific character of Mongolia.

Modern science, the technical progress, relation between the society and people, demand the main task of training youth to live in peace without war, to be human and kind. According to this, a special curriculum is available on the following subjects: morality, healthy mode of life, civil rights, economy and ethics. The curriculum includes questions dealing with customs, traditions, mode of life, relation between people and society, economy, state law, civil rights.

According to this programme, pupils of the 1-4th Form must take part in work at home; 5-7 Form pupils in school surroundings, 8-9 Form pupils in the process of the country's production. The teaching staff of the school may change 10-50 per cent of the school hours. It gives an opportunity to realize the whole programme, to support and develop the independent work of teachers, to form the pupils' ability to work, to live. The purpose of the 6-7 subjects for the 1-4 Form pupils is to give them an ability for successful study, knowledge of scientific, morals, healthy, mode of life and collectivism. There will be 8-12 pupils in the optional classes from 8 Form and they will be taught through a special programme and handbooks. There are several optional classes of the following subjects, mathematics, physics, chemistry, biology, foreign languages. These optional classes for the 8-9 Forms are organized as inter-school classes.

The 10-11 Form pupils will get general education according to modern requirements. From the 10th Form, pupils will be involved in specialized training: mathematics-computer, physics-technology, biology-agriculture, geography-economics, chemistry-technology, language-history, and so on. The specialized subjects will be taught by the special programme. But the other subjects will be chosen by the pupils according to their interests, and these subjects have the ordinary programme. This method of training releases pupils from "*compulsion*", makes them responsible, and gives them more free time for self-development and self-education.

Scientists of the Academy of Science, the teaching staff of institutions, secondary school teachers, famous honoured culture and art workers, are experiencing working together on projects of the new reforms in order to improve inter-lessons and inter-theme contacts.

The curriculum of secondary schools consists of two logically connected parts, core and optional: 30 per cent of all hours of the 1-11th Forms will be devoted to optional courses.

PHILIPPINES

The Philippines is undergoing socio-economic and political changes. Hence, education sees the job of developing the individual so he can participate and live successfully in a challenging, highly competitive, changing, technological world.

It is relevant to the goals of science education in the Philippines. These goals are:

1. to be more responsive to the needs of the Philippine society and to the national government goals;
2. to strengthen the scientific knowledge, processes and values acquired in the earlier grades for scientific literacy and the improvement of the quality of life;
3. to communicate the wonders of scientific endeavours and stimulate students with aptitude in scientific and allied careers for the development of high level scientific manpower of the country.

The Science Education in the Philippines twenty years from now is envisioned as enriched Science and Technology courses of the newly implemented New Secondary Education Curriculum. The following is a listing of the future science content in designated year levels:

Science and Technology I

(i) Introduction to Science and Technology I

(ii) Forces

(iii) Forms and Transformation of Energy

(iv) Naturally occurring changes

(v) Living things and their environment

(vi) Forms of Life

(vii) The Earth and the Universe

Science and Technology I is exploratory in nature. It presents basic concepts in physics, biology, chemistry, earth and space science.

Science and Technology II

(i) Introduction to Science and Technology II

(ii) Changes in Life on Earth

(iii) Chemical and Cellular Basis of Life

(iv) Life Energy

(v) Genetics

(vi) Basic Concepts in Genetic Engineering

(vii) Reproductive Processes

(viii) The Organ Systems

(ix) Basic Concepts in Biotechnology

Science and Technology II course is biology based. It studies natural phenomena in living things as it aims to develop understanding of man's living world and his interaction and relationship with the environment. It presents biological problems related to conservation, food production, health, reproduction and heredity.

Science and Technlogy III

(i) Introduction to Science and Technology III

(ii) Changes in matter

(iii) Molecules

(iv) The atom

(v) Periodicity

(vi) Chemical Bonds

(vii) Change, Energy and Time

(viii) Solutions

(ix) Acids and Bases

(x) Carbon and Its Compounds

(xi) The Molecules of Life

(xii) Colloids

The core of Science and Technology III is chemistry aimed at stimulating and preparing students for a career in the sciences. It presents an overview of chemistry in terms of atomic/ molecular nature of substances. It is geared towards the acquisition of an essential foundation of a student's development into a productive citizen. It considers chemical knowledge applied in technology, which has immensely influenced man's lifestyle.

Science and Technology IV

(i) Introduction to Science and Technology IV

(ii) Force and Motion

(iii) Gravity and Satellites

(iv) Electromagnetic Theory

(v) Electromagnets

(vi) Electronics

(vii) Waves

(viii) Matter and Energy

The core of Science and Technology IV is physics. It is treated as a product of experiment and theory. It aims at developing concepts as basis for the interpretation and understanding of physics phenomena. Through a historical development of concepts, physics technology is presented, and its humanistic background shown.

The incorporation/integration of concepts of the above-mentioned topics in the proposed science curricula of the secondary schools is a need. Recognition and comprehension of updated concepts will make the student: (1) conscious of the pace of technology advancement and scientific breakthrough; (2) an expert in scientific and technological investigations; (3) able to adapt, utilize and improve existing technologies.

These modern day concepts in Science and Technology will also encourage technology sharing and transfer. In totality, inclusion of these topics will contribute to national productivity and improve the quality of life of the Filipino people.

THAILAND

The Thai Education System provides for six years of primary education, three years of lower secondary education, three years of upper secondary education or three years of vocational upper secondary education, and four years of tertiary education. Primary education is compulsory for all children from the age of 6-12. Preparations are being made to extend compulsory education to include lower secondary education.

The Ministry of Education is responsible for the provision of primary and secondary education, with the Ministry of University Affairs responsible for tertiary education. There are some exceptions in that the Ministry of Education maintains some teachers colleges and technical colleges which grant bachelor degrees in various subjects. Also private agencies are allowed to run private schools and universities under terms and conditions provided by the Ministry of Education and the Ministry of University Affairs.

The Department of Education Techniques of the Ministry of Education is in charge of curriculum development for primary secondary schools in all subjects, concept in science and mathematics. As early as 1972, the Government of Thailand established a semi-autonomous body in the form of a state enterprise asked with the promotion of the teaching and learning of science. That organization is the Institute for the Promotion of Teaching Science and Technology (IPST). The IPST at present has a regular staff of about 200 persons and draws support from part-time staff joining on a secondment basis. As a state enterprise, the IPST is held accountable to its Governing Board whose membership consists of Directors General of various departments of the Ministry of Education as ex-officio members and also distinguished academics. In this way, the IPST maintains close links with the Ministry of Education and its schools and also organizations and institutes involved in the advancement of science and technology in Thailand.

Since 1972, the IPST has engaged itself in the improvement of the teaching and learning of science, technology and mathematics as an on-going activity. In the beginning stage, all textbooks in science and secondary school level and mathematics at the primary and secondary school levels were ungraded and rewritten. Science equipment and apparatus and teaching media needed for teaching new curricula were produced on a large scale and made available to all schools. Teachers were also trained to teach the new curricula. As of now, there are science and mathematics courses that are obligatory for all children upto the last year of the lower secondary schools. In the upper secondary schools, there are science courses which are obligatory for children who will take up science or science or science-related careers at the university level and also science courses obligatory for children who will study social science, humanities or such similar subjects at the university level and for those who will seek employment at the end of their secondary school years.

The time ratio between the obligatory and elective courses is about 80 to 20 per cent.

The salient features of the science and mathematics curriculum developed at the IPST include the following:

- emphases given to practical work using low-cost equipment;
- development of pertinent science concepts followed by applications;
- topics especially in science for non-science students related to students' daily life;
- inquiry methods introduced wherever possible;
- inculcation of values and attitudes that science and technology can be used to solve problems at individual and social levels;
- care for life and the environment.

As a result of the plan of the Department of Educational Techniques to reform the national curricula beginning from 1990, science and mathematics curricula for lower and secondary schools will also undergo changes. In the new curriculum system, more elective subjects will be made available for children, both at primary and secondary school levels. Elective course are to allow teachers and local education authorities more participation in the design of curricula, and permit children to choose what to learn according to their aptitude, abilities and interest.

As the manpower needs in Thailand in the fields of science and technology, especially in the area of material science, computer, electronic, and bio-engineering, will be very acute during the next decade, the science and mathematics curricula from the primary to upper secondary school will be influenced greatly by that need. It is, therefore, to be expected that new subjects related to hitech, such as laser, superconductivity, materials science, biotechnology will be introduced, hopefully in imaginative ways, to children in the upper secondary schools. New emphases will also be expected to focus on content for talented children, while science and mathematics for non-science children will be more related to applications and what children experience in their daily lives. Inquiry and scientific method will continue to receive attention, especially at the primary and lower secondary education. After that, children will be expected to apply science method and inquiry approach in a natural manner familiar to them in their early years of education.

SOCIALIST REPUBLIC OF VIET NAM

The Vietnamese education system has completed the change from the 5-3-2 to the 9-3 system, with the new education system. Compulsory education begins from the age of 6 and continues until 15. In the Vietnamese education system, the schools which provide the first nine years of the first stage of compulsory education are known as basic schools. At the end of the nine basic school years, children who pass the screening examination with good marks (about 30 per cent of the total child population), go on to the second stage school (Grades 10, 11 and 12). All students of the second stage school at the end of Grade 12 take the Exit Examination organized on a nationwide basis.

Students who satisfy the minimum grade requirement may apply to sit for the entrance examinations organized by universities and colleges. Generally speaking, only 6 to 8 per cent of the graduates of Grade 12 are admitted to higher education. Those who fail to find places in tertiary education may either receive further training at job-training centres or attend secondary vocational schools. This explains why, in the past, second-stage schools tended to organize their curriculum on the subjects that prepare students for future employment. It makes many years of experience and discussion to realize that the situation is not appropriate to Vietnamese educational development. The general education in the second stage school should give more attention to fundamental knowledge and traditional science subjects such as physics, chemistry, biology and mathematics. In facing the challenge at the close of the twentieth century, and preparing to meet the twenty-first century, Vietnamese educators see clearly that innovations in the organization of teaching/learning processes, in methodology and in the subject contents are urgent matters.

For Viet Nam, five areas of science and technology development are regarded as priority:

- Computer science (hardware and software)
- Automation in production and processing, and micro-electronics
- Bio-technology
- New Materials Science
- New types of energy (renewable as well as non-renewable)

It is expected that in the near future, students will face development problems in the above indicated areas, and this is why they should be prepared.

Trends and Issues Raised by Participating Countries

The country presentations and their follow-up discussions clearly demonstrated the common concern with the importance of well planned future content. The major motivation for such planning came from rapidly developing socio-economic trends, due to the urgent need in all countries for technological development. Participants were aware of the accelerated and continuing growth of science and technology. It was agreed that the need for secondary school learners to be aware of these developments in a fast changing world scene was a challenge best met by science education. Agreement was quickly reached among the participants, when defining new areas to be included are: bio-technology, environmental concerns, health information, electronics, renewable energy sources, with lasers and high temperature superconductivity. Another issue canvassed and supported was the general question of moral and ethical values in relation to science and technology.

Several detailed analyses of bio-technology were presented and these made it clear that this field has become an interdisciplinary subject in itself. As with the other items, the problems of definition and categorizing the subject cannot remove the urgent demands that bio-technology be explained in science classes at all levels. Similarly, environmental concerns raise broad multi-disciplinary issues, but it appears that these issues have started to filter through science syllabuses and some experience in teaching these items has been gained. In particular, praticle environmental problems have enabled many students to gain an appreciation of how science can help them protect the familiar surroundings. Health information needs clearer paradigms, but it is likely that this topic will also be readily appreciated by students at all levels. Micro-electronics, lasers, materials science, superconductivity are among the new growth frontiers of science and technology knowledge and cannot be left out of a future curriculum content. It is possible that moral and ethical questions can also enrich the context of many areas of new science and technology content.

Many new content items still require a greater depth of content analysis. This is exemplified by the various aspects of electronics, again a subject in itself, and one that is rapidly updating its content. Renewable energy resources and efficient conservation practices have become more familiar environmental issues, but as components of physical or biological sciences, they also suffer from rapidly changing trends and technological methods. Lasers, superconductors and new materials will probably retain their relevance as they become increasingly used in many technological applications. As these items are available for classroom use, it is unlikely that future secondary school programmes will be able to avoid their application. It is understood however that other discoveries may demand urgent consideration and as a consequence some of the above items could become displaced.

While the general topics such as those mentioned, have been considered, more thorough and comprehensive analyses that cover the many parameters involved, including those of ethics and values as well as prerequisite knowledge bases required for the learning of the new content areas, are still required. The present level of resolution is limited by the interdisciplinary nature of many of the new content topics as well as by different national needs. Preliminary attempts at content analysis have highlighted the need to involve a variety of resource persons from different disciplines and occupations, including those from technology.

There is a problem with the introduction of new science and technology content. If it is added on to enrich existing content, steps must be taken to prevent the accretion of too much syllabus material specially at purely factual level (the *"barnacle"* effect). Indeed the addition of new science and technology items could well demand the retention and probable extension in depth of relevant items already in the current content, to act as prerequisite foundational bases for the new content. Optional and core course structures have been used in some countries to resolve this conflict. The prescribed time allocation between core material and options varies with different countries and with different categories of students within these countries. In countries where external final examinations are taken, the options cause some concern and suspicion. Where decentralized or school based asssessment is practical, it is usually easier to meet local requirements using the core-option system.

Optional learning, in some countries, has been extended to out-of-school science and technology activities, which in several countries, have blossomed into highly creative and complex hands-on productions by students. The out-of-school modality appears to be most effective for blending science and technology in the development of an imaginative product, in the mobilization of high level human and other resources for learning and in providing considerable incentive, development of self esteem and encouragement to students to study science and technology further, especially at tertiary level. The out-of-school modality can encourage the use of process skills in science, such as problem solving, critical thinking and constructive synthesis in uncontrived situations and make them integral parts of the learning performance of students.

A second, as yet unresolved, issue arises from the extent to which technology needs to be described, as compared to the explanation of the scientific theories that undergird it. This issue becomes a very serious matter, since external sources such as the *"mass media"* are laready referring to many spectacular technologies and break-throughs, and frequently with an aura of *"magic"*. An adequate general education of students at the secondary level is required so that they can make choises with understanding, concerning these matters, particularly with ethics and values colourations. In addition, a vigorous approach is required to prepare the intellectual stream of a nation for tertiary studies in science and technology. Some countries are able to select and encourage talented students by the use of national and/or international Olympiads in the various science, technology and mathematics areas. Where such special attention is given to able students, a flexible opportunity remains for the exploration of in-depth coverage of topics from technology and science, without ultimately disadvantaging the other students.

Throughout all the above considerations, the competence of secondary school teachers to undertake the tasks involved remains a matter of deep concern, a third major issue. Some forms of in-service enrichment of teachers are available in many countries, while teachers from higher levels of education have been mobilized to assist with teaching new areas. Suitable strategies and implementation plans for this problem seem, at best, to be still at the formative stage, in most countries in the region. This situation will remain until the future science with technology curricula are more clearly defined, and resource networks become available to teachers to practice their learning to learn competencies.

Most of the successful examples of the introduction of components of new science and technoloy content, appear to come from affluent urban areas. This is not surprising, since these particular areas are also affluent in teaching and knowledge resources. This observation points to the fact that while new innovations can be tested in affluent environments, they will not necessarily spread nationwide no matter how successful they prove to be in the affluent areas. In the longer term, consideration must be given to the general provision of adequate quality support items, especially to disadvantaged areas, together with the implementation of any new science syllabus in the future.

2

Future Content

Having discussed the importance of the several new content areas for future science learning at secondary level, the Workshop undertook the task of attempting to indicate the kinds of content analyses countries would need to undertake, prior to entering the complex tasks of curriculum development. The importance of the selected new areas was also indicated. Use was made of the substantive papers and presentations of the resource persons.

Experience gained from previous reforms in science education, since particularly the 1960s, shows that (a) content analysis is an essential prerequisite exercise for systematic curriculum development; and (b) it consists of several operations, not necessarily sequential. Content analysis may start with content specialists providing a comprehensive list of knowledge elements (factual and conceptual) ordered in terms of the most significant conceptual structures of the subject. Curriculum developers would then select the content sub-set appropriate to a given learner population. This mode proved to be most productive during the reforms of the 1960s, especially for updating content in terms of concepts and for removing historical content debris non-essential to focused concept formation in the subject area. Another mode used has been the discursive description of a content areas which would indicate the scope of the content within selected boundaries, to be followed later by a detailed content analysis in the manner of the first mode.

The analyses undertaken by the Biological Science Working Group and the Physical Science Working Group are not prescriptive, either in mode or details, but explorative, and merely attempt to indicate some examples of types of steps in content analysis that may be undertaken. Even then, the few examples chosen are not comprehensive within themselves, but provide possible stimulations for further content discussions in the countries on these examples as well.

It should be *stressed* that the Working Groups only attempted the very *first step* in content analysis, a first approximation to a *"scope map"*, which also embodies the justifications for including the content. The total process of content analysis itself would involve may more steps before the intended learning outcomes, even in the cognitive domain, are identified concretely and tied to their respective conceptual structures, in preparation for developing learning sequences.

The two Groups attempted different techniques for this first step analysis, and used different extents of detail and format in the analysis. Because of the acknowledged current importance of Bio-technology, this area of learing was provided specially detailed consideration by the Biological Science Working Group. It is an example of the initiation of content analysis, of a growing edge of science today. The content analysis also places the new content items in a historical perspective, to emphasize that even if the *"present"* content is *"radically new"*, it has its own co-ordinates and roots in the stream of time and knowledge development. This analysis merely illustrates, as an example, the kind of first analysis that may be needed in other new content areas as well.

The Physical Science Group, on the other hand, focusing on Physics, considered the need for a core of foundational *"traditioinal"* basic science content on which to build the new science. The new sicence may be placed in optional and post foundational positions in the curriculum specifications. A scope map was also developed for the area, Laser.

New content cannot be merely attached to an existing curriculum. Aside from subject matter logic, curriculum overload has also to be considered. Adequate learning time has to be provided for the learning of new content, which frequently is complex, multi-disciplinary and requires other prerequisite content for the learning, especially if the learning is to be more than at the level of factual recall.

Taken together, the deliberations of the two Working Groups represent some of the important content analysis parameters, even at its first stages that may need to be considered in identifying new science content for future science and technology education at secondary level. The Working Group deliberations also portray two *different* strategies for the possible entry of future content into science education curricula.

Since science and technology are expanding at an unprecedented acceleration, it is highly likely that the corresponding content will also keep on changing with equal rapidity. Hence, the process of frequent and fast updating of content would need to be built into the content analysis activities as a "*routine*" continuous action. Aside from the specification of intended learning outcomes having to deal with very new, and often complex and interdisciplinary or multi-disciplinary content, the rapid rate of change would be an additional complication, even at first step in curriculum development. Rate of change in curriculum development would need to match the rate of change in future science content, an aspect of curriculum design that has hardly been considered by most countries of the region. The development of the "*scope map*" may well help in this direction.

A major achievement of the work of the Groups was the surfacing of options for content analysis, and for the introduction of the new content into current curricula. With the significant complication of multi- and trans-disciplinary content of the new areas, the usual subject-matter content analysis of the 1960s does not necessarily apply. A major breakthrough at the Workshop was the use of the technique of the "*scope map*" or a first contour of the new content area. Undoubtedly, a "*purely*" subject matter content analysis into the various content elements that form the new areas, structured according to the appropriate conceptual schemes, *is* possible, but it would be a long and possible contentious task, in the context of the multi- and trans-disciplinarity of the content. The "*scope map*" or contour format, however, makes it possible for a practitioner in the area of the new content (the equivalent to the content expert of the 1960s), to come up with a relatively quick description of the *"borders"* of the new content area for the purposes intended (for example, secondary education); which may then be followed by a further delving into the *"map"* to identify specific detailed content elements; and which itself may be followd with appropriate schematic and conceptual structuring, accepting that since the multi- and trans-disciplinary nature of the content is a reality, there may well be several *"helixes"* of conceptual structures inter-connected and interacting with each other (like a more complex model of the DNA type), rather than the *"simplistic"* linear scheme of content analysis, in the individual subject areas, of the reforms of the 1960s.

Deliberations of the Biological Science Working Group

The *"large new areas"* of content in the biological sciences were identified as follows:

- Human biology, health and nutrition
- Social biology and sanitation
- Human and environmental ecology (Populations and family planning, etc.)
- Marine Sciences (oceanography)
- Natural resource management involving their wise and rational use
- Bio-technology

Human Biology, Health and Nutrition

- Human body systems
- Physiology of these systems
- General hygiene, nutrition and health
- Common ailments in the region and their prevention

Marine Sciences

- Marine environment
- Marine organisms—use and ecology
- Impact of human activities on marine environment
- Conservation and use of marine resources

- Nutrient cycles
- Ocean currents .
- Movements of fishes, nutrients and pollutants
- Sea shore ecology with special reference to mangroves

Natural Resource Management Involving Their Wise and Rational Use

- renewable resources, the rate of utilization and the rate of replenishment
- destribution of resources
- community role in conserving natural resources
- efficiency in harnessing solar energy
- biomass production
- efficient use
- air, water management
- global environmental issues
- what constitutes wise and rational use of natural resources
- forest repletion and replanting

Social Biology and Human Ecology

- family life and control
- community health and sanitation
- human populations and their behaviour—interaction with environmental factors and resources
- human behaviour and stress
- human sexuality—its role under bio-technology
- agricultural systems

Bio-Technology

[This is provided detailed analysis below].

Bio-technology—A Scope Map

In basic practice, bio-technology is not a new subject. It has its orgins rooted in antiquity dating back to the early history of human beings. Its substance relates to some very ancient human activities using techniques based on biological processes. As such, food gathering, preparation and preservation have been essential components of the culture and economy of early communities around the world. The Neolithic Era (9000 BC) marks the transition from hunting and food gathering, to food production, involving cultivation of edible plants—wheat, barely, millet, rye, and malting technology.

Starting perhaps from an unexpected discovery of fermentation, human beings have being trying to improve their bio-craftsmanship for exploiting different raw materials through the use of living organisms or their biological processes. Thus, the brewing industry has been known 3500 BC; and making of wine, bread, cheese, yoghurt etc. has been a common heritage in many cultures. Although ignorant of the natural principles involved, farmers have long practised the art of improving their crops through careful selection of seeds from desirable plants. Similarly, they have also succeeded in developing better breeds of domestic animals long before the researches of Mendel. It has been common knowledge that, working with phenotypes, animal and plant breeders have been able to produce chickens that lay more eggs, cows that give more milk.

Following the discovery of Watson and Crick, much is known about how the genetic code of cells is duplicated and distributed to offspring cells. Recent researches in the field have also given scientists the ability to isolate genes from cells, duplicate them in a culture, and introduce them into other cells to achieve various results. These techniques, collectively referred to as *"genetic manipulation"*, are significant in their potential to overcome some of the natural restrictions limiting the biological variability range under conventional breeding methods. These newer techniques enable sicentists not only to develop organisms containing genetic information from diverse sources, but also to hasten the achievement of certain breeding objectives.

The *"bio-technological revolution"* is, tacitly, the re-evaluation and refinement of old knowledge and traditional practices in the light of better understanding of various biological processes, emerging new information about the genetic make up of cells, technological possibilities, and their subsequent industrial applications. The earliest techniques of fermentation originated as homecrafts and were partly rsponsible for the change from cottage industries to town-based crafts. Traditional bio-technologies in this field in early history involved natural processes. Later the process was based on mixed cultures by wild yeasts, bacteria, fungi, etc., followed by batch inoculation with selected micro-organisms and control of enzymatic reactions. It is only recently, through the use of genetic technology, that the process has become more efficient and continuous, thus acquiring high industrial capabilities.

Bio-technology as a distinct discipline of study and scientific research has emerged, perhaps only in the early 1970s. Science its emergence, it has made tremendous strides, making an ever-increasing impact on human life, with important implications and applications in industry and commercial enterprises covering agrofood, fertilizers, fuels, fibres, chemicals and pharmaceuticals, as well as crop disease and pest control. Though still in its infancy, it has already demonstrated its fruitful potential not only in intellectual endeavour, but also in partical terms.

The most significant factor behind this upsurge seems to be the rapid progress made in the field of molecular biology, genetics and gene technologies. Studies of nuclei of individual cells led to the discovery of chromosomes and their behaviour, and subsequently to the double helix of DNA, the carrier of instructions or code for the development of a future organism. As a result of a continuing series of breakthroughs in the understanding of DNA during the last few decades, it is now possible to manipulate the genetic codes of micro-organisms. With the discover of restriction enzymes in the 1970s, use of gene manipulation has resulted in the production of useful and valuable biological products such as bio-insecticides, vaccines, human insulin, human somatostatin, human growth hormone, interferons, and antifodies. The use of Restriction Fragment Length Polymorphism (RFLPs) can help to detect the presence of genetic discorders such as Huntington disease, cystic fibrosis, sickle cell anaemia, muscular dystrophy, thalassemia and haemophilia.

Further, developments in gene technology have enabled the identification in the human karyotype of approximately 50 fragile sites and 20 oncogenes that may be involved in human malignancies.

Likewise, it is also possible to use micro-organisms as vectors to induce new genetic messages into animals and plants with a view to altering their characteristics and improving their breeds. For example, viral vectors can be used to induce the gene for a missing enzyme into target cells as a possible measure for correcting metabolic disorders. Similarly, the use of recombinant interleukin-2 can help in the treatment of cancer. Genetic manipulation techniques can also be used to improve crop yield, nutritional quality of seed crops, and the resistence of crop plants to pests, pathogens and environmental changes, as well as to increase milk and meat production by animals. These successes have encouraged the industrial use of bacteria, yeasts, filamentous fungi, plant and animal cells as well as enzymes, to produce commercially a wide variety of products.

Genetically engineered microbes now form the basis of many revolutionary processes which are helping to reinvigorate, diversity and change the character of traditional land-based, biologically-based, and health-related industries, with subsequent impact on agricultural practices, medical research, waste management and pollution control. The literature is full of examples of industrial activities where bio-technologies have either already replace, or are in the process of replacing, the traditional patterns of technologies. Such cases include the manufacture of textile products, synthesis of flavourings and seasonings, production of ethanol, biogas and hydrogen, and extraction of metallic elements. Bio-technology methods are already increasingly used in the mass production of yeasts, algae, and bacteria with a view to provide proteins, amino-acids, vitamins and scores of other useful products more economically. In particular, its use in the development of new and improved crop varieties is advancing rapidly worldwide, and is an area which even the developing countries with an agricultural base cannot afford to ignore. Genetic engineering also holds a great promise to improve the techniques for diagnosing and treating hereditary diseases, cancer detection and cure, treatment of waste water and in solving problems of hunger, health, nutrition, sanitation and energy. Prospects for its use to enhance mineral and oil recovery as well as the production of energy from the world biomass, are equally strong. The recent experimentation with gene manipulation and cell fusion technology have further opened up many new possibilities within industry, of new products, improved processes, increased production, reduced costs, and reduced pollution and wastage.

In view of its universal applicability and usefulness in everyday life of people, biotechnology is now recognized as a potent tool in the future development of both rural and urban economies in the developed as well as the developing countries. As such, many nations including Australia, Great Britain, Canada, France, West Germany, Japan, USA, and O.E.C.D. are pushing it both politically and finanically and have prepared plans for encouraging its use in industry and to imporve the quality of life of their respective populations. One of the reports from the Office of Technology Assessment in the USA claims that more than 100 compounds, representing 17 different product categories, ranging from amino-acids to viral antigens, have a current market value in excess of 27 billion dollars. Recent researches and techniques of genetic technology have contribute and will continue to do so greatly, to enhance knowledge in biological science. Some of the techniques developed as part of the DNA technology have already helped to improve understanding of the regulation of the genetic mechanisms, development and differentiation of organisms, the organization of the genome, the nature of the immune response, X-chromosome inactivation, human evolution, sex determination and even the relatedness of species.

While contributing to solve many problems, the practice of bio-technology can create new ones of unknown dimensions. Inherent in this field are both benefits and risks which potentially can alter not only the environment, but also humans. The growth of bio-technology in recent years has been so fast and dramatic, that the general public's understanding of what bio-technology means, and its appreciation of the influence of research outcomes in the field on daily life, has failed to keep pace with progress. Even many scientists seem to have no time to pause and assess the full impact.

The capacity to manipulate the genetic apparatus in both the laboratory and the field has given the human creative powers that threaten to pose new dilemmas and confront critical paradoxes. The more learned about the nature of life, the more are living organisms reduced to malleable structures open to experimentation and change, at the whims and fancies of scientists. Some of the hazards of genetic engineering in relation to plants may include production of more vigorous weeds, change in the niches and pathogenicities of plant viruses and soil bacteria, increase in the breakdown of fertilizers as well as the production of nitrogen oxides (denitrification), decrease in the variability of crops. etc. More recently, there has been growing concern that altered microbes may inadvertently tip nature's balance against the human. Questions also involve legal and ethical issues in direct confrontation with traditional value systems. There are many unanswered questions especially in relation to safety, ethics, and long range effects of gene manipulation on evolution, human health, disease and the quality of life in general. Depending upon national development goals, socio-cultural and moral traditions, the answers to such questions will, of course, vary from country to country.

Disciplines and Techniques Contributing to Bio-technology

Although there are many possible ways of grouping the applications of bio-technology, the Biological Science Group classified the applications under five headings: fermentation technology, waste technology, bio-molecular engineering, environmental technology and renewable technology. The development of these applications is subject to contributions of a number of disciplines such as biochemistry, genetics, molecular biology, microbiology, mathematics, computer technology, engineering and techniques including market research. Of these, microbiology and molecular biology stand out in their importance. The latter has much advanced the understanding of the nature of living systems, in particular with reference to the molecular and genetic bases of life. Today genes are no longer regarded as abstract units without material basis, but rather as discrete molecules performing their functions in special ways. A great deal is known about single genes and their arrangements in cells. Virtually every living organism uses the same genetic code to translate its hereditary information carried in the DNA. This commonality has enabled the molecular biologists not only to slice through DNA in specific locations, but also to isolate this material and recombine it with DNA from another source to form recombinant DNA (rDNA). This technique has found great use in industry and commerce. The structure of the DNA molecule is identical among all living things, from an amoeba to the human, from a blade of grass to a tall tree. Further, it is regarded as the store house of all informatioin needed to perpetuate life or make an organism. By using complicated series of biochemical processes, the information contained in the ganes is translated into the actual stuff of which organisms are made. The ability to *"engineer"* various traits by manipulating the DNA i.e., transferring of genetic traits from the organism to another, was demonstrated in the early 1970s.

The monoclonal antibody techniques permit the production of large amounts of specific proteins such as antibodies and interferons for research and chemotherapy. Antibodies have two useful characteristics: first, they are extremely specific i.e., each antibody is produced in response to a specific foreign antigen (normally a protein) in the blood stream; and second, some antibodies, once activated by the occurrence of a disease, continue to provide resistance (immunity) to that disease (e.g. antibodies to chicken-pox and measles). This feature of antibodies enables the development of vaccines. Because of their specificity, monoclonal antibodies can be used not only as protection against disease, but also to diagnose a wide variety of illnesses. They can also help to detect the presence of drugs, viral and bacterial products and other unusual or abnormal substances in the blood. The technology underlying their production involves the fusion of antibody-producing cells from the spleen of a mouse (previously immunized with a particular antigen) with mouse cancer cells. These hybrid spleen-cancer cells are called hybridomas and can be grown in culture. They express both the spleen cell's ability to recruit specific antibodies, and the cancer cell's ability to proliferate continuously. Science each spleen cell produces only one antibody protein, the monoclonal antibody so produced corresponds with just one specific antigen.

The modern bio-process technology is an extension of ancient bio-techniques for developing useful products through natural biological activities e.g., combination of yeast cells and nutrients forms a fermentation system in which the organisms consume the nutrients to produce alcohol and carbon dioxide as the end products. Use of living organisms in this technology has many advantages over conventional chemical methods of production: they usually require lower temperatures, and pressures; they can use renewable resources as raw materials, and greater quantities can be produced with less energy consumption.

Various other themes for the basic understanding of biotechnology include: microbes and their products; cell manipulation and culture; fermentation; enzymes and enzyme technology.

Bio-technology, like any technology, aims at developing either an aboslutely new produce (or a process) or making an existing product more efficiently and at less cost, through a series of logical steps from initial ideas through process and market investigation. From the view point of the profitability of an industry, the question of market research involving identification of market requirements is very significant. This can help in designing a new product that will fit the market needs and fancies.

The main bio-technology themes may be divided into two groups, one based on the utilization of the natural processes of living organisms or cell components (Figure 1) and the other relating to utilization of living organisms modified by gene technology (Figure 2).

Figure 1. Possible bio-technology themes dealing with the utilization of natural processes in living organisms or organelles and the general biology topics, in which they can be covered (in higher grades of secondary education)—Bayzhuber, H (1989) (UNESCO)

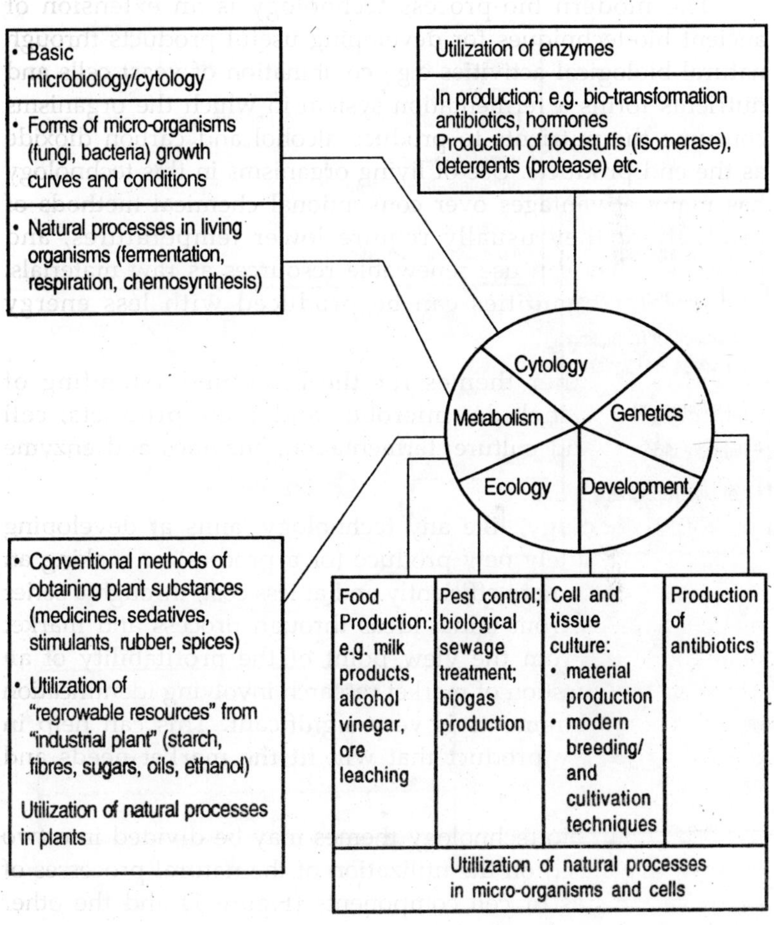

Figure 2. Possible bio-technology themes for genetics in the higher grades of secondary education dealing with the use of organisms modified by gene technology

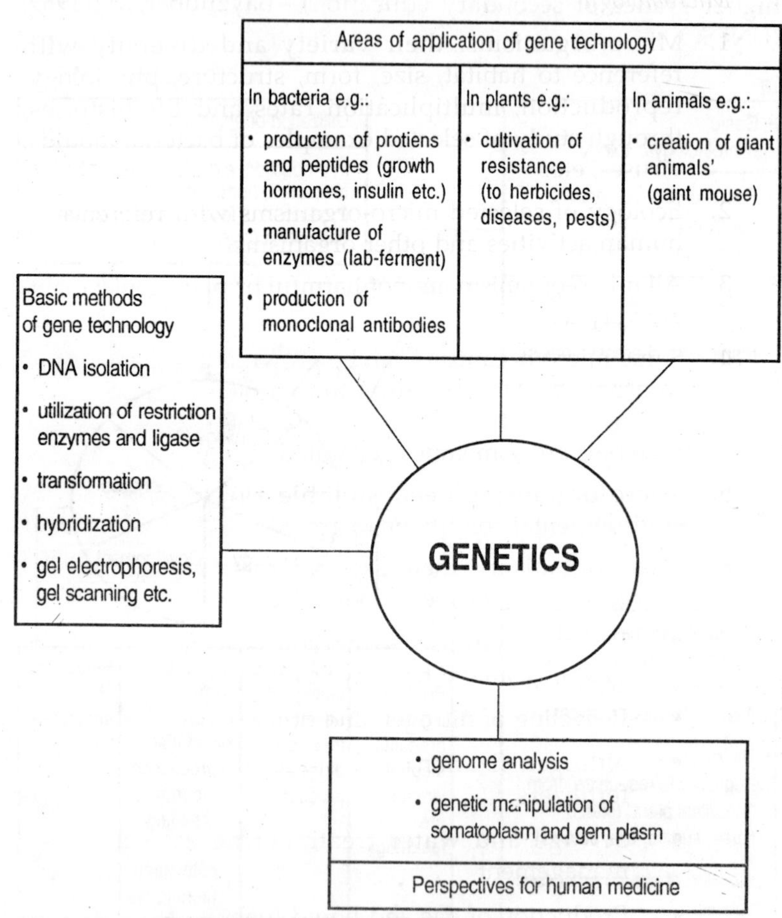

These have been further elaborated into concepts and principles for the guidance of the curriculum developers, and include the following:

Microbiology

1. Micro-organisms: their variety and diversity with reference to habitat, size, form, structure, physiology, reproduction, multiplication rates and life-histories, through study of selected examples of bacteria, moulds, viruses, etc.
2. Ecology of selected micro-organisms with reference to human activities and other organisms.
3. All micro-organism are not harmful or pathogenic; many are very useful.
4. Some micro-organisms can be grown in large quantities to produce useful products from a wide variety of raw materials. In the process, large quantities of waste materials are sometimes generated.
5. Micro-organisms need suitable raw materials and environmental conditions to grow.
6. Micro-organisms: their use and role in industry and everyday life with special reference to:
    - Production of beer, wine, spirits, vinegar, proteins, vitamins, antibiotics, soya sauce, tofu, tempe, bread
    - Recycling of nitrogen and other nutrients
    - Nitrogen fixation, and bio-fertilizer, and organic fertilizers
    - Sewage and water treatment as well as waste management
    - Production of gas and liquid fuels as an alternative to finite fossil energy supplies
    - Dairy industry
7. It is possible to produce a cheaper, better, or different product by selecting more suitable alternative organisms, changing the raw materials or by improving the engineering process.

8. General microbiology techniques, procedures and their assessments with emphasis on safety.
9. Study of a cow's stomach as a fermentation tank converting plant materials to milk.
10. Bacteriocidal and bacteriostatic methods.

Other possible themes and concepts drawn from other disciplines may include:

Molecular Biology

1. Cell structure and function
2. Cell nucleus and its function
3. The structure of DNA and RNA
4. DNA replication
5. The genetic code
6. Protein synthesis
7. Gene technology

Genetics

1. Basic principles of genetics
2. Chromosomes as the physical bases of heredity
3. Improvement of crops and domestic animals through selective breeding
4. Hybridization
5. Linkages and recombinations leading to the understanding of spatial relationship of genes on the chromosome
6. Crossing over
7. Gene and genome

Biochemistry

Enzyme structure and function as a biological catalyst.

Recognition, isolation and purification of biological molecules.

Engineering

Basic principles in relation to developing cost-effective biological processes with reference to aseptic operations, reactor design (fermenters and immobilized bio-catalysts reactors), product recovery and marketing as well as use of simple instrumentation and process control.

Theory and Practical Skills in Bio-technology

1. Recombinant DNA technology
2. Monoclonal antibody technology
3. Bacterial plasmids
4. Restriction enzymes
5. Use of DNA probes
6. Electrophoresis
7. Fermentation
8. Physical processes for separation and purification of biological products
9. Safety measures
10. Cleaning and sterilization

Cell Biology

1. Animal and plant cell
2. Forms or shapes of cells as units of life
3. Cell reproduction and growth
4. Cell or tissue culture (it is possible to grow complete organisms from single cells; cell and tissue culture techniques may be used for storing germ plasm of useful genetic varieties)
5. Cell cloning

Applications of Bio-technology

1. Human applications (vaccines, diagnostics, gene therapy)
2. Agricultural applications (natural pesticides, growth hormones)

3. Industrial applications (energy, waste management, methane production, fermentation)
4. Ecological applications (natural biological control)

Genetic Engineering Technology

1. Genetic rearrangement occurs naturally
2. Natural genetic rearrangement is one source of the variation that occurs in nature.
3. Micro-organisms can act as vectors (carriers) for genetic information.
4. Genetic rearrangement results in the expression of new traits.
5. Genetic material is universal in the living world.
6. Experiments that involve potentially biohazardous material must be conducted in accordance with established safety measures.
7. Molecular biologists have learned how to control some of the processes of natural genetic engineering.
8. New techniques allow biologists to cut apart DNA and put it together in new combinations; i.e. recombinant DNA.
9. This recombinant DNA gives organisms new characteristics.
10. Recombinant DNA technology allows biologists to produce valuable biological products.
11. Not all the information in DNA is translated into mature mRNA.
12. Many genes exist in pieces, with coding regions (exons) separated by non-coding regions (introns).
13. The ability to manipulate genetic material quickly and efficiently raises important ethical, legal and policy questions.
14. All organisms contain nucleic acid.

15. The genetic code is a universal language.
16. The evolutionary relatedness of two organisms may be measured by comparing their DNA; greater variation indicates more distant relationship.
17. Genetic technology is a powerful research tool that has improved understanding of basic biological principles.
18. Progress in genetic engineering raises important and complex ethical issues for individuals and society.
19. Ethics is the study of right and wrong behaviour and of the rules that guide behaviour.
20. Reasonable people may disagree about what constitutes right and wrong behaviour.
21. Ethical analysis is a process of critical thinking; it is based on sound facts.
22. Often times there are no clearly *"rights"* or *"wrong"* answers to ethical dilemmas.

Materials

23. Ethical positions often have implications for public policy. Public policies must generally meet several tests before they are likely to by successful.
24. Human DNA is highly variable; no two people have the same sequence of bases.
25. Variation in base sequences can create or eliminate recognition sites for restriction enzymes.
26 If the DNA from two people with the same restriction enzyme, is digested or *"chopped up"*, the variation in the DNA will result in different sized fragments for each person.
27. These fragments called RFLPs—can be used to detect the presence of disease-causing genes.
28. The genes for some disorders such as sickle cell anaemia can be detected directly. This requires knowledge of the specific mutation and restriction enzyme that cuts DNA at the mutation site.

29. Pieces of DNA that are on the same chromosomes are said to be linked.
30. During meiosis, homologous chromosomes exchange DNA in a process/called crossing over.
31. During crossing over, pieces of DNA that are closely linked will be separated less frequently than pieces of DNA that are distantly linked.
32. Some RFLPs are closely linked to disease-causing genes.
33. If one can detect such an RFLP, one can predict that the disease-causing gene is also present.
34. The predictive power of linked RFLPs depends on how closely linked they are to the disease-causing gene.
35. Linked markers allow detection of disease-causing genes in the absence of knowledge about the underlying cause of the disease.
36. The ability to detect disease-causing genes prenatally and in heterozygotes raises important ethical and legal questions.
37. Recombinant DNA technlogy permits the manipulation of genetic material in the laboratory.
38. Plasmids can be used as vectors to carry new genetic information into a bacterium.
39. Laboratory tests can determine whether the desired trait has been transferred to the bacterium.
40. Experiments that involve recombinant DNA must be conducted in accordance with established safety procedures.

Some General Concepts

1. Bio-technology has been in the service of humanity since early human history.
2. Genetic messages lead to variation in natural populations.
3. This variability can be accelerated and controlled by human intervention.

4. Modern or new bio-technology involves splicing genes to replace defective genes.
5. Gene therapy involves splicing of good genes to replace defective genes.
6. Antisense technology involves targeting and blocking the action of *"bad"* genes such as cancer causing oncogenes.
7. Bio-technology can solve as well as create problems and hence it should be guided by knowledgeable persons and decisions.
8. Bio-technology is in a state of flux and students should prepared for changes in both goals and techniques as more knowledge is acquired. Scientific research and development over the past years, particularly in molecular and cell biology, have generated possibilities of a multiplicity of new products and services or of old products produced in new ways. Likewise more research will further enhance these possibilities. The extent to which these become realities depends on complementry developments in process engineering and favourable commercial as well as socio-economic and cultural conditions.
9. The relative economic importance of various aspects of biological technology system vary from country of country.
10. The use of living organisms in the economic context can sometimes give rise to social, ethical, political and legal issues that must be examined alongside the scientific and economic aspects of a potential development of biological technology.
11. Linking school teaching to the production of goods and services and particular to local industries related to food technologies, dairy products, green house technologies, pest control, sewage treatment, etc. gives it meaningfulness.

12. Each of the pathways through the bio-technology system generate., for young people, job and career opportunities that require a wide range of knowledge, aptitudes, skills, qualifications and experience.

Comprehensive awareness of the entire bio-technology system is not possible. However, for school children to understand some basics of bio-technology they should become familiar with the following concepts:

1. Inter-relationship and inter-dependence of humans and other organisms.
2. Diverse ways in which human life-style depends on the use of living organisms in the global economic context.
3. Growing and harvesting plants and animals on farms and in factories both traditionally and by using modern bio-technological techniques.
4. Farms, forests and industries are highly organized systems with diverse and changeable inputs of raw materials, capital and labour, linked to a complex marketing system extending throughout the world.
5. Selective breeding of animals and plants can produce desirable characteristics to meet high yields of good quality animal products and plants resistant to disease and parasites.

It is further reasonable to assume that during the course of school learning, in particular with reference to biology, most school children will experience at least some examples of selected bio-technological pathways from organisms to specific consumer products or services.

The following tables point to the possibilities of several new themes and concepts being linked to existing learning areas.

Chemistry

Syllabus Topics	Reference to Bio-technology
Chemistry of Living Things	Genetics/recombinant DNA
Economics of Chemical Processes	Use of enzymes of conventional catalysts/chemical reactions (lower temperatures; fewer strong reagents; perhaps cheaper and safer).
Energy—fuels and resources; catalysis	Biomass; gasohol: biogas Use of enzymes
Food And Agriculture	a. Dairy industry—cheese; yoghurt b. Novel foods c. Improved crops—disease resistance, higher yields d. Pest control—use of fungi; genetic engineering e. Preserving foods—pickling
Metals—extraction from ores	Use of micro-organisms of leach out metals.
Nitrogen/Ammonia	Nitrogen-fixing bacteria/reduction in quantities of fertilizers and energy used e.f. chemical fixation of nitrogen.
Social Implications	a. Novel foods e.g. Mycoprotein, SCP. b. Pollution and its control c. Recycling of materials d. Health and hygiene—antibiotics; immunology/monoclonal antibodies; synthetic hormones; new vaccines; interferons.
Water	Water purification. Resorvoir to water works to mains supply. Used water treatment. Sewage works to river.

Science

Syllabus Topics	Reference to Bio-technology
Diseases and Their Treatments	Antibiotics, immunology/monoclonal antibodies: synthetic hormones; new vaccines; interferons.

Ecosystems	Importance of bacteria, fungi and algae, algae, the nitrogen cycle; nitrogen-fixing bacteria.
Fuels and Energy	Biomass, gasohol and biogas use of enzymes as catalysts. Fermentation and alcohol production photosynthesis—ways of increasing the efficiency of plant to absorb and utilize sunlight energy and minerals.
Reproduction, Growth and Cells	Genetic engineering. Cell and tissue culture.
Science and Society	Genetics. Plant and animal breeding. Economics of processes. Comparison of the use of conventional plant with one using micro-organisms.
The Earth as a Source of Materials	Biomass; formation of oil/gas by bacteria; extraction of metals from ores by micro-organisms; renewable sources of materials when suplies of oil, gas and coal run out.
Variety of Life	Micro-organisms; the importance of enzymes to all life.

Biology

Syllabus Topics	Reference to Bio-technology
Biological Resources and their exploitation	Ethanol (gasohol), methane (biogas); biomas.
Cell Biology	Fermentation processes; nutrient require-ments; SCP: cell culture.
Co-ordination. Nervous and hormonal control	Use of the plant harmones. Insulin production-genetic engineering. Sources of hormones used in medicine.
Crop and Livestock Production/Breeding	Agriculture—embryo transplants; genetic improvement.
Diversity of Organisms	Social, economic and technological impact of micro-organisms.
Ecology	Microbial pesticides. Batch and continuous fermenters.
Energy—including	Ethanol; methane; biomass.

biomass and nutrient cycles; energy flow through food chains	
Enzymes	Enzymes as products of fine organic chemicals with many industrial uses; enzyme inhibitors.
Evolution—artificial selection	Selection of variants in antibiotic production; the emergence of resistant strains; drug resistance.
Food Production —including processing	Dairy, fish and meat products; beverages; bakers yeast; food additives; novel foods; mushrooms; amino acids; vitamins; starch products; glucose and high fructose syrups; yoghurt manufacture.
Health and Hygiene —including immunity	Antibiotics; diagnostic agents (enzymes, antibodies), enzyme inhibitors; steroids; vaccines.
Heredity/Genetics/DNA, genes, chromosomes, mutation, genetic engineering	Recent advances in molecular biology in relation to biological industrial processes e.g. the use of genetically engineered microbes to make insulin human growth hormone.
Mineral Nutrition e.g. water cultures	Cell and tissue culture techniques; mineral requirements of microbes for suitable growth in fermenters.
Pest Control	Microbial pesticides.
Photosynthesis e.g. efficiency of energy conversion	Biomass.
Reproduction	Clones. Culture techniques.
Respiration	Ethanol production—as an industrial chemical or in the alcoholic drinks industry.
Saprophytes e.g. decomposition; recycling; carbon and nitrogen cycles	Sewage disposal; pollution control; ensilage and composting processes.

Symbiosis/Mutualism	Rhizobium and other nitrogen fixing bacterial inoculants; yoghurt manufacture.
Variation	· Artificial selection techniques, including genetic engineering in relation to a number of products.

As a further example of analysis of furture content in biological science, the Group reviewed the broad implications in the content of bio-micro electronics, another growing edge in today's science.

Micro Electronics and New Biology

The examplar content review indicated above, pointed to some selected content issues in the area of bio-technology, as a significant and vital component of future science content. However, the locus of movement in this selected content is essentially in the knowledge areas of biology and biochemistry. New biology has also entered as even newer and equally vital area of content, related to the integration of micro-electronics, information technology, robotics and bio-electronics. Through these new breakthroughs, human beings are emerging into a new mode of evolution itself, where human beings can change human beings and human life in a fundamental sense, to establish a new species, and challenge the very idea of "*naturalness*".

Already classical concepts like adaptation, evolution, identity, intelligence, learning, ecosystem, have undergone drastic modifications as a result of the impact of discoveries in computerized bio-microtechnology.

For example, integrated sensors are not merely in the vivid imaginations of scientists. There are already devices that convert non-electric inputs (e.g. sound, light, chemicals) into electrical impulses which may be fed into computers. They are robotic analogues of the five senses of human beings. In current advances in molecular electronics (bio-technology + micro-electronics), organic biosensors which recognize other organic chemicals, have been developed, such as the use of a monoclonal antibody as a sensor. Bio sensors now form components of artifical sense organs, and are used as control devices for heart pace makers. Field effect transistors are analoguous to neurons of the human body, in that they respond to the electrical potential created by selected ions and are dependent on ions as an energy source. Such advances have pointed the way to *"bio chips"* or natural or synthesized organic molecules instead of silicon chips, in computers. Such research leads to the horizons where compter systems embody a spectrum of biochemical features that characterize biological systems and are creative, intelligent, thoughtful. Then it would be meaningless to say that biological systems are necessarily animate in a way that artefacts can never be. This leads to questioning the very basis of distinguishing life from non-life. The issue is further augmented by the fact that technically it is feasible (though not as yet practicable) to replicate inanimately much of what life is and does, through computerization. Yet human perception has potentially an objective cognitive and a moral identity. Whether this is the fundamental distinction between bio-robots and humans has to form and essential component of future content in this area.

A related area of content is artifical learning and intelligence, which will include concepts such as stimulus, perception, purpose, behavioural response, operation path and speed, information storage and multiple processing, problem solving. Such concepts would need to be redefined in the light of the advances of micro-electronics and computerization. The horizon of organically based biochip animate brains not being confined to biological systems is a feature to be dealt with in future content.

Of special importance in future content analysis, in areas of knowledge such as the above, is that the science content published and incorporated into the current *"traditon"*of science, is not necessarily the science that present-day scientists are working on, due to the substantial phase lag between content at the growth edges of science and published content. The analysis and inclusion of the former content becomes vital to the consideration of future content. Simultaneously, the growth edges keep changing as does the corresponding content. New strategies for incorporating this unique feature of inevitable *rapid* change in content, so different to the relatively leisurely changes in traditional content, have to be developed, parallel with the content analyses indicated previously. Such strategies would naturally alter drastically the entire processes and philosophies of curriculum development and implementation.

The types of fundamental questions and issues raised earlier focused of *"life"*, *"naturalness"*, animate/inanimate, cognitive/ethical, must necessarily raise pointed questions on ethics as it manifests itself as content in these new future content scenarios. The minimum locus of consideration would relate to such aspects as bio-microtechnology's potential for usurping *"biological"* or *"human"* intelligence; its potential for integrated biological and machine organization; its growing assistance to the control of human affairs. Such issues have promoted scientists and philosophers to hasten their consideration of the ethics involved in the entire fields of bio-technology and bio-micro electronics. Already such considerations have initiated new codes of ethics for the creations of such new areas, such as the well known Asimov's Laws of Robotics:

1. A robot may not injure a human being nor, through inaction, allow a human being to come to harm.
2. A robot must obey the orders given to it by human beings, except when such orders would conflict with the First Law.
3. A robot must protect its own existence as long as such protection does not conflict with the First or Second Law.

Deliberations of the Physical Science Working Group

There was a strong contrast between the requirements of participating countries in the Working Group, in respect of a physics syllabus. Some countries needed a syllabus that provided about 50 per cent of core topics and 50 per cent of options and electives, the contrasting requirement was 80 per cent core and 20 per cent options. It was apparent, after the earlier country presentations and their discussions, that the content of a physics syllabus was not in question, so the discussion truned to providing an extended core in physics and to nominate sufficient options to make up a *traditional core* if required.

In the following step in content analysis, an extended *core* is presented. As a bare minimum, a syllabus would follow the sequence from *KINEMATICS* to *MAGNETISM*. A more adequate coverage would result if a selection down to *OPTICS* was chosen. As a rough guide, it is suggested that each core topic take about five weeks of teaching time. In this way, one year of the syllabus would take a class down to *MAGNETISM* or *INDUCTION*, while the full core might take about 90 per cent of two years learning. This guide assumes that two traditional sicences of about six periods a week are taught. If countries chose to present only physics as science for one year, they should reach *MAGNETISM* in half a year instead of one year (they would need 10 to 12 periods a week).

Where 50 per cent options are chosen, they should not be left to a second year. The opening item *KINEMATICS* would also include some consideration of measurement and accuracy, the *LAWS OF MOTIOIN* would include an historical component, while considerations of *POTENTIAL, ENERGY, KINETIC ENERGY AND WORK* would be extended to include national requirements. At this point, an option would be included; another option could well follow *OHMIC CIRCUITS* and by the time *INDUCTION* is reached classes would have gained the minimum sufficient core to enable them to draw freely from the options offered.

As only nine *special topics* are outlined (with others envisaged) it is not appropriate to suggest how long each option should take. It is difficult to imagine any option taking less than five weeks. However, some (like *ELECTRONICS*) might flow quite naturally following *OHMIC CIRCUITS* so that the time expected to cover the materials becomes a matter for individual education systems to decide.

The prescribed core, with the addition of a topic on *ROTATION* and a selection of special topics, would probably cover the conceivable needs of countries in the region, including those that prescribe a national external examination for entrance to tertiary education.

A Physics Syllabus Core

KINEMATICS. This section may start with concepts of distance displacement and time. Distance would be astronomical down to interatomic to explain orders of magnitude. The distinction between distance and displacement helps introduce the topic of vectors. In mesuring time, high precision is not required. The idea of accuracy would be introduced by this stage.

The concept of speed as a rate of change of distance, and acceleration as a rate of change of velocity, also introduce the fundamental ideas and application of calculus. The concept of integration may be followed informally, the change in velocity is the area under a plot of acceleration with time, while the distance is the area under a plot of speed with time.

The Kinematic equations follow and can be given as a useful model the can help describe motion where accelaration is not necessarily constant. Various examples of motion from the class environment should be considered and described graphically, as well as by using formulae.

FORCE AND MASS. The conditions for equilibrium include no external force and no torque, as rotation may not be further considered. The concept of moments could be examined at this point.

All familiar examples of forces can be explored and the concept of inertial mass considered for accelerating bodies.

LAWS OF MOTION. While the historical perspective of the development of Newton's Laws is interesting, students could be encouraged to consider these three laws in their own familiar intuitive environment. This topic may include an element of personal discovery.

In a similar sense, conservation of momentum need not be introduced using highly precise apparatus. Students can be given the formal principle after quite qualitative observations. The concept of impulse is a re-expression of one of Newton's Laws. A formal definition might not be necessary, although the term correctly used is useful. Again the conservation of Kinetic energy for elastic collisions is a concept that can be left to the discretion of individual teaching systems.

POTENTIAL ENERGY, KINETIC ENERGY AND WORK. The work-energy theorem of conservation of Kinetic and Potential energy (in a conservative system) can be found in one of the earlier Kinematic equations, while another will strongly suggest the second law generally attributed to Newton. It may be best to introduce these ideas of energy from previous familiar work. The idea of friction will have been introduced earlier and here, the concept serves to illustrate how, in general, energy can be lost from a non-conservative system.

Many teachers can leave the formal approach at this point and introduce enrichment material by identifying heat as energy and considering national needs, renewable and non-reneawable energy sources.

ELECTROSTATICS. While Coulombs law is the logical opening for the topic of electricity, many demonstrations require special skill in a tropical environment. It might be expedient to mention types of charges, their conservation and then move quickly through to OHMIC CIRCUITS.

VOLTAGE AND ELECTRIC FIELD. The concept of electric potential as the energy per charge is very useful. The following concept of the electric field, as the negative gradient of the electric potential, will become a matter of discretion. Some classes will need to move quickly to circuits, while others will be able to reconsider vectors and the concepts of calculus.

OHMIC CIRCUITS. Many familiar applications of electricity can be considered in terms of Ohms Law. This topic should inevitably point to syllabus extensions. The concept of power (if not already used) can be introduced in a familiar setting at this point. The basic ideas of the potential divides and current division carry through to advanced electronics. These can be simply considered in terms of Ohms Law.

MAGNETISM, FORCE AND FIELD. Unlike *ELECTROSTATICS,* there is much more scope to demonstrate this phenomena in the classroom. If the concept of the electric field was previously done in a cursory fashion, it can be reinforced by comparison with the magnetic field. Magnetism is a natural and fascinating phenomenon that provides opportunities for pupil discovery. The magnetic field generated by a current is quite weak and more than 10 Amps are normally required for clssroom experimentation. These currents are available from 12 V car batteries, but careful supervision is needed not so much to protect students, as to protect equipment.

The magnetic force on a moving charge is an abstract concept that can be introduced as a simple realistic extension of the magnetic force on current carrying conductor.

INDUCTION. This is a familiar effect in many areas of technology. However, the subject can be overdeveloped and cause confusion. Depth of treatment is a matter of choice. Lenz's Law and the concept of magnetic flux would represent a good coverage of theory, while more practical classes can explore and study electric motors and generators. In the absence of rotation, the derivation of a formula for the torque on a current carrying loop in a megnetic field, may be taking content too far.

CIRCULAR AND HARMONIC MOTION. These topics may have been introduced under KINEMATICS. Again circular acceleration may have been used to consider satellite motion. If not, it can be done at this point. While equations for circular motion follow naturally from vector differentiation, this approach might not be suitable for all. If an easy approach cannot be used, the derivation may be left out. The projection of circular motion to produce harmonic motion is useful and important to students continuing on in physics or engineering.

The discovery of a sine curve as a numerical solution to the harmonic equation is mentioned elsewhere. This approach is suitable for most classes, especially those interested in computing, even though a computer is not necessary.

WAVES. While most physics classes consider regular harmonic phenomena, this approach can restrict the number of familiar environmental examples. The initial approach would consider periodic phenomena such as annual and diurnal cycles. The basic wave equation applies to a fixed speed and period and can be illustrated by familiar examples.

Wave propagation, reflection and refraction can be explored using Hughen's approach. A closer discussion of the nature of electromagnetic waves can be used to explain interference and diffraction, while acoustic waves can also provide interesting effects.

OPTICS. This topic deals with light in particular and much valuable ground work can be laid in the previous topic. Kits of lenses and mirrors should be available for classrooms in all regions. The traditional approach considering first mirrors then lenses, ray diagrams and the familiar formulae has not been superseded. If teachers are becoming concerned over matters such as sign conventions and real or imaginary rays, they may have gone too far for this level of learning.

Much *enrichment material* can be added with optics, ranging from *astronomical observations* to *light sources* and *lasers*. For courses that offer most of this syllabus core, it really is necessary to offer special topics at this point.

KINETIC THEORY. A number of initial observations can be made regarding the properties of gases before numerical derivations are examined. It is virtually impossible to attach the original discoverers name to each gas law, so a discovery approach is more appropriate than a historical discussion. The ideal gas equation is needed for chemistry and can be simply given as another useful physical model to explain gas behaviour.

TEMPERATURE AND HEAT. As with KINETIC THEORY, there may be overlap with a chemsitry syllabus in this topic. This should not be a problem as two approaches to the same topic should ease the burden and reinforce the learning.

Working through a simple variant of the kinetic gas formula will serve to reinforce earlier concepts of the physics syllabus. The equating of internal kinetic energy with temperature remains a familiar and significant step in physics that should be of interest to advanced classes.

The concepts of heat capacity and heat transfer can be taken up by any class as a starting point for a study of heat in the physical environment, which can provide an enrichment topic.

ATOMIC STRUCTURE. This topic, along with the last two, may also overlap with a chemistry syllabus, and for this reason they appear last in the core physics material. The topic has been included as it provides a starting point for a number of special topics is LASERS, PROPERTIES OF MATERIALS, NUCLEAR PHYSICS or PARTICLE PHYSICS.

The clsses which require this subject in the core syllabus will have a particular commitment to physics as a serious study.

The identification of specific atomic properties at the turn of the century would be given and the Bohr model of the atom would be considered quantitatively. These topics will give considerable reinforcement to earlier topics in this core. Once this initial territory has been crossed, there remains a vast landscape for further study by physics students.

Some Special Physics Syllabus Topics

LASERS

Requires: WAVES, OPTICS, ATOMIC STRUCTURE

Can extend to interdisciplinary areas.

PROPERITIES OF MATERIALS

Requires: ATOMIC STRUCTURE

Can extend to interdisciplinary areas.

One particular type of material could be studied in detail.

SUPERCONDUCTIVITY

Requires: MAGNETISM, OHMIC CIRCUITS

A phenomenological approach only, useful in towns and cities where Hi-Tech superconductivity is available. Can be interdisciplinary with chemists.

NUCLEAR PHYSICS

Requires: ATOMIC STRUCTURE

Ideally this topic would include fission and fusion reactors and can become environmental.

PARTICLE PHYSICS

For physics students only.

RELATIVITY

This topic can be used to extend KINEMATICS and even LAWS OF MOTION. For less motivated students, elements of relativity may be included with the core if students want some knowkedge of RELATIVITY. Otherwise this is a topic for committed physics students.

ELECTRONICS

Requires: OHMIC CIRCUTTS

Electronics is a subject in itself. A physics class in a secondary school could choose to study either amplifiers or binary logic and simple digital circuits. Classroom kits for the latter are becoming available but will be most useful in larger towns and cities.

THERMO DYNAMICS

Requires: KINETIC THEORY, TEMPERATURE AND HEAT

This subject is interdisciplinary and environmental. However, it requires considerable physical abstraction.

PHYSICAL ENVIRONMENT

There are many environmental measurements which require the particular skills of physicists. Obviously this is an interdisciplinary subject. Many regional needs can be met by studying, for example, meteorology or the flow of water.

CONTEMPORARY DEVELOPMENTS

Superconductivity, especially the study of high temperature superconductors, is a typical example of a topic that might suddenly emerge and hold student interest for some time.

As with bio-technology, lasers represent a likely new content area to enter science and technology education at secondary level in the future. Hence, a scope map is provided below, to help identify intrinsic content as well as supportive content that may need to be considered prior to curriculum deveopment.

Lasers—A Scope Map

Optics is a traditional part in the physics text book. But usually in the secondary school physics course attention is only paid to geometric optics and wave properties of the light. Diffraction and interference phenomena are taught to explain or verify the wave nature of light. It was resonable before the invention of the laser. At that time, the most important optics industry was the lens making industry. The existence of the laser has changed the situation dramatically. The fantastic and attractive laser stimulates scientists and engineers to find so many ways of using the laser. Now lasers have been used widely in industry, such as in building construction, mineral pit drilling, ultra-precise measurement, military purposes, optical communication, as well as in medical treatment. The opto-electronic industry has grown up to be one of the most important parts of the modern high-tech industry.

Light Source

1. General introduction to light sources (structure, principles, characters)
   (a) Heat radiation source: Tungsten lamp bromine tungsten lamp, etc.
   (b) Gas discharge tube: Day-light lamp, neon lamp, etc.
   (c) Solid state light source
2. Properties of light sources
   (a) Efficiency of light source (Power converting efficiency)
   (b) The relation between the temperature and the colour of heat light sources.

Laser and Its Applications

1. The general introduction to lasers:
   (a) The structure and the working principles of the laser (take *He-Ne* laser as an example)
   (b) The properties of laser
   - Monochromacity
   - Dictionality
   - High brightness
2. The applications of laser
   (a) Application in industry
   (b) Applications in agriculture
   (c) Optical communication
   (d) Application in meteorology
   (e) Application in medical treatment and biology
   (f) Application for military purposes

3. Holography
   (a) Principles
   (b) Applications

The content analysis regarding some scientific principles involved may be illustrated (only as an example) by the following:

Early Work Related to Laser Principles

The laser owes its beginning to the maser developed by C.H. Townes at Columbia University. While working on the absorption of microwaves in ammonia, Townes used as the basic principle of his work, the fact that ammonia may be considered as having two energy states under some appropriate conditions.

A physical model of the ammonia molecule may be visualized as a pyramid with an equilateral triangular base. At the corners of the equilateral triangle, there is one hydrogen atom each, while the nitrogen atom occupies the apex of the pyramid. When subjected to an external electric field in the vertical direction (E), the plane of the hydrogen atoms adjusts itself in the plane perpendicular to the direction of the applied electric field. The nitrogen atom has the possibility of being on top or under the equilateral triangular base. Two configurations correspond to two states or represent two physical orientations of the ammonia molecule in the applied electric field.

The ammonia molecule has a permanent dipole moment (p) due to the tendency of electrons to lie closer to the nitrogen atom than to the three hydrogen atoms. This situation leaves the nitrogen atom slightly negative and the hydrogen atoms slightly positive. In the configurations depicted, the energy of the ammonia molecule with the dipole moment in the anti-parallel direction with the applied electric field is 2pE greater than the ammonia molecule with the dipole moment in the parrallel direction with the applied electric field.

Townes arranged to have a large number of the ammonia molecules in the higher energy state before he forced these ammonia molecules to flip their dipole moments to the lower energy state. By doing so, Townes obtained a coherent and thus very powerful beam of microwaves with the frequency of 24,000 MHz.

To separate the ammonia molecules in the higher energy state from the rest in the other, a beam of ammonia molecules was sent through a hollow cylinder made up of negatively charged dielectric rods. Close to the axis of the cylinder, the electric field was very weak and came close to zero, while away from the axis, the field was very strong. The ammonia molecules with the dipole moment parallel to the direction of the radial field (lower energy state) were pulled away from the cylinder and lost, while those with the dipole moment anti-parrallel to the direction of the radial field (higher energy state) were pushed towards the axis and allowed to continue their motion along the axis into the waveguide cavity. Almost all of the ammonia molecules entering the cavity were in the higher energy state.

By hitting these higher-energy state molecules with a microwave beam having the frequency of 24,000 MHz, all of the excited molecules all at once gave up their energy in the form of a coherent microwave at the same frequency. The input microwave at 24,000 MHz was in effect amplified with extreme fidelity, hence the acronym *"maser"* which stands for microwave amplification by stimulated emission of radiation. The ammonia maser even in the *'crude'* form will not amplify a microwave signal that differs from its 24,000 MHz frequency by more than 3 to 5 kHz.

The ammonia maser was quickly followed by the development of solid-state masers using para-magnetic substances as maser materials.

From Maser to Laser

It was a matter of time before the principle of the ammonia maser was applied to the visible part of the electromagnetic spectrum. Since the signal to be amplified is in the visible range of the spectrum, the device is called the optical maser. The word was eventually abandoned in favour of the word *"laser"*, which is the acronym for light amplification by the stimulated emission of radiation.

In constructing the laser, it is not possible to work with the two energy state system. The difficulty lies not in the separation of the higher energy state from the lower energy state of the laser material. Once the atom is excited to the higher energy state, it remains there for a period of about 10^{-8} seconds before returning to the ground state. This order of time is not long enough to have a reasonable accumulation of the excited states.

The way to overcome this problem is to work with a three energy level laser material such as ruby. This is a crystal of aluminium oxide with chromium impurity of the order of 0.05 per cent by weight.

Once the chromium atoms are excited from the ground level E_1 to the upper energy level E_2, they can return to the ground level in two different ways. The first is to make *'spontaneous'* transition to the ground state within the period of 10^{-8} seconds and emit photons of the same wavelength. The second is to make *'spontaneous'* transition to the lower energy level E and emit photons in the infrared region. The chromium atoms can remain at the energy level E for several milli seconds which is eternity compared with 10^{-8} seconds. The energy level$_3$ is known as the metastable state.

The chromium atoms in large numbers can be put in the energy level E_3 in a matter of a few milliseconds. This process is known as the population inversion, i.e. there are more chromium atoms at energy level E_3 than at energy level E_1.

In the ruby laser, one needs to have the optical box which functions like the waveguide cavity. The dimensions of the ruby rod are several million times the wavelength of light. Since each end of the ruby rod is fixed with a semitransparent mirror, a photon travelling back and forth has increasing chance to interact with the chromium atoms.

To raise the chromium atoms into E_2 energy level, a xenon flash tube emitting pulses of light lasting about one half to two milliseconds is used. Excited chromium atoms then drop to E_3 energy level. As one of these chromium atoms emits a photon with 6943°A wavelength in the direction parallel to the exis of the rod, interaction between this photon and another chromium atom in the E_3 energy level takes place. The interaction causes the chromium atom to undergo stimulated emission of a photon of the same wavelength. The second photon is coherent with the first. As this mechanism goes on, the ruby rod grows in intensity due to more and more photons at 6943°A are given off by stimulated emission. As the intensity of the coherent light becomes intense enough, a burst of the coherent light will leave the semitransparent mirror on one side of the ruby rod.

Types of Laser

Various types of laser have been produced using gas and liquid laser materials. Different means of pumping atoms at the ground level into higher energy states and then metastable states have also been used. Thus, we have lasers which are sun-pumped, chemical-pumped and even explosion-pumped.

Perhaps the laser that is different from the rest is the so-called injection laser. Its principle is also very simple.

When an external voltage is applied to the N-P junction semi conductor, electrons in the N-type region start to move towards and into the P-type region. At the P-type region, the electrons drop into holes and some or recombination energy is given off in the form of a photon. If the applied voltage is large enough, a large number of electrons and holes become concentrated in a very narrow region of the order of 1/10,000 of an inch wide on the P-side of the junction. A photon emitted stimulates the emission of more photons by accelerated recombination between injected electrons and holes.

Applications of Lasers for Developing Countries

The remarkable properties of lasers have lent themselves to a wide range of possible applications from basic science to medicine, biology, radar communications, microwelding, weaponry and so on.

The research and development work on the laser need not require a large investment and is within the means of many developing countries. Some areas of research work on lasers offer good opportunity for scientists to participate.

While the above scans the possible content in regard to the principles on which the laser is based, equally importantly it also points to the prerequisite knowledge the learner must have to be able to comprehend the above.

3

Learning/Teaching of Future Content

The Biological Science and Physical Science Groups continued their separate discussions, with focus on the learning and teaching of the new science and technology content, and on linking the existing the content to the new content.

Sources

Throughout the workshop, and in the group sessions, the need to establish effective contacts for academic and technical resources, was stressed. Unlike earlier curriculum reforms, which involved the updating of single discipline (content of physics or chemistry or biology), several of the new content areas were inter- or multi-disciplinary (such as bio-technology, materials science, space science), and also involved technology as well. Thereby, it was not sufficient to consult only the earlier resource persons, such as professors at universities (in physics or chemistry or biology). Very frequently, several subject-matter experts had to be referred to, and previously unused mechanisms for consultation were needed to be established.

The seekers and receivers of these resources, usually science and technology curriculum development personnel, were often themselves single discipline specialist. These persons would have to expand their content horizons to match the inter- or multi-disciplinary nature of the new content to be able to seek for effectively, and receive and use constructively, the new content aspects from the expand group of content specialists.

The curriculum specialists have also to be acutely aware of aspects like the safety of the students in conducting learning activities, which in turn would involve a still group of resource persons.

Many of the new content areas have, intrinsic to them, significant dimensions of values and ethics and possible legal aspects as well, which have to be clarified before designing the learning and teaching sequences. Once again, the potential source person "*net*" has to be cast even wider.

With such a variety of needed source persons, and many of them likely to be having little spare time for frequent consultations, the entire resource seeking and receiving operation would need to be carefully and systematically planned for. The planning needs to include the recognition that many of the resource persons would not be pedagogists, so that their content suggestions have to be reprocessed for student learning/teaching purposes.

While printed sources may be available, the vast content expanse of the new learning areas, and the rapid changes in these content areas, underline the ugent need for prioritizing the content requirements.

Prerequisite Content

In several of the new content areas of science and technology, a "*coming together*" takes place of content from several discipline areas. Some of these content components may well be beyond the scope of coverage currently at secondary level, and may demand an inordinately long time to acquire (if at all suitable for this level becasue of abstraction or sophistication), before proceeding with the learning of the new science and technology content. Yet, while it is certainly possible to provide for a general appreciation of a new technology, appreciation with understanding must needs require the prior learning of the prerequistie content components. This could become a serious problem, especially if the new content areas are learned in out-of-school situations such as science clubs. Wise judgements would be required in deciding the kinds and extent of prerequisite knowledge required for proceeding in the learning/ teaching of new science and technology content. If the model of core-cum-optional courses is chosen, corresponding implications must appear for the new core design.

Entry Points

Practical considerations would point to strategies in the learning/teaching situations which use existing content specification at secondary level. The previous content analysis of the new learning area of Bio-technology, Chapter Three, indicated specific, currently available content analysis situations, which could form entry points for the new content. Similarly, curriculum designers would need to identify, in the learning situations, equivalent entry points. The possibilities of entering the learning of a number of new content areas, via fairly *"standard"* learning sequences currently in use in several countries, but now enriched with new dimensions for moving into these new areas, as well as into such significant effective aspects as ethics and values, and concern and responsibilities about fellow human beings, provide concrete starting points in the designing of learning sequences, but with attributes quite different to those that were identified in the earlier reforms since the 1960s, when content was essentially confined to single well-established disciplines.

Designing Learning/Teaching Activities

At least as much effort would need to be devoted to the design and development of learning/teaching activities, investigations, experiments related to the new content areas, as for the detailed content analysis. Past experiences in curriculum change in science have indicated that this design and development work has to start very early in the curriculum development operation of such activities are to be made available when the learning sequences derived from the content analysis are being considered.

Some, at least, of the new content areas, have already such activities in use, though usually at higher levels of education. These would need to be reconsidered in terms of their feasibilities of use in secondary level schools. Among the many possible considerations, the reduction of sophistication by decreasing precision, has provided constructive directions for design. This implies that curriculum development designers would need to work with content specialist, (such as from universities and other institutions of higher learning and research), to decide the extent to which such reduction of precision would be possible without damaging the accurate learning of the concepts involved. It should be noted that when the new science education reforms of the 1960s were being designed, and updated content introduced together with hands-on learning activities for students, similar actions had to be taken (for such content areas as equilibrium, structure in chemistry; waves in physics; heredity and DNA/RNA in biology).

For various purposes, such as for wide commercial use, some of the previously purely university or research laboratory activities may have been absolute already. Needed apparatus or chemicals or media may be in the market now. In some countries in the region, the markets have such new resources as culture media, electronic components, and even toys, which embody new science and technology content, at relatively low cost.

Also, in several countries, development departments such as Agriculture, Forestry, Fishery, Small Industry, for their own extension services for their target populations, have developed activities based upon the new content of science and technology (e.g., cloning of plants). These are also valuable resources to be considered.

For the international market, some developed countries have produced kits that embody the new science and technology content (such as in bio-technology, lasers, computers). These sources may be considered during the design operation.

It is not always necessary for only lthe curriculum development centres to be involved in such design of learning/teaching activities. The creative energies and talents of teachers and pupils may be mobilized by stimulating design work by these vast numbers, through such mechanisms as science and technology fairs and competations, which have now become a regular feature in several countries in the region.

A few countries that have already initiated work in designing learning/teaching activities related to new content in science and technology, may be willing to share their products and expertise with other countries in the region, through such mechanisms as the UNESCO PROAP/APEID network.

To stimulate action, and to illustrate concretely the above tasks, the following *"desophisticated"* example in bio-technology, applied to plant tissue culture, is provided by the Workshop.

PLANT TISSUE CULTURE:

An example of an Activity in Bio-technology

Introduction

The techniques of plant organ, tissue and cell culture, are now established in many research lasboratories throughout the world, and are being used in various areas of plants science. Methods have been developed to propagate virus free plants by using shoot tip culture. The regeneration of plants from callus culture have proved commercially useful. Somatic hybridization, formed by the fusion of protoplasts, has made hybrids which would be impossible to create by conventional methods. These techniques have been, and can be used, to investigate a variety of botanical processes, as well as to improve crop plants. They are now important basic experimental skills required by a majority of botanists.

The methods of plant organ, tissue and cell culture, have been successfully and widely used in the micro-propagation of plants, in the production of certain chemicals, in the improvement of agricultural crops such as disease resistant plants, in inducing genetic variability, and in making hybrids between unrelated species. Since the techniques have been well worked out for many crop species, they provide a powerful tool for plant biotechnology, are relatively easy for inexperienced students to perform, and are relatively inexpensive to conduct, it is recommended that tissue culture be considered for introduction to students at secondary level.

Pre-knowledge Requirements

Basic knowledge of sterilization and aseptic techniques, and solution preparation are required. Knowledge regarding plant tissue, such as shoot tip, cambium, parenchyma, vascular tissues and plant nutrition are also required.

Objectives

At the end of the activity, learners should be able to:

1. Define and give examples of terms such as callus, re-differentiation, growth differentiation.
2. Determine growth of tissue such as callus.
3. Indicate which hormone is active in promoting callus.
4. Recognize the problem of contamination, the existence of air-borne micro-organisms, and ways to prevent such contamination.
5. Explain cell growth in vitro, and factors needed.

Isolation of Explants, Establishment and Maintenance of Callus of Carrot (Daucus Carota)

Explants isolated from the tissues of higher plants and brought into culture, like excised organs, require a nutrient medium consisting of a mineral salt mixture, a carbon source (usually sucrose), and vitamins. In addition, plant hormones (auxins and cytokinins), or their synthetic counterparts, are required to initiate and maintain cell division. Ocassionally other organic compounds are supplemented, to ensure that the excised tissue gives an established callus. On suitable media, tissus fragments from most dicotyledonous plants, particularly those containing meristematic cells, (for instance, the cambium or shoot meristem), will start to proliferate rapidly. Less frequently, some of the mature cells will also divide and subsequently become involved in callus formation. Objects best suited for such activities are explants cut from the tap root of carrot (Daucus carota). These may also be used to test the effects of different compounds of the culture medium on induction and subsequent growth of callus from explants.

Materials and Equipment

Sterile Items

1. 1.2 rimless culture tubes (150 x 25 mm) containing 10 ml of 0.8 per cent agar medium + 5 x 10^{-8}g/ml 2, 4-D sloped at an angle of 25°

2. 20 sheets of tissue paper (200 x 200 mm)
3 10 petri dishes 90 mm in diameter, either glass or plastic
4. 31 of sterile distilled water contained in 3 Erlenmeyer conical flasks (1,000 ml)
5. 50 sheets of aluminium foil (100 x 100 mm)
6. 2 beakers with lids (90 mm in diameter and 50 mm deep)
7. 2 pairs of forceps (120-150 mm)
8. 3 scalpels (c. 150 mm)

Non-Sterile Items

9. 2 tap roots of carrot (Dausus carota) at least 200 mm in length and 40 mm in diameter. The plant material may be purchased at the local market or preferably grown in open ground, in sandy soil in the garden. Most varieties will respond to the culture procedure employed in this activity.
10. 2 racks, preferably plastic or metal, to hold 12 culture tubes (150 x 25 mm) at an angle of approximately 25°
11. 1,000 ml of a solution of sodium hypochlorite approximately 20 per cent (v/v), (commercial bleach preparations can be used at a dilution of one part to five of water)
12. 1 waterproof marking pen
13. 1 glass beaker (1,000 ml)
14. 1 analytical balance for determining the fresh weight of the cultures
15. 1 Bunsen or ethanol burner
16. 1 Erleneyer flask (150 ml) containing 100 ml. 95 per cent ethanol
17. 1 role of parafilm
18. 1 small nylon nailbrush

Procedures

Use regular shaped, undamaged and clean carrot roots. Scrub the carrots with a small nylon nailbrush under running tap water, to clean the surface wall, the peel. Place the carrots (trimmed to about 100 mm in length) in a 1,000 ml beaker, cover with the solution of sodium hypochlorite and leave for approximately 30 min. During this sterilization procedure, mark each culture tube with the number of the carrot, the medium and the date. Transfer the sterilized carrots to the sterile room, making sure the UV lights are switched off before entering. (Powerful UV rays are harmful to the eyes and skin!) Wipe the working table clean with 70 per cent ethanol. Throughout the manipulation sequence, forceps, scalpels, and other small instruments must be kept in 95 per cent ethanol and flamed thoroughly before use. (Ethanol is inflammable, take great care during flaming!) Wash the carrots three times with sterile distilled water, agitating the beaker to remove completely the hypochlorite, and dry using the tissue paper. Transfer a carrot with 20 mm removed from each end, to a sterile beaker, and cut a series of tranverse slices 1 mm in thickness from the carrot root, using a sharp scalpel. Transfer each slice to a sterile Petri dish and cut explants 4 mm x 4 mm square across the cambium so that each piece contains parts of the phloem, cambium and xylem. Size and thickness of the explants should by uniform, so that a comparison can be made of the fresh-weight of the cultures after 4 weeks of growth. (Weigh 10 freshly isolated explants in order to determine the average fresh-weight). Repeat this procedure until sufficient explants have been accumulated for the activity. Always replace the lid of the Petri dish after each manipulation. Remove the closure from a culture tube and flame the uppermost 20 mm of the open end. While holding the tube at an angle of 45°, transfer (using forceps) two explants onto the surface of the agar, taking care that the root pole is touching the medium. Seal each tube immedietely with a square of aluminium foil which has been flamed, before and after it has been placed on the tube. Always flame the forceps between transfers. Repeat this procedure until all of the culture tubes have been used. Place the culture tubes in the racks and incubate in the dark at 25°C.

Sub-culture of Callus, Materials and Equipment

Sterile Items

1. 5 carrot cultures initiated from explants 4-6 weeks ago or an established callus sub-cultured 3-4 weeks previously
2. 12 rimless culture tubes (150 x 25 mm) containing 10 ml of 0.8 per cent agar medium + 5 x 10^{-8}g/ml2, 4-D sloped at an angle of 25°
3. 20 sheets tissue paper (200 x 200 mm)
4. 5 Petri dishes, 90 mm in diameter
5. 50 sheets aluminum foil (100 x 100 mm)
6. 3 pairs forceps (120-150 mm)
7. 3 scalpels (150 mm)

None-Sterile Items

8. 2 racks, preferably plastic or metal, each to hold 12 culture tubes (150 x 25 mm)
9. 1 waterproof marking pen
10. 1 Erlenmeyer flask (150 ml) containng 100 ml 95c ethanol
11. 1 roll parafilm
12. 1 Bunsen or ethanol burner

Procedures

Remove the culture tubes one at a time from the rack, and flame the top 20 mm before removing the explants/callus and placing them in a sterile Petri dish. It is preferable to accumulate six emplants/callus pieces in each dish. Usually after 4 weeks in culture, the explants incubated on medium with 2, 4-D have formed a substantial callus, and each piece should be divided into two or three pieces of not less than 5 mm x 5 mm. The cells on the lower side of the explant towards the centre are frequently necrotic in appearance and not suitable for sub-culture.

These necrotic areas should be separated and discarded. Ensure that the lid of the Petri dish is placed after each handling. Transfer the developing explant/callus to a fresh medium in a culture tube. Flame the top 20 mm of the tube containing the fresh mediumr and discard the aluminium foil cap. Using flamed forceps, remove two pieces of callus the place these apart on the surface of the medium towards the end of the tube. Take a square of aluminium foil and close the open end of the culture tube ensuring that a good seal is formed, flame the foil end place the tube in the rack. This procedure should be repeated until all the cultures have been transferred. Prolonged culture of carrot tissue produces large calluses. The procedures described for the first subculture of the developing callus are similar to those used for the routine subculture of established callus lines with a transfer period of 4 weeks.

Scheduling

Event Timing
Isolation of fresh explants from carrot root Day 0
First subculture Day 28
Market proliferation of callus c.Day 42-48
Isolation of established callus c.Day 91-98
Transfer period of established carrot callus 4 weeks

Recording of Results

Write down details of the activity in a note book, recording the starting date of the activity, the duration, number of cultures, of contaminations and the different treatments employed. Make visual observations of the cultures at weekly intervals for 4 weeks, recording changes in the morphology of the culture. Determine the fresh weight of the cultures initially, and after 4 weeks of growth.

Questions and Comments

From which tissue of the freshly isolated explants does the callus originate? Do all explants grow at a similar rate? Can liquid culture be used? If so, what should be provided?

Sterilization

Sterilize metal instruments, glassware and pieces of aluminium foil after wrapping in aluminium foil or by heating in a hot air over at 150°C for 3 hours. Sterilize the culture media, distilled water and other stable mixtures in glass containers closed with cotton wool plugs and capped with alumiuium foil in an autoclave at a pressure of 15 psi for 15 min. Paper towels and tissue paper should be wrapped in aluminium foil and autoclaved. Solutions of chemicals that will change upon autoclaving can be sterilized using a milipore filter.

Culture Medium

Chemicals	Concentration (mg/1)
Macroelements	
$CaCl_2.1H_2O$	440.0
$FeSO_4.7H_2O$	27.8
KH_2PO_4	170.0
KNO_3	1,900.0
$MgSO_4.7H_2O$	370.0
Na_2EDTA	37.3
NH_4NO_3	1,650.0
Microelements	
$CoCl_2.6H_2O$	0.025
$CuSO_4.5H_2O$	0.025
H_3BO_3	6.2
K1	0.83
$MnSO_4.4H_2O$	22.3
$Na_2MoO_4.2H_2O$	0.25
$ZnSO_4.7H_2O$	8.6
Sucrose	2% (W/V)
Nicotinic Acid	0.50
Pyridoxine	0.1
Thiamine HC1	0.1
Clycine	3.0
2, 4-D	See Text
Kinetin	See Text
Agar	0.8% (W/V)
pH	5.8

The Use of Calculators in Secondary Schools

It is likely that the new science and technology content like the current science, especially physics, would continue to make demands in mathematics and computing, thereby requiring students to have a number of prerequisite competencies in this area.

The nature of the demands need not be interpreted to mean that computers are required for each school, to permit the achievement of these competencies.

A consideration of typical secondary science syllabuses suggests that a programmable calculator will serve adequately for the most advanced topics and calculations. If students are to develop a feel for numbers and quantities, they should construct and test their own algorithms, and be left to explore the consequences of simple mathematical procedures. The cost of supplying suitable calculators is not high; if a scientific calculator is worth one textbook, a programmable calculator of 100 programme steps and 10 memories is worth two textbooks. Motivation is a key to learning. Essential mathematical tools are quickly grasped in the context of real physical problems. Very often, a programming language can be learned and used in a matter of days if it is needed for a genuine problem. Similarly statistics cannot be esily understood outside a context of real life problems. It seems imperative that some numerical computing be used in the context of physical problems. The equipment needs will be modest at the secondary level; a programmable calculator, a pencil, an eraser and some paper, including graph paper. With this minimum set, the students should become thoroughly involved in computing.

There are three important areas of numerical computing that can be introduced with a secondary school physics syllabus. The first is polynomial curve fitting, especially using straight lines to fit appropriate experimental data. The second is numerical differentiation and integration, essential becuase senior physics depends so heavily on calculus. The third possible area is the use of a mean and a deviation to describe the randomness of data points. These statistical concepts should be applied with common sense rather than with further sophistication.

Least-Squares Fitting

Least-squares fitting of a straight line or the linear regression of experimental data (with a high correlation) can be provided as an incentive to collect and refine data. Some appropriate experiments that provide data are: the detrmination of a focal length, the change of speed with constant acceleration or distance with constant speed, and the measurement of elasticity. A logarithmic linear fit can be used to study the streamline emptying of a column of fluid or the half-life of a newly leached radioactive decay product. These last two examples will deviate from a logarithmic-linear line for obvious physical reasons.

When all the data is plotted, complete with estimated uncertainties, and a best fit line has been found, commonsense judgements will usually give better estimates of the parameter uncertainties than any further statistical analysis.

If students are to understand the least-squares analysis, they should be able to appreciate how and why the various formulae are developed. There are several approaches within the scope of senior physics students. The usual derivation of the formulae from a best fit polynomial is suitable for classes with a strong calculus background, and these classes should also be able to develop strategies for fitting quadratic curves. Other students who are less familiar with calculus, could start with the axiom that mean bivariate values give a point on the line of best fit. From this point the x or y variance of lines with different slopes can be explored.

Numerical Integration and Differentiation

It is doubtful whether any student can come to terms with physics without understanding the concepts of integration and differentiation. Most traditional syllabuses start by describing motion. The reason for this approach is simply to illustrate the underlying calculus. As students become familiar with the techniques, they will be capable of exploring the solutions of second-order differential equations, a topic usually left to the second year of a university course. The ability to integrate, should lead to the discovery of the sine curve as the solution of the harmonic equation. Other functions such as the exponential can also be discovered rather than pulled out of a hat at the right time. The need to include a constant when integrating, and to use infinitely small intervals when differentiating, can also be learned from experience.

There are many ways to integrate and differentiate, numerically, but for the purposes of introducing calculus, the simplest remain the best. If interpolation of real data is attempted, students and teachers should bear in mind that fancy formulae will not make the results any more meaningful. Many of the higher order formulae are devloped on the assumption that the abscissa is divided into equal intervals. These formulae frequently become unworkable when applied to real problems, especially when uncertainties are involved.

Statistics and Packages

As science is concerned with measurement, all students should understand the significance of the mean, the standard deviation and a normal distribution. If the topic of statistics is taken further, a vast array of techniques with prepackaged programmes and programme libraries will be discovered. Similar situations exist with curve fitting and numerical calculus. It is not uncommon to find postgraduate research students who have completed very comprehensive analyses of their data and yet their results remain quite common and obvious. Science teachers in general need to take pains to ensure that the mathematical techniques presented remain transparent and simple. It the teachers are also discovering new mathematical tools, they must not let their enthusiasm bewilder their classes.

Support Use of Computers

Fifteen years ago, scientific calculators were an expensive item specially chained to the desks in teaching laboratories, and they had, at best two or three memories. At the same time, all universities and some other tertiary institutions had computers specially housed in air-conditioned rooms, surrounded by operating and service staff. These computers were only accessible using punched cards and with efficient service, output became available after about three hours. Today many school children learn to use scientific calculators at the age of about 14 years. The large institutional computers remain, but computers of megabyte capacity are available for home use.

Secondary schools, in particular, were frequently not able

to take advantage of the computer boom because small amounts of money were only spasmodically released for the purpose of buying computers. Unfortunately little staff retraining was offered and a few dedicated teachers managed to cope with the available systems. At the end of a few years, the software and possibly the hardware is out of date (or is thought to be out of date). Another chronic problem for secondory schools, that has strained their limited funds to buy computers, is the subsequent service of keyboards, disc drives, printers, etc. While chips rarely fail, just about every other component is at risk in the rugged school environment.

Much of the educational software developed, like the self-paced tutorial, is no more effective than a carefully planned textbook. There are no commerical programmes that offer more than a textbook, with dynamic graphics that illustrate particular points e.g., chemical titration, but this software is not suitable for the aging computers left in science classrooms.

The personal computer, with at least one (640k) floppy disc, has become a suitable computing standard for secondary education. These systems are easily available in mutually compatible clone forms and they are easily upgraded as required. When the intellectual development of secondary-schools students is considered, these personal computers offer opportunities far in excess of the students realistic requirements.

The advantages of investing in a computer facility to serve several schools in an area are many. It may not be cost effective in the long term for schools to act dependently. The computer facility centre would have software development staff who are aware of the content and development of the many local syllabuses (in all subjects). The centre could also have a large mainframe computer. All schools in the area can then receive updated educational software in an appropriate system code using a telephone/modern or other appropriate physical transfer of discs. Ultimately, the computer disc library will become as important as the book library. Each school will need an extra librarian who can also assist with setting up and running computers. Repairs and maintenance should be available from the central facility.

4

Recommendations

RECOMMENDATIONS FOR UNESCO ACTION

In the final stages of the Workshop discussions, a list of common problems faced by participating countries was carefully complied. Once these had been formulated, specific recommendations to UNESCO were made. There are two categories of problems in which assistance from UNESCO was sought. The first relates to those matters where direct assistance is required, or where UNESCO can approach national governments directly and advocate the requests from the Workshop. The second contains those items were UNESCO can support, and co-ordinate activities in participating countries, particularly for regional networking inputs.

Category 1A UNESCO—Governmental action

- Teachers need more time for professional improvement outside the classroom.
- The supply of science teachers should meet national quotas, or incentives are necessary to encourage science teaching as a career.
- Technological and scientific teaching cannot proceed in the absence of qualified technicians who can build and service equipment locally.
- Facilities and actual schools are needed for the designing and evaluation of new curricular projects.

- Extra-curricular activities are greatly assisted by the presence of public museums and science discovery centres.

Category 1B UNESCO Action

- Prepare a statement suggesting areas and techniques where ethical matters may be considered in the context of science and technology.
- Define the science processes that should underlie science learning and teaching, and provide guidance on a philosophical context for the learning/teaching of technological subjects.
- Provide guidance and suggestions for content, and for the integration of new topics and areas of study within existing curricula.
- Provide guidance for a holistic approach to curriculum design and teacher development.
- Set up a Resource Bank, including libraries of video tapes, computer discs, textbooks and resource notes, as well as collect and maintain examples of appropriate laboratory and domonstration equipment.
- Ensure that the science equipment offered can be manufactured and maintained by participating countries.
- Constantly revise resource materials in the light of changing content and learning/teaching practices.
- Provide schemes and assistance for the evaluation of learning and teaching.
- Provide assistance with in-service teacher training and retraining.
- UNESCO must play a leading role in co-ordinating the inter-country exchange of curriculum development, learning/teaching experiences and resources, in respect of future content.

Category 2 UNESCO—National Action

- Provide curricula updates in note form to meet local needs.

- Provide curricula amendaments that identify the local flavour of contemporary science.
- Develop low cost appropriate equipment from local materials, and at the same time discourage the idea that good science needs expensive equipment.
- Provide models of practical resource kits (equipment and notes) for remote rural areas.
- Compile resource kits for teachers (rather than students), and where necessary rewrite sophisticated technical manuals so that they can assist teachers.
- Encourage the formation and growth of Science Teacher Associations as a source of professional consultants who can provide curriculum trails and peer review.

RECOMMENDATIONS FOR SPECIFIC UNESCO ACTION

1. Provide workshops in new areas of Science and Technology that will, in turn, give participants the opportunity to privide in-service courses for science teachers in their own countries, particularly in the new content areas.
2. Encourage and co-ordinate the development of resource materials in participating countries and retain samples of these materials in the Resource Bank.
3. Organize a working party to determine the basic core requirements of the traditional science so that future content can be built on a solid base.
4. Initiate a regional project on the joint elaboration of source materials which could be called UNESCO Source Materials for New Content in Science and Technology.

Suggestions from the Chinese Delegation (as an example of a national follow-up action)

For National Action

The Beijing Municipal Bureau of Education is expected to initiate a project on the promoting of science education in secondary schools. This project will be under the auspices of and sponsored by, the Chinese State Commission of Education,

UNESCO and the Chinese National Commission for UNESCO. A Steering Committee will be set up to work out the plan of this project and to conduct the implementation of the plan.

On the basis of the DOSSSE Workshop, the contents and steps for implementation of the project would be as follows:

1. To convene a design workshop
   - to discuss and define the model of the science education system to be adopted;
   - to ensure what subjects of new science should be and could be introduced into the secondary schools.
2. To develop the curriculum, which will include
   - the traditional basic science courses, which should be retained;
   - the new science courses which should be developed;
   - the learning/teaching plan of extra-curricular and after-school activities.
3. To revise the syllabuses of the basic science courses retained, beginning with the Physics course and the Biology course for immediate attention. The requirements are:
   - to choose carefully the core unit of each course;
   - to determine the special topics (or contemporary knowledge related to each discipline) of each course and its concrate contents;
   - to determine the list of basic student activities and experiments;
   - to determine the list of indispensable demonstration experiments and video teaching-learning aids.
4. To elaborate source material for each course, including reading materials of special topics, the guide books of basic activities and experiments, audio-visual materials, and CAI software, etc.

5. To test the plan through pilot projects at several secondary schools in the Chaoyang Distrist and other districts.

For Regional Co-operation

According to the funds raised, the co-operation at two different levels could be chosen:

1. To exchange views and share experiences through UNESCO sponsored meetings on the following:
   - models adopted
   - curricula developed
   - syllabuses revised
   - source materials produced
2. To initiate a regional project on the joint elaboration of source materials which could be called UNESCO Source Materials for New Content in Science and Technology Education.

Concurrently, develop the related short term in-service teachers' training programmes which will be held within various countries.